Debra McGregor

Practice and Perspectives: Learning in practical science

Debra McGregor

Practice and Perspectives: Learning in practical science

Teachers and pupils learning about working together in secondary science classrooms

VDM Verlag Dr. Müller

Impressum/Imprint (nur für Deutschland/ only for Germany)
Bibliografische Information der Deutschen Nationalbibliothek: Die Deutsche Nationalbibliothek verzeichnet diese Publikation in der Deutschen Nationalbibliografie; detaillierte bibliografische Daten sind im Internet über http://dnb.d-nb.de abrufbar.
Alle in diesem Buch genannten Marken und Produktnamen unterliegen warenzeichen-, marken- oder patentrechtlichem Schutz bzw. sind Warenzeichen oder eingetragene Warenzeichen der jeweiligen Inhaber. Die Wiedergabe von Marken, Produktnamen, Gebrauchsnamen, Handelsnamen, Warenbezeichnungen u.s.w. in diesem Werk berechtigt auch ohne besondere Kennzeichnung nicht zu der Annahme, dass solche Namen im Sinne der Warenzeichen- und Markenschutzgesetzgebung als frei zu betrachten wären und daher von jedermann benutzt werden dürften.

Coverbild: www.ingimage.com

Verlag: VDM Verlag Dr. Müller Aktiengesellschaft & Co. KG
Dudweiler Landstr. 99, 66123 Saarbrücken, Deutschland
Telefon +49 681 9100-698, Telefax +49 681 9100-988
Email: info@vdm-verlag.de
Zugl.: PhD Thesis : Keele University : December 2003

Herstellung in Deutschland:
Schaltungsdienst Lange o.H.G., Berlin
Books on Demand GmbH, Norderstedt
Reha GmbH, Saarbrücken
Amazon Distribution GmbH, Leipzig
ISBN: 978-3-639-18762-5

Imprint (only for USA, GB)
Bibliographic information published by the Deutsche Nationalbibliothek: The Deutsche Nationalbibliothek lists this publication in the Deutsche Nationalbibliografie; detailed bibliographic data are available in the Internet at http://dnb.d-nb.de.
Any brand names and product names mentioned in this book are subject to trademark, brand or patent protection and are trademarks or registered trademarks of their respective holders. The use of brand names, product names, common names, trade names, product descriptions etc. even without a particular marking in this works is in no way to be construed to mean that such names may be regarded as unrestricted in respect of trademark and brand protection legislation and could thus be used by anyone.

Cover image: www.ingimage.com

Publisher: VDM Verlag Dr. Müller Aktiengesellschaft & Co. KG
Dudweiler Landstr. 99, 66123 Saarbrücken, Germany
Phone +49 681 9100-698, Fax +49 681 9100-988
Email: info@vdm-publishing.com

Printed in the U.S.A.
Printed in the U.K. by (see last page)
ISBN: 978-3-639-18762-5

Practice and perspectives

Acknowledgements

Prof. Patricia Murphy

Without whom all this would not have been possible……she emancipated my understanding of learning from a wide variety of perspectives. She believed in my thinking and ideas.

Prof. Miriam David

Who read and steered my reflexive writing.

Prof. Richard Kempa

Without whom I would not have made a start on the project. He believed I was capable and 'set me off' on the road of research.

The science departments of the following schools, including both their pupils and staff who patiently allowed me to video, question and survey:

Blythe Bridge High School, Staffordshire.

Coppenhall School, Cheshire.

Sandon High School, Stoke-on-Trent.

Walton High School, Staffordshire.

Weston Road High School, Staffordshire.

And last but not least my family who have patiently waited for their mother and wife to return to 'normality' and spend weekends and holidays playing, talking, reading, walking and being with them. My youngest (7) is/will be over the moon that I have completed my 'HB'!

Some personal reflections

These thoughts are to share with other readers who may also be embarking on a significant piece of educational research.

Through the experience and engagement in this level of educational research the following quotations quite aptly describe my intellectual development at various points of the thesis development.

At the beginning of this study puzzlement was often uppermost in my mind; I was, as described below, confused by the diversity of theories on research methodology and learning alone, but:

> 'Perplexity is the beginning of knowledge' (Anon).

So for me this was an incredible expansion and application of my knowledge and understanding regarding learning and teaching processes in the classroom.....what at first appeared to be 'perplexing, complex and unintelligible' became much more lucid with obvious outcomes becoming clearer with the evolution of my understanding.

At times, it [the study] appeared to be so demanding, not intellectually, necessarily, but certainly wearisome as I toiled through the files, videos, questionnaires, profuse data, associated articles and books. However, I persisted, because:

> 'Braving obstacles and hardships is nobler than retreat to tranquillity'. (Anon)

Many times I fought to 'stay on track', to retain belief in my professional capability and keep the end in sight. Many a time it would have been easier to say......'I now understand more', but to articulate the ideas, share my findings with a wider audience and influence teachers' thinking and practice was my chalice.

Contents

Contents

List of Figures, Tables and Appendixes

Figures

Tables

Appendices

Appendix 10.3 : A summary of the impact of teacher participation in interactive in-service: a comparison of scientific learning developed between pupils before and after the interactive teacher intervention.

Appendix 10.4 : Possible classification of types of formal modelling that could inform cognitive outcomes for Thinking Science at KS 4. Proposal of underpinning thinking of Reflective Science, a Key Stage 4 programme, designed to develop cognitive ability within science (now a research project funded by Esmée Fairbairn).

1. Introduction

1.1 Rationale behind the study

Throughout this study I adopted the perspective of a teacher-researcher. As a science educator, actively involved in initial and continuing teacher education, and a former teacher, I have developed a more curious researcher-like contemplation into why science teachers operate the way they do. Reflecting on my role as a classroom practitioner, I realised, in common with many contemporaries, that 'group work' strategies were often operationalised in an almost 'automatic' or routine fashion. Once a lesson's activities, practical procedures and objectives had been explained by the teacher, the pupils expected to, and indeed often did, by default, work with their neighbour or friend, resulting in the teacher withdrawing from directly influencing and managing their collaborative learning activities. The science teacher often at this stage 'facilitated' the pragmatics and mechanics of practical activities, locating an extra test-tube, re-lighting the bunsen, clearing away a broken beaker, or even applying a cold compress to a pupil's burnt finger.

In enabling practical work in groups, the teacher becomes engaged in frenetic management and co-ordination of pupils and equipment. Little attention is paid to ensuring the pupils engage in challenging mental activity as well as their physical endeavours.

I began to question, why for a significant proportion of science lessons do we encourage the pupils to work socially together in groups? What benefits are there? Does group work only support the development of social skills? Why do we feel that the risk of allowing them group autonomy, working together without direct teaching from the teacher, is an appropriate pedagogic strategy? I then contemplated how the teacher could ensure quality learning was occurring in these small groups, and what it was that we, as teachers, wanted the pupils to engage in specifically when working with their peers. I reflected on the nature of the group work. What is it about the way they interact that can help their learning? How could these kinds of interactions be best orchestrated to ensure the pupils develop intellectually when involved in practical activities? As Driver (1983:49) highlights: 'Activity by itself is not enough. It is the sense that is made of it that matters'. Practitioner experience, augmented by the opportunity to reflect on practice as a researcher has stimulated my intellectual curiosity about how children learn together. It is a reflection-on-action (Schon 1983), that I, as a former secondary teacher, postgraduate and higher degree tutor, am critically reflecting on past and current practitioner behaviour, and its effects in supporting collaborative learning between co-operating pupils. The predominance of practical work in science, usually tackled in small groups, noted by Kempa, (1994) was assumed to promote 'learning', but as Howe (1997:17) in her reviews of a wide range of studies on group interactions highlights, common practice is still as Galton and Williamson (1992) found in an earlier large-scale project, that pupils frequently sit in close proximity, but for the majority of the time work as individuals. Despite group-based seating arrangements it appears to be exceptional to find pupils working collaboratively. Pollard (2002:229) defines the commonly held rationale that 'group work is often recommended for developing social and language skills and as a means by which children can support, challenge and extend their learning together', is behind encouraging pupils to work together. Reiss (2000:153) indicates the psychological influence of working-with-peers is of potential significance, and in common with Forman and Larreamendy-Joerns (1995) highlights how plurality of goals, interest and expertise can affect learning together.

Teacher intervention or 'scaffolding' of social interaction, during science practical activities, at a cognitive level (to develop the intellectual demand) appears to be uncommon. Kempa (1979) reported that higher-level cognitive discourse, even when teachers focused on this, was rare. Kerry (1981) also supported the notion that most teacher-pupil interactions, in secondary science, were about procedure and that many opportunities for stimulating thought in pupils were lost. Boydell (1975) found the average length of conversations, between pupils, during group work was less than 25 seconds, and Bennett, Desforges, Cockburn and Wilkinson (1984) reported that when such conversations occur they can seldom be regarded as adding to the quality of task (and are quite likely to focus on last night's television or that evening's activities), they are typically limited to how much has been completed and/or how resource materials should be shared (Kutnick, Blatchford, Clark, MacIntyre and Baines 2005). Kutnick and Rodgers (1995:5), in their review of a wide range of studies, highlighted that 'groups cannot be used simply as organisational features of the classroom' and that tasks need to be presented appropriately to enable learning to take place amongst pupils. Their view that 'pupils need to discuss problems amongst themselves' to effectively learn together requires a more in-depth insight. The ways that teachers pedagogically perceive and practice how to support pupils learning together requires further development (Kutnick et al 2005). Although some teachers encouraged peer-peer discussion and analysis of practical problems in science lessons small group work was not carefully considered and supported to achieve learning aims.

In seeking to develop a clearer understanding of the nature of quality learning processes, current practice in the classroom needs to be carefully observed and interpreted from both the learner and teacher perspective. McGuinness (1999:29-30) highlights the need to consider carefully how teachers develop 'thinking classrooms' that support successful cognitive development of students through collaborative learning. Peer-peer interactions require careful reflection so that propositions can be developed about how best to support effective social construction in groups, to consequently sustain growth of intellectual capability. As Rogoff (1990) argued, it is necessary to examine situations in which children are in charge of their own activities to understand the role of peer interaction in cognitive development. In my study the pupils are provided with activities of differentiated levels of structured support (or scaffolding). It is the nature and extent of relationship between the quality of learning interactions and task structure that will be investigated first and then, subsequently, how teachers could mediate more effective collaborations.

1.2 Objectives of the study

I wish to explore pupil interactions in more depth to elicit the benefits assumed to be derived from peers working together. I wanted to find out whether a theoretical lens applied to learning interactions could inform educators about how to (re)orchestrate the classroom environment so that learners work together more effectively to enhance the quality of cognitive outcomes for all. With a deeper understanding of the processes and dynamics of quality learning interactions, is it possible to develop consistently effective practice, not intuitively hoping, through geographical proximity, that serendipitously each pupil will effectively learn from and with each other.

My study described here analyses children's interactions between each other, in a range of tasks, from open-ended investigations to highly structured experiments in an attempt to identify more clearly what kinds of learning exchanges can arise. The relationships between the structure of task and quality of interactions are examined, to judge whether or not they can effectively influence scientific learning, and whether classroom practitioners can mediate working together more effectively to promote cognitive development.

My study focused on how to support social construction in groups that enables procedural, conceptual and propositional understanding to develop. I took the approach Rogoff (1990) suggests, which explains how researchers need to address the naturalistic interaction between peers in tasks choosing for themselves, to consider how they might 'teach each other'. She describes how the collaboration and teaching processes, and perhaps the children's subsequent individual performance, may differ from those observed in the studies in which children are under the immediate direction of adults. To elucidate how children engage in mutual, interactive support, I will observe their inter-'actions', inter-'talk' and assess their final solutions.

In ascertaining the nature of learning that has arisen through pupil interactions I have adopted Bauersfeld's (1988:39) view that 'learning is characterised by the subjective reconstruction of societal means and models through negotiation of meaning in social interaction'. I will examine action and talk that is contributed by each pupil when socially engaged on task. It is through both their social and cognitive contributions to the task, that I am assuming their understandings related to the task will manifest themselves. As Bauersfeld indicates it is the nature of their exchanges to negotiate and develop meaning through task resolution that offers insight into meanings held in a cognitive sense. Thus, by examining pupils working together and reflecting on their culmination of ideas or solutions, either written or spoken, the cognitive processing engaged in and subsequent learning can be described. If the task is open-ended, as Roth (1995) identifies, there is the opportunity to identify problems and solutions, design procedures, analyse data, review and evaluate method and results, resulting in derivation of meaning and even formulation of subsequent questions. These types of 'open-enquiries', typified by a scientific investigational approach (Attainment target 1, otherwise known as Sc 1, in the Science National Curriculum) are therefore more likely to support a sharing of a wider range of ideas than a task of a highly structured or prescriptive nature. An illustrative practical providing reduced opportunities for procedural propositions, is less likely to promote scientific dialogic exchange, that encourages sharing perspectives, considering alternate methodologies or even contemplating interpretative views of evidence collected. Tasks of this varying nature of openness are thus presented to the pupils to investigate effects of scaffolding.

The notion that a scientifically richer and often higher level cognitive discourse results from participants who become more actively engaged and involved in-task is explored. My hypothesis is: when tasks are more highly scaffolded, offering few opportunities for decision-making, the task is less likely to encourage pupil engagement with the scientific concepts and procedures. This subsequently constrains the potential extent of cognitive development and scientific understanding. I contrast the effects of different levels of scaffolding within tasks, to explore what appears to best support pupils entering into more spontaneous dialogic exchange to share their cognitive resources and enter into mutually supportive interactions to reach a quality learning outcome. Transferring the differentiated nature of task scaffolding to teaching strategies, it can highlight, more explicitly, what constitutes effective (or not so effective) pedagogic support to cognitively engage the pupils.

Emphasising how to extend cognitive engagement to augment pupils' scientific understanding can then inform the design and content of professional development programmes that enhance teachers' insights and empathy into pupils' cognitive development.

My proposition is thus three dimensional; on the first plane I wish to identify what constitutes effective scaffolding to cognitively engage and develop pupils; the second plane is communicating to teachers what effective 'scaffolding' and 'learning together' means in pedagogical terms; the third plane is assessing whether informed teachers who make pedagogic changes can impact upon pupils' cognitive development, understanding and learning.

1.3 Structure of the study

There are 5 phases in my research project.

The first, introductory stage where the context of the study was explored, began with literature reviews of learning theories and current views of group work. My intention was to place my later documented research evidence, of pupils learning together, within a 'group work' and psychological 'learning theory' framework. Both teachers' and pupils' perspectives were sought through surveys amongst schools in the Keele University partnership, to explore existing routines and habits.

The second phase was collation of the observational evidence for analysis and interpretation of pupils' interactions (both social and cognitive) whilst engaged in particular tasks. The resultant findings at this stage were intended to inform teacher practice, which could be communicated through professional development activities, to more effectively support pupils in their development of scientific understanding.

The third phase became a reflective stage where I reviewed and clarified *when* and *how* it was most useful for pupils to interact and be contemplative themselves when solving problems in science.

The fourth phase was the teacher-development intervention. This informed the in-service education for teachers. This was to include dissemination to both practicing and learner teachers. The existing frameworks of professional development programmes, PGCE lectures, and mentor training days within the Education department at Keele were the intended 'vehicles' for dissemination.

The fifth and final concluding phase intended to evaluate the effectiveness on pupils' learning interactions in the classroom, of the research-informed professional development of the teachers. The effects of these changes in classroom practice were examined via a subsequent cohort of pupils, working collaboratively on similar (to phase two) scaffolded tasks.

The conclusions connect together how teachers' practice and pupils' efficacy in learning together are closely entwined. It is through illumination in empathetic professional development that teachers come to recognise how small pedagogic changes can influence the nature of interactions between peers and the subsequent learning that ensues.

Chapter two

In this chapter I intend to provide a brief overview of views and practices of group work that exist in schools. The purpose of the review is to place the reported research into a group work context. I will highlight what is known about group work generally and, where available, more specifically in science (although information is relatively scant in this area). It is my intention to consider factors that may affect pupils' cognitive achievements, when working together. I am attempting to synthesise findings to assess implications for classroom practice to inform my research, and thus identify how to influence the efficacy of peers learning together.

2.1 Introduction to group work

Kutnick and Rodgers (1994) identify how group work is not a new phenomenon, although how pupils are organised to work together and what they do in their 'groups' has changed considerably over the years. They describe how from the earliest writings about education (even Plato and Socrates) learning took place in a group context. They indicate how a variety of factors, including the nature of the task, the ethos of the school and the kind of teacher support provided are all influential upon the effectiveness of learning together. They describe how thousands of years ago Socrates would provide problem-solving tasks for his students and support their learning through 'dialogue' between him the expert (knower) and his novice pupils. The dialogues allowed the novices to generate and discuss ideas amongst themselves. As Kutnick & Rodgers (1994:2) highlight, 'this Socratic dialogue enabled two types of learning dynamic, that appropriate answers may be confirmed by the expert and that mutually naïve novices may speculate amongst themselves and thus generate new ideas to be tested'.

As the privilege of education expanded from a small elite number to the general masses in the early 1900s teaching could not be maintained in small groups, but extended into much larger classes. Over the last forty years, classrooms in developed countries have moved from large classes (50+ pupils) using 'whole-class' teaching methods to an average sized class of 30 with children sitting round tables in variously sized 'groups' (Galton and Williamson 1992).

Galton and Patrick's (1990) study identifies the frequency of different seating arrangements (location of pupils to relative to one another) which impacts directly on working group sizes.

Grouping	Seating arrangement
Small group	56%
Pairs	16%
Individual	7.5%
Whole class	20.5%

Figure 2.1 : Seating arrangements in small primary schools (Galton and Patrick, 1990)

This study showed that organising pupils sitting in small groups in readiness for working together is a pre-dominant practice in primary schools. This common practice is echoed in secondary schools too. Wellington (1994) in his review of practical work in high school science states that:

> '..... the issue of group work. Teachers commonly place pupils in small groups and assume that the group will work. Close observation shows that this is often not the case, especially in groups of three or more. One pupil may dominate while others play little part, for example, in planning, predicting or carrying out a practical. Pupils may willingly adopt different roles, some of which may have nothing to do with the science, for example one member may simply record and tabulate results with no clue as to what they mean or where they came from. ......group work must be managed – it cannot be taken for granted' Wellington (1994:137).

McAllister (1995) also identifies the lack of guidance for pupils working together and highlights that pupils need to 'know' how to 'work' in groups to operate effectively. She emphasises the many factors that can impinge on the success of group work (including pupil character, confidence, ability to communicate) and indicates the importance of teachers taking time to consider how to overcome social issues of working together.

The prevalence of small group work, in science, (Tamir 1981; Hofstein and Lunetta 1982; Gallagher and Tobin 1987) was assessed by Kempa (1991) to utilise 50% - 60% of lesson time. He also identified that applying this approach meant pupils needed to become more autonomous in their learning because this strategy, commonly adopted in secondary science classrooms, indicates the pupils:

> 'are required to assume responsibility for their own learning as the teacher's involvement in group activities is usually very limited, if not absent altogether' (Kempa 1991:341).

Kempa (1991), in his studies of secondary science laboratories, defined group work as an 'activity in which two or more pupils work together in collaboration, either on identical tasks or different aspects of the same task, usually without direct supervision or control by the teacher'. This notion of 'group work' will be extended and refined throughout this study.

2.2 Using group work

Current use of group learning in the UK could arguably be influenced by the publication of the the Plowden Report (1967), which stated:

> 'Sharing out the teacher's time is a major problem. Only seven or eight minutes a day would be available for each child if all teaching were individual. Teachers therefore, have to economise by teaching together a small group of pupils who are roughly at the same stage……'

So it was recommended that small groups should be used to increase teacher efficiency, because children working in autonomous groups could then free the teacher to help individuals with problems. The report also highlighted that group work would allow pupils to help each other and that through recognising the strengths of others they could work together more effectively. It also identified how discussion would help develop planning skills and developing explanations for each other would increase pupils' learning.

A leading researcher in this area in the mid 1980s, Bennett (1985), identified that studies over the previous 40 years in the UK had focused primarily on observing and describing practice. He identified the advantages of group work to be: helps pupils to learn co-operatively; allows children to learn from each other and removes the stigma of failure from slow learners; offers teachers the opportunity to circulate around the class and correct individuals' work; teaches pupils to be self-reliant and not teacher dependent; gives pupils a chance to work at their own pace; helps pupils to respect each others strengths and weaknesses; enables teachers to adapt tasks to be appropriate to children's needs and abilities.

As Hill's (1982) research demonstrated, another advantage of working with others was that 'two heads are better than one'; pupils working together produced a greater number of unique ideas than individuals working separately.

Bennett's summary of the ideal rewards of group work were not evidenced by observational studies. The reality was (and frequently still is) a general juxtaposition of individuals operating together without clear purpose and management. As Mercer (1999) claims, effective interactional opportunities are lost or squandered when pupils work in groups because teachers are unclear and do not provide explicit direct guidance. Bennett also identifies that although groups may work co-operatively, task enhancing interactions are rare and off-task interaction is frequent, and it appears, encouraged by lack of direct supervision.

Sands (1981a, 1981b) investigated the paucity of educational group work in science. Usually group work was organisational: members of the group seated or standing together, but working individually on the same task. External factors: size, layout of room, furniture, length of lesson and size of class, available resources and ancillary help affected the extent to which groups could be used. The most successful group work lessons were those where the teacher showed skill in handling and understanding groups, and gave a positive lead to a lesson before the group work began. The teacher was regarded differently by the pupils during group work compared to a whole-class teaching situation. The teacher's role shifted to that of a consultant and facilitator rather than an instructor. The role was active (and tiring) as work was monitored, directed, information gathered and processed, questioning and explaining carried out with speed and at different levels, while groups were controlled, motivated and supervised.

In science, Sands (1981) describes typical occurrences, still familiar today, in lessons where grouping is utilised as a teaching strategy. Groups were rarely more than two pupils, they usually followed instructions or a work sheet as they proceeded through a piece of practical work, recorded the results and cleared up. Individual writing up usually followed. In 90% of lessons observed each group was given the same task. In some science lessons the science topic under study was presented by several different approaches using different work-cards, again appropriate for varying levels of ability. In only 5% of observed groups were group members working for less than half the time. Talk mainly related to work in hand and was never at a particularly high level. Simple questions were asked, instructions repeated, straightforward comments made. A certain amount of chat went on, and if not excessive, probably played an important part in keeping the group working together. Many groups were allowed to select their own members and therefore were long lasting, consisting of friends of the same sex, and with a similar outlook, usually of the same ability. Where a group was formed consisting of members of widely differing ability, the teacher reported that its members might lose patience with each other and re-form in to another group.

Another researcher, eminent in the field of group work, Johnson (1981), in the US, collated reflections on groups of people working together in a variety of situations (including business), and not just classroom settings. Johnson and Johnson (1996) developed their ideas to include descriptions of both the processes and outcomes of co-operative working.

2.3 Views of effective group work

Johnson and Johnson (1996) provide much argumentation for 'effective' group work. They focused particularly on how to structure and influence patterns of interactions. Johnson and Johnson (1991, 1992, 1996) claim that to work together effectively, regular working habits with regular partners are necessary.

A co-operative learning group, they state, has a number of defining characteristics that include responsibility for performance; accountability working toward group goals; doing real work together, to promote each other's success; and the utilisation of taught social skills to co-ordinate efforts and achieve goals. Their emphasis on the social interaction is even more clearly emphasised through their definition of a 'small group' as

> 'two or more individuals in face-to-face interaction, each aware of positive interdependence as they strive to achieve mutual goals, each aware of his or her membership in the group, and each aware of the others who belong to the group' (Johnson and Johnson 1996:12).

They say creating and maintaining truly committed co-operative learning groups is far from easy because many educators are 'confused' about what is (and is not) a co-operative learning group as well as about the characteristics that make co-operative learning groups work. They too, like Galton and Williamson (1992) highlight the lack of understanding that educators have to inform how best to utilise a small group approach in classrooms.

They connect group development with Tuckman's (1965) work, who describes how as a group develops it goes through a series of stages, from forming, storming, norming, performing to adjourning[1]. Johnson and Johnson (ibid) illustrate the five keys to a group's productivity are: positive interdependence, individual accountability, promotive interaction, social skills, and group processing. They describe these as effective components of co-operation that can promote higher student achievements. Cotton and Cook (1982) and McGlynn (1982) in their critique of the research of Johnson and Johnson, argued that earlier work did not clearly connect findings and conclusions. Their later work (meta-analyses) does not provide apparent evidence of improved achievement in classroom situations. However, recognising influential factors such as understanding and commitment to goals, decision-making processes, communication of ideas and feelings (Johnson and Johnson 1996:33) are important, but are not clearly illustrated from classroom locations. Their discussions recognise the components of effective groups, including the need for members to engage in controversy by disagreeing and

[1] Description of the developmental stages groups progress through:

Developmental stage	Description
1. Forming	Members become orientated towards each other, being accepted, and learning more about the group
2. Storming	Members often confront their various differences and the management of conflict becomes the focus of attention.
3. Norming	The group develops some consensus regarding a role structure and a set of group norms and increase group cohesion.
4. Performing	Group works as a unit to achieve the group's goals.

challenging each other's conclusions and reasoning, thus promoting creative decision making and problem solving. They also argue that decisions should be made by reaching a consensus to promote distributed participation by group members. Their findings appear to be derived from numerous business contexts, but are arguably applicable to classroom situations.

Slavin (1985) also highlights positive effects derived through co-operative learning. In his studies he applies a number of strategies[2] that encourage co-operative working and compares the sum of individual performance in control and experimental classes. His findings indicate that pupils' enjoyment level, self esteem and intergroup relations are increased and as a consequence their academic achievements are improved.

Sharan (1985) looked at co-operative learning and illustrated how 'groups' carrying out investigations could improve academic achievement, compared to whole\class instruction, promoting learning on a high level cognitive functioning without loss of basic information. The results were particularly marked in lower class, low status groups in Israel and replicated to some degree in Johnson's work with middle class American children. Johnson's (1981) work in particular highlights the problem solving abilities developed in the group and retained by the individual.

Sharan (ibid) concludes that co-operative learning in general has led to an increase in academic achievement and social skills development when compared to the traditional method of teaching, which is primarily only concerned with academic achievement.

Johnson and Johnson (1996) developed a learning group performance curve (Johnson and Johnson 1996:16) to elucidate the difference between traditional classroom groups, described by Kelly (1997) as organisational groups, co-operative learning groups and high performance co-operative learning groups. The characteristics of these groups are summarised in Table 2.1 below. They describe:

> 'a pseudo-learning group is a group whose members have been assigned to work together but have no interest in doing so. Members may block or interfere with each

[2] Slavin (1985:7) co-operative strategies : Student Team Learning; Jigsaw; Learning together; Group-Investigation.

other's learning, communicate and co-ordinate poorly, mislead and confuse each other, loaf or seek a free ride' (Johnson and Johnson 1996: 17).

The interaction among group members detracts from individual learning without delivering any benefit. The result is that the sum of the whole is less than the potential of the individual members. Johnson and Johnson (1996) describe a *traditional classroom learning group* as one whose members have accepted that they are to work together but see little benefit from doing so, interdependence is low. The assignments are structured so that very little if any joint work is required. Members do not take any responsibility for anyone's learning other than his or her own. Members interact primarily to share information and clarify how the assignments are to be done. They each do the work on their own and their achievements are individually recognised and rewarded. Students are accountable as separate individuals, not as members of a team. Students do not receive training in social skills, and a group leader is appointed to be in charge of directing members' participation.

Johnson and Johnson (1996) argue that a *co-operative learning group* is more than a sum of its parts. It is a group whose members are committed to the common purpose of maximising each other's learning. It has a number of defining characteristics: i. shared and individual responsibility for performance; ii. shared and individual accountability working toward group goals; iii do real work together, promote each other's success; iv. utilisation of taught social skills to co-ordinate efforts and achieve goals. A *high performance co-operative learning group* meets above criteria for CLG *but* outperforms all reasonable expectations. Members' mutual concern for each other's personal growth enables this. Groups like this, Johnson and Johnson argue, are rare. They claim that creating and maintaining truly committed co-operative learning groups is far from easy, and that CLG's are rare because many educators are confused about what is (and is not) a co-operative learning group as well as about the basics that make co-operative learning groups work.

Type of group	Definition
Pseudo group	A group whose members have been assigned to work together but they have no interest in doing so. The structure promotes competition at close quarters.
Traditional learning group	A group whose members agree to work together but see little benefit from doing so. The structure promotes individualistic work with talking.
Co-operative learning group	A group in which students work together to accomplish shared goals. Students perceive they can reach their learning goals if and only if the other group members also reach their goals.
High performance co-operative learning group	A group that meets all the criteria for being a co-operative group and outperforms all reasonable expectations, given its membership.

Table 2.2 : Group performance categories according to Johnson and Johnson (1996:17).

They even suggest that educators lack the discipline to implement the basics of co-operative efforts in a rigorous way, but that is something worth considering as co-operative learning offers a way forward to prepare students for the social interactions they will face outside schools. The achievement of real collaboration in groups so that pupils genuinely share their ideas and their knowledge of how problems can be solved is an important aspect of teaching which needs to be carefully planned for. Research into collaborative group work in the early 90s (Galton and Williamson 1992; Bennett and Dunne 1992) indicated that pupils needed to be taught how to work in co-operative groups, Galton et al (1992) identified that they needed a range of skills, including those cognitive skills involved in completing a task or activity set, and social skills of working as a productive member of a team. Galton emphasised the importance of teachers making it clear to pupils that they value the performance of these skills, and drew attention to the importance of self-esteem and self-confidence in the context of an activity and the method of instruction. He also acknowledged that pupils need to know the purpose of the task, the desired outcomes of the task, and the role each child is expected to play in achieving success. He reiterated that tasks need to have the potential to achieve success and to enable the pupils to work at the edge of their understanding.

Through exploring perspectives and descriptions authors use to define their use of group work, it appears that much observation descriptively summarises what group work (effective or not) looks like. These descriptions, often of a social nature, emphasise that co-operation is important, but do not explain what it is that happens between peers, and teacher and pupils to cause improvements in understanding or achievements. Many factors are offered as possible influences, but exactly how the nature of learning, in a group work situation, is influenced remains blurred. It appears that because researchers have ignored theoretical perspectives developed by social psychologists, studies have been of a rather descriptive nature.

However, in the last decade, in the UK, there has been somewhat of a shift to focus and explore more carefully the nature of the learning interactions, cognitive processes and outcomes (Kempa et al 1991, 1995; Howe et al 1990, 1992) of group work in science. Researchers have re-adjusted their lens and sought to examine through deductive evidence what is happening in the minds of the learners within the context of co-operatively working together. The emphasis on analysis has shifted from that of a very theoretical social nature to one of a more cognitive or psychological *and* social character. In the late 1990s, underpinned by the constructivist approach, there appears to be much more detailed analysis of how pupils socially interact to construct and re-model their ideas. Social interaction between pupils to learn as a group (rather than within a group) thus can be defined as collaboration. The research has begun to examine more closely the social interactions and how the exchange of ideas through conversations and other (actional) means, between members of a group, can influence their developing understanding.

2.4 Factors influencing group work

Desfountain and Howe (1992) have claimed that pupils need 'worthwhile opportunities to work together in small groups, making meaning through talk, supported and challenged by their peers'. The notion that talk enables two or more pupils to pool their experiences and achieve new levels of understanding beyond that which either had before was an important finding. Cobb et al (1997:1258) considers collaboration between peers as that involving 'collective reflection' as 'the joint or communal activity of making what was previously done in action an object of reflection.' Hendley and Lyle (1995) consider that collaboration is not only important as a valuable learning mechanism between peers, but also between teacher and pupils. They consider problem solving in Design and Technology and argue its suitability for the development of collaborative learning, a method of learning which encourages decision making after a period of critical enquiry and experimentation. They further argue that:

> 'the successful implementation of the design and technology curriculum hinges upon the development of classroom talk, because talk plays the central role in the development of critical thinking, reflection and evaluation, all important features of design and technology' (Hendley and Lyle 1995 : 363).

It is engaging in evaluation, which enables pupils to reach 'higher ground' as they distance themselves from the process and reflect on the finished product. As Bruner (1986) says:

> 'This process of objectifying in language or image what one has thought and then turning around on it and reconsidering it' (Bruner 1986 : 129).

is a prime task of education. The key to this reflective process is language; it is talk in collaborative groups, which Hendley and Lyle argue, that can provide the means through which evaluation can take place. Collaborative group work is an important strategy which can be used to help children develop evaluative skills, considering the 'values' of such things as 'aesthetics, function, safety, reliability and cost'. A concern here, is if the teacher retains control over what constitutes knowing, the pupils will miss the opportunity to make use of what they know as the basis for extending their learning, and to collaborate with others in the co-construction of meaning.

In summary, thus far, it appears that group work is a widely and regularly used teaching strategy, the relative success of which may depend on an extensive range of influencing factors. It appears that it may be the nature of the interactions between pupils that is key to achieving academic progress. The following discussion indicates how each of the more prominent factors may influence and support learning and achievement in small groups.

2.4.1 Group work and talk

There is a significant body of research, much dating from the 1970s and into the early 1980s that indicates how classroom talk has changed from the day-to-day running of the classroom, presentation of information, or questioning to test pupils' factual recall to becoming of real use in the process of learning. Flanders (1970) claimed that about two thirds of each lesson was taken up with talk, and two thirds of that was done by the teacher.

Barnes (1976) claimed that:

> 'When children are talking in a group without an adult present, responsibility for the management of the talk falls on themselves. They must negotiate whom talks, when and how. They must cope with occasional episodes of conflict and with silences. They must encourage group members with useful contributions to make, and at the same time, control any attempts to dominate the talk for irrelevant purposes.'

Barnes and Todd (1977) explored the value of small groups for encouraging exploratory talk. They carried out studies on unsupervised small groups, working on tasks set by the teacher, in a secondary school. The teachers were often surprised by the quality of the discussion and cited a number of instances where the contribution of a pupil within the group far outweighed the quality of their performance during whole class discussions.

Barnes and Todd argued that children were able to increase their understanding in such situations without needing to call on an adult resource. Tough (1977) reached similar conclusions, also as part of the Schools Council Project, but focusing on Communication Skills in Early Childhood. Tough studied language development in nursery and infant children and concluded that even at this young age children were capable of engaging in extended exploratory discussions.

These studies did not, however, explicitly explore the relationship between the group interactions and pupil achievement, there was an implicit assumption that whilst pupils were 'discussing' they were consequently learning. Tann (1981) began to explore the context in which these 'scholarly' discussions took place. She also explored in some detail the interaction processes and began to relate this to 'grouping' policies. Her study entailed recording pupils' individual contributions to conversations whilst carrying out tasks. The tasks were mostly open-ended problem solving scenarios, the group collectively decided on the solution they thought most appropriate. Tann identified three key stages in the discussion process. The first identified as 'orientation', involved pupils defining the problem, interpreting the task and setting limits[3] on the activity. The second stage, 'development', involved what others define as 'brain-storming', where ideas were generated and reasoning strategies began to evolve. The third, 'concluding' stage included increasing acceptance of each other's ideas and more progressive focusing on specific strategies necessary for a successful resolution. Tann identified three determinants of success; pupils' ability to raise questions, to listen attentively to each other and to manage disputes whenever these arose. Webb (1980) categorised these kinds of interactions as 'explanatory help', but she found, that there was very little use of questioning by either the teachers or the pupils. She highlighted that pupils were given little instruction about 'how to work in groups'. Biott (1987) supports this view. In Biott's study the early stages of group discussion were observed to be mainly concerned with precision matters. There was little evidence that children listened to each other's views. Over time, however, there was some evidence that the nature of tasks was being reconsidered and that ideas for accomplishing them were reviewed. Biott argues that this apparent lack of early achievement can result in teachers abandoning group work, which in turn causes pupils to develop low expectations about the effectiveness of working together because it is curtailed before anything meaningful is accomplished.

[3] Define 'setting limits'.

Bennett (1985) studied transcripts of pupils working on mathematics and language based tasks. Unlike other studies (Kelly 1982), but similar to Kempa (1991, 1994) he found that two thirds of pupil talk was task related. Most of the conversations revolved around the quantity of work completed by each pupil or involved disputes regarding use of materials. Bennett found that a small proportion of the discourse was 'task enhancing' talk helping to improve the pupils' performance on the task. The most frequent kind of task enhancement conversation (less than 10%) Webb (1985) labelled 'explanations'. Comparing heterogeneous and homogenous groups and quality of discussion, Bennett and Cass (1989) examined explanations offered and appropriateness of the premise on which the explanation was based. They noted that whilst 43% of explanations were both correct and appropriate, 42% were correct but inappropriate, and in each case explanations were offered by high attainers. A little under a third of all instructional talk consisted of suggestions. Of these 54% were from higher achievers compared to 32% from low attainers and 14% from average attainers. 69% of all suggestions were inappropriate but a large number of them were accepted by other members of the group. The tendency to accept inappropriate suggestions was twice as great in mixed groups than in homogenous groups. In post task interviews high ability children were very successful in articulating the reasoning behind decision making during the task. The researchers felt this was a positive benefit for the low ability pupils.

In Roth's (1993) analysis of types of talk he found, somewhat differently to Boydell and Galton, that overall, three quarters of all talk (including pupil-pupil, pupil-teacher and teacher-pupil) was task related talk. There was no indication of gender effects; boys and girls appeared to converse freely and frequently without bias. However, little of the task related talk was task enhancing; i.e.: furthered task performance. Much of the talk was not of the task itself, but reports of how much work each had completed, arguments relating to materials or discussion concerning each other's academic status or competence.

Latham (1992) identified four assumptions about learning which he believes underpin the requirement for attention to spoken language and group work

that is found at all key stages and in all subject areas of the National Curriculum. The first assumption is that learning is likely to be more effective when learners are solving problems or making use of information; and that secondly there is a need to acknowledge and use what learners already know as a basis for extending their learning. Thirdly, he says, reflection has to be an essential aspect of learning, to help learners make explicit to themselves, as well as to others, what they know, understand and can do. He finally describes that learning should be a social and collaborative enterprise.
The key skills guidance for all subjects of the National Curriculum (2000) emphasize the importance of teachers helping pupils to work effectively in groups, for it is not just change in the status of talk which is important, but the settings in which the talk takes place between peers without the teacher's presence. Latham claims that in such settings, where the discourse status of each member is equal, they learn to collaborate in order to make meaning. More recently there seems to be accruing evidence that collaborative talk in small groups has been successfully developed in some classrooms, Cobb 1997; Mercer 1995, 2000; Mercer and Littleton 2008; Murphy 1999; Murphy & Henessey 1999, have provided examples of classroom talk which show children working in collaborative groups and using language to make meaning for them selves.

2.4.2 Group work and ability

Solomon (1987) established that working in small groups, did bring advantages, but that these were not uniformly spread. Due mostly to the work of Webb (1980):

> 'we know that benefit accrues mostly for the groups which have a range of abilities, only for high and low ability students in these groups, and for the former only if the subject material has already been learnt. The proposed interpretation is that the more able pupils 'tutor' the less able; this helps the able consolidate their learning, and gives extra help to those who need it most. The middle ability students it seems, are either ignored or just do not join in, and the discussions may even distract them from learning' Solomon (1987:71).

The present practice to commonly 'set' and organise pupils of similar ability to work together because they are then easier to teach, the content can be narrower, more specific (less need for differentiation) and pacing, working through the material, can be much higher than would be the case in a class of wider ranging abilities. Boalar (1998) describes this perception that similar ability groups are easier to teach and are more likely to improve attainment. Her evidence suggests, however, that pupils are bored, because they do not have time for reflection. This is particularly true in a class judged to be capable; the pace of lessons is so rapid that pupils were often reprimanded for 'not keeping up'. In her studies of high ability pupils working together, high performing boys were unhappy and girls wanted to be moved to lower ability sets.

2.4.3 Group work and gender

Webb (1984) has shown that different gender groupings affect the learning outcomes. Females and males showed equal achievements in groups with equal male and female numbers. However, when there were fewer females than males in the group, the males tended to ignore females with the result that the latter did less well. In groups with fewer males, the females diverted their attention to the males and again did less well.

Tann (1981) duplicated elements of Webb's (1985) findings, that boys tended to offer more suggestions whereas, in contrast, girls tended to be more consensus orientated and avoided challenging each other. Dissonance with Webb's study was the 'interaction' effects in that low ability boys in mixed ability groups tended to take an active part in discussion whereas slow learning girls within these groups tended to remain very silent and allowed the most able girl to emerge as leader.

Conwell et al (1993) have considered verbal and non-verbal interactions and their gender and racial differences in unstructured learning groups in a science activity. She found that females were better facilitators (encouraging others to participate and engage in the task) than the males.

Murphy (1999) in studies on collaborative learning has found that boys' and girls' goals for learning differ in both science and technology. They differ in how they conceive the problem. In technology, for boys the problems are to do with the device or product and are generally technical. For girls working on similar products the problem was to do with the context of use of the product. Similar difference were noted by the APU survey:

> 'Girls appeared to work fundamentally from human needs dealing predominantly with issues. They were often cautious in their entry to a situation, wanting to know how, why and whom it was for. While studying and designing the minutiae they were constantly seeking to keep the implications of the whole in view and for some this complexity became intolerable to the point where they capitulated. Boys, on the other hand, seemed able not only to start into the activity without knowing much, but were prepared to work on specific parts of it without considering the whole...possibly to lose sight of it altogether' (Kimbell at el 1991).

Howe (1997) discusses whether schools perpetuate behavioural differences between males and females, and whether classroom interaction reflects the gender divisions in society and whether it contributes to its continuation. She highlights that classroom interaction leads boys and girls to perform differently in different subjects, providing them with objective evidence of contrasting suitabilities. She claims that this would amount to interaction exerting a direct influence upon academic achievement and as a consequence an indirect influence on occupational choice.

2.4.4 Group composition

Bennett (1985) found instructional output was highest in groups consisting of high and average ability pupils compared to groups of low and average pupils. In groups containing above-average pupils the mean proportion of instructional input was 15% compared to 2% in the low ability groups. Bennett and Cass (1989) studied pupils engaged on history problems using computers. Comparing homogeneous and heterogeneous groups Bennett et al found there were the highest number (805.8) of interactions in the mixed group and the lowest (277.6) in the analogous group. Within the heterogeneous groups the greatest number of interactions were evident in the group containing two low and one high attainer. Contrary to other studies Bennett and Cass found that girls tended to speak more frequently, despite the fact that there were fewer of them in each group.

Biott (1987) examines the issue of leadership within groups:

> 'the official leader did little more than give turns, do the writing or read out the task and children who were expected to be leaders were sometimes bossy and impatient. They acted in ways which precluded slow pace reflection, tentative thinking aloud, question raising and exploratory testing of ideas.' (Biott 1987:10)

Biott (ibid) suggests that it is useful to identify roles of responsibility for group members:

> 'Encouraging and supporting others especially weaker members;
> Holding the group together in difficult moments;
> Questioning others to invite participation;
> Expressing doubt in a way, which invites others to comment;
> Trying to express a half formulated idea in a way which encourages others to join;

Summarising progress in a tentative way and slowing the pace to make the group more reflective or speeding it up to test more ideas' (Biott 1987:11).

Both Webb (1989) and Biott argue strongly for the need to develop a structured approach to group work. Biott identifies shared understanding between teacher and pupils, particularly 'rules' regarding intra-group activity. He also highlights the idea that pupils should self evaluate their inter-group contributions, although this kind of subjective reflection is something generally recognised is difficult for children to do (Adey 1991), without support.

2.4.5 Group management and organisation

Bennett and Dunne (1989) working with fifteen primary teachers compared different kinds of grouping organisation. In one group children worked individually on identical tasks with individual products, while other pupils worked individually towards a joint outcome in a jig-saw pattern. A third group worked co-operatively on a single task leading to a shared outcome (see table below). They used Piagetian classification to analyse the children's conversations and they compared conversation relating to action and conversation relating to abstract thought (involving the ability to conduct genuine argument). The evidence suggested that when the task was structured (so the children had to work together) the level of task-related talk was much higher than in the more common situations where grouped children were seated in close proximity but worked individually. They found that overall 88% of the talk in the 'co-operative' groups was on task compared to 66% in the more individualised situations.

	Type	Task demand	Intended outcome	Example
1	Seating groups	Each pupil has a separate task	Different outcomes: each pupil completes a different assignment	Writing stories on themes chosen by the pupils
2	Working groups	Each pupil has the same task	Same outcome: each pupil completes the same assignment independently	Mathematics worksheet
3	Co-operative groups	Each pupil has separate but related task	Joint outcome: each pupil has a different assignment	Making a map
4	Collaborative groups	Each pupil has same task	Joint outcome: all pupils share same assignment	Problem solving e.g.: discussing a social or moral issue

Table 2.3 : Classification of different grouping arrangements in the primary classroom (taken from Galton & Williamson 1992:10).

However, there does not appear to be a consensus about the relative importance of these characteristics. Other researchers debate 'symmetry' or not, of roles within groups. Within symmetrical groups, all pupils are given equal responsibility for ensuring success. Within asymmetric groups, some are more 'expert' than others and help or peer-tutor others. Research thus far suggests that symmetric roles are preferable when the content of the learning task is conceptual (Rogoff 1990; Damon and Phelps 1989), and asymmetric roles are preferable where the emphasis is on skills.

2.4.6 Group work and nature of tasks

Dunne and Bennett (1990) found that tasks involving 'action', i.e.: manipulating materials enabled talk (although related to the activity) to 'flow' more easily. If more difficult abstract reasoning was involved (i.e.: theoretical mathematical problems) talk often faltered compared to the spontaneity of 'action' related talk. Dunne and Bennett reported that teachers regarded the latter discussions as less worthwhile and less suitable for use with collaborative groups.

Galton and Williamson (1992) reported that:

> '1. When children sit in groups in a classroom they are likely to achieve more if they are encouraged to co-operate either by working towards a common shared outcome or by making an individual contribution towards a common goal, including decision making, planning of individual contributions and their combined presentation. Such groupings seem to improve pupils' self-esteem and increase pupil motivation.
>
> 2. Groups function best when they are of mixed ability but such groups must include pupils from the highest ability group within the class. A crucial factor is the teacher's ability to encourage pupils to assume overall responsibility (ownership) for the activity, thus reducing the dependency upon the teacher for approval of group decisions.
>
> 3. Children perform in different ways according to nature of the task. Levels of conversation are highest when pupils are engaged on 'action' tasks. Levels of conversation will be more sophisticated during more abstract tasks.
>
> 4. Problem-solving tasks with a clear testable outcome tend to generate a greater degree of collaboration than more 'open-ended' tasks. Pupils do not like challenging each other by debating the value of each other's solutions. They tend to assert rather than hypothesise or raise questions in this kind of discussion.
>
> 5. For successful collaboration pupils need to be taught how to collaborate. They require immediate feedback on their collaborative performance.
>
> 6. The value of individual rewards is debatable. Group work is a two-stage process, the initial and subsequent encounters requiring the use of different strategies by the teacher' (Galton and Williamson 1992 : 42).

Galton and Williamson also suggest that

> 'the above findings offer considerable reassurance to advocates of group work. It appears to have considerable cognitive benefits for pupils of different ability, gender and race, although there are issues still to be resolved. They argue that because researchers have ignored theoretical perspectives developed by social psychologists studies have been of a rather descriptive nature' (Galton and Williamson 1992 : 44).

So, although advantages claimed for group work are supported here and well documented by Barnes and Todd (1977), Edwards and Mercer (1987) and Cowie and Ruddock (1988) reviews of research evidence, indicate that even though pupils were seated in groups, most of their time was spent on individual tasks (Galton et al 1980; Bennett et al 1984; Tizzard et al 1988; Howe 1997). As Galton and Williamson reiterate classroom observational research has repeatedly come up with the finding that there is little collaboration among pupils in the primary classroom and that teachers, as a whole, show marked reluctance to use it as a major teaching strategy.

Murphy and Spence (1997) and Murphy and Davidson (2002) have explored the influence of scientific task on social interaction within groups of children. They considered the responses of different groups of children completing similar tasks (cleaning dirty water, dissolving sugar, investigating friction etc). To judge whether the pupils were working collaboratively together, they focused on gleaning evidence of shared goals, shared task responsibility, shared resources, shared thinking, shared decision-making. They found that the tasks used in classrooms influence the kinds of thinking in which children engage and this in turn influences learning outcomes. The nature of task impacts on the interaction between students' understandings, expectations and interactions and those of the teacher. They identified that pupils must exchange thinking with each other in the process of completing the task, and therefore teachers need to actively monitor students' engagement and interactions during group work. They need to be able to distinguish when it is the children's; i) scientific understanding which limits their participation in activities; ii) their communication skills which limits their ability to articulate their views, attend to others and to negotiate resolutions and hence their participation; and iii) their differing views of salience which prevents them agreeing a common task and shared reference hence preventing participation in shared activity.

If pupils are placed in a *predict outcome – test prediction – interpret results* format there are major implications for both group interaction and subsequent learning (Howe et al 1995; Tolmie et al 1993). Howe (1998) indicates that when she compared groups producing original explanations or selecting from a list produced by the teacher, the former is more effective. She explains 'Research is just beginning here, but it is unlikely that such results will turn out to be isolated examples once the issue of task structure is explored systematically' (Howe 1998:20). Recent studies have shown how the nature of tasks engaged in can influence the learning demands (Galton, Hargreaves and Pell 2009). However, there still remain un-answered questions, especially in secondary science classrooms, about the differences in learning processes and outcomes, when small groups of learners tackle similar but differentiated tasks.

There is a paucity of information offering insights into group learning interactions within differentially structured practical situations including investigational work in secondary science. Therefore a study of collaborative interactions whilst performing experimental work is an area that presents itself as one that merits investigation.

2.5 Influence of interaction on achievement

Interactive experiences can make individuals feel uncomfortable, even if they are not explicitly told that their presence is unwelcome. The classroom is a public forum in which it is necessary to display one's problem-solving and managerial skills. Although not the workplace, the classroom might be the place where interaction might provide boys and girls with different opportunities to acquire and practise particular skills. Howe (1998) argues that the 'non-displaying' sex might respond in such a way that academic achievement is at risk, indeed the lack of interpersonal relations may result in withdrawal altogether. Academic achievement might be preserved if interpersonal relations of a private, individualised nature are possible with a more expert learner or teacher. Howe (1998) postulates that it is possible that girls adopt alternative and seemingly 'compensatory strategies', i.e.: Good et al (1980) and Dart and Clarke (1988) note girls make more individual approaches to teachers than boys, and Jones and Gerig (1994) find that by virtue of these approaches girls' questions are more likely than boys' to be answered.

She reviews a variety of research on whole class interaction and suggests that

> 'pupils play an active part in bringing the gender differences in classroom interaction into being boys are more likely than girls to create conditions where their contributions will be sought by teachers, and they are more likely than girls to push themselves forward when contributors are not explicitly selected' (Howe 1997:11).

In analysing feedback to pupils, Howe summarises 'higher levels of negative feedback to boys than to girls, a finding which is consistently attributed to male misbehaviour.' There are, however, studies where no gender difference in 'criticism' is found (Smith and Glynn 1990). She deduces that boys probably receive more positive feedback, too.

In reviewing the effect of the sex of the teacher and its potential impact on class interaction, Howe (1997:13) notes that there are few indications that teacher variables of any description exert much influence. She notes, however, that pupil variables may be more relevant, particularly ability. Good et al (1973) and more elliptically, Morgan and Dunn (1988) suggest that high-ability boys are particularly favoured while low-ability boys can sometimes contribute the least of all. This may be significant when trying to interpret the finding that the dominance of boys reflects the talkativeness of a subgroup (Dart and Clarke 1988).

Kruger (1993) states that 'two novices can facilitate each other's acquisition of a complex concept'.

Her experimental evidence indicates that when naïve children solve a problem together, they advance more in their understanding of it than they do when they work alone. This has been shown with tasks such as conservation (e.g.: Doise and Mugny 1979), spatial co-ordination (e.g.: Emler and Valiant 1982), legal thinking (Roy and Howe 1990), moral reasoning (e.g.: Berkowitz, Gibbs and Broughton 1980) and mathematics (Phelps and Damon 1989).

Kruger reiterates that :

> 'The beneficial effects of peer collaboration ......is a well documented phenomenon' (Kruger 1993 : 165).

She considers (ibid) however that:

> 'what is more controversial is the mechanism by which peer collaboration promotes cognitive development in the child.'

Howe (1997) concludes in her review of current research that principles of effective group work are beginning to emerge, and that sooner or later these are likely to exert an influence upon classroom practice. She discusses how

> 'virtually all classroom interaction research is limited to descriptions of what takes place' .... 'with very few [studies] relating 'interaction' to measures of academic performance' (Howe, 1997: 5).

Interaction as a catalyst

Howe, Rodgers and Tolmie (1990) and Howe, Tolmie and Rodgers (1992) have found that pupils can benefit academically from collaborating even when group performance is low. This is because 'group interaction can act as a catalyst for subsequent reflection and learning, regardless of the quality of the interaction itself' (Howe, 1997:20).

Howe (1998) argues that even if group work is not working effectively in its current form, there may be other approaches which achieve greater success. She argues that as group work has always seemed desirable on social grounds, the quest for different methods has been high on the research agenda for the past ten years. She suggests that the issue of task structure is one that may provide useful insights into more effective learning interactions. This issue is initially addressed by my research project here, and subsequently informs discussion of implications for secondary science teachers' professional development and practice in the classroom.

2.6 National policy on group work

Kutnick (1990:8) identifies the tension between governmental and teacher ideologies. The UK government has argued that traditional whole class practices should be increased. Ideologically from the teacher's perspective a more child centred, active participation in learning is desirable, but is difficult to bring about in practice, especially with regard to effective groupings.

Alexander et al, (1992) and OFSTED, (1993) have found teachers use a range of groupings in their classrooms, and define 'fitness for purpose' as an analytical tool for making choices about the nature of working groups. Fitness for purpose applies to size of group, social context of instruction, teacher and pupil preference and how composition might be determined by ability, friendships, or social skills. This notion has been constrained somewhat by governmental policy cited in 'Excellence in Schools' (DfEE 1997), whereby 'setting'[4] was advocated in science, mathematics and languages. If, however, schools can justify other forms of effective grouping, that provide 'support for those who need it most while continuing to challenge all pupils' (DfEE 1997:38) setting is not compulsory. Some teachers continue to be advocates of alternative grouping strategies to support pupils working together, because as Heathfield (1999) describes, 'it reflects the true nature of learning'.

In the National Curriculum guidance for learning across the curriculum, social development in science is rationalised (2000:8) as 'helping pupils recognising how the formation of opinion and the justification of decisions can be informed by experimental evidence, and drawing attention to how different interpretations of scientific evidence can be used...' . Also highlighted is the key skill of 'working with others through carrying out scientific investigations', but no further elucidation of the pedagogic approach is offered.

---

[4] Setting:Pupils are regrouped into classes for different subjects on the basis of their attainment in the subject concerned.

It seems though, that policy generally, is to promote 'working together' skills through practical work and that this should be carried out with groups of pupils of similar ability.

The DfEE group work directives add gravitas to the argument that more careful studies need to be undertaken regarding the nature and influences on effective collaborative learning, as Howe (1997) indicates, so that teachers can make informed pedagogic decisions in planning and practice.

Chapter three

3. 1 Introduction

The intention of this chapter is to elucidate various fundamental psychological learning theories, which are then drawn upon later, to illuminate and inform how current practice in science classrooms could be improved when employing small group work strategies. Much of the theory is discussed in detail to explicate the variance between differing interpretations of constructivism. As Roth (1995:11) explains, 'we make sense in various ways, and understand the world not merely by means of one theory ....or interpretative repertoire, but in a multi-faceted way and from different (ideological) positions'. In my efforts to understand and interpret classroom happenings, successive theoretical frameworks were the varifocal lenses through which I observed and theorised. Thus my reflections on the (re)application of these theories later in the thesis requires this literature review to present a balanced, descriptive account of contrasting psychological learning theories. The intention is that they will serve as referents for locating and discussing my findings in an intellectual sense.

My role as a science educator

In my role at Keele University, as a science educator, supporting and guiding local teachers in their pedagogical and curricular developments I was questioned on several occasions concerning evidence that the Cognitive Acceleration through Science Education (CASE) project improved children's performance at GCSE[5]. The cognitive acceleration approach offered evidence that suggested an interventional programme (Thinking Science) taught to Key Stage 3 pupils effects 15 – 20% improvements in A – C grades (of Mathematics, Science and English) in GCSE examinations (Shayer 1996; 2000) at Key Stage 4. I was aware of the various associated theories of cognitive development, but had not considered in detail what this meant in terms of secondary science pedagogy, especially as CASE emphasised group work as an integral, but overt teaching strategy. Thinking Science, the curriculum materials of the CASE project, it seemed, was predicated on

[5] GCSE is the abbreviation for General Certificate in Secondary Education, the culmination examination used at the end of Key stage 4 to assess pupils' academic attainment.

Piagetian tenets (with some Vygotskian methodology). Alongside this curiosity regarding 'cognition' and factors affecting its development, I began to consider how inextricably linked learning and pedagogy were. At this time O'Loughlin's (1992) claim that science education needs 'rethinking' also stimulated me to explore the various theories of learning and their associated potential impact on the children's cognition. O'Loughlin questioned pedagogy founded on constructivism, a teaching approach promoted by many science educators at that time. As a professional leader of teaching and learning in the context of secondary science I strove to understand the development of cognition to objectively review and evaluate the underpinning philosophy and mechanisms involved in CASE. The following discussion in this chapter is intended to describe and place in context the various perspectives science (and other) educators hold of 'cognition' and 'learning theory'. Terms such as constructivism, social construction, learning, knowledge and understanding, often inconsistently and inappropriately applied, will be reviewed. I will consider from an evolutionary perspective the theoretical grounding and development of constructivism, (arising from Piagetian perspectives) and latterly (discussing developments in understandings) from a Vygotskian viewpoint. The characteristics of the ideas within the theories will be considered, focusing particularly on the 'agency' of learning, the nature of knowledge and how that influences the perceived learning processes. The interactions between individuals within a 'social' context that appear to support learning will then be discussed. I will then attempt to clarify my view on learning and indicate how it has determined the issues for the research and influenced the focus and methodological approach adopted in this study.

3.2 Theoretical perspectives of learning

Defining the issues

In the ensuing discussion of the theoretical grounding of educational theories the commonalties and contrasts are considered. Although many theorists agree that the child is the 'constructor' of knowledge (or the agency of learning), there are disagreements about how learning occurs (the processes involved), and where it occurs (solely in the mind, or combinationally through bodily engagement and the mind, or through language), what influences might have a greater or lesser bearing (context, structure, historical, social, cultural) and what outcomes are a measure that learning has occurred (knowledge; 'expertise'; skill; reality; understanding). The various issues surrounding perspectives of learning are addressed in this chapter.

3.3 Constructivism

The theoretical underpinning of constructivism is based on Piagetian notions of how children learn. Piaget, a Swiss psychologist, with a background in biology and natural sciences, studied the evolution of children's thinking. In his studies, which involved detailed questioning of children, he argued how knowledge was constructed through his descriptions of the development of understanding such things as number, time, space, velocity, geometry, chance and morality from birth to adolescence. He theorised that there was a genetic influence to higher order mental processes, in that thinking evolved from biological mechanisms, rooted in the development of an individual's cognitive structures, ie: nervous system.

He also believed there was a maturational influence, that the processes of concept formation follow a pattern through several clearly definable stages (Figure 3.1: The Piagetian stages of development) which are hierarchical and each must be experienced before any subsequent stage of development is possible.

Piaget takes an 'active' rather than 'passive' view of the part played by children in their own development. It is through a child's experiences in the world, that a child can 'construct their own knowledge'. He argued that conceptual development occurs through action (with materials), and that 'thought is internalised action' so therefore children have to be active and 'constructive' in order to develop their understanding of the world. This is illustrated by an attractive metaphor, utilised by Margaret Donaldson, on the front cover of her book '*Children's Minds*' (1978) which provides an image of a learner, a young girl manipulating two pieces of wood presumably in the process of actively constructing an understanding of some phenomenon. The image portrays the learner as an active, constructive knower, empowered to take charge of his or her own learning. This presents an archetypical image of constructivism. It is whilst they are actively attempting to adapt to the environment, that they organise actions into schemata through the processes of assimilation and accommodation.

Period	Stage	Mental age range in years
Sensori-motor	I Sensori-motor	0-2
Preparation for,	II Pre-operational	
and use of,	(A) Pre-conceptual	2-4
concrete operations	(B) Intuitive	4-7
(or latency)	III Concrete operations	7-11.5
Formal operations	IV Formal operations	11.5 onwards

Figure 3.1 : The Piagetian stages of development (Adopted from Brown, G. and Desforges, C. 1979).

Assimilation is when the learner re-organises the cognitive structure to accommodate the new learning. Schemata are kinds of understandings or types of thought (Rommetveit 1985:193), which Piaget classified into distinct patterns of cognitive behaviour; e.g.; Combinations, relating to chemical combinations in a dye, an inhibitor or neutralising agent; correlations and probability, discovering the correlational relations between a pair of variables hair and eye colour (Gruber and Voneche 1995:397) or recognising how sample size can affect measured outcomes; proportionalistic thinking, recognising the ratio of one thing to another, like, for example, gearing ratios of differently sized cogs (Adey, Shayer and Yates 2000).

The sensori-motor stage describes the progressive development from inherent reflex systems to the onset of language use. The pre-conceptual stage describes how children use transductive reasoning in order to form pre-concepts. A young child sees her mother combing her hair. She says 'Mummy is combing her hair. She is going shopping'. The child links the two actions, although both are carried out at other times linked with other activities. Egocentricism also pre-dominates because the child is unable to view things from another person's point of view. The intuitive stage is very much superficial perceptions of the environment. This is because the child appears to be unable to consider all aspects of a situation simultaneously. A child will usually fixate on one dimension of an object or event to the exclusion of all others, which Piaget calls *centring*. Concrete operations are those where a child can reason, but largely based on the perceptual facts or happenings before them. They can identify, and qualitatively describe relationships between variables, but not necessarily explain them. They can classify at this stage, (group things together with similar characteristics) unlike the pre-conceptual stage, sorting between similar (and dissimiliar) relevant properties. Formal operations are the highest levels of thinking. Understanding, and developing a mental model to explain, for example, volume, density, dissolution, justice or cruelty requires this *abstract* thinking capability without needing the concrete materials to provide substance to the argument.

Thought or thinking, according to Piaget, has its origins physically performed and then internalised. So thought is internalised actions.

3.3.1 Defining the learning process

Knowledge, according to Piaget, is accrued within an individual (all processes are 'intermental'). Through experiences, new knowledge is acquired, that is 'checked' against existing self-knowledge. These may be triggered by disequilibrium (conflict with existing beliefs or pre-conceptions). This 'new' experience or information has to be accommodated and assimilated as a 'reconstructed' concept. The empirical evidence for this 'rearranged' concept is embraced within the individual's inner mental model. It is only through experience that ideas are amended. His account of knowledge comprises 'mental constructions', which the child creates to make sense of his or her experience of the world. In applying his stages of development theory, he argues that attempts to question, show or explain things to children before they are mentally 'ready' cannot foster *development*, though the child may learn 'empty' procedures. Indeed, premature teaching and questioning may demoralise or frustrate a child who can not begin to understand what he is being 'taught'. He argues that immature pre-operational thinkers can learn *procedures* but not develop *conceptual* understanding. Fosnot (1989) argues that constructivism is equated with the kind of rational scientific reasoning processes familiar in Piaget's theory:

> 'A constructivist takes the position that the learner must have experience with hypothesizing and predicting, manipulating objects, posing questions, researching answers, imagining, investigating and inventing, in order for new constructions to be developed. From this perspective, the teacher cannot ensure that learners acquire knowledge just by having the teacher dispense it; a learner-centred, active instructional model is mandated. The learner must construct the knowledge.'
>
> Fosnot (1989:20)

Fosnot also highlights that resolving cognitive dissonance, at the child's initiative, in Piaget's view, is essential to the development of cognition.

Piaget viewed the entire purpose of intellectual growth as one of coming to know reality more objectively through developing increasingly de-centred and hence more objective perceptions of reality (O'Loughlin 1992:793). For Piaget 'the structure of the mind is the source of our understanding of the world' (Venn and Walkerdine 1977:73). Piaget was not an innatist who believed that interpretative schemes pre-exist in the mind, nor did he believe that we could apprehend reality through direct experience as behaviourists do. Piaget suggested that our interpretative schemes evolve as a result of successively more complex interactions with the world. Piaget's theory is developmental in orientation, suggesting that we begin by developing operations to act on our world, and eventually, by the stage of formal operations, we have acquired abstract, logico-mathematical reasoning capacities that allow us to detach ourselves from the object world so that we can reason about it in strictly logical terms. Piaget conceptualised the process of coming to know in biological terms because he viewed intellectual adaptation as merely a specific case of the larger process by which organisms engage in biological adaptation to the environment.

As O'Loughlin (1992) notes, Piaget focussed primarily on logico-mathematical reasoning, the kind of 'purposive-rational, goal-directed behaviour' (Broughton 1981:270) that is normally equated with mathematical problem solving and empiricist conceptions of scientific rationality.

He argues that Piaget's hypothetico-deductive method of systematic hypothesis testing is similar to that which empirical scientists arguably engage in (although Knorr-Cetina 1981; Knorr-Cetina and Mulkay 1983; Latour and Woolgar 1979, would argue actions of scientists are much more constructivist in nature than many empirical scientists might care to admit).

3.3.2 Views of knowledge

Child is the meaning maker (Bruner 1983; Newson 1978) through constructing his or her own understandings of the world. At the core of constructivism is the belief that human beings build up knowledge in a slow process, and that the expanding mental model of the world that he or she inhabits is the result of the child's constructive effort, achieved through a progressive and cumulative process of hypothesis formation, testing and modification. Each new step in the constructive process results from a transaction in which what is already known is brought to bear on new information, creating new meaning and enhancing understanding.

Epistemologically there is debate regarding knowledge; radical constructivists (Von Glaserfeld 1984) assert, also, that knowledge is not passively received but actively built up by cognitising the subject matter. However, their definition of knowledge is not objective 'reality', that which scientists accept is a universal 'truth', e.g.: Enstein's theory of relativity[6], Newton's law of gravity. Radical constructivists argue that knowledge is experientially accrued to inform our personal model of the world. Arguably, the function of cognition is adaptive and serves the organisation of the experiential world, not the discovery of 'ontological' reality. In other words as an individual interacts with the world, 'knowledge' is confirmed or refuted, 'knowing' is only within our own, self-constructed world. The perception of (not-so-radical) constructivists is that knowledge is 'objective' and independent of particular individuals who know.

As Sigel (1978) describes, (non-radical) constructivism is:

> '……that process of constructing, in effect, creating a concept which serves as a guideline against which objects or people can be gauged. During the course of interactions with objects, people, or events the individual constructs a reality of them…this mental construction then guides subsequent actions with the objects or events' (Sigel 1978:334).

[6] Einstein's theory of relativity explains the relationships between space, time and matter in a mathematical way.

He further clarifies his thinking by adding another dimension to his view by arguing that

> 'for the necessity of considering each individual as a scientist, constantly engaged in dialectical interaction with reality, and constantly evaluating information for its congruence with current representations of reality.' (ibid)

Sigel focuses on the development of mental representations of reality. He argues that to develop abstract representations we need to detach ourselves from our own reality, and to increase the accuracy and complexity of our representations we need to be confronted with contradictions and discrepancies that induce cognitive conflict and thus force us to re-evaluate our existing interpretations in light of the discrepant information. His perspective considers absolute scientific reality as knowledge. Bauersfeld (1995:143) summarises the differing views that constructivists hold of 'knowledge'; one is that knowledge is an object, a finite issue or goal, a truth; the other is that of knowledge as an action or process, as 'something that works', as Von Glaserfeld (1984) suggests.

In my view the interpretations that individual learners place on what they hear or read depends on their existing understanding and on their interpretations of the total context in which the propositions are encountered, and if (as is often the aim in classrooms) learners are to come to know what their teachers percieve, more is required than the presentation of propositional knowledge through talk or text. There also needs to be extended opportunity for discussion and problem-solving in the context of shared activities, in which meaning and action are collaboratively constructed and negotiated. In other words, education must be thought of in terms not of the transmission of knowledge but of transaction and transformation (Bruner 1990; Moll 1993).

Reflections of constructivist perspectives of learning, lead me to take Goodman's (1984) view that there are as many worlds as there are knowers. He argues, quite successfully, that the world can only be described within our own frames of experience, and as we all experience a unique permutation of formal and informal learning or life experience our self-constructed models of the world must be particular. As Rommetveit (1985) asserts

> '..knowledge, ... propositions,...... formulations cannot be identical from one knower to another because for each knower the propositions are embedded in a unique structure of personal knowing arrived at through a particular, socially situated learning biography.'

Goodman and Elgin (1988) consider the meaning of 'knowledge':

> 'Taken as pursuit of knowledge, that (*cognitive*) endeavour starts from sure truths and seeks by means of derivation, observation, and experiment to discover others and so to arrive at an accurate and comprehensive description of 'the real' ready made world. The foundation is supposedly solid, the methods prescribed, and the goal eternal transcendent truth. In contrast, taken as the advancement of *understanding*, the cognitive endeavour starts from what happens to be currently adopted and proceeds to integrate and organise, weed out and supplement, not in order to arrive at truth about something already made but in order to make something right – to construct something that works cognitively, that fits together and handles new cases, that may implement further inquiry and invention' Goodman and Elgin (1988:163).

It is the perspective of a learner, as an active constructor of personally (and socially) referenced, checked and accepted or rejected information that I have assumed in my pupils.

3.3.3 Role of language

Piaget's perception of the role of language is similar to visual perception. It is a way of representing the world. He purports that language exerts no formative effect on the structure of thinking. It is a medium, a method of representation, within which thought takes place. He describes how mental actions and operations, the processes of thought, are derived from action, not talk. He does, however, more subtly add that language can facilitate the 'emergence' of thought. Through talking to others, particularly other children, the child's thinking becomes socialised.

Donaldson (1987) emphasises the promotion of sense making and thoughtfulness in classrooms that can only occur when students feel comfortable enough to talk in their own tentative voices in order to reach for their own tentative understandings. Both Duckworth (1978) and Donaldson (1987) emphasise the importance of perplexity and confusion in the process of coming to new understandings, and both emphasise the slow and messy path to the construction of personal meaning. Both are clear too, that although the teacher's role is to try to promote the kind of intellectualism that will enable students to move forward to what Piaget might call abstract thinking, and what Donaldson refers to as 'disembedded thought' (Donaldson 1987:75), this can only be done by acknowledging individual learners' frames of reference and by raising questions that cause learners to become reflective about their points of view:

> 'To the extent that one carries on a conversation with a child, as a way of trying to understand a child's understanding, the child's understanding increases *in the very process*. The questions the interlocutor asks, in an attempt to clarify for herself what the child is thinking oblige the child to think a little further also...... [for example] What do you mean? How did you do that? Why did you say that? How does that fit in with what she just said? Could you give me an example? How did you figure that? In every case these questions are primarily a way for the interlocutor to try to understand what the other is understanding. Yet, in every case, also they engage the other's thoughts and take them a step further' (Duckworth 1987: 96-97).

Duckworth takes the Piagetian view of thought and language a step further to explain how verbal exchange (or interaction) of this kind, between teacher and learner can help clarify the pupils' understandings. The perspective that reflective verbalisation can offer insight into a child's cognitive processing informs the nature of the evidence I intend to seek in my observations of pupils-in-action.

The following section considers the contrasting views of social constructivism, childrens' understandings brought about through social interactions of some kind, underpinned by Vygotskian perspectives of knowing and learning.

3.4 Social Constructivism

Vygotsky, a Russian psychologist, was concerned with the influence of societal factors on individual intellectual development. He postulated that children's cognitive development could not be understood without regard to the social interaction with others. Leont'ev (1981:55) highlights Vygotsky's view of the importance of social interaction in the development of thought:

> 'higher psychological processes unique to humans can be acquired only through interaction with others, that is, through interpsychological processes that only later will begin to be carried out independently by the individual.'

Juxtaposed to Piaget's more individualistic perspective of learning, Vygotsky (1978, 1987) perceived these higher mental functions: thinking, reasoning and understanding as social in their origin. Central to his notions of learning is the concept of the 'zone of proximal development' (zpd), the region within which a child could be sensitively guided to complete a task. He emphasised that children could engage in joint problem solving with the support (guidance or scaffolding) from a more expert other, to develop another's zpd. The concept of zpd has since become an integral component of other teaching theories, eg: Tharp and Gallimore (1988) who developed the term 'assisted performance' and describe it as offering social guidance to learners. Vygotsky's perception was that the child's interactions with other people serve to mediate between the child and the world-to-be-learned-about. Understanding learning arguably, depends on understanding the types of interactions that serve to foster it.

In contrast to Piaget's developmental theory which focused to a large extent on individual, isolated minds that construct knowledge from experiences in the world, Vygotsky's view of learning regards individual cognitive development as subject to dialogic interplay between nature and history, biology and culture, the lone intellect and society. His perspective on psychology reflected his views on the historical and cultural origins of the way in which people in different societies come to act upon, construe and represent their world.

Vygotsky also focussed closely on the links between modes of discourse and modes of thought, he believed that language and communication (and hence, instruction) promoted intellectual and personal development. He thought that instruction lay at the heart of development, enabling a child's potential for learning to be revealed when working with more knowledgeable others.

Arguably, the two most important dimensions of Vygotsky's work in relation to developing arguments to clarify how understanding develops in learners are:

1. The 'zone of proximal development' (offering a contrasting view of cognitive or mental 'readiness' to Piaget).
2. The general genetic law of cultural development.

3.4.1 The zone of proximal development

Vygotsky's (1978) notion of the zpd'[7] (offering a contrasting view of cognitive or mental 'readiness' to Piaget[8]) is described as 'the distance between a child's 'actual developmental level as determined by independent problem solving' and the higher level of 'potential development as determined through problem solving' under adult guidance or in collaboration with more capable peers' Vygotsky (1978:86). Wood (1998:17) defines this interactional process as one which can result in:

> 'Children's knowledge' as 'a product of the 'joint construction' of understanding by the child and more expert members of his culture.'

The extent to which peers can assist each other, then, will influence learning outcomes.

Conventional explanations of the zpd view learning as a process by which a learner internalises knowledge, whether 'discovered', transmitted' from others, or 'experienced in interaction' with others. This focus on internalisation, in social constructivist theories, does not just leave the nature of the learner, of the world, and of their relations unexplored; it can only reflect far-reaching assumptions concerning these issues. It establishes a sharp dichotomy between inside and outside, suggesting that knowledge is largely cerebral, and takes the individual as the non-problematic unit of analysis. Furthermore, learning as internalisation is too easily construed as an unproblematic process of absorbing the given, as a matter of transmission and assimilation. The notion of zpd has received vastly differing interpretations, roughly classified into three categories. One of these interpretations (discussed in detail later in this section) directly informs my research about how to 'assist' pupils when working together.

The ways in which others have drawn on Vygotsky's perception of the zpd concerns the nature of the child's interactions with other people which serve to mediate between the child and the world-to-be-learned-about. Understanding

---

[7] Vygoskian notion of readiness relates to the 'region of sensitivity to instruction' (Wood and Middleton, 1975), or bandwidth of competence (Brown, 1979; Brown and Reeve, 1987), where students are ripe for new learning.

[8] Piagetian notion of 'readiness' defines whether a child has reached one level of cognitive competency and is ready to move to the next.

learning, arguably, from this perspective depends on understanding the types of interactions that serve to foster it.

In contrast to Piaget's developmental theory which focused to a large extent on individual, isolated minds that construct knowledge from experiences in the world, Vygotsky's view of learning regards individual cognitive development as subject to 'dialogic' interplay between nature and history, biology and culture, the lone intellect and society. His perspective on psychology reflected his views on the historical and cultural origins of the way in which people in different societies come to act upon, construe and represent their world. Vygotsky also focused closely on the links between modes of discourse and modes of thought, he believed that language and communication (and hence, instruction) promoted intellectual and personal development. He thought that instruction lay at the heart of development, enabling a child's potential for learning to be revealed when working with more knowledgeable others.

3.4.2 Mediation

Vygosky argued that to mediate 'higher mental functioning', i.e.: to enable a learner to move into their zpd, would require "psychological tools" (particularly speech) (Daniels 1996: 7), in the form of either signs or symbols, individual activities or interpersonal relations. Vygotsky claims that a defining feature of human mental functioning (on both the intermental and intramental planes) is mediated by tools and signs. He describes mediational means as a way of organising one's own or others' action, using signs such as various forms of speaking or social languages (Wertsch 1985). For Vygotsky, teaching is important as a particular form of interaction or mediation between a more knowledgeable other and a novice. It is in this interaction that we see children 'appropriating' adult language, using it as a pseudoconcept, and then internalising it until it becomes transformed into a useful intrapsychological construct, often then regulated by such language processes as inner speech. Vygotsky's view of the teaching-learning interaction is described by Brown and Ferrara (1985):

> 'Vygotsky's theory of cognitive development rests heavily on the key concept of *internalisation*.......The child first experiences active problem solving activities in the presence of others but gradually comes to perform these functions independently.

> The process of internalisation is gradual; first the adult or knowledgeable peer controls and guides the child's activity, but gradually the adult and child come to share the problem solving functions with the child taking the initiative and the adult correcting and guiding when she falters. Finally, the adult cedes control to the child and functions primarily as a supportive and sympathetic audience. (Brown and Ferrara 1985: 281)

Mediation then, is a form of scaffolding, to help or support pupils who can not solve a problem unaided. Mediation can take many forms including a cue of some kind, be it a (verbal or written) psychological tool, which could be a series of progressive questions or a gesture toward equipment to be used; or a psychological sign such as a nod or shake of the head or symbols such as a diagrammatic representations of experimental work.

3.4.3 Thought and speech

Vygotsky studied the development of childhood speech. He discerned that language was both social and communicative in origin and intent, and that there is an important stage of transition between two quite different functions of language. Initially speech serves as a regulative, communicative function (i.e.: child communicating to adult....hungry, pain, help me), later it also serves other functions and transforms the way in which children learn, think and understand. It becomes an instrument or tool of thought, not just providing a 'code' or system for representing the world (as Piaget perceived). For Vygotsky, then, not only do physical actions that serve to manipulate and organise the world get internalised to become (non-verbal) thinking: the physical activity of speaking, which serves to regulate the actions of others, also becomes internalised to create verbal thinking. Vygotsky describes all forms of thought, then, as *activities.* Vygotsky (1986:251):

> 'Thought, unlike speech, does not consist of separate units. When I wish to communicate the thought that today I saw a barefoot boy in a blue shirt running down the street, I do not see every item separately: the boy, the shirt, its blue colour, his running, and the absence of shoes. I conceive of all this in one thought, but I put it into separate words. A speaker often takes several minutes to disclose one thought. In his mind the whole thought is present at once, but in speech it has to be developed successively. A thought may be compared to a cloud shedding a shower of words. Precisely because thought does not have its automatic counterpart in words, the transition from thought to word leads through meaning.'

He provides a perspective on 'inner speech' too, which could be described as verbalised or conscious thinking, and its role in developing thought.

> 'The transition from inner speech to external speech is not a simple translation from one language to another. ...It is a complex dynamic process involving the transformation of the predicative, idiomatic structure of inner speech into syntactically articulated speech intelligible to others.' Vygotsky (1986:249)

He goes on to elucidate how thought should be transformed to an external means of communicating one's ideas. The complex transition from internal to external speech depends on

> '...shaping a thought first in inner speech, then in meanings of words, and finally in words.' Vygotsky (1986:253).

Vygotsky strongly believed that articulating thoughts was an effective method to process, connected or random, thoughts in a conscious way to raise the awareness of mental activity and subsequently create organised logic and meaning for ones self and others from these utterances.

Thinking and doing.....

Vygotsky (1978) says in an early essay:

> 'Children solve practical tasks with the help of their speech, as well as with their eyes and hands. This unity of perception, speech and action, which ultimately produces internalisation of the visual field, constitutes the central subject matter for any analysis of the origin of uniquely human forms of behaviour' Vygotsky (1978:26).

Central to his notions of learning is the concept of the 'zone of proximal development' (zpd), the region within which a child could be sensitively guided to complete a task. He emphasised that children could engage in joint problem solving with the support (guidance or scaffolding) from a more expert other, to develop another's zpd. The concept of zpd has since become an integral component of other teaching theories, e.g.: Tharp and Gallimore (1988[i]) who much later developed the term 'assisted performance' and describe it as offering social guidance to learners. Vygotsky's perception was that the child's interactions with other people serve to mediate between the child and the world-to-be-learned-about.

Vygotsky (1978) says in an early essay:

> 'Children solve practical tasks with the help of their speech, as well as with their eyes and hands. This unity of perception, speech and action, which ultimately produces

internalisation of the visual field, constitutes the central subject matter for any analysis of the origin of uniquely human forms of behaviour' Vygotsky (1978:26).

Central to his notions of learning is the concept of the 'zone of proximal development' (zpd), the region within which a child could be sensitively guided to complete a task. He emphasised that children could engage in joint problem solving with the support (guidance or scaffolding) from a more expert other, to develop another's zpd. The concept of zpd has since become an integral component of other teaching theories, e.g.: Tharp and Gallimore (1988[ii]) who much later developed the term 'assisted performance' and describe it as offering social guidance to learners. Vygotsky's perception was that the child's interactions with other people serve to mediate between the child and the world-to-be-learned-about.

3.4.4 The genetic law of cultural development

Vygotsky and Luria argue that systems for representing and communicating knowledge generate important transformations in the minds of those who master them. So when children learn how to read, and how to make use of mathematical symbols, they acquire new ways of thinking as they master and internalise activities needed to work upon and exploit these new mental tools. As Shotter (1992) describes, children first have to learn *the ways* to make sense of others and construct knowledge which allows them to organise and relate self to circumstances. In this endeavour, words become transparent means through which children make meaningful contact with their surroundings and others. When there is difficulty in this contact, the transparency disappears, and meaning has to be derived through a process of interpretation. Meanings, using words, have to be negotiated (to develop shared or common understandings of objects, observations, processes) and socially constructed. So individuals are interacting and functioning as members of intellectual communities, constructing meaning collectively (not individuals who build understanding independently of others) before Self-understanding develops. Vygotsky identified the roots of intellectual functioning found first in our surroundings and through interactions with Others before appearing internally:

> 'Developmental processes....... operate only when the child is interacting with people in his environment and in co-operation with peers' (Vygotsky 1978).

From this perspective Vygotsky formulated his general law of development:

> 'Any function in the child's cultural development appears twice, or on two planes. First it appears on the social plane, and then on the psychological plane. First it appears between people as an interpsychological category, and then within the child as an intrapsychological category. This is equally true with regard to voluntary attention, logical memory, the formation of concepts, and the development of volition.......it goes without saying that internalisation transforms the process itself and changes its structure and functions. Social relations or relations among people genetically underlie all higher functions and their relationships' (Vygotsky 1981:163).

These assertions of Vygotsky's notions of individual mental functioning support the underpinning idea that higher mental functioning retains its origins in social processes. Vygotsky does not elaborate in detail on how social and individual psychological planes might be similar or different, but he does describe how mental (internal) processes, are quasi-social in nature, because internal thoughts are processed in a person's own private sphere, thus retaining the functions of social interaction, or as it could be described 'talking to ones self' inter-mentally.

Mercer (1998) elaborates on the social-ness of meaning-making, he describes how different kinds of talk can illustrate whether pupils are engaged in effective social construction. In his analysis he clarifies how one pupil building positively on another's utterance is cumulative talk, but engaging critically and constructively with another's idea is exploratory. He clarifies how different types of talk are distinctive social modes of thinking, because 'knowledge is made more publicly accountable' and 'reasoning is more visible in the talk' (Mercer 1998:104).

3.4.5 Concept development

Vygotsky described differences between scientific and everyday life concepts. He argues that both are important in the formation of mature concepts (Daniels 1996:11). He describes scientific concepts as systematic, organised and hierarchical (like classifying and sorting objects with various criteria in mind, solving logical problems, quantifying relationships), whereas everyday concepts are tightly linked to particular contexts and lack an overall system.

Vygotsky emphasised the role of metacognition to 'meld' scientific thinking with everyday referents, to enable concepts to 'come to life' and be applicable across a range of situations.

> 'Vygotsky made it a point to argue that scientific concepts far from being assimilated in a ready made form, actually undergo substantial development which essentially depends on the existing level of a child's general ability to form concepts. This level of comprehension in its turn is connected with the development of spontaneous concepts. Spontaneous concepts in working their way upward toward greater abstractness, clear a path for scientific concepts in their downwards development toward greater concreteness' (Kozulin 1987:xxxiv).

Howe (1996) explains this by arguing that whilst pupils may be able to define or explain a given concept on a verbal level and be able to use words to express their understanding, a concept remains an abstraction and is not fully understood unless or until it can be applied to specific examples. In applying generalised concepts to specific examples student thinking becomes concrete, moving from the plane of abstract thought to the phenomenon represented by the words or symbols. In contrast, everyday concepts develop outside a definite system; therefore to be understood in relation to what has been learned in school, thinking about a given phenomenon must move upward from the known specific example toward abstraction and generalisation. The child must eventually come to see everyday concepts as part of a system of relationships and at, the same time come to see how the experienced object or phenomenon fits into the scientific system he or she has been taught. West and Pines (1985) suggest a metaphor that provides a useful image. The metaphor is of two vines: one vine representing spontaneous concepts grows upward while the other vine, representing scientific concepts, grows downward. Under the influence of instruction that encourages integration and consolidation the two vines intertwine and grow together as conceptual understanding develops.

Vygotsky also emphasised that only through interaction with adults, can children infer a sense of a concept. The need for teachers to understand how learners make sense of the world is highlighted by Duckworth (1987):

> 'Meaning is not given to us in our encounters with the environment, but it is given by us – constructed by each of us in our own way, according to how our understanding is currently organised. As teachers we need to respect the meaning our students are giving to the events that we share. In the interests of making connections between

> their understanding and ours, we must adopt an insider's view: seek to understand their sense as well as help them to understand ours' Duckworth (1987:112).

Bruner (1990) described earlier constructivist views of meaning making 'to discover and to describe formally the meanings that human beings created out of their encounters with the world' (p.2-3), he highlighted how it focused upon 'symbolic activities human beings employed in constructing and in making sense, not only of the world, but of themselves'. He later discusses how 'folk psychology' (p.35) can provide additional insight into the social and cultural effects on the processes by which, and situations in which, we develop meaning.

In Piaget's view the flow of construction is from one's interactions with one's non-human environment toward an exchange with others. In Vygotsky's view, the flow of conceptual development is reversed, from inter to intra exchange. What neither theorist addresses particularly well is the interaction between these two types of construction. Bruner (1986:126) elucidates somewhat on the connection between social worlds (of teacher and pupil) and the ways in which learners might engage with and come to understand scientific concepts. He describes an experience in a science lesson as a young boy:

> 'I recall a teacher, her name was Miss Orcutt, who made the statement in class, "It is a very puzzling thing not that water turns to ice at 32 degrees Fahrenheit, but that it should change from a liquid into a solid," She then went on to give us an intuitive account of Brownian movement and of molecules, expressing a sense of wonder that matched, indeed bettered, the sense of wonder I felt at that age (around ten) about everything I turned my mind to, including at the far reach such matters as light from extinguished stars still travelling toward us though their sources had been snuffed out. In effect, she was inviting me to extend *my* world of wonder to encompass *hers*. She was not just *informing* me. She was rather, negotiating the world of wonder and possibility. Molecules, solids, liquids, movement were not facts; they were to be used in pondering and imagining. Miss Orcutt was the rarity. She was a human event, not a transmission device' (Bruner 1986:126).

Explaining how conceptual understanding develops, Roth (1995) refers to Greeno's (1991) use of 'environment' as a physical metaphor of an intellectual domain with resources spread throughout. Using the environmental metaphor, knowing means to know your way around, to know where the resources are (buses, maps, streets, shops, pavement) and to be able to use them appropriately. Learning in this metaphor is equivalent to moving to a new place, finding your way around and using the resources available to support you. Taking a cognitive perspective, the knower, the learning and the known are inseparable. The knower develops cognitive structures which represent an ontological 'reality' (like Newtonian laws of gravity or Watson and Crick's structure of DNA). In the environmental metaphor, knowing refers to the abilities to find and use concepts rather developing a unique personal representation of the concept(s).

3.4.6 Interpretations of the zpd

The interpretations of Vygotsky's notion of the zpd can be roughly classified into three categories, scaffolding; cultural interpretation and the collectivist or societal perspective.

Scaffolding

The concept of scaffolding construes the zpd as the distance between engagement and mastery of a task. It has informed how to support or scaffold learners in their problem solving progress. Introduced by Wood, Bruner and Ross (1976), it captures the sense in which, through encouragement, focusing, reminders and suggestions, a learner can be supported in mastering a task or achieving understanding. Light and Littleton (1999:9) describe the building analogy of scaffolding:

> '..imagine building an arch with bricks it is easy to see the vital role played by the wooden *framework* used to assemble the arch. However, the role of this scaffolding is temporary, when complete the arch will hold itself up, without scaffolding it could not have been built.'

This interpretation has inspired pedagogical approaches that explicitly provide support for the initial performance of tasks to be later performed without assistance (Greenfield 1984; Wood, Bruner and Ross 1976; Tharp and Gallimore 1988). Tharp and Gallimore (ibid) even identify progression in the scaffolding. In the first stage the expert other directs the novice. In the second stage the learner takes over the role of 'scaffolder', often entailing 'talking oneself through' a task, remembering advice, reminders and injunctions previously given. The third stage is labelled as 'self-guidance' as the scaffolding is removed. The final fourth stage they recognise as one where there might be regression to earlier stages, when the task may be slightly different or other un-known factors affect performance. Scaffolding in this sense is flexible and characterised by the teacher's responsiveness to the needs of the learner; as Pearson (1996) highlights it allows teachers to intervene to provide the cueing, questioning, coaching and information required to enable students to complete a task before they are able to complete it independently. Scaffolding then is a way teachers (or more able other[s]) can mediate learning. Differing levels of support 'that enable a child or novice to solve a problem, carry out a task or achieve a goal which would be beyond his or her unassisted efforts' (Wood, Bruner and Ross 1976:90) are possible through a variety of strategies, for example, the simplicity or complexity with which a task is presented; the nature and sequence of questions a teacher might ask.

Cultural interpretation construes the zone more widely as the distance between the cultural knowledge provided by the socio-historical context, usually made accessible through instruction and many tasks, and the everyday experience of individuals (Davydov and Markova 1982). Hedegaard (1996) calls this the distance between understood knowledge, as provided by instruction, and active knowledge as owned by individuals. In these two classes of interpretation of the concept of the zone of proximal development, the social character of learning mostly consists in a small 'aura' of socialness (Roth 1995) that provides input for the process of internalisation viewed as individualistic acquisition of the cultural given. There is no account of the place of learning in the broad context of the structure of the social world.

Collectivist or societal perspective.

Engestrom defines the zone of proximal development as the 'distance between the everyday actions of individuals and the historically new form of the societal activity that can be collectively generated as a solution to the double bind potentially embedded in....everyday actions' (Engestrom 1999). Under such societal interpretations of the concept of the zpd researchers tend to concentrate on processes of social transformation. They share our interest in extending the study of learning beyond the context of pedagogical structuring, including the structure of the social world in the analysis, and taking into account in a central way the conflictual nature of social practice. Lave and Wenger (1991) also discuss Vygotsky's theory of learning as a dimension of social practice. This perspective places more emphasis on connecting issues of sociocultural transformation with the changing relations between newcomers and old timers in the context of a changing shared practice.

Although each perspective differs, they also share some key ideas, that in varying degrees they draw upon the concept of activity developed by the cultural-historical school of psychology (Leont'ev 1978; Wertsch 1981). All three put a heavy emphasis on the role of mediating artifacts in human cognition and learning.

3.5 Comparing Piagetian constructivism and social constructivism

There are educators who perceive that Piagetian and Vygotskian views can co-exist as complementary perspectives. There are others who articulate the incompatibility of the two oft quoted polarised paradigms. Bidell and others (e.g.: Marin 2000) consider closely the inter-relationship between Piaget and Vygotsky. Bidell (1992) explores the social dimension of Piaget's ideas and suggests that it is pertinent to make a distinction between Piaget's stage theory of development and Piaget's constructivist theory of knowledge:

> 'Piaget's stage theory of development tacitly reflects the idealogy of individualism. The stage theory is based on an interactionist metaphor in which the relation between the person and the social world is conceived as an individual standing apart from and interacting with a social environment. Piaget's constructivist theory of knowledge in contrast rejects the Cartesian Tradition of reductionism (in both nativist and empiricist versions), affirming a relational and even dialectical view of development' (Bidell 1992:307).

Bidell's analysis moves the Vygotsky versus Piaget debate forward, in that he argues that the internal inconsistency within the Piagetian notions opens the door to integrate Piaget's constructivism and Vygotsky's dialectal methodology. He suggests that:

> 'Piaget's constructivism implicitly supports a contextualist approach to knowledge development and stands in contradiction to the individualism and interactionism of his stage theory.....Vygotsky presents a dialectal conception of the relations between personal and social that differs diametrically from reductionist views......dimensions of reality such as the social and personal are not separate and self-contained but

> have a shared existence as differing tendencies united within real developing systems .....replaces the reductionist metaphor of separation and interaction with the dialectical metaphor of participation' (Bidell 1992:307).

This begins to illustrate how constructivist perspectives of developmental psychology might begin to acknowledge more appropriately the relative personal, social and cultural influences on learning.

3.6 Social interactions: Piagetian and Vygoskian perspectives

To examine how pupil exchanges can contribute to conceptual understanding Rogoff (1990) recognises that researchers need to address the naturalistic interaction between peers in tasks they do well or choose for themselves, and consider how they might 'teach each other'. She goes on to speculate that the collaboration and teaching processes, and perhaps the children's subsequent individual performance, may differ from those observed in the studies in which children have been under the direction of adults, participating in tasks in which adults are more skilled. She believes that children play special roles in one another's cognitive development and are not merely unskilled foils for comparison with skilled adults. To explore the role of peer interaction in cognitive development, Rogoff argues, it is essential to examine learning situations in which children are autonomous.

Rogoff (1990) states that:

> 'Rather than viewing individuals, their social partners, and the sociocultural context as independent 'influences' or factors of development, I argue that they represent differing angles of analysis of an integrated process. Although researchers and scholars find it convenient to focus their investigation on a specific angle, looking at the complex process of development through a particularly interesting window, the different angles or windows may artificially divide a unified, whole developmental process. For convenience of study or discussion, we may focus on one or another, but we must remember the integrated nature of the developmental process' (Rogoff, 1990:26).

To inform what my research addresses the following discussion looks more closely at influences on, and perspectives of peer-peer learning.

Piaget (1977) specifies during the stage of concrete operations (from about 7 to 11 or 12 years), children become capable of co-operating and coordinating points of view.

> 'Thus the child becomes capable of discussion - and from this internalised discussion, and that conducted with oneself, which is reflection-of collaboration, of arguments that are orderly and understandable by another' (Piaget 1977:157[9]).

Piaget, it appears, suggests that exchange between peers acts as a stimulus to order thought in a logical way that involves a system of propositions that become understandable and are free from contradiction and are reversible:

> 'Thinking in common promotes non-contradiction: It is much easier to contradict oneself, when one thinks for oneself (egocentrism) than when some partners are there to remember what one has said before and the propositions that one has agreed to admit' (Piaget, 1977:158).

The importance of social interaction and societal influence becomes more obvious in the next stage of development, the formal operations:

> 'Things are even clearer in the formal stage, which begins after 11-12 years, since hypothetico-deductive thought is above all thought supported by a language (common or mathematical) and is thus collective thought' (Piaget 1977:158).

Vygotsky's perspective contrasts with Piaget's in its assumption that from the beginning the child is a social being, involved in social exchanges that support and guide the development of higher cognitive processes:

> 'The child's rich and complex social contact leads to an early development of means of social connection. It has been clearly demonstrated that simple though unique reactions to the human voice are present in the third week of life (i.e.: presocial reactions) and that the first social reactions appear by the second month.....laughter, babbling, pointing and gesture emerge as means of social contact in the first months of the child's life......However, the most important event in the development of the child's thinking and speech occur at approximately two years of age.....This critical moment, the moment when speech becomes intellectual and thinking verbal, is marked by two clear and objective symptoms.....First, the child who has attained this level of development begins to actively expand his vocabulary by asking the name of each new thing he encounters. Second, these efforts result in an extremely rapid increase in the child's vocabulary' (Vygotsky 1987:110-111).

As Rogoff explicates (1990:146) Vygotsky assumes that social guidance aids children in learning to communicate and to plan and remember deliberately from the first years of life. This guidance provides children with the opportunity to participate beyond their own abilities and to internalise activities practised socially, thus advancing their capabilities for independently managing problem

---

[9] Piaget 1977:157 ref: Les operations logiques et la vie sociale.

solving. Light and Littlejohn (1999:10) quite appropriately, highlight that current Vygotskian standpoints tend to view effective teaching and learning exchanges as essentially incidental to ongoing joint activities, and should be given more attention. In attempting to illuminate what is happening in the classroom, Edwards and Mercer (1987) explored how skilful guided classroom discussion maintained a focus of shared attention and provided children with a language in which to describe their own experiences and using that language to build up a body of 'common language' about the topic in hand, thus demonstrating social-construction-in-action.

Vygotsky argued that rather than deriving explanations of psychological activity from the individual's characteristics plus secondary social influences, the unit of analysis should be social activity, in which individual functioning develops (Wertsch 1985). Piaget's approach was the reverse - to focus on the individual as the unit of analysis, with social influence overlaid on the individual's activity, after the child becomes able to take another person's perspective. These differences in timing and centrality of social influence may relate to Vygotsky's focus on development of understanding and skills in using cultural tools and Piaget's focus on qualitative shifts in perspective.

Rogoff (1990) describes how it is difficult to dis-entagle the social from the conceptual

> '..the notion of interaction often involves an assumption that the interactive entities are separable. In the nature-nurture debate, nature and nurture are regarded as independent influences - definable in terms not involving each other - that happen to co-occur. In much of psychology, the roles of the individual and of the social world are treated as separable. In such an interactional perspective, researchers assume that if the elements (nature and nurture, or the individual and the social world) are well enough studied, it will be possible to put them together to examine the 'dynamic' process of interaction and interdependence.'

In this study the entwined nature of conceptual and social discourse and activity are taken as interdependent factors affecting and informing the course of the interactions. The interactions, as Bauersfeld describes here are analysed and interpreted to elicit the usual 'patterns' of hidden grammar'. Bauersfeld (1988) describes his notion of 'patterns of interaction'.

> 'Obviously the common principle of 'cause and effect' is to a certain extent difficult to apply here. Neither the teacher nor the student alone can be blamed for the course of the process; they are not aware of the covert pattern of their joint actions. As a product from *social* interaction, the patterns develop from the mutual reflexive expectations and interpretations of the actors and their related moves, from the implicit 'obligations for action', which are typical for the insitutionalised educational processes, and from the teacher's and the student's routines as acquired across many shared classroom experiences. .....through the analysis, reconstruction, and comparison of many cases, the patterns of interaction appear to function as a quite reliable hidden grammar of classroom activities' (Bauersfeld 1988:37).

He illustrates how the learning situation influences the interactional 'pattern of grammar' that develops as problem solving proceeds and suggests that the core of the notorious school-generated failure of so many mathematical school careers, is the adoption of the 'funnel pattern of interaction' (p.36) whereby the teacher is satisfied and convinced that he has 'carefully reacted to the different difficulties of individual students' (Diederich and Lingelbach 1977). The student has 'followed the teacher's 'recipe' to solve a task. He describes the pattern as 'narrow and impoverished' because 'knowledge from an instructional situation is not automatically transferred to a different situation of possible application.' As Parkinson (2002) highlights this is similar to some extent, in science, teachers may consider themselves 'good' if the pupils have been quiet, looked attentive and the teacher covered significant subject matter in the 'transmitting of knowledge'.

Peer-peer interaction versus peer-teacher interaction

Piaget (1926) emphasised peer interaction, with its exploration of cognitive conflict between companions of equal status. Rogoff (1990) exemplifies this by describing the following situation. Two five year-olds quarrelling over drinks of soda that had been poured into glasses of different shapes (an everyday situation resembling Piaget's conservation task). An adult had attempted to pour equal quantities for the two children, but since Valerie's glass was tall and thin, and David's was wide and faring at the top, the quantities were not obviously equal. Valerie attempted to convince David of the fairness of the distribution:

'Yours is fatter and mine is thinner, that's why it looks like I have more. See, I have to squeeze my hand to get it into my cup, but not into yours. [She squeezes her fingers together and puts them into the opening of each cup to demonstrate.] It's just that mine is thinner so it looks like it has more' (Rogoff 1990:147).

It is such interaction between peers that Piaget argued can lead children to reconsider their ideas. A more asymmetrical collaboration, between adult and child Piaget felt would be unlikely to lead to cognitive restructuring, because compared to adults children's ideas are often poorly formulated and exist only as an 'orientation of the spirit' that cannot compete with more exact, clearly articulated views of adults. In such cases children are likely to agree without examining the idea, and therefore do not verify it for themselves. Piaget (1977:230) argues that it is not until adolescence that they begin to learn to discuss as equals with their teachers, when they have 'conquered their internal liberty'. He did postulate that adults and children could interact in a reciprocal way that enables pupils to advance their understanding to a new level of equilibrium:

'It is despite adult authority, and not because of it, that the child learns. And also it is to the extent that the intelligent teacher has known to efface him or herself, to become an equal and not a superior, to discuss and to examine, rather than to agree and constrain....'

For Vygotsky (1978) interaction with equal peers is not the ideal way to bring about cognitive growth; he argued that the partner should be more capable in using intellectual tools of society. However, his perspective is essential to understanding cognition in social contexts. Vygotsky's developmental theory, emphasises the gradual process of learning to use intellectual tools through social interactions with more expert others.

'The greatest change in children's capacity to use language as a problem solving tool takes place somewhat later in development, when socialized speech (which has previously been used to address an adult) is turned inward. Instead of appealing to the adult, children appeal to themselves; language thus takes on an intrapersonal function in addition to its interpersonal use' (Vygotsky 1978:27).

Hence the most effective social interaction is one in which joint problem solving occurs, guided by an individual who is skilled in the use of these intellectual tools. Other conditions that should be in place to render the social interaction effective is that the problem solving activity also occurs within the participant's zpd.

Damon (1984) suggests that different types of learning may be differentially facilitated by equal or by more expert partners.

> 'Peer tutoring may be used whenever students need to acquire information or skills that do not extend beyond their conceptual reach. Learning historical facts……becoming adept at multiplication tables….even figuring out how to make use of a computer…..draw upon features of basic understanding that the child has already developed……
>
> Peer collaboration, on the other hand ,…..is an ideal technique for encouraging children to wrestle with intellectual challenges in difficult new principles. Learning to communicate accurately through written and spoken language, grasping the logic behind scientific formulas, and realising the political rationale underlying a societal governance system can all be fostered in a collaborative peer interaction context. Such intellectual accomplishments stretch the boundaries of children's mental abilities. Consequently, they flourish best under conditions of highly motivated discovery, the free exchange of ideas, and reciprocal feedback between mutually respected equals. These are precisely the characteristics of collaborative interchanges between children' (Damon 1984:340).

Piaget's speculations on the benefits of peer interaction focused on the cognitive conflict occurring when children of equal status bring different perspectives to bear on a problem, interaction between conservers (those that understand the notion of conservation of volume, mass etc) and non-conservers (those that don't understand conservation of matter) is not really interaction between equals, since according to Piaget the conserver has a better understanding of reality, not just a different understanding of reality, than the nonconserver (Tudge and Rogoff 1989). Hence it is possible that within Piagetian research, benefits derive from working with a partner who has more advanced skills, consistent with the Vygotskian position. In Piaget's view, cognitive conflict provides an impetus for children to seek equilibrium at a higher level, some authors suggest that children would be most likely to change their thinking when faced with a perspective that fits reality better than their own, especially if it involves problem solving at a level *just* beyond that of the child (Azmitia 1988; Kuhn 1972; Mugny and Doise 1978; Tudge and Rogoff 1989). The benefit of a partner whose perspective is not too far in advance of that of the child is also consistent with Vygotsky's concept of interaction within the zone of proximal development, where an expert and a novice work together at a level just beyond that of the novice.

Rogoff (1990) discusses the relative capability of peers working together:

> 'Working with a partner who is slightly more skilled may be most effective, working with a partner equal in skill, or even one less advanced, may still yield progress (Forman and Kraker 1985; Glachan and Light 1982; Light and Glachan 1985; Rubtsov 1981; Rubtsov and Guzman 1984-1985). In some studies, however, there is no progress, as when partners are equal in understanding of seriation problems (Heber 1981) or there may even be 'regression', as when children interact with less advanced partners on balance-beam problems (Tudge 1985). The significance of relative expertise of partners is not yet resolved, but it appears that even within Piagetian tasks, the benefits of social interaction may relate to the expertise of the child's partner' (Rogoff 1990:173).

Hogan and Tudge (2000) note, that there has been relatively little research on peer collaboration, as opposed to peer tutoring, approached from a Vygotskian standpoint. However, since the mid-1980s Vygotskian ideas have begun to influence interpretations offered by researchers for peer facilitation effects in experimental studies. As Galton and Hargreaves (2009) summarise there have been several recent studies in primary education that have endeavoured to contrast a Vygotskian and Piagetian perspective of peer-peer learning. It is within the predominantly Vygotskian context, that I have applied theoretical lenses to peculiarly examine learning in secondary science. I have sought to illuminate and interpret learning interactions between peers of similar status and consequently inform appropriate pedagogy.

3.7 Community of learners

This section provides an introduction to a more socio-cultural perspective of learning, that suggests quite directly how teaching could be orchestrated. It should be apparent that it has been developed *from* the theories previously outlined in this chapter.

Brown (1993) argued that the historical roots of this pedagogic approach are embedded in the changes undergone in psychological learning theories over the past 30 years. The key underpinning ideas are, firstly, the notion that learners are no longer passive recipients of others' expertise, but have become more widely viewed as 'active constructors of knowledge'. Secondly, that human learners have knowledge and feelings about learning (Tulving and Madigan, 1970) and sometimes even control over it, which she describes as metacognition. Thirdly, that we now recognise that some humans are predisposed to learn certain things more readily than others (Carey and Gelman, 1991).

Brown defines 'guided discovery' as key to the pedagogy, but often difficult to orchestrate. The teacher needs to be sensitive (emotional understanding, Goleman 1995) knowing when to intervene and when to leave alone. To be successful, the facilitator must be continually engaging in diagnosis of student understanding, and be sensitive to the current zpd where students are ripe for new learning. Guided discovery places a great deal of responsibility in the hands of the teacher who must foster, and guide the 'discovery' process into forms of disciplined inquiry that may not be reached without expert guidance.

In a Vygotskian sense the zpd within which the children learn is mutually and actively created by teachers and students. What is orchestrated here is a 'collective' zone of proximal development. One approach within this 'community of learners' theory is 'Reciprocal Teaching'. In a typical reciprocal teaching session each participant in a reading group of approximately six members takes a turn leading a discussion. The 'learning leader' begins by asking a question about the core content and ends by summarising the gist of what has been read. Questioning provokes discussion, and summarising helps students establish where they are in preparation for tackling a new segment of text. On chosen occasions the leader asks for predictions about future content and attempts to clarify any comprehension problems that might arise. The key activities of questioning, summarising, clarifying and predicting provide the repeatable structure necessary to sustain discussion, a structure that can be faded out when students are more experienced in leading and taking part in discussions (and so 'scaffolding' is reduced Henessey (1993).

Brown argues that this approach is likely to contribute to a new theory of learning. Her ideas encompass a number of accepted psychological theories (Vygotsky 1978; Bruner 1969), develop existing notions of the active, strategic nature of learning (Brown 1974, 1975) and metcognition (Brown 1975, 1978, Brown, Bransford, Ferrara and Campione 1983; Adey, Shayer and Yates 2001) to create what she describes as 'Steps toward first principles of learning'.

Within this framework the students are perceived as apprentice learners and the teacher is the master craftsman of learning that they must emulate. In this role, the teacher models scientific inquiry through thought and real experiments. The teacher's role also includes efforts to model habits of mind by which children are encouraged to adopt, extrapolate and refine the deep underlying themes to which they are exposed. As Bruner (1969) argues, education:

> 'Should be an invitation to generalise, to extrapolate, to make a tentative leap, even to build a tentative theory. The leap from mere learning to using what one has learned in thinking is an essential step in the use of the mind. Indeed, plausible guessing, the use of the heuristic hunch, the best employment of necessarily insufficient evidence- these are the activities in which the child needs practice and guidance. They are among the great antidotes to passivity' (Bruner, 1969:126).

Brown acknowledges that this approach requires the expert guidance of a talented teacher, and that dissemination of this new theory it is not straight forward to apply in a different school. Even implementation with a different class in the same school requires adaptation of the model depending on interests of students and teachers, the age of the children, the relative importance of literacy versus content knowledge etc. The eventual goal is 'implementation as evolution constrained by first principles' (Brown and Campione 1995).

It is dissemination of the 'first principles' and not surface procedures, already utilised widely by teachers that need emphasising so that any adaptation or modification will still realise the educational objectives of *more effective learning*.

Key ideas of 'The first principles of learning'.

Three key principles of this approach are 1. that multiple zones of proximal development should be encouraged and supported; 2. that dialogic exchange is means by which ideas are communicated, considered and developed and 3. there is distributed expertise within the community of learners.

In a community of learners, the environment is seeded with ideas and concepts. Participants in the classroom are free to appropriate vocabulary, ideas, methods and solutions that appear initially as part of the shared discourse, and by appropriation, members transform these ideas into personal knowledge. The classrooms are intentionally designed to promote shared discourse. The activities can take a variety of formats, face-to-face in small or large groups, or even mediated via print or electronic mail. Dialogues provide the format for novices to adopt the discourse structure, goals, values and belief systems of scientific practice. Over time, the community of learners adopts a common voice and common knowledge base, a shared system of meaning, beliefs and activity that is often implicit as it is explicit (Brown and Campione, 1995). It is through the participation in increasingly more mature forums of scholarly research that these citizens are enculturated into the community practice of scholars. The classrooms encourage the development of a community of discourse pervaded by knowledge-seeking and inquiry processes. In this type of learning community Brown argues expertise is distributed, everyone is a teacher, writer, or expert at something. Everyone is involved in a plan-prepare-practice-perform cycle (with tangible results) and indicate they feel ownership of their learning (Brown and Campione, 1995). This approach embraces situated activities to avoid the oft quoted lack of continuity between school activities and out-of-school cultures (Roth, 1995). Enlisting students as both designers and evaluators of their learning is one of the most important activities of the Community of Learners. The philosophy behind this is an outcome of long-standing interest in 'metacognition'. Brown and Campione, (1995) claim it is a fundamental right that students should understand, evaluate and orchestrate their own learning.

3.8 Key educationalists' views of learning, pedagogy and group work situations in science

Here I offer an indication of notable and influential science educators' views from the UK. I have considered their views because their influences have impacted nationally (and internationally) over the past couple of decades. I have described how they perceive pupils should be taught, and extended my discussion to illustrate tensions between theories of learning and their views of science teaching.

In the early 1980s the late Rosalind Driver and others focused much research effort on identifying children's misconceptions in science. Driver's (1983) view paralleled strongly with early Piagetian ideas. She asserted that (1983:52) 'As childrens' experiences get more extensive the structures they develop become more encompassing'. She perceives the child as the 'architect of its own knowledge' (Driver 1983:53).

She discusses Piaget's notion of active learning whereby the learner constructs his or her knowledge through interaction with the environment and the resolution of cognitive conflict. She noted that, it is the need to resolve the cognitive dissonance that provides the intrinsic motivation for learning. Driver argued that:

> 'what is assimilated depends not only on the environment, but on the learner's existing cognitive structure. If there is no dissonance between an experience and a learner's cognitive structure then the information is assimilated without a change in the structure taking place at all. This suggests that for effective learning the principle of *moderate novelty* needs to be applied.' (ibid:53).

She alludes to, but doesn't elaborate on the notion of pupils comparing ideas with one another. 'Social construction' was not prominent. She described how the processes of disequilibrium and subsequent equilibrium result in new intellectual structures being developed....and in Piaget's view although maturation and various social and physical experiences are necessary for development, the essential dynamic process is that of equilibration.

Driver (1985:8) described how she perceived the process of learning:

> 'learning is seen to take place through the interaction between, on the one hand, a learner's experiences and, on the other, the 'mental entities', the 'ideas' or 'schemes', used to interpret and give meaning to those experiences.'

She recognises that pupils may have 'subjective' ideas, that although a pupil has 'seen' or experienced the same phenomenon or experiment, the interpretations are personal to him or her:

> 'Individuals internalise their experience in a way which is at least partially their own; they construct their own meanings. These personal 'ideas' influence the manner in which information is acquired. This personal manner of approaching phenomena is also found in the way in which scientific knowledge is generated. Most philosophers

of science accept that hypotheses or theories do not represent so-called 'objective' data but that they are constructions or products of the human imagination.' (1985:2).

In this way of thinking, observations of events are influenced by the theoretical frameworks of the observer. The observations children make and their interpretations of them are also influenced by their ideas and expectations.

Driver goes on to hypothesise on a possible model of learning (1985:4):

> 'Pupils' minds are not blank slates able to receive instruction in a neutral way; on the contrary she states that students approach experiences presented in science classes with previously acquired notions and these influence what is learnt from new experiences in a number of ways. These include observations made of events, the interpretations offered for such observations and strategies students use to acquire new information, including reading from texts and experimentation. What children are capable of learning depends, at least in part, on 'what they have in their heads', as well as on the learning context in which they find themselves.'

Driver described how she believed what we say and do depends on our 'elements' or 'groups of elements' of stored information we hold. She defined a 'scheme' as an individual's knowledge about a specific phenomenon (e.g.: the sensation of cold elicited by a metallic object) or a more complex reasoning structure (e.g.: association of one variable with another) that leads children to anticipate that 'the brighter the light bulb, the larger the shadow will be'. Thus, in her view, the term 'scheme' denoted diverse things that are stored and interrelated in memory. These 'schemes' also influenced the way a person behaved and interacted with the environment, which in turn could be influenced by feedback from the environment. She used an analogy to explain how new information is assimilated:

> 'Consider a group of students in a class. The students relate to each other, they form different groups for different activities such as sports, drama and science lessons. These groups are not static, they change as friendships and interests change; some students may not relate to others at all but remain isolates. Consider what happens when the new boy arrives in the class. When he arrives, there are various possibilities for what might happen, he might not relate with the other students at all and remain isolated, he might join a group that already exists, or his presence might provoke a re-organisation of friendship groups of the class as a whole. The same student could also be integrated differently depending on the class that receives him.'

This analogy illustrates how Driver perceived new information was assimilated. She explained how each of us has a characteristic organisation of schemes, and that because acquired information is linked to other information, even if this new information is the same for several people, the links established between this and existing information will be unique.

Driver suggested that even if a pupil experiences, recognises, observes an event or information that does not 'fit' the preconceived ideas the learner will not 'automatically re-adjust' his or her cognitive structures. Driver's view implied that the teacher should provide a wide range of experiences to enable the pupils to deduce the scientific truth. She recognised that to help students re-organise their thinking about natural phenomena it 'takes time and favourable circumstance'. These notions of providing dissonance with preconceived ideas, presenting sufficient scientific evidence and enabling individuals time to re-construct their ideas (and consequently cognitive structures) underpin the philosophy and methodology suggested in the Children's Learning in Science Project (CLIS), led by Driver et al (1994).

The Children's Learning in Science project (CLIS)

The CLIS project was predicated on pupils' current (mis)understandings, as Ausubel (1968) described:

> 'The most important single factor influencing learning is what the learner already knows. Ascertain this and teach him accordingly.'

The Ausubelian school of thought argues that there is no optimum age for learning (in contrast to Piaget who describes characteristics of several progressive stages of cognitive development and identifies typical ages of these). The CLIS approach builds on this and ascertains that children's ideas should be considered and the teacher should orchestrate the opportunity for the pupils to re-visit scientific evidence and consequently re-structure (correct) their misconceptions. The teaching process that Driver developed through her work on pupils' conceptual understandings in science has become recognised in science education as the constructivist approach to teaching (Figure 3.2).

ORIENTATION

↓

ELICITATION

OF IDEAS

↓

RESTRUCTURING

OF IDEAS

i. Clarification and exchange

ii. Exposure to conflict situations

iii. Construction of new ideas

iv. Evaluation

↓

APPLICATION

OF IDEAS

↓

REVIEW

Figure 3.2: Stages in the constructivist teaching sequence – *A summary of the constructivist approach.*

Modern constructivist approaches to teaching emphases the need for pupils to engage in activities that allow them to construct their own knowledge and understanding. What is constructed depends crucially on what the learner brings to the situation as well as the nature of the learning situation provided by the teacher (Brown, 1995). The next stage it is argued is to present pupils with the appropriate scientific ideas and statements of key facts. Pupils then go on to perform appropriate (interactive) practical activities and relate their findings to the previously presented scientific explanation. Finally they are encouraged to reflect on how their final ideas contrast with their (now rejected, but earlier misconceived) understandings. The important point about this strategy is to recognise that the pupils do not begin their thinking from a blank sheet. They carry ideas to the situation gleaned from a range of prior experiences many of which originate from outside the school as a part of everyday events. These ideas are often held tenaciously and function as blocks to the learning of correct scientific ideas (Driver et al, 1984).

Solomon (1987) extended pedagogic discourse to consider social and cultural influences on pupils' ideas in science. She presented a theory of the social construction of meaning in which she argued that:

> 'Social interaction, whether in the general culture, the peer group, or even, in its most tenuous form, via relationship with a television character'……. 'can permeate both the learning and application of science.'

She also argued that two types of knowing can co-exist and that the context, whether in unequivocally scientific or real-life settings, can affect pupils' application of associated knowledge. This culminated in a conclusion highlighting the difficulty of embedded social influences that should be accounted for in the oft-regarded abstract paradigm of school science.

In the early 1990s the view of constructivism within science education begins to consider a much wider perspective than hitherto. There has been a very staunch Piagetian viewpoint, where effective science teaching meant placing appropriate challenges or tasks in front of the child (Solomon, 1998). The tasks are designed to elicit predictions from the child in increasing sophistication in relation to the mental structures the child brings to bear on the problem. Progress in conceptual development was perceived as the child's ability to through structured activities, develop from sensory-motor responses to internalisation of complex abstract analysis of scientific phenomena. This engendered 'scientific' approach (of Piagetian constructivism) translates well to the 'personal construct theory' (Solomon, 1998), whereby many science educators tend to think that pupils or learners have an innate capability to think things out for themselves, and that previous experience, interaction with others, and other socio-cultural influences are of little or negligible importance. When introducing the notion of 'Personal constructivism,' Solomon describes a mature and a juvenile learner as ‘sophisticated thinkers with conceptual schemata which they had developed for themselves in order to model natural phenomena’. She went on to describe them as able to ‘articulate their theories and be willing to test them’. Her discussion of these learners indicates very strongly a belief that an individual determines his or her own mental prowess and that their innate ability alone drives them to their ‘ceiling’ of thinking.

Alongside these epistemological views of how knowledge is constructed, that have influenced teaching, there has also begun to be more debate about the role and significance of reflection on one’s own thinking processes or metacognition. Adey (1991) developed this notion of metacognition, as an integral element of the Cognitive Acceleration through Science Education (CASE) project.

The Cognitive Acceleration through Science Education project (CASE)

The CASE programme is a two-year intervention designed to be taught at Key Stage 3 (11-13 year olds). It is a series of 30 activities designed to challenge and develop pupils’ thinking. The teaching approach is based on both Piagetian and Vygotyskian principles. Adey and Shayer (1994) describe the important features of the CASE programme as:

- Duration and density
- Concrete preparation
- Cognitive conflict
- Construction
- Metacognition
- Bridging

Duration and density (1994:60) they clarify as a steady rate over two years, i.e.: an interventional lesson once a fortnight during year 7 and year 8. The lesson framework comprises of 5 phases (or pillars of wisdom) informed by Piagetian perspectives of the learning process. The first is concrete preparation; this is establishment of unfamiliar vocabulary and apparatus. It is perceived as the preparatory part of the lesson. The cognitive conflict, often in the form of problem solving, is the presentation of somewhat surprising data, information or experiences. This is applied directly from Piaget’s view of cognitive growth developing through dissonance. Construction is drawn from

Vygotsky's concept of zpd, described by Adey and Shayer as 'construction zone activity', that is mental activity going beyond children's present limits of assured competencies. Construction is the process the learner is engaged in when re-establishing (Piagetian) equilibrium. Yates (2001) offers an analogy of pupils as puzzle solvers, each contributing a 'piece' of information to the task solution. Metacognition means 'thinking about one's own thinking, becoming conscious of one's own reasoning'. Informed by the Piagetian view that 'children's reflections on problems and consideration of possibilities before acting are important aspects of cognitive development' (Adey and Shayer, 1994:68). They add that Vygotsky rightly says: 'control of a function is the counterpart of one's consciousness of it', and 'if a child is going to control and direct his own thinking, he must become aware of it' (ibid). Bridging is the final link in the chain of developing, abstracting and generalising reasoning. It is taken from Feuerstein's Instrumental Enrichment programme, where students are encouraged to summarise strategies used to solve problems and then consider where similar tactics might be used elsewhere in or outside school. Adey (1998) states that children's ability to learn depends to an important extent on their ability to process new information. The CASE intervention programme enhances the pupil's information processing capability, by setting challenges and encouraging the pupils to reflect and become more conscious of their own thinking. He states that from a Piagetian perspective that all information needs to be processed by the receiver. The effectiveness of this information processing depends on a) the existing network of understandings that the receiver already has, and b) the power of his/her information-processing capability.

The 'objectives' of CASE are the understanding of reasoning patterns (or schema) identified by Piaget, described earlier. The CASE approach recognises that pupils cannot be taught these reasoning patterns (control and exclusion of variables, classification, ratio and proportionality, compensation and equilibrium, correlation, probability, formal modelling) or scientific ways of thinking about relationships between variables; they should be supported in 'constructing' their own understandings. The processes of retrieving data and using it effectively is an essential step from being a knowledgeable novice to being an expert, as Adey (1991:30) adds:

> '...it is only after one has solved a problem that one can learn most effectively how one should have solved it.'

Adey et al (1989; 1994) have remained focused on intra-mental development, although there is consideration of inter-personal activity and social transaction. In the CASE approach the 'language of reasoning mediates metalearning'. Shayer (1997) discusses the notion that Piaget and Vygotsky are a necessary marriage for the successful implementation of this educational intervention. He states the Piagetian contribution as the 'framing of the tasks themselves', i.e.: the 'hardware' of the lessons, and the 'conduct' of the lessons as drawn from Vygotskian approaches. He summarises:

> 'the objection is frequently met, from Vygotsky enthusiasts, that if one is pro-Vygotsky one must be necessarily anti-Piaget. In physics, who can doubt that Einstein gives a better understanding of action at a distance than does Newton? Yet 99% of current engineering calculations are done in Newtonian terms.'

This suggests that the teaching programme was originally theorised on Piagetian concepts alone. Vygotskian influences on the development of the CASE approach extend to consider mediation through social interaction with adults or peers. In applying the notion of proximal development, Adey and Shayer (1994) recognise that 'instruction is good only when it proceeds ahead of development, when it awakens and rouses to life those functions that are in the process of maturing or in the zpd' (Wertsch 1985:165). They identify '*probable* value in peer collaboration', and add that

> 'translating it into practice, the mediating role of the teacher lies in developing the skill of first framing the tasks for the pupils in such a way to direct their attention to the problems they will meet and should discuss with each other. Then the whole class is encouraged to share the different insights and difficulties which the working groups have encountered. The zpd is thus established collaboratively, and all pupils benefit.' (Adey and Shayer 1994:119)

Through my increasing involvement in CASE professional development programmes my perspective of its impact on pupils' cognitive development increasingly focused on the nature of interactions between peers and the dialogic exchanges between pupils and teacher. Although Adey (*ibid*) emphasised that Vygotskian ideas were key to the pedagogy of the thinking activities, there did not appear to be clear guidance for teachers explicitly defining how they should support group work. This absence of this kind of pedagogic advice was a stimulus for me to explore, through this study, *how, when* and in *what form* should these Vygotskian notions of learning be transacted into group work practice (and pedagogy)?

In the mid 1990s Driver's view shifted to acknowledge a stronger influence and importance of the role of interpersonal exchange (between peers; learner and teacher). Her view of knowledge acquision became informed by considering the nature of scientific knowledge, individual (or personal construction) as well as perspectives on social processes that may influence learning. The viewpoint (Driver et al, 1994) took was that knowledge and understandings, including scientific, are constructed when individuals engage socially in talk and activity about shared problems or tasks. They state that:

> 'making meaning is thus a dialogic process involving persons-conversation, and learning is seen as the process by which individuals are introduced to a culture by more skilled members' (Driver et al, 1994:7).

They continue by discussing the notion that:

> 'within a culture more experienced members can support less experienced members by structuring tasks, making it possible for the less experienced to perform them and to internalise the process, i.e. convert them into tools for conscious control' (Driver et al, 1994:7).

They claim that if knowledge construction is seen solely as an individual process, then it is similar to what has been traditionally identified as discovery learning. If, they argue, learners are to be given access to the knowledge systems of science, the process of knowledge construction must go beyond personal empirical enquiry. They identify important features of mediation, that intervention and negotiation with an authority, usually the teacher, is essential. The two important components of the teacher's role are to firstly introduce new ideas or cultural tools where necessary and to provide the support and guidance for students to make sense of these for themselves. The other is to listen and diagnose ways in which the instructional activities are being interpreted to inform further action. They state

' teaching from this perspective is thus also a learning process for the teacher' (Driver et al, 1994:11)

and that

'Learning science in the classroom involves children entering a new community of discourse, a new culture; the teacher is often the hard-pressed tour guide mediating between children's everyday world and the world of science.' (ibid)

Howe et al's (1990) work on groups of primary pupils, their interactions and development of ideas of flotation also supported the notion that learning would be enhanced, even maximised, if children explore their conceptions while working with peers whose alternative conceptions are different. However, in a subsequent study exploring understanding of motion down an incline, Howe (1992) amended her view of the impact of children collaborating with alternative conceptions. She argued that the task given, and the composition of the group could influence the resultant understanding. If, for example, children with conflicting ideas worked together to predict results and then explain outcomes, there was a definite gain over those who only had the opportunity to discuss outcomes. The pupils also measured as 'low' made most gains in their understanding.

Millar (1989) compared various views of constructivism and indicated that social constructivists should reject Piagetian constructivism because he argued constructivism is too closely associated with an instructional mode and that a better route would be that of curriculum technologist utilising the constructivist model flexibly to inform science learning. His view, juxtaposed to many other science educationalists, illustrates how the emphasis in science education has long been concerned with 'how to teach', but has not reflexively anticipated how pupils learn, to subsequently inform pedagogy.

Marin et al (2000) considered the changes in science teaching paradigms over the past couple of decades. They claimed that 'social constructivism….is not an easy bedfellow for Piagetian constructivism, even though both have the same thing in mind…a study of the learner'. They discuss Piagetian and social constructivism from a conceptual development standpoint. They consider characteristics of social constructivism, including the more dynamic nature of constructing academic knowledge, that ideas are often deep-rooted and cannot be easily changed by instruction (Hierrezuelo and Montero, 1991; Olivia, 1996, Driver 1986); the notion of coherent conceptions helping explain daily phenomena, which is of little scientific value but well adapted to explain what they see (e.g.; sugar dissolved in water...becomes water); same concept, but different meanings not arousing explicit contradiction (e.g.: weight frequently associated with aspects of volume, density and pressure, (Driver, 1988). They argue that social constructivism (Driver, Asoko, Leach, Mortimer and Scott, 1994; Driver, 1988):

> 'has shown the need to understand the evolutionary sequence of children's thinking to elucidate whether students' net results, which appear similar at different ages or after the teaching and learning processes, are due to a methodological problem or, on the contrary, may be due to obscuring reasoning which is becoming more sophisticated' (Marin et al. 2000:233).

And...

> 'The extensive catalogue of social constructivism on students' conceptions for a variety of phenomenologies provides much of the specific content which is lacking in Piagetian theory and which would make its application to science teaching more useful and effective' (Marin et al, 2000:235).

They proceed by arguing that

> 'many authors have opted for the conciliation between social constructivism and piagetian constructivism (cited:Aliberas et al, 1989; Lopez Ruperez, 1990; Perales, 1992; Pzo et al, 1992) and in light of this (Matthews 1994; Solomon, 1994; Duschl, 1994; Gilbert, 1995; Ritchie et al, 1997; Kelly, 1997) perhaps now is the moment to continue with this tendency' (Marin et al, 2000:235).

There is a strong indication here that if this notion is widely held then the science education community has not yet fully assimilated and accommodated the theories of social constructivism and embraced it within their epistemological views of how learners learn.

Ann Howe (1996) acknowledges that :

> 'Vygotsky's work has received increasing attention in recent years from psychologists and educators outside of science education but has received little attention from science educators themselves' (Howe, 1996:35)

This assertion is supported through a review of recent publications that claim to emphasize what science teachers should be doing in their classrooms to model good practice. There is no section in the following publications; 'Issues of science teaching' (Sears and Sorenson, 2000); 'Good practice in science teaching' (Monk and Osborne, 2000); 'ASE[10] Guide to Secondary Science' (Ratcliffe, 1998) 'The effective teaching of secondary science' (Parkinson, 1994); 'Secondary science – contemporary issues and practical approaches' (Wellington, 1994); which addresses pupils working together in science classrooms. Osborne (2000; 1998) does, however, mention social construction, in one example, as a method by which pupils recognising there could be more than one interpretation of scientific evidence. The classic work carried out by Tinbergen, in 1951, of stickleback courtship indicates females are passive recipients of males' attention. More recently, however, the red colouring of the male has been found to reduce the likelihood of other males attacking. Further work focussing on the females has since shown they are more aggressive than males in defending their territory. Commenting on this research, Reiss (1984) highlights that this demonstrates that the way scientists interpret evidence depends on their previous ways of thinking and 'that even the most famous piece of research is not necessarily correct'.

Howe (1996:46) highlights that the cognitive stage theory of development, held by Driver, Adey, Shayer and others, has been used as the basis for curriculum materials and recommendations for teaching strategies (not only in science education). The subject-specific embeddedness of the constructivist theory has begun to be challenged, and is acknowledged by Adey (1991), using empirical evidence of the contextual nature of knowledge. Rogoff and Lave (1983), Newman et al (1989), Girotto and Light (1992) among others, have shown that a child's response to a cognitive task or problem in one setting or in one knowledge domain, may be, and often is, different from the response in another setting or domain. This also challenges the view that a cognitive skill or capacity is stage dependent with cognitive abilities that are generalisable across a range of tasks regardless of content, context or structure of the task.

Howe (1996) explores Vygotsky's ideas on the interrelationship between spontaneous everyday concepts and non-spontaneous scientific concepts, the

[10] ASE is the Association of Science Education.

interdependence of thought and language, and the relationship between school instruction and mental development. She argues, whilst pupils may be able to define or explain a given concept on a verbal level and be able to use words to express their understanding, a concept remains an abstraction and is not fully understood unless or until it can be applied to specific examples. In my study I offer the children everyday contexts (eg: candle burning in lantern, slipping in training shoes) to explore whether they can, and if they do, how they solve the problem applying scientific concepts (that combustion requires oxygen) and investigational procedures (like fair test, controlling variables, analysing data). As West and Pine's (1985) metaphor of two entwined vines, one representing everyday concepts and the other scientific concepts, do the two support each other to enable the children to come to a more meaningful understanding of the task and its solution.

Parkinson (2002:22) in his review of learning in science, recognises learning situations where there could be interactions between the zpd's of all members in a group, whereby one pupil may affect the partially formed ideas of others. He does not elaborate on the nature of interactions between learners, but does highlight the role of the teacher scaffolding the 'learner on the right track' through activity, questioning, explanation and discussion. He does not elaborate on the nature of cognitive processing expected of the pupils, nor explain further what teacher intervention is necessary to obviate pupils 'off track'.

As highlighted, at the beginning of this chapter, O'Loughlin's (1992) claim that Science Education needs 'rethinking' and re-defining in line with current understandings of learning appears to be substantiated in a number of ways when referencing literature regarding effective science education. He provides an epistemological critique of forms of pedagogy founded on Piagetian constructivism. He discusses that despite the appeal of the notion that learners construct their understanding, he argues that constructivism (which tends to privilege one form of knowledge, namely the technical rational) needs to take account of a learner's social and historical experiences, and the situated nature of knowing. He highlights the essentially collaborative and social nature of meaning making and questions assumptions made that children learn by doing. Driver et al (1989) argued, teachers need to recognise that 'the role of science educators is to mediate scientific knowledge for learners, to help them make personal sense of ways in which new knowledge claims are generated and validated, rather than to organise individual sense-making about the natural world'.

It appears then that there is a somewhat evolutionary development of the view of learning, knowledge and teaching in science education. It began with Piagetian constructivism and has since developed a more social, interactional dimension, described as social constructivism and is currently moving toward a more socio-cultural perspective of the learner.

3.9 Summary

Prominent views about how children learn in science and how we should teach them have been discussed in this chapter. The notions explored here indicate that the general view still revolves or centres on the nature of scientific knowledge and how the epistemological view might inform pedagogy. As O'Loughlin points out, if a constructivist notion of learning is maintained then pedagogically the teacher's role is perceived more as effective presenter, facilitator and/or demonstrator of the appropriate task. How the pupils collaborate and interact with each other is significantly less important than how they internalise meaning directly from engagement with the specified task. Pedagogically pupils' interactions with each other do not require mediation, so intervention is concerned with ensuring individuals develop conceptual understanding of the scientific truth, reached primarily through interaction with the task. If, however, learning is perceived as essentially social in its origin then pedagogy requires more thoughtful intervention to mediate, and nurture appropriate and meaningful interactional discussion that addresses conceptual aspects of science, with account taken of influences of the intrinsic nature of science and its associated methodologies. Pedagogically supporting pupils to propose ideas, exchange views and offer rationale is appropriate. It should be justifiable that pupils are encouraged to explain phenomena, not just produce a description (that the teacher expects) of the scientific 'truth'. For example, presented with teaching dissolution to young secondary school children, engaging in simple activities where pupils add solids to liquids and attempt to construct explanations for the disappearance of the salt or sugar (applying previous knowledge of particles), I would argue that contrary to Driver, because there are no agreed or unified scientific truths or theories regarding dissolution (there are currently 4 hypotheses[11]; Selley, 2001) for example, it is quite justifiable for pupils to develop their 'own' rationalised and evidenced constructs to explain what happens when solids dissolve. In applying their model of particle theory to explain why solids disappear to each other is likely to provide a range of plausible ideas[12]. To consider scientifically the plausibility of the various hypotheses provides quality learning opportunities. To 'scaffold' and mediate their learning, by asking a series of sequential, reflective questions[13] would engage them in their zpd's.

In my study I will attempt to explore how peers learn together. The pupils will work in small groups (mini-learning-communities), to illuminate how they would naturalistically interact and mutually support each other. Some interacting peers will have more task support (or scaffolding) than others to explore whether the level of scaffolding impacts on the nature of their interactions and the quality of their learning. I have taken a social constructivist view (of their task resolution) that through their interactions they are all working together to reach a solution, and to achieve that they should engage in explicit dialogic exchange that verbalises thoughts. Their actions are also taken be a manifestation of their individual contributions to the group task, whether it is demonstrating how to use, organise or arrange equipment. Through analysis of these exchanges and their final solution I am attempting to identify what constitutes quality-learning interactions in scientific problem solving. My interpretative analysis should offer insight into the nature of the interactions (not just talk, but action as well) to inform how teachers could

[11] Four explanations for dissolution: 1. The liquefaction theory; 2. The spaces or assault theory; 3. The hydrate theory; 4. The interaction theory.

[12] Plausible ideas could include: the solid melts, the solid becomes a liquid, the solid becomes invisible.

[13] Example of the kinds of questions to provoke thinking: (i.e.: what happens to the solid particles? We can see them at the top of the tube, but they disappear further down. The liquid is changing, what might that mean? How does the water change? When does it become a solution? Will the mass of the solution be more, less or the same? So are the 'solid' particles still there? Somewhere? How could solid particles change or 'disappear'? What do you know about particles that might help you explain how they could interact?).

more effectively support cognitive development through social interaction in secondary science classrooms.

Chapter four

4.1 Outline of intentions

As a science educator (and former teacher) closely involved in supporting teachers working with pupils in secondary schools, my study is intended to inform current practice and suggest how to further enhance interactive group learning. In my capacity as a tutor for both beginning and experienced teachers my focus has been on how to avoid pupils 'doing' habitual practical work that does not result in meaningful learning (Hodson 1990;1992). I aspired to inform 'best practice' and enable teachers to become more effective through their reflections on praxis.

4.2 The phases in the research project

As my study progressed, so my methodology evolved, I shifted from a scientific educational stance, when developing the initial questionnaires, to one of a more 'interpretative', ethnographic stance, with an overtone of the critical dimension. As I progressively analysed and interpreted my observations of current practice, it became apparent that the community of teachers were disempowered regarding their knowledge and constructs of 'learning' and, more particularly, what constitutes effective peer-peer interaction, to support cognitive development.

There were five stages in my research project. The first, introductory phase where the context of the study was set, providing the rationale behind the observational studies; the second concerning gathering the evidence from observations, of pupils in-action; the third was reflecting on the meaning of the findings; the fourth was the development and delivery of in-service training, informed by the research findings; and the final concluding part reviewing the effects of professional development on teachers and connecting these effects with pupils' learning.

My study begins by examining the literature regarding learning theory and current group work practices. My initial data was gathered from teachers I work with to explore the ways in which they utilised small group opportunities in the classroom and examine how they perceived their pupils were learning together. I used questionnaires to uncover the nature and extent of their use of these groupings and how they managed, organised and perceived its efficacy as a pedagogic strategy in the science classroom. I consequently wished to investigate the pupils' perspectives of working in this way, to consider their views alongside those of the teachers. My strategy was to gather a more comprehensive view of existing habits and routines within science classrooms in the local schools where I was engaged in supporting both training and qualified staff. I intended that these first two steps in data collection would provide a qualitative and complementary view from two perspectives (orchestrator and participant) of and within, group work practices. The resultant data from these surveys provides the context and background to this localised study, to provide indicative insight into the extent and nature of social interactions, which have (or not, as the case may be) been cultivated to promote learning within the Keele University Initial Teacher Training (ITT) partnership.

My intention in the second phase of the study was to re-construct typical practices that teachers utilise when employing group work in learning situations to elucidate consequences of their approaches. Resultant interactions were interpreted to inform under what circumstances cognitive gains through social exchanges are made. I explore the influence of task structure on cognitive development through observations of various groups of co-operating children. With theoretical frameworks of learning in mind, I interpreted the recorded group interactions, (verbal and non-verbal) to ascertain pupils' subsequent understandings arising through differentiated scaffolding.

The third phase of the research was reflective, contemplating *when* and *how* teacher intervention best supported cognitive development whilst pupils were working together on scientific tasks.

During the fourth phase of my study I intended to develop suggestions regarding pedagogic practice to support pupils' interactional learning. Through contrasting the nature and extent of actional and dialogic exchanges and resultant learning outcomes developing from various groups I hoped that the ways in which collaborating peers could be better supported would become pedagogically clearer. I decided in the fifth stage of the research to evaluate the success of the pedagogic ideas to support more effective learning. I intended to explore whether the teachers' practice could be influenced through engagement in professional development. My philosophical stance was to place the teachers in the role of learner, to afford them the opportunity of empathising with their pupils, when in a unique learning situation themselves. So that, as Roth (1999) says, 'through enlightenment, it is possible to emancipate the pedagogical thinking of both science educators and science teachers'.

During the fifth phase of the research I also re-examined pupils-in-action post teacher-professional-development. This stage in the project was to explore whether the teachers had affected pupils' learning interactions.

Attempting to understand and interpret how and why pupils interact in the ways they do, consider influential factors and inform a theory of effective pedagogic practice to support cognitive development, whilst solving problems, in small groups, is the crux of my study.

4.3 My methodological stance

4.3.1 The nature of the study

The stance I have taken in this investigation is that of an educator (social scientist) exploring science education pedagogy. I postulated that currently the ways in which teachers support peers working together can affect the nature of their learning interactions and consequently their cognitive development. The context of the study is a group of science teachers (and their teaching of pupils within the Keele University Initial Teacher Training (ITT) partnership schools), with whom I collaborate regularly to support developing trainee students. The background to the study has been acknowledged through purposive sampling of 69 teachers' views of their practice and perspectives on pupils, in their schools, working together. As Denzin and Lincoln (1994:202) describe:

> Many qualitative researchers employ...purposive, and not random, sampling methods. They seek out groups, settings and individuals where ..the processes being studied are most likely to occur.

This is juxtaposed by analysis of a tenfold sample (652) of their pupils' perspectives of their learning with each other. With the survey findings in mind, I begin by applying scientifically informed methodology, adopting initially a view that, independent or experimentally controlled variables, such as task structure, gender, expertise, achievement or social status can influence interactional dependent variables such as amount of talk and type of talk (e.g.: number of disagreements or explanations, Azmitia, 1988; Bearison et al, 1986; Kempa, 1994). My hypothesis was : 'How does the extent of scaffolded-in-task support affect peer-peer learning interactions?' I set up a 'standarised method' (triads [normal working partners], standardised tasks, non-participant observation through video recordings) to collect the data, which would be examined to refute or 'prove' that the degree of scaffolding results in particular kinds of interactions that affect cognitive outcomes. Reflectively, though, I recognised the complexities of interactions between children in different situations; as Layder (1994:19) identified, 'human beings exercise agency' (individual choice and intention), so the approach I subsequently took was one of a more interpretive nature (Bassey, 1999:43).

4.3.2 Becoming more interpretive

Collecting a range of observational data (transcript of dialogue alongside measures of passive and active participation, reviewing pupil behaviour over a temporal period as well as subjective individual responses to each other and also collating pupils' written notes) suggests methods typical of a qualitative approach (see exemplar data Appendix 4). With a case-study approach in analysing group interactions, I recognise the complexity of both the social and cognitive nature of participants' responses to the task and each other. With a teacher-researcher perspective I interpreted the data gathered both quantitatively (to explore whether there were correlations between types of interactions and quality of task outcomes) and qualitatively (as explained earlier), in contrast to the semi-quantitative, approach to collate teacher and pupil perspectives of current practice. By subsequently interacting with the teachers to inform them, and monitoring their interpretations through their pedagogic practice in the classroom, my study has become more ethnographic. Silverman (2000:77) describes ethnomethodology as that:

> 'which encourages us to look at people's everyday ways of producing orderly social interaction'.

My methodological stance developed ethnographically because I wished to explore 'how the members of the group being studied understand things' (Denscombe, 1998:68) and also the 'meanings they attach to happenings' and 'to grasp the *native's* point of view....to realise *his* vision of *his* world' (Malinowski, 1922:25). As a teacher-researcher I had a practical interest in how and why these pupils interact they way they do, (as a result of teacher orchestration or intervention) so this 'ethogenic' (Cohen, Manion and Morrison 2007:21) method assumes that in analysing the 'actors' participation in social episodes there is construction of understanding of what the pupils are doing in response to particular (practical) events. I assumed that the pupils acted with intent (to complete the task) and in so doing were making meanings in and through their activities (Blumer, 1969). This ethnographic perspective of co-learners through verbal and non-verbal, interactions actively constructing their social world, which as Malinsowski (1922) explicates:

> '...should deal with the totality of all social, cultural and psychological aspects of the community, for they are so interwoven that not one can be understood without taking into consideration all the others' (Malinsowski, 1922: xvi).

in other words the social, cultural and cognitive components of learning need accounting for. I observed these small groups, operating as mini-learning communities, responding to the task set and interacting with each other to achieve a solution. As an interpretative study my research sets out to extend beyond just a description of prevalent practice (as Howe [1997:49] indicates is a constraint of previous studies), to glean meaning and understanding of the processes and outcomes of interacting individuals in practical science. My findings were intended to subsequently inform the professional development work in which I am currently engaged in when supporting secondary science teachers to develop their pedagogy. I sought to also to judge how far I might influence teachers' pedagogy (through reflective questionnaires and examination of subsequent pupils-in-action) after sharing with them my findings of the ways in which pupils' interactive learning together could be enhanced.

4.3.3 Interactionism

In seeking to interpret the interactions between co-learners, I have assumed that the pupils are acting towards things (tasks and equipment presented) on the basis of the meanings they have for them. My interactionist stance focuses on the world of subjective meanings and what the pupils communicate about their understandings to their peers. I think that the process of ascribing meaning is a continuous dynamic one, so during the completion of a task I believe the pupils construct, modify, re-construct, contemplate benefits and problems, piece together and negotiate understanding in a social context. As a symbolic interactionist Cohen et al (2007:24) would identify the 'nature of the interaction, not the individuals, their personalities but the dynamic activities taking place between people' as the important foci for research. He says that individuals align their actions to those of others, that they empathise with others' assertions and circumstances and deliberate on or even manage how 'others' might perceive them and so doing they 'influence' the situation. A symbolic interactionist, then, holds the view of an active human being and rejects the image of a passive, determined individual. Underpinning concepts held by the interactionist are that individuals determine their own actions, that the ways in which they react to others, how they attribute meaning, interpret actions of others, define the situation, is subjective (relating to self). Negotiation (by verbal predominantly, but also non-verbal means) is paramount and is the means by which understandings are continually developed, refined or modified. It is from this interactionist stance of learning that I am seeking to clarify how a teacher could most effectively support useful peer-peer interactions.

4.3.4 The critical dimension

In attempting to understand learning from the pupils' perspective to inform pedagogy in an 'interpretative' sense, the 'lens' of the study is later re-focused on interpreting the observations of the pupils or 'actors' as Cohen et al (2007:28) describes and attempting to interpret why 'what' is happening in the 'interactions' between the pupils. In trying to assess a variety of factors and their potential influence on the inter and intra interactions, I, as the observer, attempted to come to an understanding of the meanings children make in different learning situations. As Habermas (1984 in Cohen et al 2007:27) indicates this is hermeneutic; in other words, striving to (re)interpret and understand further what has already been interpreted by others (Kempa, 1994, Bianchini, 1997, Howe, 1994, 1998). In so doing I later apply a different theoretical interpretation of findings made by others, I recognise the intellectual sensitivity, and in that way employ a more critical dimension of educational research. My ultimate purpose here is to attempt emancipation of disempowered teachers and science educators (lacking acquaintance and understanding) to redress inequality in opportunity for members of small groups of co-learners to promote more intellectual freedom in learning situations. In the words of Cohen et al (2007:26):

> 'critical theory seeks to uncover the interests at work in particular situations [....]. Its intention is *transformative* [....]. In this respect the purpose of critical educational research is intensely practical.....'.

Habermas (1974:8) postulates that understanding and interpretation, predicated on 'practical' interests, is an attenuation of the scientific method and is exemplified in the hermeneutic, interpretative methodologies outlined in the qualitative symbolic interactionism approach described earlier. Through these methodologies, I am as researcher seeking to clarify, understand and interpret the communications of 'speaking and acting subjects' (ibid). Hermeneutics involves recapturing the 'meanings' of interacting others, recovering and reconstructing the intentions of the other actors in a situation. This approach then seeks to develop understanding of meaning in a social context. Meanings rather than phenomena take on significance in this paradigm (Cohen et al 2007:29). The parallel in this study is that teachers regularly allow peers to work in friendship groupings. This routinised practice without specific interactional guidance can result in pupils being cognitively constrained in the nature of their social exchanges. The teachers not recognising and developing appropriate support and settings for effective interactive learning can result in limited or constrained social interaction bereft of cognitive development. This is certainly the case when teachers assign pupils to work together for disciplinary rather than educative reasons (Kutnick et al 2005). Habermas (1974:230) suggests that through reflective practice teachers could become emancipated. Smyth (1989) identifies stages in this reflexive process, which I recognise are closely aligned with the research approach taken in this study. He describes the first stage as one of 'A description of the existing situation'. Which in my study is explored through the literature review and the extensive questionnaires to both teachers and pupils to 'uncover' the nature of various learning practices in small groups in classrooms, and associated perceptions of both teachers and pupils regarding this approach to learning situation. This first stage then identifies 'What is currently happening?'. Smyth (ibid) would describe the second stage as the 'What does it mean?' phase. This echoes the approach of the interpretative paradigm previously explained. This is explored through the observations of pupils to probe more closely what is happening in particular learning situations. Smyth (ibid) views the third stage as that focused on *confrontation* 'How did this come to be?'. The parallel in my study would be clarification of the influence of task scaffolding (and lack of teacher understanding about how best to support) on the quality of peer-peer interaction and learning outcomes. Reflecting on the influences effecting learning outcomes in this situation elucidates further 'How this came to be' in the schools studied.

In stage 4, described by Smyth as *reconstruction* 'How could things be done differently?' would be paralleled by the development of pedagogic suggestions that can elucidate for teachers how to better support more effective learning interactions amongst pupils working together. It is this more critical perspective, informed by an interpretivist stance, which Crotty (1998:112) describes 'Critical inquiry...[is not] a research that seeks merely to understand..[it is] a research that challenges ...that [takes up a view] of conflict...that seeks to bring about change', which is my ultimate aim, through enlightening the teachers about social and cognitive processes and raising awareness of cultural influences to support pedagogic change.

I add a stage beyond Smyth where I attempt to evaluate (from teacher and pupil perspective) the efficacy of evolved pedagogic strategies.

Stage 5 in my project is the intervention on teachers' practice. Within this stage I enact for teachers *how to* change their practice, I seek their views on the ways they *have transformed* their action-in-classrooms and finally assess the pedagogic *impact* on pupils' learning.

Stages in the reflexive research process (Adapted from Smyth, 1989)	Focus of the stage
Stage 1	What is currently happening? • What is known about group work and learning? • What do teachers and pupils perceive happens in science lessons when children work together to carry out practical work?
Stage 2	What does it mean? • How do pupils socially interact and learn together? • How do teachers support this (or not)?
Stage 3	How did this come to be? • Reviewing observations and reflecting on interpretations of peer interactions. • Exploring the link between support, talk and cognitive processing.
Stage 4	How could things be done differently? • Developing the connections between scaffolding, talk and cognitive development to elucidate pedagogy. • Considering the potential influence of teacher intervention on pupils' interactions and learning.
Stage 5	Pedagogic intervention. a. Enacting changed pedagogy. b. Reviewing teachers' transformations. c. Assessing impact on pupils' learning.

Table 4.1 Summary of the stages in the research (adapted from Smyth, 1989).

4.4 My methods explained

Teachers frequently organise pupils to work together in small groups. Kempa (1994) assesses the frequency to be 'in the order of 50%-60%'. Kempa and Ayob (1991) add 'this strategy commonly adopted by science teachers requires that pupils assume responsibility for their own learning as the teacher's involvement in group activities is usually very limited if not absent altogether.' I knew from experience in my role as a tutor in teacher education, through regular supportive visits to mentors and trainees, and informal observations of existing practice that pupils working together in groups was routinely utilised in practical science. It seemed appropriate therefore to investigate further, through the network of schools within the ITT Keele University partnership, the extent and nature of group work in local secondary science classrooms.

4.5 Seeking teachers' views

I used a questionnaire to gain insight into the teachers' beliefs and prevalent practices because it potentially enabled collection of a significant, representative sample of science staff views. All mentors and their science departments, within the ITT partnership, were personally invited to be involved. The research project, including intended aims and outcomes, was outlined. I explained to the teachers that I was attempting to ascertain the characteristics of group work being used, how is it being orchestrated, the frequency with which it happens and why they are carrying out these pedagogic routines in their particular ways. I thought that the teachers' responses would provide an insight into typical practices of a range of relatively local schools. A copy of the questionnaire is included in Appendix 4.1, and more detail regarding its design is given in the next section. I hoped the findings would present a broad indication of contemporary habits that placed the more detailed later 'interactional' analysis into a wider context. I intended that this broad based survey should provide a macro-perspective of local teachers' views and predominant routines.

4.5.1 Sampling teachers' perspectives

The questionnaire was distributed to all science mentors, within the Keele partnership. This ensured that each school within the University ITT partnership that supported science students was invited to participate. Each questionnaire was supplied with a SAE to return to Keele to encourage rapid responses (Denscombe, 1998:96). The Keele University Secondary ITT partnership encompasses a consortia of 38 schools. Most are LEA comprehensive schools within Staffordshire, Stoke-on-Trent, Shropshire or Cheshire (see Figure 4.2 below), although there are a number that are Grant Maintained and selective according to religious practices.

Schools:	LEA	Male teachers	Female teachers
Alsager Comprehensive	Cheshire	1	
Biddulph High	Staffordshire	2	1
Blessed Wiiliam Howard RC	Staffordshire	1	
Blythe Bridge	Staffordshire	2	2
Brine Leas High	Cheshire	1	1
Burton Borough	Shropshire	1	1
Cheadle High	Staffordshire	1	1
Clough Hall Technology	Stoke-on-Trent	1	3
Coppenhall High	Cheshire	3	2
Haywood High	Stoke-on-Trent	1	1
Eaton Bank/Congleton High (was Heathfield High)	Cheshire		3
King Edward VI, Stafford	Staffordshire		2
Kings Grove	Cheshire		1
Leek High	Staffordshire	1	1
Madeley High	Stoke-on-Trent		1
Malbank High	Cheshire		1
Newcastle Community College (was Sneyd High)	Staffordshire	3	2
Newport Girls High	Shropshire		4
Rising Brook High	Staffordshire	3	
Sandon High	Stoke-on-Trent	1	
Sir Graham Balfour High	Staffordshire		1
Sir John Talbot	Shropshire	4	2
St Thomas More RC	Stoke-on-Trent	1	1
Walton High	Staffordshire	3	2
Weston Road High	Staffordshire	3	3
Totals		33	36
Total returned questionnaires		69	

Table 4.2 Showing the schools and LEAs of the teachers that returned the 'Investigation into group work in Science at Key Stage 3 and 4' questionnaires.

Thus there was a mix of urban, rural, 11-16 and 11-18 schools that were invited to contribute 4 questionnaires were given to each school (5 of the larger schools requested further copies). Of the 152 questionnaires distributed 69 were completed and returned. The 69 science teachers who responded were from 25 of the 38 schools, the survey therefore appeared to provide an indicative sample of typical, local, partnership practice. The range of teaching experience of those teachers that responded extended from 1 year to 30 years, of all the 69 teachers that replied the average teaching experience was 7 years. 52% of the sample were female, the remaining 48% were male. In discussions with staff that returned their forms, many stated that it was colleagues' lack of time to complete the questionnaire, as the reason for not replying.

4.5.2 The initial teacher questionnaire

As Davidson (1970) would say the ideal questionnaire possesses the same properties as a good law:

> 'It is clear, unambiguous and uniformly workable. Its design must minimise potential errors from respondents....and coders. And since people's participation in surveys is voluntary, a questionnaire has to help in engaging their interest, encouraging their co-operation, and eliciting answers as close as possible to the truth.'

The questionnaire was designed to be as succinct as possible, clear to follow, easy to understand (using appropriate language) and reasonably quick (20 - 30 minutes) to complete; as Munn and Drever (1990) indicate these are appropriate characteristics to aim for.

At the beginning of the questionnaire (see Figure 4A.1) the range of different question styles teachers were offered were exemplified and the corresponding method of response explained.

The content of the questionnaire was determined by the identified areas for research exploring the current situation in schools.

The first section sought general information, to elicit background information, such as specialist subject, level of qualifications, extent of teaching experience etc. The second section explored the extent and typical features of group work. I asked the teachers about regularity of different types of learning activities they utilise, how often they do this, what size of group they usually employ, and the rationale for organising their pupils to work together for practical and non-practical work.

In this section, for example, I wanted to find out how regularly pupils worked together in groups, when engaged on particular tasks, so a 5-point scale: never, rarely, occasionally, fairly frequently, always was offered. This type of data meant that a semi-quantitative analysis could be collated. As Wilson and McClean (1994:21) indicate, this type of question is quick to complete, easy to code for computer (and statistical analysis) but does not usually allow for 'other' ideas. I had to ensure categories were exhaustive, and that there was no bias (Oppenheim 1992:115) in the possible response options. The third and fourth sections were concerned with how they organise and manage group work. These questions were designed to explore the pedagogic support strategies utilised, and the extent to which the teachers intervened and interacted with the pupils in their learning. The final, fifth, section sought to elicit more subjective feelings and opinions regarding the educational value(s) of working in small groups; these responses were more difficult to predict, so open questions were offered to elicit free, not predetermined, responses (See Appendix 10).

4.5.3 Analysing the responses

All 69 teachers' responses were entered into a datafile in SPSS. Each question was coded (becoming the 'case variable' in SPSS) and 'labelled' to enable rapid logical retrieval; e.g.: Section B of questionnaire (Appendix 4): The extent and nature of group work. Question 1. Learning activities. A. Conduct of practical work, including the collection of data and information, was labelled as 'S3_con' for responses at Key Stage 3; responses at Key Stage 4 were labelled 'S4_con'.

Some questions were best explored by providing a scale of the range of responses expected - the teachers would then select from options which best reflected their normal practice, e.g.: Section B, Question 1 - designed to examine the regularity with which various activities are utilised, when working in groups, was asked on a variation of a likert scale: always, fairly frequently, occasionally, rarely, never. This provided a useful, although rather subjective, measure of how often teachers conducted practical work in groups, facilitated discussion of practically derived data and provided the opportunity to plan practical work in groups. The responses to these questions were then converted to a numerical scale: always = 5, fairly frequently = 4, occasionally = 3, rarely = 2, never = 1. This meant that statistical and graphical representations of the data using SPSS (a software package providing the user with the tools for semi-quantitative or quasi-quantitative analysis) could be made. Open-ended questions, allowing free response from the teachers were listed and then typed into word processing file. The complete set of responses were then classified and categorised (Appendix 4).

4.6 Eliciting pupils' views

I wished to elicit the pupils' perspective of group work to explore as an interpretative researcher how their stance might illuminate understandings of the learning processes and outcomes. To gain a non-biased, informative view I decided a questionnaire to elicit a significant number of perceptions from children in the ITT secondary schools was appropriate.

My intention was to explore pupils' ideas about working together. I wanted to gain an insight into their perspectives about working with each other; and secondly to contrast these findings with those of the teachers to see whether they corroborated each others' views. I assumed that two juxtaposed perspectives (from 69 teachers and 643 pupils in a range of Keele ITT partnership schools) would provide an illuminating insight of present routines and rituals in science classrooms.

4.6.1 Sampling pupils' perspectives

I asked teachers (as a question at the end of their questionnaire) if they would like to be further involved in the research project. Staff from several schools replied positively. For expediency (as there was no funding for the project in resources or time) the five closest schools (in promixity to Keele) from the replies received were chosen to provide an indicative, purposive sample of pupils' views within the ITT partnership. The five schools happened to also provide differing pupil experiences in terms of co-operative working. The questionnaires were distributed to each of these schools. I intended to gather information from two mid-ability classes in each of years 7 – 10, from each of the five schools, with the intention of gleaning a macro-view of 'typical' local experience. All the questionnaires were distributed in the summer term (1998). The five schools involved were typical of the Keele partnership consortium, i.e.; one was an inner-city 11-16 Stoke-on-Trent comprehensive; and four contrasting 11-18 Staffordshire comprehensives, one in a deprived semi-urban area and two others of average achievement, and a third of very high achievement, each located in semi-rural settings.

School A is an 11-18 Staffordshire school. It is described by Ofsted (1999) as an average sized mixed comprehensive school. There are 981 pupils (515 boys and 466 girls), only one from an ethnic minority background. The school is oversubscribed. It is a school that shows above average performance in KS 3 and GSCE science; attendance is above average and the school has a good ethos. It provides a positive learning environment with good attitudes to work on the part of the students. Behaviour is noted to be good. In science the knowledge and understanding in particular areas is good, most students have investigative skills that match their attainment in other aspects of science. The exception is in year 9 where some students find it difficult to relate their investigative findings to their scientific understanding. However, during year 7 and 8 opportunities for investigative work have improved and students are doing better than expected for their age.

School B is an 11-18 mixed, grant-maintained comprehensive in a socially deprived area (number of pupils eligible for free school meals is above average; with 180 pupils registering for Special Educational Needs) of Stafford in Staffordshire. It is relatively small, with just under 600 students. Unusually for a school of this size it has sixth form provision. The proportion of A* – C at GCSE and KS 3 SATs performance are below the national average. "Students develop slowly their capacities to think and carry out investigations. They can, in the main, devise fair tests and make sound predictions. However, their ability to interpret results is unsatisfactory" OFSTED, 1999. The school's ethos is noted to be committed to creating a positive learning environment, students' attitudes to learning are good, they work well with each other and with their teachers.

School C is a medium sized 11 – 16 mixed comprehensive school, situated on the edge of the city of Stoke-on-Trent. The number on roll is approx. 750. It is a popular school, which has been oversubscribed. 8% of schools pupils required SEN support, 32% are eligible for free school meals (above national average 17.5%), the number of EAL[14] pupils is below average. The ethos is described as very positive and purposeful, in which pupils are encouraged and expected to attain highly, both in academic and personal achievements. Relationships are very good and a strong community spirit prevails. Science achievement is generally above the national average. In 1999 there was 4% improvement in pupils reaching level 5. Compared to similar schools results are well above average. In investigative work at key stage 3 by year 9 pupils have developed the basic skills ready for GCSE.

School D is a large 11-18 mixed comprehensive, with an expanding sixth form. The catchment area is largely residential with a high proportion of owner occupied houses. Pupils eligible for free school meals is well below the national average. The number of pupils requiring SEN support is below average, as is the number of EAL. Pupil attainment on entry is high (above national average of eleven year old tests). In all three core subjects pupils' attainment at 14 is well above national average (in mathematics, 38% surpassed expectations of typical 14 year olds). 'These high standards have been sustained for several years', OFSTED (2000).

School E is an 11-18 large mixed comprehensive of 1059 pupils in a semi-rural situation. The number of pupils entitled to free school meals is in line with the national average, the proportion of EAL and ethnic minorities are also below the national norms. The attainment levels on entry in year 7 are below average. The achievement in KS 3 Science SATs is a little below average, but A* - C grades at GCSE in Science are above average. 'Pupils make good progress in all aspects of science, including experimental and investigative science' OFSTED (1999).

[14] EAL identifies English as an Additional Language, which provides background information regarding ethnic diversity in the school.

Professional mentor and trainee meetings provided the opportunity to distribute and collect the questionnaires. I provided 240 questionnaires for each school (maximum of 30 pupils in eight classes).

School	Year 7		Year 8		Year 9		Year 10		Totals		Total
	B	**G**	**B**	**G**	**B**	**G**	**B**	**G**	**B**	**G**	**All**
A LEA: Staffordshire	**27**	**21**	**15**	**11**	**22**	**12**			**64**	**44**	**108**
B LEA: Staffordshire	**13**	**16**			**28**	**15**	**29**	**17**	**70**	**48**	**118**
C LEA: Stoke-on-Trent	**20**	**22**			**16**	**22**	**7**	**23**	**43**	**67**	**110**
D LEA: Staffordshire	**23**	**35**			**28**	**30**	**25**	**29**	**76**	**94**	**170**
E LEA: Staffordshire	**22**	**22**			**42**	**29**	**16**	**15**	**80**	**66**	**146**
TOTALS	**105**	**116**	**15**	**11**	**136**	**108**	**77**	**84**	**333**	**319**	**652**
	221		**26**		**244**		**161**		**652**		

Table 4.3 : The response rate from pupils completing 'Pupils working together in science' questionnaires from Schools A, B, C, D and E.

Schools A, B and C returned almost half (108; 118; 110 respectively); school D returned 170 scripts and school E returned 146. Of 1200 questionnaires provided, 652 were returned completed (Y7 = 221; Y8=26; Y9=244; Y10=161). The reasons for incomplete pupils' responses were explained, by staff, that in the summer term pupils were often missing from class (holidays, extracurricular activities), that the timetable was often disrupted, lessons were re-organised or re-scheduled and there were decreased opportunities to question targeted classes. Others had existing teaching (to complete schemes of work) pressures and could not afford opportunities for pupils to respond.

4.6.2 Piloting the questionnaire

To validate the language and intent of the questions, the content of the questionnaire was trialled with a group of Y7 children in school A. They read through the questions and answered them. Post questionnaire completion, I discussed the questions and their responses in a 'focus group' situation.

4.6.3 Questioning the pupils

I developed a questionnaire booklet (Appendix 4.3) of manageable A5 size entitled 'Pupils working together in science' to explore pupils' thoughts about working with others. The questionnaires [to gather a large amount of data in a relatively short space of time in a comparable way (Munn and Drever 1990:11)] provided the appropriate tool to glean proportionally almost tenfold the teachers' views. Teachers were provided with an introductory script (see Appendix 4.4) to explain to the pupils the purpose of the questions, which were designed to encourage them to reflect on the nature of their learning and social interactions with each other and also the extent to which they are guided and supported to work collaboratively.

The first section of the questionnaire elicits personal background information, such as which class they belong to, how often they have science etc, for use as reference and background information. Section B explores the frequency and regularity with which they work together (to ascertain whether pupils and teachers have similar views). The next section asks them about how their working together is orchestrated to elicit whether the pupils self-select their working partners, or whether the teachers strategically group learners. They are also asked about the number of peers they normally work with to ascertain usual group size. In sections D and E they are asked for their views about how successfully they feel they interact and learn from each other and whether or not they are co-operating and collaborating effectively. They are also asked whether or not they perceive that they might need further support in working more effectively together.

4.6.4 Analysing the responses

As with the teachers' questionnaires, similar coding, 'labelling' and interpretation of open responses were utilised. The data were then entered into an SPSS dataset, similar to the responses from the teachers' questionnaire.

4.7 The observations of peer interaction

4.7.1 Aims of this aspect of the study

Having explored teachers' and pupils' perspectives of the nature and extent of existing practices to support learning through social interactions, I wanted to investigate and understand better how the children gain from effective working with others. There is general agreement that small group work is beneficial and an appropriate strategy to use to develop learning (Kutnick and Rogers 1994:2). Group work has been recommended for effective education in the Hadow Reports (1926, 1931) in the US, and in the UK by the Plowden report (1967), which highlights using small groups to increase teacher efficiency, so that autonomously working groups would free the teacher to help those with difficulties. The Plowden report goes on to emphasize how group work allows pupils to recognize and work with the strengths of each other, offer explanations that can help increase learning and enable discussion to plan. My observations were intended to add depth to the current descriptions of group work that Howe (1999:49) recognises require application to wider contexts. I wished to analyse further observations to attempt to understand under what circumstances cognitive gains, generally acknowledged by Galton and Williamson (1991), Howe (1998), Mercer et al (1999) and Murphy (1996; 2001) to exist.

As Pheasey and Underwood (1994) identify 'there are essential differences in the level of interaction in co-operative versus collaborative group work'. My investigation was to explore whether there appeared to be simply non-confrontational co-operative interactions in the sense that Kempa (1994), Bianchini (1997) and others define group work, or whether they were engaging in truly collaborative work, where, as Henessey and Murphy (1999) would describe, all members of a group share in the decision making process and work on the problem as a team. The effectiveness with which a group interacts and thus collaborates has been shown by Murphy (1997; 1999) and Howe (1999), in their analyses of interactions in primary science problem solving situations, to be influenced by task structure. Murphy (1997) suggests that 'tasks used in classrooms influence the kinds of thinking in which children engage and this in turn influences learning outcomes'. Howe (1999:20) identifies how small variants in task structure can have major implications for interactions and subsequent learning, she explains how related pedagogic strategies can affect learning, but highlights the need for 'the issue of task structure' to be 'explored systematically'. This is exactly what I attempt to do in my series of case studies. As Adelman et al (1980:59) identifies, the advantages of case studies are that they may enable generalisations to develop irrespective of (school) situation, but that they do allow for the complexity and embeddedness of social truths. In my project they are intended to inform 'a step to action'. I hope that in their 'world of action' I am interpreting insights from the interacting peers that can then be put to use. My study, at this point, focuses on the extent to which task structure can influence peer-peer interactions. My interpretative paradigm adopts learning theory that highlights the interplay between discourse, action and cognitive processing. The on-task-interactions were recorded to enable later transcription and further analysis. The nature of dialogic exchange, actional interplay and task outcomes were used as measures of cognitive engagement and development indicating subsequent levels of procedural and conceptual scientific understanding.

4.7.2 A series of case studies

In my pilot study a variety of groups, all single sex triads, were presented with tasks of differing context (combustion, friction, density), and differing levels of structure (more detail is given in chapter 7, section 7.3). The pupils were observed, carrying out the tasks in their schools.

My intention was to 'interpret' the ways in which they interacted to see whether any 'fuzzy generalisations', Bassey (1999:51) could be offered that highlighted the potential for more effective collaborative group work. What became apparent through piloting differing contexts with the same groups of pupils was an indication of sustained patterns of interactions (Bauersfeld 1988) between pupils regularly working together (see Appendix 7).

4.7.3 Gathering evidence of typical learning interactions

Forman (1994:5) discusses peer collaboration and how many previous studies have taken either an individualistic or sociocultural perspective. The individualistic perspective views the social context as an environmental variable influencing cognitive performance; i.e.: the social interaction may assist or prevent learning from occurring but the learning itself is regarded as an individual process and knowledge is something one may or may not acquire. In a typical scientific research study, independent variables such as gender, expertise, achievement or social status are experimentally controlled or interactional variables such as amount of talk and type of talk (e.g.: number of disagreements or explanations) are treated as dependent variables (Azmitia 1988; Bearison et al 1986; Kempa 1994). Early analyses of learning from peer collaboration were dependant upon specifying the input and output conditions that result in different cognitive outcomes. For example, Doise, Mugny and Perret-Clermont (1975) contrasted pupils working individually and with a partner in post-test scores. More recently assessments of students' social interactions and then correlation of these dependent variables with the cognitive gain scores; e.g.: Bearison, Magzamen, Filardo (1986) have become more commonplace.

Much of the literature on peer collaboration describes research that has been conducted in an experimental setting. An experimental setting allows one to control all extraneous variables so as to better observe the variables of interest in the study. Early research from a Piagetian perspective on the benefits of collaboration (working with and without a computer) tended to focus on outcomes (Doise et al 1979). This is similar to my initial approach where potential pupil or teacher interventions were controlled and the variables investigated were initially task structure and task context. Further into the study I refined my approach, and varied only task structure.

The socio-cultural perspective focuses more closely on the nature of the interactions and the mutualistic learning that arises as a result of participants' interpretations being continually negotiated. My study considers initially the more individualistic perspective and subsequently, more reflectively, adopts a more socio-cultural model, by focusing on actors engaged in situated activity, recognising connections between what an actor does, feels, thinks and believes, the constraints and supports provided by other actors and artefacts. I recognise that these actors are not disembodied minds; they derive their identity from their cultural mini-community (friendship driven) practices set in a much larger, more complex learning community (the school). In taking a more socio-culturally aware approach, my perspective of learning begins to lean toward that of communities of practice, within which, as the participants become more involved in the problem solving activities, they move from the peripheral (Lave and Wenger 1991) into more centrally sharing in the learning process. More recent work based on writings of Vygotsky has begun to examine and articulate the processes mediating productive interaction (Forman and Cazden 1985). My later more interpretative study (somewhat different in nature to these earlier perspectives on peer interactions) re-explores the nature and extent of the learning processes and outcomes. In analysing the video transcripts, actions, reactions, implicit understandings, dialogic exchange, procedural and conceptual development and task outcomes (indicating the complex nature of learning) have all been considered. My analysis of talk is informed by Mercer's (1999) work. He classifies talk according to its interactive nature. He provides a method by which exchanges between participants can be classified to indicate relative levels of cognitive involvement in the group task.

4.7.4 Pupil observations

These have been carried out at four schools within the partnership. Schools A, C, D (from the pupils questionnaire sample) and school F (described in Appendix 4) were involved. This was stage two in my research, finding out what working together meant for pupils and teachers. All the schools were involved because they were keen to find out more about how their pupils worked together and had previously indicated an interest in further involvement in the study and offered immediate observational opportunities. This sample provided a mix of 11-16 and 11-18, urban and semi-rural, with two schools in Staffordshire, one in Cheshire and a third in Stoke (typical of the Keele ITT consortia). Triads of (regularly working together) pupils were randomly chosen, and given differentially scaffolded tasks to solve.

With no funding to support the selection and bringing together for comparative purposes ideal representative samples from each school involved, as Bryan (1988) highlights:

> 'How do we know ... how representative case study findings are of all members of the population from which the case was selected?' (Bryan 1988:88).

I needed to define my 'cases'. The Y7 classes involved were randomly determined by timetable and researcher availability constraints. Each teacher who volunteered their school involvement was asked to identify typical working groups of their Y7 classes: again, in this way I hoped to illuminate through this kind of purposive sampling indicative behaviours and practices. I videoed several groups in each volunteered Y7 class, in each school. As Wolcott (1990) identifies the analogy of a zoom lens is useful when considering how you might view your data. The on-task-interactions of Y7 pupils working in their own school were videoed because I knew that interpreting the data would require the application of a variety of focal 'lenses' to my raw material (both actional and verbal) to explore 'what' was happening and 'why'. Therefore, a method to 're-observe' the original peer exchanges was required. With a wide-angle lens I gleaned general observations of pupils in action, before applying the macro-lens to analyse in detail the interactions between the triads.

4.7.5 Recording the pupils working together

I gave the pupils no guidance on how to tackle the tasks, apart from reminding them to 'work and talk as you normally do in science'. The worksheets provided the differentiated task support. The pupils' interactions whilst carrying out activities were recorded using a video camera with desktop microphone. This was similar to Tann (1981) who just recorded individual voices, then amalgamated them as a whole; Bennet et al (1984) also taped conversations. But as many have indicated previously (Tann 1981; Biott, 1987) group interactions are extremely complex so consideration of additional none-auditory interaction was also possible through video recording of the groups whilst completing tasks. Many researchers have utilised video technology and subsequently analysed transcripts of the tapes (Issroff, Jones and Scanlon 1994; Conwell 1994). The need for a permanent record of my 'actors' in their worlds of action that could be re-visited for differing foci of analysis was essential. Video recording in this way could be described as a pluralistic approach (Forman and Larreamendey-Joerns 1995:550) extending beyond individual performance to incorporate 'multiple learning indices and analyses of group functioning over time within particular activity settings'. It takes into account the 'various perspectives in the task that participants bring to bear in the learning situation'.

4.7.6 Development of the tasks

School activities as Roth (1995) argues should be authentic; the tasks created here are adapted or designed so that the 'context' is related to a pupil's everyday experience.

Hiebert at al (1999) supports a problem solving approach (to engender the opportunities described above) because 'allowing the subject to be problematic means allowing students to wonder why things are, to enquire, to search for solutions, and to resolve incongruities'. They build on Dewey's view of reflective enquiry to argue why "this approach yields deep understandings" of the kinds that we value as science teachers. Watson (1997) working on a project with ASE and King's college identified that making decisions and being involved in developing procedures, planning, measuring, observing, analysing data and evaluating methods were important learning opportunities in investigational work.

Roth (1995) clarifies this further by linking problem characteristics with the learning potential; he identifies open inquiry type tasks as those which provide the opportunity for students to:

a. identify problems and solutions, and test these solutions,
b. design their own procedures and data analyses,
c. formulate new questions based on their previous claims,
d. develop questions based on their prior knowledge,
e. link their experience to activities, science concepts, and science principles,
f. share and discuss procedures, products and solutions (Pizzini, Shepardson and Abell 1991).

During the process of task resolution I am looking for evidence of these kinds of cognitive processes. Watson and Wood-Robinson (1998:90) elucidate further that it is the thinking opportunity that is important in investigations, and that: 'It is important to provide time for discussion and to encourage pupils to make their ideas explicit'. They go on to highlight how the balance between support 'which gives students enough freedom to make decisions for themselves, and imposing a structure in which the teacher has made most of the important decisions' is vital, and how 'autonomous learners need to be aware of the educational purposes of activities in which they are engaged'. Howe and Tolmie (1994) identify that 'seemingly small changes to a task structure can have major consequences for the effectiveness of group work; the changes can influence both the process and outcome of learning' providing strong endorsement to the 'significance of task.'

Tasks of differing context and structure were standardised through the use of a task sheet (and no other intervention), this allowed me, as researcher, to compare the performance of different groups attempting similar tasks. Activities of this kind, typically investigational, appear to offer the greatest potential for supporting cognitive development.

In exploring further the effects of in-task-support I provided also semi-structured activities, which provide a lesser degree of openness, so the undertaking is in essence 'scaffolded'. The highly structured practicals do not provide problem-solving-authenticity, because the challenge and steps toward the 'solution' are clearly defined and because of the 'closed' nature of the task offers few ambiguities and uncertainties. There is no 'driving' of problem solving in these kinds of illustrative[15] practicals because discussion required to clarify, and make decisions has been reduced to solely 'mechanical' issues related to the 'carrying out' of the task. There is therefore, little opportunity for the pupils to consider 'what' they should or could be doing, and therefore to engage in developing procedural ideas; thus, potential deliberation and consideration of the scientific methods adopted is minimised. Interactions are more likely to focus on managing, operating and handling apparatus. However, the given method, is more likely to yield higher quality, reliable evidence, providing a basis for explanatory discussion of the related science.

[15] APU Definition of Illustrative = an experimental activity that 'demonstrates' or verifies a law or principle

Talk is more likely then to focus on 'what does the evidence mean?', rather than 'how should we collect our data?' Discussions, could be cognitively constrained in this learning situation, however, because the pupils are less likely to relate methodological processes to anomalous results, for example.

Context of the tasks

Using my professional experience as a teacher, I developed practical activities that were appropriate in context, and linked to the conceptual demands of Key Stage 3 schemes of work (e.g.: considering combustion in the context of same sized candles in differing sized jars, offers opportunity to consider the limitations and consequences of differentiated volumes of air (oxygen) available for burning) so that teachers would not be resistant to providing the time for the pupils to carry out the tasks. I attempted to provide less familiar practical activities (not in published Key Stage 3 schemes), so that the experimental work would be of interest as well as directly useful for the pupils.

4.7.7 Interpreting the interactional observations

My approach was to try and empathise with the different learners in their groups, in each problem-solving situation, were there any commonalities? Or was each situation so unique that no generalisations however, fuzzy, could be made. There was constant zigzagging between the data, analysis and underpinning theories and aspects of existing literature. As Hitchcock and Hughes (1995) describe:

> 'Qualitative data analysis .... refers to the ways in which the researcher, finding a series of individual cases, begins to look for relationships between them. Once a series of relationships is observed, the researcher attempts to formulate a series of insights or hunches in the light of the relationships observed, into a theory, which will cover and account for all cases as far as possible. This is not unlike the way in which many social scientists proceed, but the important feature of the role of induction in qualitative analysis is the significance of the researcher's experience. The hunches and ideas are generated out of the interaction of the researcher's own personal and, in our case, professional experience and the nature and content of the data' Hitchcock and Hughes (1995:297).

4.8 Video analysis

I watched each video clip on a minimum of four occasions, once to transcribe the pupils' conversations and then to identify and measure, in turn, other aspects of each child's interactions (with the others) and learning. A full example of this initial analysis is provided in Appendix 4. Conwell (1994) utilises an approach whereby she identifies the different ways pupils contribute to an unstructured task. Non-verbal actions were registered, using a similar coding system to SPOC category (Simpson and Tuson 1995:37).

After the transcription was written, each pupil was observed in turn from the videotape. Every minute of 'action' of each pupil was noted on the observation sheet (Appendix 4). I used this standard ethological technique to analyse in a semi-quantitative way behaviour patterns of my actors. The behaviours of each pupil (were colour coded) in a group were then overlaid onto the same observation sheet to review visually the 'interactions' between them.

4.8.1 Transcription

For each group carrying out each task, the time (from beginning of task), utterances stated and by whom, and general actions or behaviours were recorded.

Time (mins)	**Transcript**
0	All read papers
0.40	**A** to **B** 'you work the timer'
	A 'Let's do the smallest tube, then the middle then the biggest'
0.53	**A**, **B** and **C** spend a minute or so writing.
	A looks at **C**'s writing
	A 'Let's do this one first' - reaches smallest jar and spill
	C 'I'll light one of the candles'
1.41	**B** to **A** referring to timer 'How do I start this?'

Figure 4.1 : An extract from a typical transcript of a triad of pupils.

Tolmie et al (1993) video recorded group responses to differing tasks, he coded

> 'exclusively on dialogue, and enumerated the 'turns' (defined as distinct attempts at communication by any participant) devoted to:
>
> 1. Factor discussion; i.e.; any positing of a factor affecting outcome, elaboration of its role, agreement or disagreement with the role ascribed, or reference back to previous statements about a factor and its role.

2. Prediction discussion, i.e.: any statement of predicted outcome, and agreement or disagreement with that statement.
3. Chairing i.e.: requests for someone else to make a prediction or statement about a factor, or any other attempt to direct group progress (e.g.: 'we have to agree on what we think first', 'we have to turn over to the next page').

This enabled a measure of the impact of task condition upon in-group dialogue. In Appendix 4 there is an example of analysis of this kind where the number of times a pupil asked a question or the number of times one agreed with another was registered.

4.8.2 Analysis of the talk

Underwood, McCaffrey and Underwood (1990) noted that where performance varied between pairs of children working on computer tasks, there was also a variation in discussion.

Pheasey and Underwood (1994) studied discourse through problem solving and found that:

> '...lack of in depth discussion between pairs when they are not experiencing any difficulty with the task. It is only when the children hit upon some problem that 'real discussion' begins to take place.'

The groups in the study here were posed purposely designed 'problems' to provoke discussion.

Mercer et al (1999) defined 'exploratory talk' described as 'that in which partners engage critically but constructively with each others' ideas. Statements and suggestions are sought and offered for joint consideration. These may be challenged and counter-challenged, but challenges are justified and alternative hypotheses are offered. In exploratory talk, knowledge is made publicly accountable and reasoning is 'visible'. They assessed the success of talk by considering reasoning that was illustrated through 'key linguistic features', such as length of time at a turn of talking, incidence of 'because' and 'cause' 'I think' and 'agree'. Through their transcript analysis they found that where there was a high incidence of these features the pupil scored higher in a Raven SPM test.

Pheasey and Underwood (1994) studied discourse through problem solving and found that:

'...two sessions is probably not long enough to develop a stable working style'. As the pupils in my study were working in their normal groupings, I did not perceive that 'usual style' would be an issue. Bauersfeld (1988) refers to the types of exchange that develop over time as interactional patterns.

A temporal perspective

Issroff, Jones and Scanlon (1994) adopted a time line approach to analyse qualitatively behaviours between students. Their analysis showed differences both between and within, the pairs of pupils, in terms of the symmetry of their behaviours and the nature and timing of different types of talk. They also found evidence of development of modes of interacting (historical interactional patterns mentioned by Bauersfeld, 1988) over time in two of the five pairs studied. Similar to my study the co-workers were self-selected. I mapped the actions of each member of the group to explore whether historical (or other) interactional patterns became apparent. The timeline approach was intended to contribute to i. Identification of behavioural differences between members of a group; ii. the nature and extent of collaborative (or co-operative) action (verbal or behavioural) within particular groups; iii. Comparisons within groups completing the similarly structured tasks; iv. Comparisons between groups completing the same tasks.

4.8. 3 Assessing task processes and outcomes

Verbal evidence

I analysed the discourse for evidence of task resolution. The formative discussions and final task solution as verbalised by individuals within the group was noted in the transcript. The scientific accuracy and evident quality of scientific procedural and conceptual understanding, indicated by individuals and groups was also noted (see Appendix 7 and 10).

Written evidence

I provided the pupils with paper to freely scribe their thoughts. There was no imperative to write anything; a blank sheet was provided for each pupil. This provided another dimension of the articulation of intra-mental activity.

4.9 Developing teachers' experiential knowledge of pupils' learning interactions

Craft (2000:197) identifies a teacher's view 'of teaching will....tend to be affected by their experience and the type of schools they teach in'. I intended at this point, to develop an interventional in-service training approach, which was the initiation of stage five in my research. My intention here was to re-enact learning settings for teachers as *persons-acting* (Lave 1997:180) to encourage them to rethink how pupils learn. As a result of their [the teachers] direct experience, I hoped that they would mutually engage with each other (like groups in this study) to 'reflect on the full complexity of doing things together' (Wenger 1998:77). I intended that their reflection-on-experience should inform their reflection-in-action (Schon 1989).

4.9.1 The teachers involved in professional development

The professional development programme(s) were offered to teachers who were involved in the Keele ITT partnership as well as science and technology teachers from other LEAs (see Appendix 4.7a – f). The first group of teachers (all from the Keele consortium, including school A) involved in an INSET programme, informed by early findings from this study, have already been shown to change their practice in a number of ways (McGregor and Gunter 2001). The study here reports on subsequent cohorts of teachers from a range of LEAs (Appendix 4.7 a-f) and their subsequent changes in praxis. Each school represented was given two questionnaires to complete, teachers attending on the final day of the programme were asked to complete the survey over their lunch-break. I recognised the various issues associated with this, including proximity of the researcher that may influence the respondents' responses, however, the practicality of a feasible, immediate, purposive (Bell 1999:157) data collection outweighed the probability of few elective returns.

4.10 Assessing the impact of changed practice

Zeichner and Liston (1990) identify several kinds of reflective teaching. I assumed that through the professional development I offered, informed by my research findings, that I would encourage several aspects of each these. Shulman (1987) identifies reformed practice that stresses reflection upon subject matter the representation and translation of subject matter knowledge to promote understanding. Ross and Kyle (1987) emphasise the thoughtful application of particular teaching strategies that have been suggested by research on teaching. Duckworth (1987) views reflection developmentally and describes improved teaching that is sensitive to students' interests, thinking and patterns of intellectual growth. Maher and Rathbone (1986) describe a social re-constructionist view that emphasises reflection of a social and political nature to ensure greater equity and justice in schooling. To glean an indicative assessment of the potential change in practice, I will purposively sample a reasonable number of teachers for their subjective views, to explore the nature of the changes in practice. This questionnaire will explore how they think their practice and actions in the classroom has changed to improve pupils' cognitive development. The semi-quantitative nature of some pre-determined responses will indicate how prevalent particular practices are (Appendix 9.1). Juxtaposed to this personal subjective view of change I will collate more objective evidence of pupils-in-action. I will re-apply my analytical framework already explained (section 4.8) to the videoed recordings of the pupils working together. The impact of changed praxis through the teacher questionnaires and re-observation of pupils-in-action will triangulate the evidence collated. This second case study, will include a further series of observations of Y7 pupils, in school C, where staff have been involved in professional development. The findings of this part of the study should provide evidence from the teacher perspective and pupil actions of improved, higher quality learning, through supported social interactions.

The table below summarises the stages of the research, the focus at that point and the methods applied:

Stages in the reflexive research process	**Focus of the stage**	**Methods of the stage**
Stage 1	What is currently happening? • What is known about group work and learning? • What do teachers and pupils perceive happens in science lessons	 Literature review of group work and learning theories. Survey of 69 teacher perceptions, of group work in science, from 3 LEAs.

	when children work together to carry out practical work?	Survey of 652 pupil perceptions, of their experience working with others, from 5 schools within Staffordshire and Stoke-on-Trent.
Stage 2	What does it mean? • How do pupils socially interact and learn together? • How do teachers support this (or not)?	Observations of 36 triads of pupils from 4 schools in Staffordshire, Stoke-in-Trent and Cheshire LEA. Case study analysis focussed down to detailed interactional-cognitist examination of action and discussion occurring between members of 12 groups whilst on-task.
Stage 3	How did this come to be? • Interactional analysis to elucidate the impact of differentiated structure and support within tasks on the nature and extent of talk and cognitive development.	Analysing pupil exchanges for evidence of occurrence of 'exploratory' (cumulative and disputational) talk and inter-thinking. Comparison of procedural and summative task outcomes between 12 groups offered 3 levels of differentiated support.
Stage 4	How could things be done differently? • Considering the potential influence of teacher intervention on pupils' interactions and learning.	Linking support and scaffolding to elucidate, through reflective scrutiny of pupil exchanges (of 12 triads, from stage 3, with particular focus on un-supported tasks) in practical contexts, when (and how) intersubjectivity becomes a key issue to support the development of effective learning.
Stage 5	Pedagogic intervention. d. Enacting changed pedagogy. e. Reviewing teachers' transformations. f. Assessing impact on pupils' learning.	a. Designing, adapting and enacting teacher support in professional development activities to elucidate for teachers-as-learners the importance of inter-subjectivity. b. Reflective survey of 83 teachers' (from wide variety of LEAs) perceptions of their change in practice. c. Case study of 12 triads from two Y7 classes from school C.

Table 4.4 : Summary of the research stages, the focus at each point and the methods used.

4.11 Ethical considerations

The headteacher of each school was approached to seek permission to involve their staff and pupils in the research project. The questionnaires for both teachers and pupils assured that the data would be treated confidentially for research purposes only. The aims and procedures were explained to each member of staff and pupil involved, either through the covering letters or verbally, either collectively as mentors or as individuals within the schools. No pupil or teacher was involved without his or her informed consent. To retain anonymity and confidentiality of data pertaining to the pupils and teachers involved in this study, details are available, but are not clearly disclosed here. Pupils, their groupings and teachers are represented using a numerical system. Case study schools are identified by letters.

Chapter five

5.1 Introduction

The purpose of this chapter is to examine the nature and extent of group work from the teacher's perspective. The chapter begins with a description of the findings from the surveys and concludes with a summary and suggestions regarding the implications of their views.

5.2 The extent and nature of group work

This analysis should provide some insight into teachers' perspectives and practices in local secondary science classrooms. The foci of the questionnaires was to elicit what kinds of activities the teachers directed the pupils to do in groups, how they orchestrated the pupils to interact and how much of this kind of learning opportunity arose in the classrooms.

Frequency of group work

Teachers were asked to indicate how often they used group work in science (see table 5.1). Nearly half the teachers spent more than half the lesson time facilitating pupils working together in groups. This supports Kempa and Ayob's (1991) view that 'the proportion of lesson time spent by pupils on group work is in the order of 50-60%', indicating that generally a significant proportion of class time, in secondary science, is spent working in small groups.

Proportion of time (%) working as small groups	**% of teachers**
Less than 10	3
10-25	14
25-50	38
More than 50	45

Table 5.1: Teachers' perceptions of the proportion of time pupils spend working as a small group

Practical work in groups

The teachers were asked to assess the regularity with which they carried out various aspects of practical work (see Table 5.2), conducting the experiment itself, discussing the outcomes and planning the practical, either previously or subsequently, using a five point likert scale (never, rarely, occasionally, fairly frequently and always). The results are shown in Table 5.2 below.

Learning activities	Extent of use at KS 3[16] % teachers					Extent of use at KS 4[17] % teachers				
	never	rarely	occasionally	fairly frequently	always	never	rarely	occasionally	fairly frequently	always
Conduct of practical work, including the collection of data and information			7	62	31			10	62	28
Discussion of data/information collected from practical work		3	33	48	16		5	20	55	20
Planning of practical investigation	2	12	57	21	8	2	20	41	31	7

Table 5.2: Extent of planning, discussing and conducting practical work in small groups.

The extent of planning opportunities

Rather surprisingly, it appeared that, relatively few opportunities are offered to groups of pupils for the planning of practical work (see Figure 5.1 below). The most frequent practice is to enable 'planning' occasionally in small groups. About a third of the teachers enable pupils to always or fairly frequently 'plan' in small groups. About a fifth of the teachers indicate that they rarely or never provide the opportunity for the pupils to 'plan' together. In comparison of

[16] KS 3 represents Key stage 3, pupils taught; usually at the beginning of their secondary school experience are aged 11- 14.

[17] KS 4 represents key stage 4, pupils in the age range 14 – 16 are taught during this period.

practice at both KS 3 and KS 4, a similar pattern of opportunity for planning emerges, with this kind of opportunity most commonly occurring occasionally.

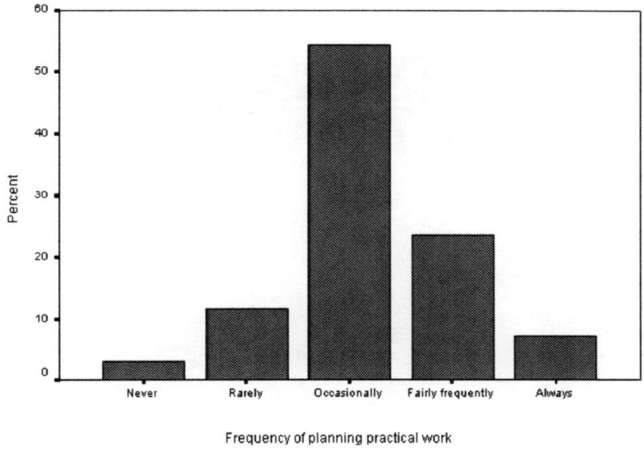

Figure 5.1: The frequency with which teachers perceive they allow their pupils to 'plan' practical work in small groups with KS 3 classes .

Although 'planning' an original experiment was not frequently proffered to small groups, when they were provided with the opportunity 45% of the teachers asked would usually check the intended procedure for possible safety risks (see Figure 5.2) and then allow the pupils to proceed rapidly to the experimental work. Just under a third would discuss the practical and consider the safety implications before allowing the pupils to proceed. Just over a tenth would utilise some pupil suggestions and consider them with the whole class. A small number allow pupils to proceed immediately to do practical, whilst a few others apply combinations of the previous approaches.

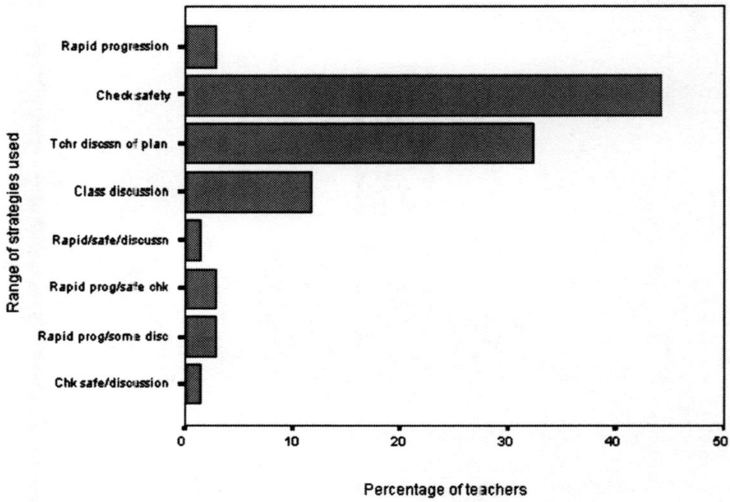

Figure 5.2 Indication of the strategies teachers use to enable pupils to apply their planning ideas to a practical situation.

Performing practical work

As anticipated, it would appear that almost all the science teachers questioned predominantly utilise group strategies for the act of conducting practical, which includes manipulation of apparatus, observation of variables (controlled and changing) and recording of results very frequently (see Figure

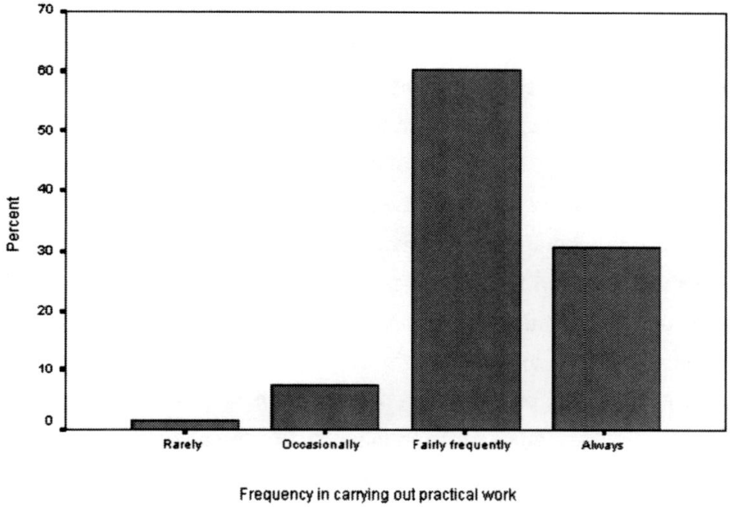

Figure 5.3 Teachers' views of how often they allow their pupils to work together in small groups to conduct practical work at KS 3 .

5.3 and 5.4). Practical work appears to be conducted by groups frequently or always in over 90% of the cases at both KS 3 and 4; no teacher stated they never conducted practical, and only 8% purported to effect practicals occasionally.

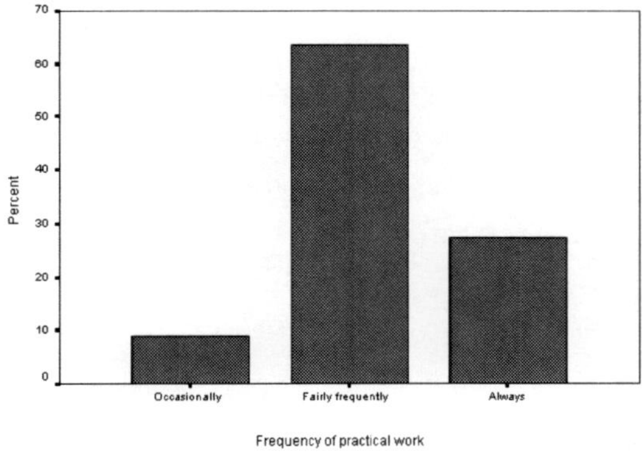

Figure 5.4 Teachers' views of how often they allow their pupils to work together in small groups to conduct practical work at KS 4 .

Opportunities for discursive consideration of experimental data

The teachers also reported that discussions of outcomes were less frequently divulged in groups, only 63% of teachers regularly and 33% occasionally allowed groups to engage in this discursive type of activity. Discussing outcomes (i.e.; results, meaning of data; conclusions) derived from practical work was, as with 'planning', relatively less frequently organised between pupils than anticipated. Again there was a similar trend at Key Stage 3 and 4.

The reduced opportunities to either plan experimental work or discuss practical outcomes in small groups may be a result of the pressure of Sc1 assessment, with teachers wishing to utilise as many opportunities as possible to evaluate individual performance in planning and interpretation of results. It could also be that much practical work is of an 'illustrative' nature and only provides limited opportunity for collaborative planning, as the methods appear to be largely 'predetermined' by the teacher to provide particular sets of results or data (see Table 5.3). Interpretation and the meaning of data is not frequently considered by the pupils in a peer-peer interactive manner either; it may be because teachers have to ensure the whole class reach the 'right' conclusions through a teacher-led approach or that assessed 'individualised' responses are required. This then raises questions as to why teachers organise pupils in groups for practicals, as they say in response to later questions that they do it in order to provide the opportunity to share ideas but, when planning and interpreting results from practical situations it appears that they relatively infrequently organise working groups to achieve this through peer-peer interactions.

When asked about the strategies they used to introduce practical tasks, the following practices were observed (Table 5.3).

Strategy used	Frequency of use..... (% of teachers)		
	Normal practice	Occasional	Exceptional or never
Practical task is pre-determined. Pupils are expected to follow instructions provided.	59.4	34.8	5.8
Practical tasks are generally pre-determined, but modifications are required in the light of outcomes of prior class discussion.	27.5	62.3	10.1
Practical tasks are only loosely pre-structured. Actual practical strategies emerge from discussion with pupils.	13.0	55.1	31.8
Practical work is not pre-structured, but arises from the context of the lesson topic and in the light of suggestions received from pupils.	3.0	19.4	77.6

Table 5.3 The frequency of differing strategies teachers use to introduce practical work.

Almost 60% of the teachers introduce practicals that are pre-determined, with pupils expected to follow the instructions provided, just over half introduce pre-determined experiments occasionally and only a small number (5.8%) organise pre-determined practical work.

Just over a quarter provide the opportunity for pupils to modify the pre-determined tasks, almost two thirds may do it occasionally and 10% said it was exceptional. Normal practice does not appear to be devising practical strategies through discussion with pupils, although this kind of practice was intended to be promoted through the introduction of Science 1[18] investigations in the National Curriculum; only 13% do this normally and occasionally over

[18] Sc 1 is the common label for Attainment Target One (Scientific enquiry) in the Science National Curriculum.

half do it. More than a quarter find it exceptional practice, a handful stated they never do it.

Practical work developing in the context of a lesson topic and in the light of suggestions from pupils is not frequent practice (as one might expect where there is direct pressure to deliver a prescriptive, overcrowded curriculum) is the exception rather than the rule, with over a quarter of the teachers never managing practical work in this way.

The relatively fewer opportunities for pupils to create or develop their own practical procedures, because they are largely pre-determined by the teacher, implies that much experimental work carried out by pupils, will, therefore to be illustrative in nature rather than genuinely investigative. It may also be that practical experiences are purposefully orchestrated to develop basic practical skills (setting up apparatus; using different measuring equipment; making observations). This supports to some extent the notion that the teachers are organising groups for practical work largely as a response to apparatus and/or resource constraints rather than to purposely promote discursive, interactive activity between pupils to exchange ideas, develop propositions or, indeed, promote cognitive development.

Other learning activities carried out by small groups

Teachers were asked to consider the range of learning activities employed when organising pupils to work in groups. In addition to practical work they claim they organised games (occasionally 13%; frequently by nearly 3%) or simulations, quizzes (occasionally 13%; frequently or always 4%), and debates (occasionally by 4%; frequently or always 1.5%). One or two individuals mentioned that they never or rarely utilised role play at Key Stage 3, but occasionally employed it at Key Stage 4. A few teachers recounted rare or occasional use of data searches, planning group presentations, preparing display work and supported self-study activities. Other activities that featured as occasional learning activities for groups were, discussion of examination type questions (nearly half the teachers), with just over a fifth providing this type of theoretical discussion opportunity regularly. One teacher stated he fairly frequently organised groups to demonstrate to their peers.

Sizes of groups normally organised for practical work

Group size (number of pupils)	% teacher responses		
	Frequently	Occasionally	Never
2	53	44	3
3	62	36	2
4	30	63	8

Table 5.4: Sizes of groups used in practical work

When questioned about the regularity with which they used either two, three or four pupils in a group for practical work, teachers indicated three in a group was the number most frequently utilised (62%). 36% stated that they occasionally opted for three, and only 2% said they never used groups of three. When questioned about the use of two pupils in a group, 53% said they frequently used this number, almost a third occasionally used two, and 3% stated they never organised pairs for practicals. Groups of four pupils were less common than two to carry out practical work; a little less than a third (30%) frequently utilised groups of this size, although 63% stated they occasionally used four in a group, with 8% stating they never used four.

There was no obvious correlation between size of group used and teacher experience or gender or school.

5.3 Teacher reviews of their organisation and management of group work

Reasons for arranging practical activities in groups

Teachers were asked to explain why they organise pupils in small groups to carry out practical activities. Each teacher was invited to provide up to 3 reasons for organising their pupils to work in groups. The most prominent reason (given by almost a third of the teachers) for using groups to do practical work was limited resources. 15% indicated that sharing ideas was important. Efficient strategy for learning, task motivation and development of social skills were proffered, each by about 10%. The remaining reasons each amounted to less than 5% of the teachers' responses. Rather unexpectedly, it appeared that physical limitations dictated the strongest rationale for organising pupils to work together in science. The prominence of resource constraints over the development of social skills prompted a further exploration of the prioritisation of the teachers' views. Further consideration of the initial rationale provided by the teachers is indicated in Table 5.5 (below).

Nearly half (47.8%) of the teachers stated that they used groups for practical experimental work because of the shortage of resources or equipment, an additional 5.8% added the constraints of space to this, so more than half (55%) of the respondents stated that physical limitations (not educational reasons) determined their use of group work strategies. This is corroborated by earlier research reporting on classroom groupings (e.g.: Tann 1981; Galton 1990; Good and Marshall 1984; Dreeben 1984) that found classroom organisation and physical structure constraints determined classroom organisation into groups, rather than any concern or aim to maximise learning capabilities. Comments such as 'rarely enough for individuals to work alone', 'limitations of availability of practical apparatus', 'lack of facilities' 'uses less equipment' indicated that teachers wished that there were sufficient resources for pupils to work individually or in even smaller groups.

The second most common reason (14.5%) for organising pupils in groups was so that they were afforded the opportunity to share their ideas, 'pupils learn from each other', 'cross fertilisation of ideas', opportunity to let pupils discuss scientific ideas' 'sharing of ideas and expertise' were typical responses. A few (5.8%) stated that this would lead to more efficient learning. Categorising the responses indicates that about two thirds of the teachers questioned reasoned physical constraints dictate their teaching approach; and about a third stated reasons that indicated they used grouping to promote more co-operative ways of working.

<table>
<tr><th>Category of response</th><th>Percentage of teachers indicating this reason</th><th>Percentage responses in associated categories</th><th>Percentage responses in either 'physical' or 'co-operative' categories.</th></tr>
<tr><td>Classroom management</td><td>1.4</td><td rowspan="4">56.4
Resource limitations</td><td rowspan="6">60.7
Physical limitations</td></tr>
<tr><td>Resource limitations (general)</td><td>1.4</td></tr>
<tr><td>Resources limited (equipment/paper resources)</td><td>47.8</td></tr>
<tr><td>Resources and space limited</td><td>5.8</td></tr>
<tr><td>More complex tasking (groups more able to tackle more difficult problems)</td><td>4.3</td><td rowspan="2">5.7
Time constraints</td></tr>
<tr><td>Rapidity of tasking (groups can work through tasks faster)</td><td>1.4</td></tr>
<tr><td>Sharing - generally</td><td>1.4</td><td rowspan="4">26
Sharing</td><td rowspan="7">33.2
Co-operative working
(consequences of social interactions)</td></tr>
<tr><td>Sharing ideas</td><td>14.5</td></tr>
<tr><td>Efficient learning</td><td>5.8</td></tr>
<tr><td>Task motivation</td><td>4.3</td></tr>
<tr><td>Social interaction</td><td>2.9</td><td rowspan="3">7.2
Social skills</td></tr>
<tr><td>Social skills development</td><td>2.9</td></tr>
<tr><td>Personal skill development</td><td>1.4</td></tr>
</table>

Table 5.5 The comparative reasons teachers initially provided to explain why they use groups in practical work (n=69).

Analysis of teachers' additional rationale for organising pupils to work in groups, indicated that sharing ideas and social interactions become more prominent after consideration of constraining resources. This indicates that uppermost in teachers' minds are often the pragmatic and temporal issues related to practical work and the notion of beneficial learning interactions in small groups is secondary.

Reasons for arranging non-practical activities in groups

Teachers were also asked to explain why they used group work for non-practical activities. As anticipated the most prominent reason, in a non-practical situation, for using groups in non-practical lessons was to share ideas, results, findings, tasks etc. amongst the group members, see Figure 5.5 below.

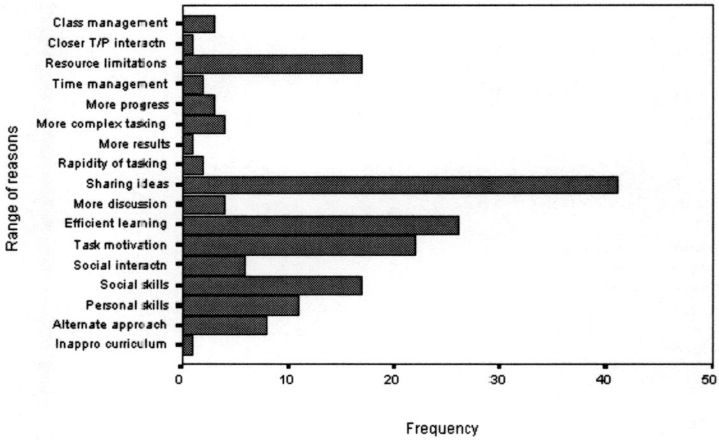

Figure 5.5 The variety of reasons teachers organise pupils working together when carrying out non-practical activities .

It appears that sharing ideas was the predominant rationale for organising pupils to work together, to enable them to 'bounce ideas off each other' and 'pooling of ideas' to consequently enhance and augment individual opportunity for thinking and discussion through peer-peer interactions or 'pupil-pupil interactions' as one teacher described. Another noted that working in groups 'makes pupils think for themselves rather than it being a passive activity'. The notion that interaction between group members would also benefit individuals because they could 'check understanding' against one another 'by question and answer' and because they 'have to think and present their arguments clearly' and that in so doing they 'can learn from one another' was also advanced. Other teachers recognised benefits where there are asymmetric groups; the 'weaker pupils listen to discussion rather than sit blankly doing nothing', also if 'they find reading/writing difficult they can still play an active role' within the group. Other teachers recognised the more active support for less able pupils because the 'more able assist less able' and generally 'better pupils help weaker ones' and that this can enable 'pupils to gain confidence', 'especially the quieter ones'.

Some teachers remained focused on physical constraints and mentioned that pupils can 'share the workload' and if there is a 'range of abilities in group' then the tasks set can utilise

the 'different skills of individuals' and the experience of the 'combined' or 'team effort' of the individuals is beneficial.

Particular social skills that the teachers noted were developed were the 'skill of listening and valuing others' opinions'; being able to 'co-operate' with others, noting that to do so meant 'tolerance improved'. Several teachers mentioned the promotion of 'co-operation' and the development of co-operative skills through the experience of working in a 'team' or 'group'.

Categories of reasons for using groups in non-practical work	**% Teachers**
Class management	2
Resources sharing	4
Time constraints	6.7
Sharing ideas/results/tasks	59.4
Social interaction	24
Alternative approach	3.3
Inappropriate curriculum material	0.7

Table 5.6 The relative importance teachers attached to working in groups on non-practical activities.

Reasons for using groups in non-practical activities

Teachers were asked to give three reasons why they used group work for non-practical activities. Teachers appeared to find this much more difficult than reasoning why they used groups in practical work (because there were more blank responses).

Teachers' rationale for using group work

Category of response	Practical activities	Non-Practical activities
Class management	1.1	2
Resources sharing	18.2	4
Time constraints	11.2	6.7
Sharing ideas/results/tasks	43.9	59.4
Social interaction	23	24
Alternative approach	2.7	3.3
Inappropriate curriculum material	0	0.7

Table 5.7 Categorisation of teachers' rationale for using group work in science lessons

This indicates (generally) that the teachers questioned tended to reason that it is appropriate to use groups in non-practical situations predominantly for social and intellectual (sharing ideas) development of individuals (59.4%), but that this is of lesser importance (43.9%) when carrying out practical work, with resources and time constraints becoming much more prominent.

Organising pupils to work together

Nearly half (45%) the teachers questioned allowed pupils to select their own working groups, almost a third instructed them to work with their neighbour (usually a friend). Only a small number (not quite 10%) determine the group composition. A handful of teachers operate a range of strategies when organising pupils working in groups (as indicated in Table 5.8 below).

Teachers' usual practices when organising groups	% respondents
a. allow pupils to select their own working partners	45
b. instruct pupils to work with neighbour	29
c. form working groups by placing pupils together for particular reason (criteria applied indicated below in Table 5.9)	10
a & b	3
a & c	5
b & c	3
a, b & c	5

Table 5.8 To show strategies teachers use when organising working groups.

Of those that stated they would form groups (10% above) for particular (educational or otherwise) reasons almost half said they would consider ability a significant factor. Slightly more than a fifth thought the social composition important and slightly less thought both ability and social composition important.

Criteria (teachers above) used to form groups	% respondents
Ability of pupils	47
Social mix of pupils	24
Ability & social	18
Rotation (strict/random)	12

Table 5.9 To indicate criteria the teachers (10%) used when forming working groups (n= 7).

Predominant practice is not to pre-arrange or organise pupils in groups according to the task(s) or learning outcomes to be addressed; the usual 'default' practice is to allow pupils to work with their neighbour (inevitably a friend) or choose with whom to work with (also likely to be a friend).

When asked about preferences regarding the composition of groups they would like in their classrooms, about a fifth indicated they prefer mixed gender groups, a small number 2.4% said they did not wish to see boys and girls working together in groups, and one individual felt that single sex groups were best. 14% said they prefer mixed ability groups and almost 6% indicated they preferred similar ability groups. There did not appear to be strong views or feeling about the ways groups should or definitely should not be composed. There was little indication that teachers carefully thought about the effects of particular 'mixes' of group members on the learning interactions and outcomes. Fewer than a fifth indicated that 'mixed' or similar ability, or mixed or similar gender groups was likely to have a significant impact on the working groups (either the outcomes or the interactions).

Nearly three-quarters (73%) of the teachers questioned said their working groups remained 'unchanged'; when pupils did switch working groups it was usually because the teacher felt 'rebalance' was necessary socially so that dominance by an individual was averted. They also reorganised to balance ability, or to control miscreants, rejuvenate interest or vary the experience for the pupils. Infrequent, pupil-initiated, changes would result from shifts in friendship groups.

Teacher views of difficulties related to organising pupils into effective working groups.

When asked about the difficulties or problems teachers encountered when utilising group work approaches, the predominant concerns revolved around intra-group management, including issues like 'weak groups who can't get started' and 'fast groups that run out of things to do' and the issue of 'ensuring active participation from all members'. Teachers talked about how a 'passive approach is taken by some group members leaving others doing everything' or 'brighter pupils (even within a brighter group) do more of the work', so equity of individual involvement on a group task is a significant issue. This concern is strongly linked to the composition of group members, because '*mousey* pupils are difficult to stimulate and are easily dominated – making no real contribution' and 'clash of personalities which leads to arguments' illustrate discord through disharmonious mixing of co-workers.

Issues of difficulty	% teacher concerns
Group composition (not harmonious/productive)	38
Intra-group management (maintainance on task/equitable contributions etc)	38.2
Inter-group management (standardised experience for all groups/teacher support)	4.7
Time management (lack of progress)	3.9
Resource constraints (insufficient resources/safety issues/limited space)	15.6

Table 5.10 Teacher perceptions of the difficulties faced when organising pupils to work in groups (n = 43).

It is interesting to note that teachers' immediate response when asked about difficulties were dominated by concerns of negative peer pressure and the issue of distraction of pupils resulting in 'off task' behaviour and generally disharmonious mixes of pupils in groups.

Resource and space constraints are also an issue, with the imbalance of contributions by individuals within groups then becoming more significant. The reasons given as major difficulties and problems encountered by science teachers when organising group work were predominantly related to social interactions in some way, i.e. absence of leadership, disharmonious mix, peer group 'pull' etc. The second main category of difficulty was related to intra-group management, which included how to sustain and monitor individual learning, ensuring that each pupil interacted and contributed appropriately etc. The third most common category of response was that of resources (and space) constraints, mentioned by 15.6%. This appears to be a little contradictory as teachers had responded earlier, with nearly half (49.2%) stating that they used groups for practical experimental work because of the shortage of resources or equipment.

Teacher involvement in intra-group task management

In the organisation of tasks amongst individuals in a group, over a third of teachers try to initiate group responsibility for task organisation and distribution; allocating a group member responsibility for task allocation is rare, but more than half the teachers made suggestions as to the tasks that might be entailed in an activity, but left the group members to decide for them selves who did what. Less than 3% assigned specific tasks to specific members of the groups. Providing clear guidance on exactly what and how each participant in a group should contribute to that group was not common practice.

To monitor and maintain groups on task almost half the teachers (47.8%) 'systematically move around to all working groups and discuss their work with them', just under a fifth (18.8%) monitor general progress of the pupils and do not intervene unless necessary; a sixth (15.9%) say they oversee the class but stay close to groups that tend to deviate from the task in hand; just over a tenth (11.6%) retain an overview of the class, but focus attention on 'low ability' or 'slow learners'. The remainder of the teachers (3.1%) carry out combinations of the above.

Teachers were then asked to consider the strategies they might use if groups finish their tasks set at different times, in other words how would they 'intervene' to encourage completion of tasks or provide further learning experiences.

Strategies teachers employed for fast working groups included 'extension work' (often undefined further); this was mentioned by almost 70% (69.7%) of those questioned. Additional practical tasks (modify experiment, collect more data; look at extra variables) were offered by 15.2%; just under tenth said they would provide supplementary theoretical work (questions, further data to interpret), 3% would ask the pupils to repeat data collection (to check for reliability, look for more detail etc). One teacher said rapid workers could then support others.

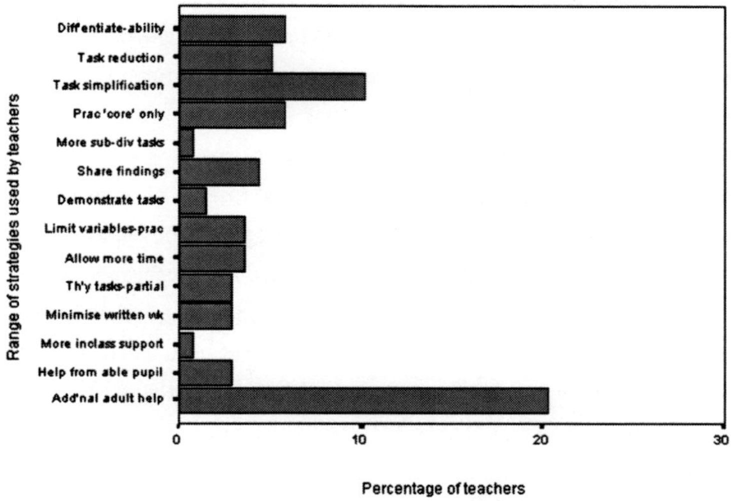

Figure 5.6 Graph to illustrate the range of strategies that teachers use to deal with 'slow-working' groups.

With slower groups the teachers suggested that they would present the tasks in a simpler, more appropriately differentiated way, the practical tasks would be reduced, streamlined, even demonstrated or only the 'core' work done. Theoretical work would be given much less emphasis, reduced or simplified. More in classroom support would be provided either by the teacher or from more able peers.

It would appear that predominantly faster working groups would be provided with generally more 'to do', albeit additional extension practical activity or more questions to answer. There does not appear to be additional teacher-peer interaction, or purposeful provocation of meaningful peer-peer interaction where discussion of the quality of outcomes or meanings of the findings could be discussed at length.

There appears to be much more intervention if a group is struggling with a task (see Figure 5.6). Either the teacher or other more capable peer is likely to offer support. The tasks themselves are also likely to be modified in some way to accommodate the capability of the pupils.

5.4 Teacher views and opinions about group work

This section of the chapter seeks to describe what views and opinions teachers have of the benefits and disadvantages of children learning together in small groups.

Suitable and unsuitable occupations for groups

When asked if there were any specific kinds of tasks that were particularly suitable for groups to tackle, over a quarter of the teachers stated investigations (20.8 % specifically mentioned complex investigations). Project work was thought to be appropriate by 11.3%. A wide range of other activities including field work, other discursive types of activities such as debates, presentations, experimental planning and analysis, simulations and role plays were all thought to be appropriate.

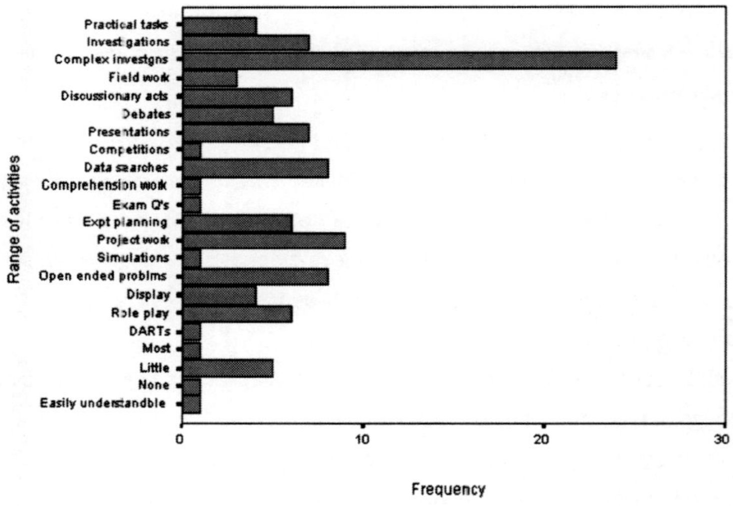

Figure 5.7 Teacher perceptions of activities suitable for small groups.

Activities judged to be unsuitable involved assessments of pupils' performance in Science 1 investigations, planning, reporting or concluding and any practical or theoretical examinations. Practicals of a highly complex nature, utilising expensive or limited materials or specialist equipment and those that involved high level safety hazards were also deemed unsuitable. The data suggests that the inherent nature of technically demanding practical work thus limits or constrains what teachers perceive pupils should do in small groups.

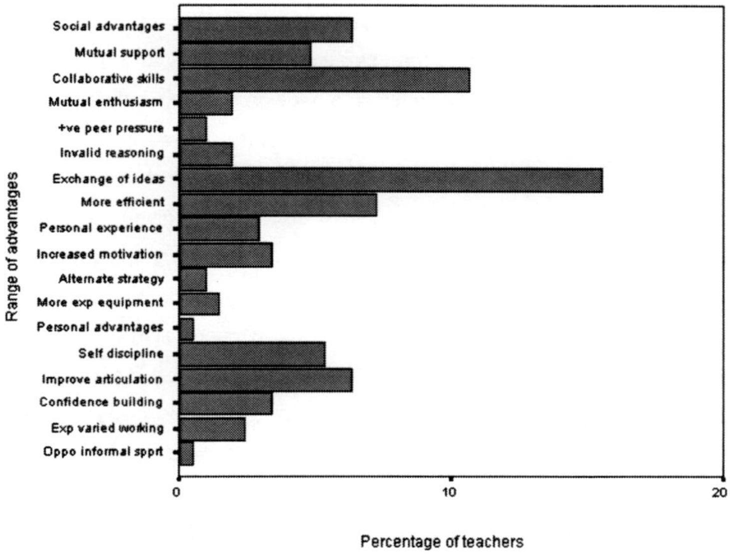

Figure 5.8 Teachers' views on the educational advantages of pupils working in small groups.

Teachers' opinions of educational benefits of working in small groups

Teachers were questioned about the educational advantages they thought group work could offer their pupils. Exchange of ideas was the most common response amongst the teachers. Providing the pupils with the opportunity to '*learn from each other*', '*cross-fertilising*' their thoughts, '*discussing their ideas*' and '*enlarging their ideas*' were specifically quoted. Collaborative and social skill development appears to be the next category of perceived advantages, illustrated by views highlighting the advantage of '*co-operation*' and '*team-work*' even noted to infect the whole classroom to create a '*better …atmosphere*' infiltrated with a '*feeling of co-operation*' to '*help each other*'. One teacher recognised that the variety of differing skills members of a group might have could contribute to team work because '*each person can adapt a role most suited to their personality – can be given a chance to try new roles in new groups'*. Another noted that the sorts of '*collaborative skills*' that could develop are '*important in later life*'. The teachers generally appear to think that within such situations the pupils will '*learn to 'get-on' with others*', '*learn to work co-operatively*' and as a consequence '*learn the importance of team work*'. Some teachers indicated that '*skills*' such as '*listening*' and '*articulation*' or '*oral communication*' would develop, alongside '*valuing others' opinion*' or '*learning to appreciate other peoples' viewpoints*' as a result of working together. These in turn would then augment individual *'confidence'* because pupils feel *'less self conscious'*. Some stated that given '*a degree of independence*' they took more '*responsibility for their learning process*' and this *'improved self discipline'*. A considerable number of teachers also regarded time efficiency to be an advantage with pupils able to '*collect more data*' because their are more '*hands*' available, they can '*progress better*' so that '*more can be done in a given time*', as the pupils generally operate '*quicker*'. Also *'the combined efforts of the individuals lead to a more complete activity'* because they '*use each other's ideas to progress better*', another also noted that *'better motivated pupils can stimulate others*'. The quality of learning experience was noted by some too, indicating that '*sharing ideas lets them [the pupils] develop concepts/further [their] own knowledge*' and that '*discussion of ideas leads to the best solution*'.

This overview provides the rationale for teachers organising their pupils to work together. There does appear to be, however, a 'hope' that particular collaborative skills will develop, being co-operative, taking joint responsibility, developing self discipline, appreciating others' view points, because when asked how they support group activity there is little suggestion about how they might support pupils beginning to share task responsibility. Slower or less able pupils are those that receive most support through teacher scaffolding or intervention and possibly peer generated (proximal development). The contrasting view of the disadvantages teachers perceive exist could provide some insight into the barriers for groups working more frequently together and the difficulties teachers perhaps do not have the pedagogical strategies to overcome.

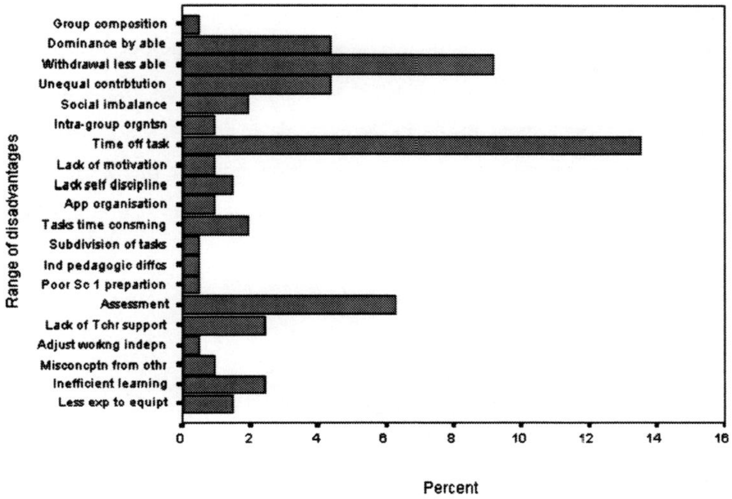

Figure 5.9 Teachers' views on the educational disadvantages of pupils working in small groups.

Teachers' opinions of educational problems when working in small groups

A much wider variety of views were elicited when teachers were also asked to relate any disadvantages that might be associated with group work in science. Their perceived shortcomings encompassed aspects of pedagogic difficulty e.g.; poor Science 1 preparation, meaning pupils wouldn't be adequately prepared for the investigational assessments; difficulties in assessing individual performance; providing individual support; picking up from others the 'incorrect' or 'incomplete ideas' or concepts. These appear to illuminate teachers' views that pupils do ***not*** learn from each other, and only learn from themselves (the expert, information and knowledge providing teacher).

The most frequent concern teachers stated with regard to working in groups was pupils 'off-task'; the 'time wasted due to too much distraction', 'opportunities to mess around' and the noise levels resulting in 'pupils deviating' from their set tasks were typical of disadvantages quoted by teachers.

The second area of concern was that regarding the composition of the groups, 41.3% of the respondents mentioned either social imbalance, dominated by an able member of the group or withdrawal of a less able member and the inequality of contributions made by individuals to the task set. Nearly 40% were concerned with the intra-group organisation, how the pupils could/should motivate themselves, organise the resources they were to use, subdivide the tasks or labour etc.

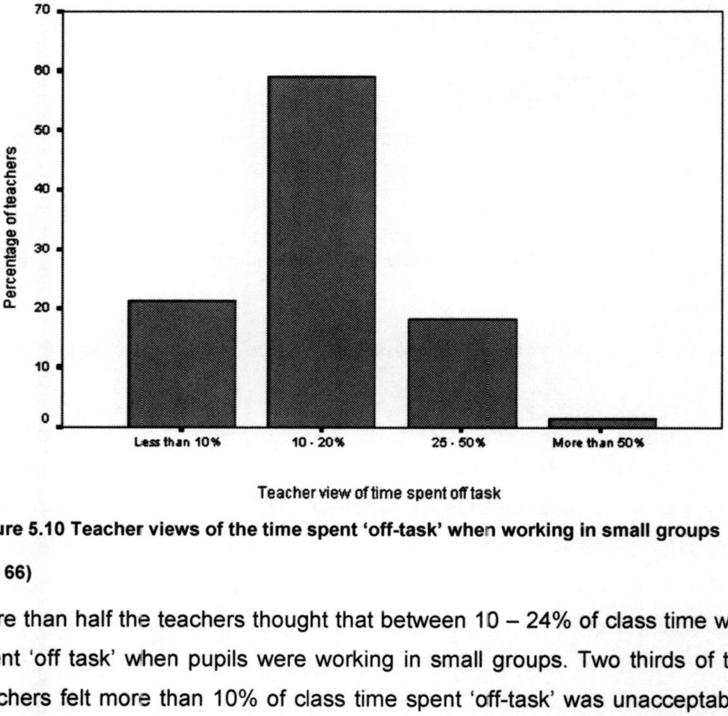

Figure 5.10 Teacher views of the time spent 'off-task' when working in small groups (n = 66)

More than half the teachers thought that between 10 – 24% of class time was spent 'off task' when pupils were working in small groups. Two thirds of the teachers felt more than 10% of class time spent 'off-task' was unacceptable, and as about 80% thought 10% or more was 'off-task' time they were correct to allow this to be a significant concern.

Teachers were asked (in the light of their own experience) which types of groups they felt were educationally most effective. Over a third (35.9%) thought that groups composed of pupils of similar academic aptitude were educationally most effective. More than a quarter (28.1%) thought that personality compatible groups were most effective, whilst 14.1% thought that friendship groups were best. Nearly 8% thought mixed ability groups most effective, and even fewer (6.3%) thought a group in which one pupil could 'lead' would be most educationally useful. A tenth of the teachers said that various combinations of friendship, ability and personality were important. Only one teacher mentioned that the most effective composition of a group 'depends on the activity'. These responses indicate that teachers do not predominantly think that differing ability pupils within a group, mixed gender groups and non-friendship groups are likely to promote effective working interactions between pupils.

5.5 Summary and further questions

There are a number of issues raised as a result of this initial investigation of this indicative sample of teachers' views of pupils working together.

It appears that working in small groups is commonplace practice in secondary science classrooms (in the Keele ITT partnership), but that teachers often organise their classrooms to operate in this way because of resourcing constraints. It appears that these teachers do not pro-actively manage and organise pupils into particular kinds of working groups, they predominantly allow children to self select whom they associate with. It appears that they are aware of many difficulties of peers working more independently in a small group, but that they usually only intervene, in the group processes, for disciplinary reasons. If they do direct group membership it tends to be predominantly with ability in mind. In Alexander's study (1992) mixing abilities in a group is not often employed by core subject teachers, although curriculum areas such as art and craft featured this strategy in their teaching. There appears then to be little or no regard for the potential to create particular group memberships to maximise social interaction and subsequent construction of knowledge and understanding. It seems then that these teachers do not appear to consider carefully the educational outcomes they may wish to achieve (apart from 'exchanging ideas' and 'developing social skills') that may serendipitously emanate from placing particular pupils to work together. Thus, it seems, resources (or physical parameters) are often a very strong influence on the how, why and when small group work is utilised. This was also found to be the case in Alexander's (1992) study of primary ICT and science teachers who determined size of working groups according to amount of apparatus available, rather than being guided by pedagogic considerations. Tann (1981), Galton (1990), Good and Marshall, (1984) also found that the physical structure of rooms influence number and size of groups rather than learning intentions.

Although these teachers recognise there are benefits to working together, their general view is that very little or no meaningful *learning* takes place as a result of peer-peer interactions.

They appear to believe that effective learning occurs predominantly as information given from them, the more 'expert' teacher. There appears to be little consideration of the nature of interactions that they need to support or how to effectively scaffold peer–peer learning interactions. There does not appear to be an acknowledgement or even tacit understanding that the type of practical activity, and the inherent structure within in it, will (or will not) support collaborative planning, debate and attempts at co-constructing meaning out of data gleaned, through discussion.

Although this sample of teachers articulate a predominant reason for pupils working together in small groups to discuss, share, and develop ideas, they often instigate much illustrative, 'recipe-like' practical work with very little opportunity to devise, create and pursue investigative approaches in a group. There appear to be relatively few opportunities for pupils to consider planning investigations or practicals to discuss the outcomes of their experimentation in small groups, and participate in the types of discussions and subsequent verbal and cognitive interactions that provoke thinking.

The teachers' concerns about problems regarding social difficulties, 'off task behaviour', lack of leadership, individual assessment problems and other issues that can often arise through children working together appear to impact on their view of the interactions they wish to support. Thus a cohesive, co-operative, non-argumentative type of interaction, rather than supporting much more intellectual debate and discussion of interpretations concerning the conceptual and procedural issues of the tasks in hand, appears to be uppermost in their minds. Consequently it seems accurate to note that, for these teachers, co-operation is more prevalent as a concern, rather than provoking effective learning interactions that can underpin cognitive development.

Placing children in groups that purposely *spark,* develop and consider ideas would suggest a change in culture is needed, and explicit reasoning by the teacher to guide why pupils should share their thinking more openly, and become more deliberately explicit themselves, and enter into deliberations regarding possible solutions, discussing their reasoning used to make decisions about their methodology or findings. The teachers therefore need to be aware of pupils' differing interpretations (role of intersubjectivity explained later in chapter 8) of the same methods, results or conclusions in a practical situation and its subsequent effect on cognitive processing and the development of more effective working together. To explore the nature of peer-peer exchanges and associated social development *experienced* by the pupils appeared then to be an essential dimension to examine, before offering suggestions to teachers regarding pedagogical change needed to support more effective learning interactions. To elucidate whether purposeful discussion and exchange of ideas was developing spontaneously between pupils when they work together was the focus of my survey of their views of *happenings* in the classroom. The next chapter discusses the findings of this survey and begins to highlight issues that require consideration when offering pedagogic advice to science teachers supporting pupils in their practical work.

Chapter six

6.1 Introduction

The purpose of this chapter is to provide some insights into pupils' perspectives of group work in secondary science classrooms. The following is a discussion of the nature and frequency of small group work alongside pupils' more subjective views about how they perceive they interact to work and learn with their peers. The opinions and stances of a wide range of pupils were sought, to provide a general view of their experiences and reflections and to also compare and contrast teachers' and pupils' perspectives, to explore whether their perceptions were corroborated when considering group work. A comparative analysis of this kind can then illuminate current routines and practices of teachers. Of the 900 questionnaires distributed to the five schools in the partnership, 652 were returned. 221 of the respondents were from Y7; 26 were from Y8; 253 were from Y9; 197 were from Y10. The majority were therefore from KS 3; with just under a third (28%) representing KS 4. In the discussion where there are contrasts between general views of the pupils and more specifically Y7 (early KS 3) perspectives the differences are highlighted. The questionnaire was designed to elicit both social and scientific insights into *what* they usually did in groups and *how* they did it.

6.2 The frequency and nature of group work

Time spent working in a group

Pupils' responses suggest that 40% think that they spend more than half their lessons working in groups. Of the sample 49% of them think that about 25% to 50% of the lesson time is spent working in groups; about a sixth think less than a quarter of the lesson is spent working with others in a group. In Y7 a much larger proportion perceive they spend more time working in groups.

Over half the lesson		Chapter 2 Between a quarter and a half		Less than a quarter	
All pupils	**Y7 only**	**All pupils**	**Y7 only**	**All pupils**	**Y7 only**
39	59	46	38	14	4

Table 6.1 : Pupils views of the proportion of time they spend working in groups (n = 652; for Y7 n = 221).

Every science lesson		Most science lessons		Some science lessons		Never	
All pupils	Y7 only	All pupils	Y7 only	All pupils	Y7 only	All pupils	Y7 only
6	6	48	52	44	40	2	2

Table 6.2 How often in science lessons pupils think they work in groups (n = 652; for Y7 n = 221)

Often		Ocassionally		Rarely or never	
All pupils	Y7 only	All pupils	Y7 only	All pupils	Y7 only
15	22	58	63	26	15

Table 6.3 How often pupils think they work in groups when doing things other than practicals (n = 652; Y7 n = 221).

It would appear that not only do Y7 do more practical activities, but also they work generally more often in groups, carrying out a wider variety of tasks or activities, not just experimental work.

Usual size of group when doing practical work?

When carrying out practical work, a comparison of all years and Y7 (percentage of pupils reporting on size of group they are working in) indicated the predominant group size to be 3.

Usual group size:	All years	Only Y7
2 pupils	22	26
3 pupils	36	27
4 pupils	31	39
more than 4 pupils	4	1

Table 6.4 To indicate the usual size of group to carry out practical work (n = 652; Y7 = 221).

In science, to do practical work, just over a third of the pupils report they most commonly work as a triad (in Y7 this appears to be a little lower). This 'perception' of pre-dominance of triads is confirmed by the teachers' responses (Chapter 5). In non-practical situations this changes and more than half of them are likely to work as a pair (see Table 6.9).

When working with others, not practical, but in science, what is usual group size?

Usual group size:	All years	Only Y7
2 pupils	51	55
3 pupils	22	21
4 pupils	17	19
more than 4 pupils	5	1

Table 6.5 : To indicate the group sizes used for non-practical work (n = 652; Y7 =221).

There appears to be a significant increase in the frequency of dyads utilised to carry out non-practical activity in science. Pupil perception is again corroborated by teachers' responses that they organise groups of children in larger groups, greater than two, to do practical work, they say, predominantly, because of resource constraints.

The nature of group work

Pupils were asked to indicate how often they carried out various kinds of activities in small groups. The results (Table 6.6) suggest that the most common activity carried out in small groups appears to be practical, experimental work. It appears that planning the practical and discussing the results of the experimental work was not so commonly carried out in groups. Discussing questions or problems appeared to be about as frequent (a little less than half the time spent in groups) as discussing results of practical work. Creating a piece of writing or researching and role play were much less common practice in small groups.

	Activities linked to practical work:			Activities not directly linked to practical work:			
Indication of frequency of activities:	Carrying out a practical or experiment, including collecting results	Discuss the results or how the experiment has gone	Plan a practical or investigation	Discussing questions, problems set or information provided by the teacher	Creating a piece of written work (e.g.: poster or letter) together	Finding out together, using CD-ROM or encyclo-pedia, library	Role-play, using drama/acting in some way
Frequently	63	44	25	44	17	6	3
Occasionally	33	44	56	43	46	20	5
Rarely	3	11	17	13	36	73	91

Table 6.6 Pupils' views of regularity of working within a small group to carry out various activities (n=652).

	Activities linked to practical work:			Activities not directly linked to practical work:			
Indication of frequency of activities	Carrying out a practical or experiment, including collecting results	Discuss the results or how the experiment has gone	Plan a practical or investigation	Discussing questions, problems set or information provided by the teacher	Creating a piece of written work (e.g.:poster or letter) together	Finding out something together, using CD-ROM or encylopedia, library	Role-play, using drama/acting in some way
Frequently	70	57	32	44	18	3	1
Occasionally	29	32	45	46	50	13	2
Rarely	1	10	21	10	31	83	95

Table 6.7 : Y7 pupils' views of regularity of working within a small group to carry out various activities (n = 221).

Carrying out practical work

The majority (over 60%) indicate that they frequently work in a group to carry out an experiment; just under a third occasionally or sometimes work in a group to 'do' the practical with only a very small proportion (3%) rarely working with others in this way. In year 7 there appears to be more emphasis on organising the pupils to do practicals in groups (commonly 70% frequently work in groups; with 21% sometimes working in groups; 1% rarely work in a small group). Thus, in later years the practice of small groups doing practical together appears to decrease.

Discussing results

Generally fewer than half (44%) frequently discuss results; fewer than half (44%) sometimes discuss results. 10% rarely discuss results. There is an increase in the frequency of discussion with Y7, with well over half (57%) frequently discussing results and just less than a third (32%) sometimes discussing results. Although there are obvious opportunities for pupils who are often, regularly working together to carry out practical work, they do not, it seems, perceive or indeed discuss their findings to the same extent as 'doing' the practical (corroborated by the teachers' views Chapter 5, Fig 5.4).

There appears to be, as with carrying out practicals, a decrease in the discussion of results later in Key Stage 3 and 4.

Planning practical work

Generally most pupils think they have opportunities to plan together in groups sometimes, it appears to be less frequent to design a practical together regularly and a significant number say they do not plan at all together as part of a group. A greater number say they only occasionally plan or do not 'plan' together at all in Y7.

Alternative group activities (other than practical)

In asking pupils about the other activities they engaged in as a group, the following activities were suggested for consideration to explore the potential nature of co-operative work in addition to the obvious practical experimentation.

Discussing questions

Questions (i.e.: from examination papers or tests) are discussed in groups frequently by nearly half of the pupils and occasionally by most of the other half. About 10%, a relatively small number, rarely discuss questions or a problem set by the teacher.

Creating written work together

Almost half the pupils do this sometimes, just under a fifth do it frequently and about a third rarely do it. Thus it appears, co-operatively (or even collaboratively) working together to create a written group 'outcome' does not appear to be common practice.

Researching together

About a quarter of the pupils indicated they did this often or sometimes. Almost three-quarters rarely did it. In Y7 it appeared to be much less frequent than in the later years. Thus, again, it appears that another collaborative type of activity is infrequent.

Using role-play

Very few pupils indicated that they were engaged in this kind of activity, from the data gathered, it also appears to be less frequent with younger pupils (Y7) than later years.

In general, then, engagement in scientific practical work is more prominent in Y7 than in later years, where there appears to be a wider variety in the types of activities pupils are directed to do in small groups.

Variations between the schools

There appears to be some indication that school D, reputably, the most successful academically (according to OFSTED), is the one that allows pupils to work most often in groups to do practical work (91% of the time). The less academically successful schools, B and C, and to a lesser extent school E, appear to offer much less opportunity to carry out practical work within small groups of pupils. Similarly the more academically challenged schools appear to offer less opportunities to discuss results after experimental work and also less opportunity to collectively plan investigative work (perhaps because of disciplinary and control concerns). However, opportunities for discussion appear to be higher in the academically challenged schools when not directly linked to more traditional experimental work.

Generally there does not appear to be frequent verbal interaction although the learning opportunities might appear to be appropriate.

	Schools				
Nature of frequent group work	School A (sample size 108)	School B (sample size 118)	School C (sample size 110)	School D (sample size 170)	School E (sample size 146)
Practical activity	76	36	44	91	58
Discussion of results	59	24	37	54	40
Planning practical activity	22	24	23	39	16
Discussing (non-practical) questions, problems etc	55	33	59	15	38

Table 6.8 : Indication of the nature of the group work frequently carried out.

Other non-practical activities considered carried out in groups indicated very similar practice between the schools for using role play, or finding out together, see Table 6.9 below.

	Schools				
Nature of frequent non-practical group work	School A (sample size 108)	School B (sample size 118)	School C (sample size 110)	School D (sample size 170)	School E (sample size 146)
Role play, drama, or acting in some way	0	9	1	4	1
Finding out together	0	7	8	10	4
Creating a piece of work together (writing or poster)	10	19	38	15	10

Table 6.9: Indication of nature of frequent non-practical group work in the different schools.

Attempting to provide opportunities for pupils to work together to produce a piece of written and or graphic outcome appears to be more widespread in school C than in the other schools.

6.3 Management and organisation of group work

How is group membership determined?

Pupils were asked about how they were organised to work with others in groups. From the pupils' perspective they respond saying that the majority of the time they are able to choose their working partner(s). If the regularity with which teachers also instruct pupils to 'work with their neighbour' is true then it is only a small proportion of the time that pupils are directed to work with specific partner(s). The vast majority of the time, then, pupils self select whom they wish to work with, so peers, it seems are likely to be working in friendship groups.

	Teacher instructs that working partner(s) should be 'neighbour')		Teacher allows pupil choice of working partners		Teacher instructs exactly whom to work with	
	All pupils	Y7 only	All pupils	Y7 only	All pupils	Y7 only
% pupils' views	14	19	76	61	7	13

Table 6.10 : Pupils' views of group membership.

There appears to be an indication that Y7 have less choice about whom they work with than the older age groups.

Comparing pupil experience between the schools indicated that teachers frequently allowed pupils to work with whom they liked, especially if one presumed that the teachers did not 'place' children specifically adjacent to particular neighbours.

	Teacher instructs that working partner(s) should be 'neighbour')					Teacher allows pupil choice of working partners					Teacher instructs exactly whom to work with				
School	A	B	C	D	E	A	B	C	D	E	A	B	C	D	E
% of pupils' views	15	26	25	3.5	6	62	64	67	95	84	17	6	6	1	3

Table 6.11 : Pupils' views within the different schools

The stability of the groups is indicated by how often they change. Just over 60% of the pupils indicated they remained in the same working groups. Just less than a third indicated they changed their groups. A few more pupils (40%) from school B, school C and school D indicated they changed their groups sometimes. Less than a tenth of the pupils said they changed their groups often. Of the minority that did change groups occasionally, when asked about why this change occurred pupils provided a very wide range of responses.

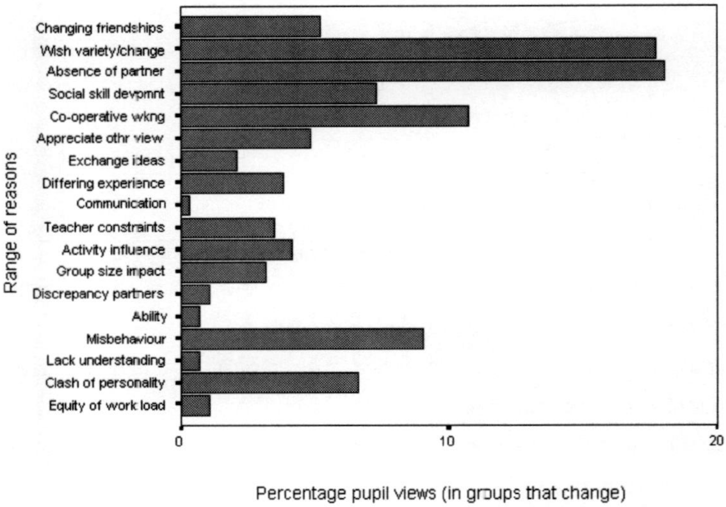

Figure 6.1: The range of reasons pupils (from five schools) gave for changing whom they worked with.

It would appear that where members of groups appear to change more often, the major reason (stated by a quarter) is a wish for variety or change, they 'want to work with different friends' because 'sometimes you get tired of working with the same people' and would like 'variety in who you work with'. The re-grouping of co-workers for this reason, it appears, is organised by the pupils; 'We just decide to work with different people in each lesson'. The second most common reason given was associated with development of social skills in some way, through a recognition that they could learn by observing or working with different people, for example, 'so we can get to used to working with other pupils because we won't always work with the same people all our life'; many others indicated they wanted to 'get to know other people' and find out how 'other people listen and learn', 'see what other people are like to work with…boys as well as girls' another specifically said 'because it allows you to work on your social skills.' It appears then, that pupils have a very social view of reasons to change working partners in recognising resultant social skill development to 'get on with each other' and work 'co-operatively' is important through working with peers. They also seem to value others contrasting views that through social interaction, group work can provide a varied, differing learning experience. In Figure 6.2 there is an indication that some pupils (almost 15%) also recognise teacher directed change of group membership can be utilised as a disciplinary measure to control misbehaviour.

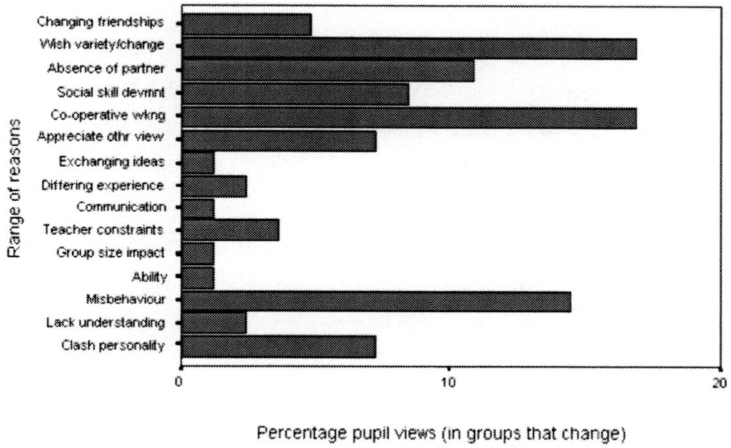

Figure 6.2 : The range of reasons pupils from school A gave for changing whom they worked with.

In school B absenteeism (of the regular partner) predetermines whether or not a child works consistently with the same pupils. Misbehaviour is also quoted as a reason for change, by a slightly larger number than those in school A.

In school C, similar to school A, pupils wished to ensure variety in whom they work with and also recognised that social skill development was important, to 'learn to work with different people' and become 'better' at working with others.

In school D surprisingly, absence of usual working partner was the prevalent reason for change. Co-operative working 'helping get along with people' and 'to get used to other people working with you' was also an important rationale for choosing partners. Absence of 'misbehaviour' as a reason for teachers to move group members reflects the 'relaxed' ethos of this school.

In school E, less academically successful than D, almost a quarter of the pupils liked to change working partners for variation (Figure A6.3).

Selecting working partners

Pupils were asked about whom they would choose to work with in a group. Almost two thirds (62%) said that working with friends was most important. 16% said they would like to work with pupils of similar ability and a small number (3%) said they would like to work with pupils who were better at science than themselves. A small number (3%) said they would like to work with other pupils who listen indicating concerns over a significant problem where an individuals contribution is not listened to. Almost a tenth (9%) said they did not mind whom they worked with. A small number (3%) said ability and friends were equally important.

School	Friends	Pupils better at Science	Pupils similar ability	Pupils who listen	Don't mind
1	61	2	16	15	3
2	50	8	16	5	9
3	66	4	11	5	8
4	75	2	14	1	4
5	53	3	22	3	8

Table 6.12 : Indication of relative importance (percentage of pupils' views) of preferred characteristics of working partners.

Pupils largely prefer to work with their friends, although in school B, a challenging school, where there is little group work, only 50% of those asked agreed with that idea. In school D, where group work is much more commonplace, three-quarters of the pupils preferred working with their mates. It appears then that pupils prefer to work with their friends, but recognise that changing membership of a group is also valuable socially and can provide heterogeneity in learning. In school E, there is recognition of the variation in learning experience, contributed to by contrasting views and exchange of ideas through different working partners.

Management of group work tasks

To explore how teacher's perceive pupils should work together, their management and organisation of group learning was examined. In the previous section it became apparent that teachers were happy to allow friends to work together and usually organised groups of three for practical work. They usually created many opportunities to carry out practicals, but orchestrated less opportunity for discussion of the meaning of results, and provided even less opportunity for planning In non-experimental situations. Other activities where opportunities for discussion that could explore pupils' ideas and facilitate their cognitive development appear to be rather scant.

The pupils were asked about the way in which the teacher usually introduces the work each member of a group should do. The majority of pupils (77%) indicated they are provided with instructions for the group or general information about what to do – but are then left to work out exactly who should do what themselves. Only 22% indicated they were given guidance by the teacher as to what individuals could contribute when working with others.

In school D, where group work is most prevalent, just over a tenth of the pupils said they were given guidance about what individuals within groups should do. The most guidance given for individual sub-tasks was to about a third of the pupils from school A.

Teacher involvement in intra-group work

Whilst pupils are working on their tasks in groups the most common practice, for teachers in each of the five schools studied, was to walk around the classroom occasionally talking to pupils. Virtually half (49.4%) of the pupils report this usually happens. Just over a fifth (22.4%) say their progress is regularly checked and 15% report that the teachers provide assistance when needed. A small proportion indicate they are left to themselves (5%). This practice is broadly corroborated by the teachers' view of their practice (see chapter 5). About half the teachers systematically monitor group progress, and about a fifth intervene when it appears necessary. A smaller proportion retain an overview of the class, but remain in the proximity of lower ability groups or potential miscreants. It would appear that intervention from the teachers is usually to monitor progress, support less able or slow learners or to control misbehaviour.

It appears that the majority of teachers, most of the time are allowing their pupils to organise themselves and determine the direction of their work with very little or no direct guidance or intervention form the teachers.

6.4 Pupils' views of interactions between peers in the groups

The nature of peer-peer interactions is explored in the next section, and pupils' views of these different aspects described.

Pupils learning from peers in the group.

Pupils were asked about how much they think they learn from each other. Almost half (46%) say they learn as much from their partners as they do from themselves. Almost a fifth (19%) say they learn a lot from their working partners.

Less than a tenth (7.5%) say they don't learn much from their partners, but think the others learn more from them. About a quarter (26%) say they don't learn much from each other, and indicate their learning comes mostly from the teacher.

Interestingly there is a high correlation between the pupils perceived ability and how much they think they learn from others in the group (Appendix 6.4). The more capable the child in science the more they learn from their partners, they say.

The less able scientists said they didn't learn much from their peers but mostly from the teacher.

Feeling confident and understanding how to work together

Pupils were asked to indicate how confident they feel about the task they are engaged on when working in a group. Over a fifth (22%) felt they always knew what to do. Nearly three-quarters mostly knew what to do, but indicated they were sometimes not clear. This indicates that tasks are not spontaneously engaged in by all group members when tackling a problem. A task has to be worked out or 'discovered' (Newman, Griffin and Cole 1989:33). It appears also from the lack of teacher intervention that maybe this is not an area clearly addressed when pupils embark upon practical work.

Less than a tenth were often unclear and tended to misunderstand the work they were asked to do. When asked whether they debated or argued about who should do what, only just over a tenth said they always argued; just over a third (38%) said they sometimes argued and virtually half (49%) said they rarely argued. It appears then that there is relatively little discussion, dispute or debate about what is done and by whom. It seems there is relatively little verbal social interaction that explicitly considers alternative perspectives or view points of the task, its associated methodologies or individuals' responsibilities for them.

Pupils' perception of the efficiency of working together in a group.

Just less than a third (29%) said that they always felt they worked more quickly in a group rather than as an individual. Nearly two thirds (63%) said they sometimes worked more quickly in a group. Only a small number (7%) indicated they work faster working alone. Collectively pupils perceive they work more effectively.

Thinking about and sharing 'ideas'

Asked if they felt they collectively produced more ideas, nearly two thirds (60%) said they did, about a third (32.3) said they sometimes created more ideas. A very small number said they rarely produce more ideas when a member of a group. The social interactions are productive through exchanging thoughts (nearly two thirds (62%) said they share ideas and always exchange thoughts, a third (33%) said that sharing ideas sometimes happened, a small number (4%) said they rarely shared ideas.) and subsequently pooling and generating divergent thinking. Again just under two-thirds (61%) said they always worked out results together, a third (33%) said sometimes worked out results together and a small number (4%) said they rarely worked on their results together.

Talking about the task

When asked about how often they talked about 'things' other than the science tasks set, over a fifth (22%) said they always talk more often about things not related to work set; over half (58%) sometimes talk more about things unrelated to the task set and just under a fifth (19%) rarely talk more about 'other things'. When asked about the proportion of time spent not talking about science just under half (48%) of the pupils said they only spent a little time; almost a third (30%) said between quarter and a half of the lesson; almost a tenth (9%) said about half the lesson and a tenth said they spent more than half the lesson talking 'off task'.

Reflecting more about the science

A third of the pupils indicated that when there was more discussion they always thought about the science more. Just over half (51%) said they sometimes thought about the science more as a result of more talking about it. A smaller number (16.5%) said they rarely thought about the science as a result of discussing it more. Talking appears to stimulate the pupils to consider the 'content' of the lesson more carefully.

Increased enthusiasm and motivation

Asked about their relative enthusiasm working with others rather than alone, nearly half (48.4%) said they were always more enthused; just over a third said (35.1%) they were sometimes more enthused; a small number (14.5%) said they were rarely more enthused.

Asked about whether they worked as hard as they could, just over a tenth (13%) said they don't work as hard as they could just over half (51%) said they sometimes don't work as hard as they could and just over a third (36%) say they always work as hard as they can.

6.5 Pupils' perceptions of difficulties when working together

The nature and frequency of difficulties encountered when working with others. In attempting to inform what strategies might be successful in supporting more effective group work, the various kinds of difficulties pupils experienced were assessed. Strategies that could support more effective interactions, both socially and cognitively were sought. So pupils were asked about what kinds of difficulties they encountered when working with others and how often these kinds of problems arose.

Problems working with others was not an issue for the majority. Only a minority, under a tenth (7%) say they always have a problem and less than a third (28%) sometimes have a problem.

The kinds of problems they encounter are making enough effort to discuss the work set, decision making, dominant individuals, listening to others, understanding what to do and lack of guidance. A tenth say they always lack the effort to discuss, under half (44%) say they sometimes lack effort and a similar number (42%) say they rarely have problems discussing what they are trying to do as a group. The decision making process, deciding who does what is an issue for nearly 70% of the pupils asked. Only a relatively small number (15%) said they always had problems deciding whom should do what, just over half (54.5%) have difficulties sometimes deciding whom should do what and just under a third (29%) said they rarely have problems. Just over half the groups found the presence of a dominant leader was an issue.

Just over a fifth (22%) always have the problem that one person dominates, just under a third (32%) sometimes have this problem and over two fifths (44%) rarely have this problem. Almost half the groups found others listening to them was problematic, with just over a tenth (12%) recognising this as a regular problem, almost two fifths (38%) sometimes have this difficulty, and nearly half (48%) rarely had this difficulty.

Understanding what to do was a concern for just over half, with just under a tenth (7%) have a problem with this, under half (44%) said they sometimes have a problem and almost half (46%) rarely have a problem with this. This could be explained by the lack of spontaneous discussion to clarify between peers their views of the task set. Of concern to the majority was the lack of guidance on how to work with others. Of all the pupils asked a third (33%) say they have been given help or advice on how to work with others, whilst two thirds (64%) say they have been given no guidance at all. There is interesting variation between the schools that indicates in school D, where group work predominates, very little support or advice is given so the majority of pupils, it seems, are left to work out for themselves how best to co-operate and collaborate on group tasks.

	Schools				
	School A (sample size 108)	School B (sample size 118)	School C (sample size 110)	School D (sample size 170)	School E (sample size 146)
Percentage of pupils	44	32	32	19	39

given guidance					

Table 6.13 : Data to indicate how much guidance on how to work with others pupils perceive they receive in the different schools.

Those that reportedly received guidance were asked who provided the support and whether they provided some or a lot of guidance. The following table indicates the summation of some and a lot of guidance provided by their current science teacher, their previous science teacher, their form tutor or some-one else.

	Schools				
	School A (sample size 108)	School B (sample size 118)	School C (sample size 110)	School D (sample size 170)	School E (sample size 146)
Current science teacher	42.1 (21.7 + 20.4)	39.3 (17.9 + 21.4)	41.4 (20.7 + 20.7)	15.3 (4.7 + 10.6)	28.7 (7.5 + 21.2)
Previous science teacher	26.4 (5.3 + 21.1)	29 (5.1 + 23.9)	26.1 (4.5 + 21.6)	14.1 (3.5 + 10.6)	21.8 (4 + 17.8)
Form tutor	28.3 (13.8 + 14.5)	21.4 (12 + 9.4)	23.3 (8 + 15.3)	14.1 (5.3 + 8.8)	23.3 (4.8 + 18.5)
Someone else	23.8 (5.9 + 17.8)	27.3 (12.8 + 14.5)	24.3 (6.3 + 18.0)	15.3 (1.8 + 13.5)	30.2 (15.8 + 14.4)

Table 6.14: Indication of the proportion of pupils to whom guidance on how to work with others was provided by various members of staff in school.

It would appear that the current science teacher offers the most advice on how to work with others. The previous science teacher, form tutor and other members of staff appear to provide guidance to less of the pupils (about a fifth). In school D there appears to be much less obvious guidance on how pupils should work together. It appears that the pupils themselves deal with how to work effectively together. School A,B and C appear to offer the similar levels of support, with the current science teacher providing most assistance in how to work together.

More advice on how to work with others in groups

When asked whether they would like more help to work effectively with others, just over a third (35%) said yes. But almost two thirds (62%) said '*no*' they did not require assistance in collaborating with others. Many pupils indicated that they liked working in groups because it was '*more interesting*' , '*more fun, learnt more and concentrated more*' that they worked more quickly and that it was easier if you had some-one to '*discuss your work with*' because there is mutual in-built support, there is '*always someone to help if you get stuck*' and '*you have someone to discuss ideas with*'. Others more thoughtfully highlighted that they would like more autonomy in their working together, '*I think you would learn more if you had the chance to decide which experiments you would need*', others recognised that they needed to develop their social skills to be able to '*understand my partner's points of view because they don't always know what they are on about*'. Others recognised '*how to organise time and resources better*' was the kind of guidance they required. Pupils themselves also noted size and composition of groups as an issue. Single gender groups mean '*girls gossiping*' so '*mixed groups would be better*', and they said if the group is '*too large* ', '*some people end up not doing anything and letting everyone else do the work*'. They said they '*prefer if we are told individually what to do*'.

6.6 Summary

Orchestrating group work

About half the pupils perceive they spend about half their time working in groups. For Y7 working with others appears to be commonplace with nearly two thirds discerning they spend more than 50% of their time in a group.

In practical situations triads appear to be the most common sized groups, defaulting to dyads when scientific apparatus is no longer a concern [of the teacher].

The group membership is usually determined by the pupils. Changing working partners appears to be usually through their desire for variety in experience (to promote exchange of different ideas) or because their normal working partner is absent. Less than a tenth of the 'changes' are due to teacher intervention.

Whom they work with is predominantly their choice, although there are indications that in KS 3 teachers select groups for just over a tenth of pupils. It appears for the most part that teachers do not pro-actively manage 'learning' groups. The pupils perceive that they 'control' mostly whom they work with, and that teacher direction of group members is applied for disciplinary purposes (or to avoid personality clashes) to control mis-behaviour (see Figure 6.1).

By choice most pupils would wish to work with friends (this was most prevalent in school D), but some did indicate that other pupils of similar ability was a consideration.

A small number said *'someone who would listen'* to them was important; whilst surprisingly about a tenth didn't mind whom they worked with.

Pupils primarily work in small groups to do practical work. This appears to be commonplace in Y7 and less so by Key Stage 4. The pre and post practical discussion, however, appears to be much less prominent in small groups, and again there appears to be less planning and post practical discussion linked to the experimental work later in Key Stage 3 and 4.

Working in groups to discuss questions or problems set by the teacher appears to happen frequently for just under half Key Stage 3 and 4 pupils, but surprisingly other tasks are not commonly tackled by co-operative or collaborative working together.

Guidance and support in how to work effectively as a group (and how to allocate sub-tasks amongst themselves) was not commonplace. Often the pupils are told what the group as a whole should achieve and left to their own devices as to 'how to get there'.

Learning interactions

The pupils perceive that the teachers did not generally 'intervene' in their learning activities, but mentioned the following support from teachers: progress through tasks, checked behaviour and provided assistance if slower or less able group needed it.

Most pupils perceive they learn from each other to varying degrees. However, about a quarter of them questioned felt they learnt mostly from the teacher. As there appears to be a correlation between pupils' perceived ability and how much they think they learn from others; less able pupils will perceive they do not learn from their friends (likely similar lower ability), so therefore observe that learning and information is derived from their teacher.

Most pupils think they work faster than when working alone, only a small number think they work best solo. They think they produce more ideas, work out what their results mean, discuss relevant science more and are generally more enthused by working in a group.

Perceived difficulties when working together

Generally the majority do not think they have a problem. This is exemplified by one pupil's remark when asked if she felt she should have more advice on how to work with others, she said '*no because people know how to work in groups because we've done it since nursery or reception'*. However, over half, at least sometimes have problems making the effort to discuss the tasks set and then to understand what they are meant to do. Only a third never had problems deciding whom should do what. Less than half do not have the problem that one group member wants to lead or dominate. Less than half said there was never a problem with listening to each other.

On asking about advice pupils might need to work more effectively together they realised they needed to hone their social skills. To *'appreciate or understand others' views'*, to discuss ideas or suggestions and give each member of a the group equitable opportunities for their 'say', to make decision making and other task processes more inclusive.

They also noted they needed to be kept on task more effectively, to ensure appropriate group members worked together, that the task was appropriate and that '*too large'* numbers were avoided so opportunities to participate in activities were maximised.

Some obviously relish challenge and would welcome more independent ways of working because not only did several pupils ask for more autonomy in their learning they also requested more opportunities to 'plan' and 'do'.

They also recognised it was valuable to work in different groups to '*find out how other people learn'*.

6.7 Comparing teachers' and pupils' perspectives

Comparing the teachers' and pupils' perspectives indicates juxtaposed views of the similar practices in the schools surveyed. It appears that the pupils offer more insights into working together effectively, probably because they *experience* it, as '*persons-acting'* in a setting (Lave, 1997:180), rather than a person located outside the activity. Most pupils perceive they work faster and better (produce more ideas, work out what their results mean, discuss appropriate science more) in small groups than when working alone. Their reflections on working with others appear to be have more insightful into what constitutes better learning together, than the inexperienced *persons* (Lave, ibid) or teachers. They comment on improved motivation levels when working with others, that there is mutual support available, and that through discussion they can exchange ideas and appreciate the views of others. Some pupils recognise the importance of communication, underpinning working cohesively together, not only discussing, but also listening to ideas. The opportunities to make decisions, about *how* to do things, has also been highlighted by pupils, to support better learning, which both Rogoff (1991) and Roth (1998) would indicate is essential to develop autonomous working groups. Pupils have even indicated they value working in mixed gender groups, recognising both social (working together more effectively) and cognitive benefits through sharing *what* and *how* others think. Teachers however, maintain quite a different viewpoint of group work, they appear to perceive it, primarily, as an organisational tool through which they can maximise access to limited resources. Their perspective of the educative potential of learning through interaction with peers it seems is very limited. These findings suggest they currently support pupils by monitoring progress-on-task, checking general behaviour and offering support to slower or struggling groups. They are not addressing what the pupils describe they need to support more effective working together. The pupils say they need help in appreciating and understanding each others' views. They also comment on how discussion with others renders the problems easier to solve so they are less likely to be 'stuck'. Teachers need help in understanding how they can best support and develop a classroom culture of regular, autonomous, non-threatening discussion to share and make explicit the ideas and thoughts that pupils have, that could contribute to problem solving in an investigational situation. Experience working-with-others, in a group, to become '*persons-acting*' Lave (ibid), solving a problem, would inform teachers about the learner's situation. Consideration of appropriate intervention (to ensure cognitive processing is made explicit to support reaching a decision) between teachers working-together would enable them to experience interactive learning, themselves, with others. This experiential knowledge could then inform how best they [the teachers] could more effectively support pupils working together in the classroom.

Chapter seven

7.1 Reviewing teachers' perceptions regarding peer-peer interactions

Chapter 6 indicates that teachers' perceptions about supporting peer-peer learning during experimentation are dominated by concerns about practical issues. Pragmatics of resources and sufficient space are priority. Working groups are usually self-selected by the pupils themselves, because there is a prevalent view that learning and understanding is not significantly affected by collaboration with peers. Learning is perceived by many of the science staff (and some pupils) as a much more straightforward procedural matter of the more expert teacher *transmitting* the information required. The teacher's lack of acknowledgement of interactive peer learning results in little or no consideration about how to effectively support working collaboratively. Teaching approaches do not regularly include encouraging peers to exchange and discuss each others' ideas and interpretations to clarify the task and develop shared views of their goals and aims and enter into debate about which tactics or strategies might be best and co-constructing understanding from their findings. So, in a semi-naturalistic way I decided to explore peer-peer interactions, by analysing behaviours that characteristically arise between working partners (triads), without either teacher or other pupil interference. This provided illustrations of, arguably, typical widespread 'micro' level learning interactions. As Rogoff (1990:173) identifies 'to understand the role of peer interaction in cognitive development, it is necessary to examine situations in which children are in charge of their own activities'. In the re-enactments of intra-group interactions examined here, small groups of pupils are working together, they have autonomy over the ways in which they choose to carry out the practical work.

In the interpretative paradigm, I analysed the talk and action exchanges to illuminate how, as a result of peers working together, they develop solutions (to the tasks given) and understandings (of associated scientific concepts) between each other. The initial tasks for each group were to 1. find out how the volume of air (determined by the size of gas jar) affected the burning time of a candle inside (see Figure 7. 1); 2. investigate how change in mass (weights inserted into a training shoe) affected friction (see Figure 7.2) and 3.

determine the relative density of various objects and liquids (see Figure 7.3). Each group was provided with the same equipment for each task (as detailed on the following task sheets).

Candle Race

John noticed that when Jo lit a candle in a small lantern it often flickered and went out.

When Sue lit a candle in a much larger lantern it usually burnt brighter and for much longer.

Jo said "I bet a candle with more air around it will burn better than one in a small space".

Can you design an experiment to find out if this is true.

Equipment you might use:

Figure 7.1 : The open Candles task sheet

This task was designed to provide the opportunity for the pupils to explore how length of burning time (dependant variable) is related to the amount of air (oxygen) available in the jars (independent variable). The apparatus comprised 3 different sized jars, 3 similar sized candles, a ready lit bunsen burner (yellow flame), goggles and spills. The timer was provided for them to measure exact burning times, if they wished.

SPORTING SHOES

Sam and Mary both have new training shoes of the same type and size.
They were both running, but Mary slipped.
Mary asked 'Why should I slip and not you?'
Sam replied 'Perhaps it's because I'm heavier than you.'

Can you design and carry out an investigation to see if there is any truth in Sam's suggestion?

Equipment you might use:

Figure 7.2 : The open Sporting Shoe task sheet.

This task was designed to provide the opportunity for pupils to explore the relationship between mass (independent variable) and slippiness/lack of friction (dependent variable). The groups were provided with 100 g slotted weights that could be hung on a hooked bottom mass (a little different to the illustration). They were also given a hooked forcemeter and a training shoe (with string loops at the front and back so pupils could attach the forcemeter and/or masses if they wished).

DENSITY RATINGS

A group of teenagers were discussing floating and sinking.

Sarah said "rubber will sink in water, but cork will float".

Peter said " I agree, but would it be the same in oil? or syrup?"

Sarah replied "Umm, and would other objects like a nail, paper clip, pasta, piece of candle and a grape all sink in any liquid?"

Can you design an experiment to find out which of the liquids and solids mentioned are more or less dense than each other?

Equipment you might use:

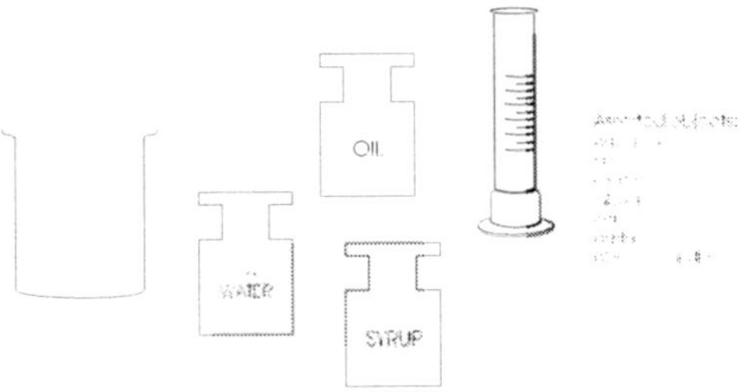

Figure 7.3 The Open Density task sheet

This task was designed to provide the opportunity for pupils to explore the behaviour of objects (and liquids), floating or not and whether they could explain what happened (why some objects sank, but others floated in different liquids). The apparatus the groups were given for this task was a jar of golden syrup, cooking oil, and coloured water, 3 measuring cylinders, 3 beakers, a spoon (for retrieving objects) paper clip, nail, grape, rubber (bung), cork (bung), piece of dried pasta, a piece of candle wax (from birthday candle) and paper towels. I intended that the pupils should consider adding the three liquids together in a beaker and then lower the objects to observe their floating and/or sinking. I deliberately provided more than one beaker to remove an obvious clue (placing all liquids and objects in one beaker).

I varied the tasks in the level of scaffolded support[19] they provided (either open ended [no scaffolding, similar to an Sc 1 investigation], semi-structured [scaffolded through questions focused on the investigational method] or highly structured [significant scaffolding with all practical steps clearly given, with a few questions provoking explanations]. The differing levels of scaffolding are exemplified here, the candles task, Figure 7.1 illustrates the open ended nature of an un-scaffolded task. The following diagram illustrates how additional questions were added to the semi-scaffolded sheet, to remind and focus the pupils attention on relevant procedural issues.

Candle Race

John noticed that when Jo lit a candle in a small lantern it often flickered and went out.

When Sue lit a candle in a much larger lantern it usually burnt brighter and for much longer.

Jo said "I bet a candle with more air around it will burn better than one in a small space".

Can you design an experiment to find out if this is true.

Equipment you might use:

Think carefully about the following before you start to carry out the experiment.

- How can you accurately measure how long the flames burn in different sized jars?
- How can you make sure that your tests are fair?
- How will you present your results?
- How many times do you need to repeat the experiment so you know your results are reliable?

Figure 7.4 Semi-structured candles task sheet

[19] Scaffolding purely related to task support through differentiated worksheets in this case. Not physical gesture, verbal prompt or dialogic discourse as Stone (1998) would describe.

The questions included in the semi-structured task (Figure 7.4) were intended to provide a support structure that engaged the pupils in careful consideration of the scientific methods they were devising. This task sheet provided a scaffold for the groups working on the problem. The following task sheet (Figure 7.5) provides all the instructions needed to carry out the task, and is therefore a highly structured support that obviates the need for pupils to discuss and design their practical approach.

Three Candle Race

John noticed that when Jo lit a candle in a small lantern it often flickered and went out.

When Sue lit a candle in a much larger lantern it usually burnt brighter and for much longer.

Jo said "I bet a candle with more air around it will burn better than one in a small space".

This is an investigation to find out if the amount of air available in the lantern affects how long it remains alight.

You will need:

3 candles of the same size
small jar
medium size jar
large jar
stopclock

bunsen burner
safety mat
goggles
spill

What to do:

1. Light the bunsen burner (remember you must have goggles on).
2. Set out each of the candles, with a jar close by, ready to light with a spill.
3. Light each candle.
4. Start the clock and at the same time place the jars over each candle as in diagram above.
5. Record how long each flame burns for, and fill in the results below.
6. After each try turn the jars upside down several times before repeating the experiment.

Time that candle burns for	Small jar	Medium jar	Large jar
1st try			
2nd try			
3rd try			
Average of all three tries			

6. Can you explain your results?

Figure 7.5 Highly structured or prescriptive candle task sheet

The differentiated task sheets for the other practical activities are illustrated in Appendix 7.

The groups were given 3 different tasks (of similar scaffolding) to complete successively. I wished to check for patterns and consistency of interactive behaviours. I analysed the interactions from an interactive cognitist perspective. Applying a social-constructivist view of the role of peer-peer interactions (Bearison 1991; Sigel and Cocking 1977) I embraced the notion of socio-cognitive conflict arising through dissonance with others, which could be resolved through pupils socially interacting to engage together in problem solving. I took the viewpoint that through engagement with others in solving a task they are able to 'decentre' and re-construct their own understanding. The comparative and evaluative consideration of each other's views would then inform the group decision-making process and extend the shared perspectives on a solution. I recorded the interactional processes engaged in to facilitate later in-depth analysis that could examine both the nature and extent of peer-peer interactions. As Durkin (1995) states, 'cognition' was perceived 'as a product of social interaction'.

7.2 Interactional-cognitist perspective

Without direct mediation from the teacher, it was only through inter-'talk' and inter-'action' that pupils could progress to complete the tasks. Thus the interpretative analysis has included the extent to which they have engaged both verbally and non-verbally in problem solving together.

The initial analyses were carried out of the same group proceeding through three successive tasks (of differing context, but similar support) and indicated that the pupils interacted in similar ways even though they were attempting contrasting tasks. As my analysis progressed the findings from the detailed scrutiny of pupils tackling the candle task provided rich indicative evidence of interactions, that appeared to be fairly consistent in nature. So, I decided, once my analytical framework was established, to compare the variance of interactions between pupils attempting differentially scaffolded candle activities.

Through applying the interactive-cognitist perspective this analysis seeks to gauge the level of verbal and non-verbal involvement, on both a cognitive and social plane that the pupils engage in to complete a task.

More recent studies (Tolmie, A. et al 2009; Kutnick et al 2005; Howe et al 2007; Galton et al 2009; Baines et al 2008; Mercer and Littleton 2008) highlight the importance of talk and language as the means by which pupils communicate and render their thinking explicit. Light et al (1999) have highlighted how having to use language to make plans explicit, to make decisions and to interpret feedback seem to facilitate problem-solving and promote understanding. In these studies talk and language are considered integral to make explicit egocentric thought. Vygotsky (1999:248) proffered that speech was 'a distinct plane of verbal thought'.

Inter-'actions' such as passing equipment, instructing how to use a timer or recording results can be seen as indicators of levels of inter 'actional' social engagement. Vygotsky (1978) says in an early essay:

> 'Children solve practical tasks with the help of their speech, as well as with their eyes and hands. This unity of perception, speech and action, which ultimately produces internalisation of the visual field, constitutes the central subject matter for any analysis of the origin of uniquely human forms of behaviour' Vygotsky (1978:26).

As Bruner (1986:72) goes on to describe:

> 'Language is (in Vygotsky's sense as in Dewey's) a way of sorting one's thoughts about things. Thought is a mode of organising perception and action'.

Discussion, deliberation and decision-making regarding the procedural methods used, and the conceptual meanings made from the practical experience and observations, (both of which will connect with prior knowledge and understanding) enable cognitive development to become more evident. I have interpreted, as Mercer (2001) would argue that, language in this way is thinking 'out loud'. Their 'talk' alongside their 'actions' can both implicitly and explicitly illuminate their cognitive processing. It is through this constant (but often jerky) seesawing of ideas, suggestions, clarifications that they dialogically expose their strategic or tactical approaches, with the implicit understandings (or not) becoming obvious through actional and linguistical manifestations. The emergence of their procedural and conceptual understandings (often inter-woven, like the DNA double helix, with two visible, inextricably-linked, threads) often occurs in staccato like reactions to each other's utterings and actions. Thus through both talk and actional interactions, the development of understanding is accrued in a spiral-like fashion, between the pupils gradually attributing and cumulating their 'public' knowledge and understanding.

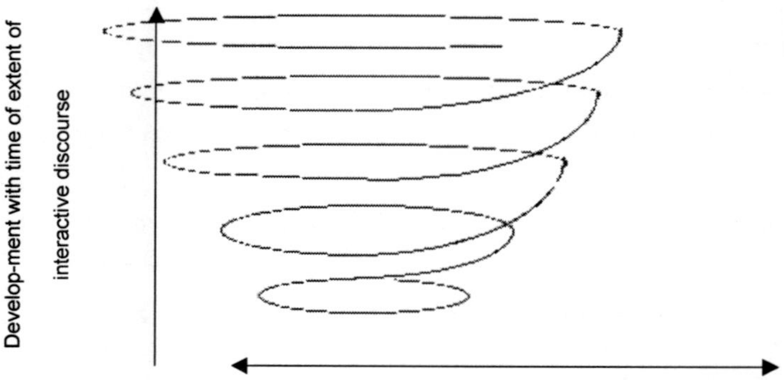

Increasingly enriched (becoming more complex) cognitive nature of the discourse

Figure 7.6 : Cognitive development depicted as a developing spiral.

The diagram above illustrates how I have perceived cognitive development as a developing spiral, resulting from seesawing inter-'actions' and inter-'talk'. The upward, broadening nature of the spiral is indicative of the developing, subsequent enrichment of the talking and thinking that develops as a result of the social interactions over time.

Cognition is perceived here as arising not only through talk, but also through 'mindful' actions. Bredo (1999:36) describes the role of mind in relation to the body; in his chapter on reconstructing educational psychology; as

> 'a property of the interaction between individual and environment rather than as something inside the individual or tucked away in the cranium'.

Clancey (1992:7) supports this stating that

> 'perception and action arise together, dialectically forming each other'.

My study encompasses analysis of both action and thought, as forms of communication which are complementary dimensions of active participation in social interactions; i.e.: through active contributions of either a verbal and/or non-verbal nature the individuals are participating in a social way with each other to solve a given task. Verbal exchanges between peers can be both social and cognitive. As the theoretical perspective applied here is that of interactive cognitist, both elements of social and cognitive exchange and development are analysed.

Mercer (2000) describes particular kinds of talk as 'explicit inter-thinking'. Applicable to the study here are three types of social talk he identifies, as disputational, cumulative and exploratory.

7.2.i Analysing the social nature of talk

The three distinctive social modes of thinking through talking identified by Mercer (1995:104) are elaborated upon below:

Disputational talk

Mercer characterises this by disagreement and individualised decision-making. He goes on to say that this is often when one pupil gives an instruction to others, which is undisputed, and is therefore 'potentially' disputational talk. Within this type of talk, he clarifies; there are few attempts to pool resources, or to offer constructive criticism of another's suggestions. Characteristically these are often short exchanges consisting of assertions and challenges or counter-assertions. Within this there is likely to be, as Light et al (1994) have identified, focussed talk on practical procedures, verbal explicit planning; suggestions about how procedures should be carried out, and stating what something means in an individual's view. Within the context of the study here, it appears, from my observations, that action can become disputational too, ie: a decisive individual pushing apparatus towards another is indicative that that person should use (and even carry out a particular task associated with) that equipment, eg:passing a pencil, task sheet or spill toward another without debate or discussion can still be widely interpreted as potentially disputational talk.

Cumulative talk.

Mercer (ibid) describes cumulative talk as that where speakers build positively but uncritically on what another has said. Partners use talk to construct a 'common knowledge' by accumulation. He argues that cumulative discourse is characterised by repetitions, confirmations and elaborations.

Exploratory talk.

Mercer (ibid) describes exploratory talk as that where partners engage critically but constructively with each other's ideas. Statements and suggestions are offered for joint consideration. These may be challenged and counter-challenged, but challenges are justified and alternative hypotheses are offered. In his discussions, when compared with the other two types, in exploratory talk, knowledge, he strongly argues is made more 'publicly accountable' and reasoning is more 'visible' in the talk.

7.2.ii Analysing the scientific content of talk

To assess the 'quality' of scientific discussion, evidence of procedural understanding through discussion and consideration of tactics and strategies were noted. In the Candle task, for example, recognising the relationship between the independent and dependent variables is essential. Recognising that the amount of air (independent variable), determined by the size of jar, affects the burning time (dependent variable). Which strategies or methods they use to investigate the relationship is important, they may lower the three jars over three candles simultaneously or utilise just one candle three times or they might use each of the three candles in succession; making judgements about methods which are fair (e.g.: same flame size at start, ascertaining beginning and ending of burning (standardised start and end point); measuring and collecting data in appropriate ways (Assessing the relative [first or last] or absolute [tenth of second, second, minute] time the candle burns; deciding how much data is needed (only one or several results for each jar size); recognising data trends and developing appropriate explanations given the nature of the data collected and their prior knowledge (which factors can affect combustion of a candle? Oxygen, carbon dioxide, size of jars, candle flame? flushing of jars). Recognition of validity (how many times before can say with confidence, does the method chosen give evidence for conclusions) and reliability (how representative or dependable are these results?) in their data collection and linking this to verifiable (are the assertions made supportable from the evidence collected?) solution outcomes and endpoints were also noted.

7.3 Scaffolding and the tasks

Daniels (1998:5) defines Vygotsky's notion of scaffolding where a distinction is made between support for the initial performance of tasks and subsequent performance without assistance, "the distance between problem-solving abilities exhibited by a learner working alone and that learner's problem solving abilities when assisted by or collaborating with more experienced people". Wood (1998) links Vygotsky's notion of ZPD[20] and scaffolding. He describes scaffolding as varying levels of control, ranging from minimal where a learner might be asked a very general question, such as 'what might be done here?' to a highly controlled situation where the tutor actually demonstrates the steps needed. The interactional processes that result from highly scaffolded tasks to low or virtually no scaffolding are investigated in this study.

The task sheets (Figure 7.1 etc and Appendix 7) provided differentiated support, at three levels, for different groups of pupils. At the highest level of support or control (as Wood describes it) pupils were offered an observation and challenged to explain it, but they were guided in a prescriptive way through the practical work step by step (like following a recipe). This method is frequently used by teachers to illustrate concepts; i.e.: there is little scope for developing an original method because the purpose of the practical is to clearly *illustrate* a scientific concept or *verify* a principle. In the candle task, the relationship between the amount of air (and thus oxygen) and the length of time a candle burns, i.e.: the more air (oxygen) there is the longer the candle burns. With this task the questions asked were designed to encourage the pupils to come up with a description of the data pattern and offer a scientific explanation for the observations. These were highly structured (or highly controlled as Wood (ibid) would describe) tasks.

At the second level the same observations and challenge were given as with the highly structured tasks, but a few prompting questions were asked to deliberately guide the pupils to consider important aspects of the practical

[20] ZPD - Zone of Proximal Development, where both the actual developmental level and the potential development level are considered to ensure the distance between the two is not too great that the problem is unsolvable. Vygotsky (1978:86)

work, and then reflect on the meaning of their observations. This was much less structured than the first types of task. These were semi-structured.

At the third level, the same observation and challenge to explain was given as with the first two types of task, but there was no suggestion at all about how to carry out the practical work (so control or scaffolding was minimised), although diagrams of useful apparatus were provided and actual equipment given. It was a completely open-ended task, which emulated a typical investigational approach regularly used by teachers to assess Sc 1 skills (referred to as scientific enquiry in the Science National Curriculum). As Watson (1997) identifies, investigations (like this) offer a learning situation where pupils have to make their own decisions either individually or in groups because they are given some autonomy in how the investigation is carried out. Roth (1995) also considers 'investigational' approaches and recognises, there is the opportunity to identify problems and solutions, design procedures, analyse data, review and evaluate method and results, resulting in formulating new questions. These types of 'open-enquiries' , typified by an Sc1 investigational approach are therefore more likely to provide opportunities for sharing a wider range of ideas than tasks of a highly structured or prescriptive nature. Watson and Wood-Robinson (1998:90) go on to highlight the idea that:

> 'Investigations involving practical work are essentially thinking activities'.

Quite justifiably then, in posing open-ended investigational work to children, we are triggering them to think, and in analysing how they perform in the tasks we can make assumptions about their cognitive ability. Using this technique the tasks have been scaffolded to re-enact strategies that teachers typically use in practical secondary science work (when aiming to illustrate scientific concepts, to highlight procedural points and to develop scientific skills respectively) to explore the impact on the character, content and magnitude of learning interactions.

Anticipated impact of the scaffolded tasks

The diagram below (Figure 7.8) illustrates how I perceived scaffolding affected the development of discussion and the resultant cognitive engagement with the scientific tasks presented to the pupils.

Model A The effect of no scaffolding	Model B The effect of some scaffolding	Model C The effect of significant scaffolding in task
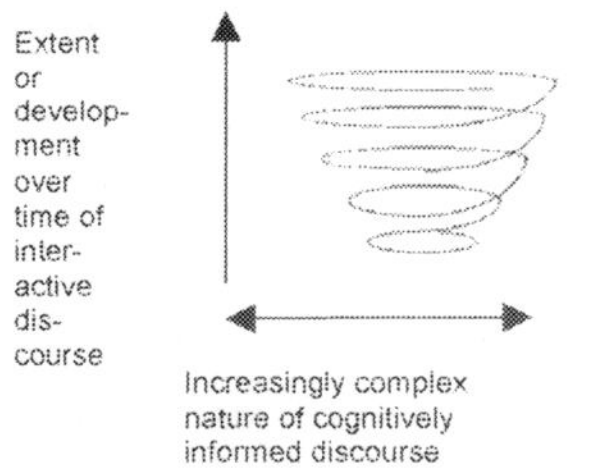		
High quality talk focussed on both procedures and concepts reflecting high level thinking demanded through the open nature of the task and the inherent decision-making needed.	More cognitive engagement with both methodology and scientific explanations than model C. Less cognitively developmental than A	Fewer cognitive developmental steps likely because the need for decision-making is reduced, thus the subsequent level of interaction is diminished.

Figure 7.8 : My cognitive-interactionist prediction of the influence of scaffolding on cognitive development.

The highly structured tasks (Figure 7.5; Appendix 7.2, 7.4)

I anticipated that this level of support was not likely to promote extensive discussion on procedure, but more likely to uphold the collection of quality data, which would provide high quality evidence for pupils to enter into discussion about what the data means. This was developed to provide the opportunity to engage in quality dialogue regarding conceptual understanding, applied to explain the evidence.

The semi-structured tasks (Figure 7.4; Appendix 7.1, 7.3)

I intended to guide the pupils to consider the most prominent procedural issues in these tasks. Through this measured and controlled level of scaffolding I predicted that the resultant discussionary debate should be more concerned with the nature of their observations and being able to explain them and subsequently consider how the data was derived and thus support the pupils becoming more conceptually and procedurally aware.

The open tasks (Figure 7.1; Appendix 7.2; 7.3)

I provided these to assess how pupils interact when undertaking an investigation. Viewed through a cognitive interactionist lens this should support high quality interactions that embrace both procedural and conceptual matters. As Armitia (1993) would identify, and I predicted, without scaffolding, an investigation is a demanding task, but it should provide potential opportunities for higher-level transactive exchange required to resolve dissonance, explicitly rationalise proposals and opinions to solve the task.

7.4 Some general findings from the interactive-cognitive analysis

I carried out the micro-analysis of interactions on 24 different groups from 4 schools. The detailed analysis is too extensive to present in the appendices, so exemplars have been provided. An example of an interactive-cognitive analysis of pupils' responses is presented in Appendix 4 which provides an illustration of an initial exploration (including transcript of actions and discussion and subsequent scrutiny of the interactions between a triad of girls (group 1A) from School A. This illustration is intended to provide the reader with insight into the depth and detail of analysis applied to various (transcripts of) groups' learning activities in this study.

Generally the pupils, although working in close proximity to each other, and used to working in this way, did not exhibit all the anticipated cognitive developments through social interactions. There was much co-operative work (little or virtually no discord) and practically all the pupils were, for most of the time, actively engaged on task, but there did not appear to be many interactions that significantly affected the quality of cognitive development and resultant learning.

Azmitia et al (1993) found that when friends worked together on scientific tasks they were more likely (than acquaintances) to evaluate their solutions, spontaneously justify their proposals, elaborate and critique each other's reasoning and engage in transactive[21] discussions. In my study, with no teacher intervention, there was no obvious culture, amongst the pupils from four schools, of spontaneous dialogue centred on consideration of advantages and constraints of differing practical procedures, the meaning and explanations for data patterns or trends. Justifications and explicit reasoning was not offered by all participants readily. Plausible proposals or suggestions from a member of the group tended to be either unquestionably accepted (through silent acquiescence or an 'actional'[22] response) or quietly ignored. There was relatively little responsive 'debate' or overt reasoned argument or agreement. There were many obvious missed opportunities for explicitly describing and clarifying data patterns or trends and attempting to explain the phenomena observed. Spontaneous pooling of ideas in the sense that Mercer describes 'exploratory' talk offering ideas for critique or 'public' scrutiny was rare. There were infrequent disagreements or questioning of each other's propositions and contradiction of anothers' ideas was not at all common.

More detailed and specific findings

I am going to consider firstly the nature of the talk entered into at different stages in the pupils' practical procedures and consider the relative extent and frequency of these different types of talk. I will then relate the nature and extent of discourse to the scaffolded or 'controlled' support level of the tasks. The quality of science outcomes (in terms of practical tactics adopted and application of conceptual understandings to explain observations) are finally considered in the instances of the differentially structured tasks.

Ways of talking

7.4.1 Disputational talk

This often occurred at the onset of a task. When deciding what to do, an individual often made an initial suggestion, as illustrated here :

[21] Transactive dialogue defined as discussion in which an individual's reasoning operates upon another's, resultantly developing awareness of contradictions between the two participants logic, Azmitia etc al (1993: 206)

[22] 'Actional' in this sense meaning a non-verbal, but physical active response; e.g.: A suggests lets light all candles, B proceeds to light the candles but does not say anything.

A to B "You work the timer"
A "Let's do the smallest tube, then the middle then the biggest"

After they each jot down some thoughts, A then continues directing...

A "Let's do this one first" Reaches for smallest jar and spill
C "I'll light one of the candles"
B to A referring to timer. "How do I start this?"
A to B "Just press start then I'll tell you to go"
A lights first candle with spill
B to A "Tell me when go"
A "Not yet"

A decides what they should do. The other two do not question her directives. Although Mercer (1995) identifies disputational talk as that which is characterised by decision making, often in the groups studied here, there was very little 'decision making', experimental design was usually directed by a confident or capable individual who was not questioned by his/her peers. The dominance of an individual appears to prevent discussion, and clarity in decision making and planning before they begin to manipulate the apparatus and launch into 'doing'.

Other typical examples that illustrate maybe some pupils have very scanty ideas, but they still do not consider them carefully to any significant extent before launching into practical work, include another group of three boys who read the task sheet quietly, then B mutters for a few seconds,

A demonstrates lowering jar over candle.
B says 'light the candle'
A lights the spill
B directs smallest jar first
C lowers small jar over candle
C tries to time how long the candle burns

With no careful planning they launch into lowering the jar over the candle so quickly that C hasn't got the timer organised and subsequently B estimates how long before the flame extinguishes.

Another group 3A, doing the sporting shoe activity, do not clarify what they are going to do before they do it:

ABC all reading from the instruction sheet
A 'No I haven't done this one before'
C 'I have, I know what you have to do because...'
A 'I don't'
C 'you could,...emm..put the weights on because....'
A 'put a weight on like this...'

A	*grabs the shoe and then puts it down.*
C	'because it might because... heavier ....emm'
A	'put different amounts of weights on'
C	'cos if you're pressing down on it more then like you haven't got much chance of falling over'
A	*smiles as C's pen rolls off table* 'like your pen'
A	*picks up force meter and fiddles*

Neither do 7D, another group of three girls:

A + B + C read task sheet	
C	"... gram mass in the shoe...to..."
B	Leans over , picks up the weights, takes one and puts the rest back
B	"This looks good"
C	"Yes"
B	"100 grams" Stands up and puts the weight in the shoe
A	Leans over, picks up the force metre and attaches it to the strings on the shoe.

They clearly do not share with each other and make explicit their intent (although they pick up and move equipment). They do not enter into any kind of planning or explicit decision making based on discussion of potential or possible procedures.

Another group, 1C, (the most collaborative of the sample) enter into some discussion, but they still do not debate and clearly articulate and agree what it is they are going to do **before** they do it.

A	indicates the jars will be needed
C	indicates the candle is needed
A	suggests there will be 'less oxygen in each of them' (the jars)
A	suggests B goes first
	They discuss lighting the candle
B	suggests they have a different sized jar each (to lower over candles)
A	asks whether they will do it simultaneously
	They count 1,2,3 each lowers a jar over the candle nearest them
	Candle in larger jar extinguishes last
B	says 'not a lot of air.....so it will go out' meaning smallest jar
A	then notices timer and asks should we time them? She indicates she thinks they are 'stupid' not to have realised.

There is postulation from A that the amount of oxygen differs in the jars, but what effect that may have is not predicted clearly beforehand. It appears that the equipment acts as a series of visual clues to inform how they should carry out the practical, the girls implicitly assume each piece of apparatus should be used in some way, but again do not explicitly clarify how. As there are three jars, they take one each, they do not consider any strategy other than lowering the jars simultaneously. In fact only after the experience of doing it in an exploratory, qualitative way does A notice the timer and realise they could measure how long the candles burn.

Another example of a lack of planning, influenced strongly by directives from a dominant pupil, early in a practical activity (group 2F; before 1 minute has elapsed):

A	Picking up small gas jar "..put them over that" lowers jar over candle.
B	"Light the candle"
	All three put on safety goggles.
A	Picks up spill and lights it, then lights candle with spill
B	"small…first"

And later when the candles are lit, A is still directing whom should do what when…:

A	"Ready" (Lights candle)
B	"Yeah"
A	"Put it on…"
B	"Yeah…"
B	lowers gas jar on candle, C starts and stops watch quickly

When they are ready to start the next trial pupil A again takes a lead:

A	"Yeah that's right, that one is, it's this one and then that one " Picking up medium gas jar and candle, meaning the large jar later
C	Records results
A	"B it's this one and …."
A	"….that one now"
B	"Eh?"
A	"This one and that one" Pointing to jar and candle "I'll light this one now" Lights spill.

In another group, each individual tells the others what they will do (group 2D; after 30 seconds, but before 1 minute elapsed) as well as directing others:

B	"OK, I'll light this one". Indicating candle in front of her.
C	"I'll light this one", then to A "You do this one". Indicating candle closest to A.
B & C	pick up a spill.
A	picks up the candle and puts it down and gets a spill.

The level of planning is often compromised through this kind of talk because there is an absence of explicit reasoning, that others should feel comfortable considering and debating (group 4D; within the first thirty seconds):

A	"Do the small jar first" Picks up and sets the stop clock.
B	"umm.."
C	lights first candle

A in this extract is 'directing' which order the jars should be investigated in. Neither B nor C dispute this, however, C 'decides' he will light the candles. He doesn't verbalise this, he 'actions' his decision. This is also typical of many groups, without any verbal discourse at all, they 'do' something, this could be viewed as 'disputational action'. Another example of this is seen here (3D: after 10 minutes):

C "A…going to do this one?" Pointing to candle they have just used
A "It doesn't matter……. no." Writes.
C Lights the candle with the spill
B Places the small jar over the lit candle
C Starts timer
The three girls observe the lit candle which is inside small jar
Candle goes out
C Stops timer "Twelve." Resets timer.
A writes
C places timer near to **A** and **B**

There are lots of incidences with this group of 'disputational action' regarding roles. With virtually no discussion they 'fall' into particular kinds of roles (candle lighter; timer and recorder; jar operator).

Other examples of disputational talk regarding pupil proposals are not often disagreed with by others. In fact it is unusual for the peers to challenge or counter another's 'plausible' suggestion; in fact more typical of the groups studied here are 'declarations' regarding individual roles and responsibilities. This is a group about to run their trials a second time:

B	removes gas jars from candles
C	"Right do it again"
A	"Yeah I'll light them" Gets up to light the spill.
C	picks up timer "I'll do this this time"
B	"You record them"
C	"Yeah I'll record". Sits down next to B (in A's place)
B	"Do you want me to write?"
C	"No I'll write". Picks up pen. "There you go"
A	lights first candle
B	picks up smallest gas jar
A	lights other two candles

A has previously operated the jars; with no negotiation he 'declares' he will 'light' the candles. C has previously lit the candles, again with no verbalisation he claims the timer, and 'declares' he will time 'this time'. B operated the jars last time, by default he is carrying out the same role again. Disputational talk, it seems here, develops into disputational action and declarative action or talk. This group 9D, 3 girls, carrying out the shoe activity, demonstrate the frequent lack of debate regarding proposals from peers:

All three read the task sheet

C	"Now pull gently on the..."
B	"Put your findings in the following table"
A	"Pull gently on the force metre until the.."
B	"Shoe"
A	"Do you want to make a little line, see whether it moves, see whether it moves?"
C	"Yeah"
B	"On the table!"
A	"Yeah, we can wipe it off after"
C	"Yeah"
A	makes a mark on the table at the front of the shoe

Throughout various groups' activities dominant pupils sometimes declare what they are doing, or intend to do with virtually no disputes, dissention or even comment from other group members.

It appears then, that disputational communication (talk or 'directive' or 'declarational' or even 'actional' sub-categories of this) can focus on the scientific methods to be used, and the roles each pupil might take. As Vygotsky says the cognitive functions occur first on the social plane, and in many cases here cognitive understanding of procedure is initiated through social interaction.

Mercer claims that 'disputational' talk is a significant aspect of learners learning together, however, in this study there does not appear to be too much 'dispute' amongst co-learning friends. Of all the clips studied the following is probably the most 'disputative' incident. The three boys here have some anomalous results (in the three trials so far, the medium jar candle has burned for longer than the large jar candle twice), B suggests they should do a fourth trial, and initially suggests each of the three jars on each of the three candles in turn (2C: nearly eighteen minutes into the task), which C reminds him he proposed much earlier in the task:

B	"three of each on each one"
C	"yea, that's what I said"
A	"but you've gotta be sure haven't you?........another six.." indicates each jar in turn over the each candle "three of them on that one...three of them on that one....three of them on that one..."
B	mutters "three on each...that's another nine!" whilst tossing a pencil.

A "‥ don't be spiteful"
All three boys writing again drawing out results tables
A mutters

A responds to the dispute by saying 'don't be spiteful' indicating, perhaps why 'friends' working together rarely disagree, as the individual who is criticised will feel it is a personal indictment, and peers do not wish to compromise their social relationships. This may suggest why there is much 'conformity'[23] in the dialogues studied here.

7.4.2 Cumulative talk

Mercer (1995) has identified this as uncritical, but positive talk. This is the most common type of social dialogue identified in this study.

It is prevalent amongst all groups. It is significant in single sex girl groups, when developing their plan and procedures (and when attempting to describe what is happening, re: data collection and then explain why their results are as they are) for the practical investigation, typical verbal discourse is a little like this (1F: before 1 minute has passed):

B "If you light a candle under each of them, right, in order of size, erm, find out which one goes out quicker"
A "Yeah, see how much air in it"
C "turn that upside down" (pointing to largest gas jar)
A "Yeah" (picks up jar)
B "So what you do is light a candle and then you put it on like that" (indicating by moving arm over candle)
A (picks up gas jar and moves it over candle)
C "Yeah, so shall we light the candles with the splint" (reaches for splint, A picks up another gas jar, B fiddling with gas jar)

Each girl builds positively on the previous utterances, notice they also 'action' preparatory operations without overtly telling the others what they will do. In this next episode of talk, there appears to be a quick 'switch' to disputational talk, which is followed by 'actions' triggered by B being decisive about what to do with the candles. Again notice no verbalised commentary on the actions they carry out, or intent to undertake. Cumulative type talk is entered into again when A checks with B about where to place the jars.

B Reaches for watch glass. "Put that on the bottom …..stick your candles on there"
C "OK" Puts candle on watch glass.
A Puts candles on other watch glasses.

---

[23] Pupils 'conforming' or agreeing with each other's ideas, rather than entering into discord with them.

B	Puts on safety goggles.
C	Lights candles.
B	Picks up gas jar.
A	Holding gas jar. "Do you want that putting on the top of it"
B	"You can go in order of size can't you, bigger..." Pointing from left to right at candles.
A + B	put gas jars on two of the candles, C reaches across and puts the medium jar on the middle candle.

In this instance 'action' carried out by each pupil is complementary to each other, so the essential preparations that are required to undertake the practical are completed without verbalisation, this could be identified as cumulative 'action'.

In discussing the data collated there tends to be support for each others' notions, in cumulative talk, especially if there is no controversial idea presented by any pupil, e.g.: (1F: two and a half minutes into the task):

B	"We can say there's...the bigger one goes out first"
A	"Yeah but...the first time we did it that one went out first, didn't it" *(Pointing to smallest gas jar)*
B	"Yeah"
A	"And then that one" *(Pointing to biggest)* "then that one" *(Pointing to middle)*
B	"It's something to do with carbon dioxide and oxygen"
C	"Yeah inside the, inside the, inside the"
A	"..jar.."
B	"Yeah, ...is that..." *(Pointing to smallest)* "Because it's got less oxygen"
A	*(picks up smallest jar to examine...she turns it around to examine from different angles)*
C	"They are all the same candles aren't they? So"
A	"...umm..."
B	"That's got less oxygen" *(Pointing to smallest)* "So that means the candles going to burn more carbon dioxide....or something"
A	*(puts smallest jar down and picks up medium jar)*
C	"Yes" *(Picking up smallest gas jar)* "It's all steamed up inside hasn't it"
B	"Yeah"
A & B	*(pick up large jar together & examine)*
A	"Yeah, that one in the middle hasn't got much on it" *(Puts down the large jar, picks up medium jar to examine)*
B	"No"
A	"That ones got loads" (Pointing to large) "That ones quite...hasn't it"
C	(Puts down small jar) "Do you want to try one more time then"
B	"Yeah if you like"
A	"Yeah...(???)"

They begin by affirming what the results were (small jar candle extinguished first, then large jar, finally medium jar), and they then enter into cumulative dialogue focused on what is inside the jars that may help explain what has happened. B makes most of the suggestions, C adds to some of the proposals, accumulating 'common knowledge' as Mercer, 1995 would describe it. B initially proposes that the carbon dioxide and oxygen may be important; C refines this to add 'inside', indicating that 'something' is happening, A latches onto this and adds 'jar' clarifying where 'inside' is. B affirms and extends this knowledge further to quantify that the amount of oxygen is linked to the size of jar, she focuses on the small one first saying 'it's got less oxygen'. A picks up the jar and inspects but does not add to the accumulation of shared understanding. C is considering that the candles may have some influence and checks that the others think they are the same and thus can not affect the outcome. B is attempting to clarify how the other gas she previously mentioned (carbon dioxide) might be connected with less oxygen in the smaller jar. She suggests the candle 'burns more carbon dioxide or ...something', her hesitancy suggests she is not sure. C now inspects the jars further and adds 'its all steamed up' A builds on this idea and compares the middle jar, saying it doesn't have much on it. A links the significant condensation in the large jar. C thinks they ought to try it again.

The constraint of the conversation, entered into by A and C only 'describing' what they can see rather than attempting to 'explain' it, or at least hypothesize, like B, limits the cognitive value of their dialogue.

This is another episode where the pupils are finishing their task, they are attempting to describe the data pattern derived but can't 'see' the general pattern (as mass increased force required to just 'move' the shoe increases). They are looking for a much clearer directly proportional pattern:

A	"If you times that by 2 you get that, well say it was 15 instead of 1.5, if it's 15 times by 2 that'll be 30, if you times that by 2 it'd be 48, well that's close to that, it's close to 50 isn't it"
C	"Mmm"
B	"So this ones" Pointing to results table
A	"See erm"
C	"That'd be 18 there"
A	"60, 74"
B	"Yeah?" Pointing to results table
A	"Yeah but that's....."
C	"I think we've gone wrong"
C	"Don't know"
A	"There is no proper pattern in there is there"
B	"No"
A	"5,6,7,8,9, then 1"

They supportively add to each others' justify their expectations.

Other episodes, although with a more expert peer might support their cognitive development further into the zpd, do illuminate how cumulative talk can support construction of 'common knowledge' (1C: after 4 minutes):

A	"Yes, it's because that's got less space"
C	"Yes, so we can write that down couldn't we? So just put like..."
B	"The smaller the..." Writing.
A	"With less oxygen"
B	"Jar didn't have lot of..."
A	"Air, space"
B	"Didn't have a lot of space in it did it, oxygen, is that how you spell it?"
A	"No, it's got a 'y' before the 'g', oxy, like the spot thing"
A & B	*..giggle..*
C	Fiddles with timer.

Through their dialogue they have accumulated the concept of the size of the jar constraining how much air and space (and thus oxygen) is in it.

Later this group extend and enhance their understandings when discussing their conclusion through this type of talk (1C: after 6 minutes):

B	"It took longer to go out, yes?"
A	"Yes, so the..."
A	"....so put, the conclusion is, our conclusion is it, Joe was right"
B	"Conclusion is..."
A	"Or was it that John, yes, Joe was right"
C	"So just put our conclusion is..."
A	"You just need..."
C	"Our conclusion is that the one, more space, I mean air..."
A	"Yes"
B to A	"It depends on the space of, the light is..."
A	"If it's got more oxygen it goes out....."
A	" ..... it takes a longer time, it burns for longer, that's it"
B	"Yes, so our conclusion is that if the lantern has more room"
A	"More oxygen..."
C	"No, our conclusion is that the.."
A	"The candle will stay alight...."
C	"The jar with the more oxygen would make the candle, the candle, the jar..."
B	"With the less oxygen"
C	"Will make the candle blow out first, this is because it hasn't got enough oxygen in it...."

Other groups, however, do not accumulate observations and ideas in the same way. Observations are not frequently described, they are rarely discussed and debated, and conclusions are not regularly rationalised and clarified.

A typical response to collecting data is just to record or note it. There is no spontaneous effort to clarify for each what they have seen, and then share their ideas on what they think has happened, accompanied by an explanation. The response of group 1A, is that once the pupil operating the stopclock announces how long the candle has burnt for, each child jotted down the result. There was no discourse considering what this meant or projection forward to consider what might happen to the next candle in the next jar. One pupil in group 1F predicts what might happen once she has seen clearly from the first experimental run that the candle in the smallest jar will extinguish first and the largest jar last. Prediction is not common, but appears more prevalent amongst the groups carrying out the semi-scaffolded tasks.

7.4.3 Exploratory talk

It was anticipated that much 'exploratory' talk would materialise through pupils working on open tasks, where many (Watson et al 1998; Roth 1993) have recognised is the potential opportunity for decision making and the preludes of consideration of alternative ideas, consideration of appropriate and inappropriate proposals, prioritising what is most relevant (all requiring high level cognitive capabilities). Evidence of exploratory talk was rare, generally, in engagement on any of the tasks. There was no obvious substantiation of more exploratory exchanges on the open tasks compared with the scaffolded tasks.

In one group (1F: after four and a half minutes) they were on the verge of extending their talk into 'exploratory', on several occasions, in this first example, they have watched the three candles burning in the three jars, three times, and they are contemplating why the small jar candle didn't consistently extinguish first and the large jar candle burn consistently longer:

All contemplating the results.

C "I think it's with less air"
A "Yeah, I do, I reckon that one should go out first" *(Pointing to smallest jar)* "it's smaller isn't it"
B "Yeah, that one goes out first, then that, then that" *(Pointing from largest to smallest)*
A "There's more air trapped in that isn't there" *(Pointing to largest gas jar)*
C "Yeah"
B "Yeah so it's going to take longer"
C "Yeah there's more air in there"

B "Mind you'd think the more air the longer it would take to burn out wouldn't you" Pointing to large jar
A "Mmm"
B "Cos it's got to burn all the air in there, all that oxygen"
B "Confusing"
A *lifts small jar off candle.*
B *lifts medium jar off candle*
C *lifts large jar off candle*

In their method they do not check the initial candle flames are consistent before they lower the jars, they do not lower the jars with similar force (in the second trial B and C lower the jars very quickly creating a draught which blows the candles out almost immediately), they don't consider 'flushing' the jars (they are placed open end down on the bench trapping most of the gaseous products until the next trial). They certainly do not consider 'timing' the length of burning to 'average' the results and explore if overall the large jar candle burns the longest.

On another occasion, this same group were still considering their anomalous results, and are about to try a fourth time (1F:after six minutes):

B "Hang on"
All pick up gas jars: A smallest, B medium, C largest
C "That ones got a bigger flame"
A "That ones got a small one, that ones got a bigger one"
B "That's because of the amount of wick"
A "..don't we...."
B "It's the amount of wick that's on it though isn't it"
C "Lets swap them around and see if it makes any difference" (*Offering gas jar to others*)
A "Why didn't we light them at the same time, all one stump each, then you light them at the same time, cos by the time you light that one, that ones burning out"
B "Yeah I see what you mean now"

They do not question each other's ideas; they readily accept any 'plausible' proposals from their peers and 'go with' them through either actional or verbal acquiescence. B thought earlier it was just the synchronicity of lowering the jars; A has now focused on the 'flame' of the candles. A suggests a method of each lighting simultaneously, but none of the girls propose further that they could utilise the same candle repeatedly to create a 'fair test'.

Another group (1C:after five and a half minutes) in their concluding discussion again engage in 'cumulative' talk that becomes 'exploratory' when C disagrees with B about the amount of oxygen in the medium jar, and A connects oxygen with volume in the jar:

B Is speaking aloud as he is writing. ".... went out in 7 seconds. Large jar"
C "Went out in 11 seconds, because it didn't have this, well it did but..."
A "Well that one had....". Points to large jar.
B "The large jar had a lot of...". Still writing.
C "No, here you put exactly the same" Correcting B's writing.
B "Yes, because..."
A "It didn't have a lot of oxygen, so the medium jar burned a bit more"
B "Didn't have a lot of oxygen"
A "It didn't have a lot, it just had a bit more"
C "Yes"
B "Look the medium jar also didn't have a lot of oxygen, so that went out in 7 seconds"
C "Yes, it had a bit more than, you know, you need to put that, it had more though, because if you didn't then that's just going to, we need it to compare it"

Through C disagreeing with B's writing they clarify the relative amounts of oxygen each jar holds (in their view) and how it affects the burning time of the candles. Discussion before and after this difference of opinion is typical of the usual 'cumulative' dialogue, where peers confirm and support each others views, but rarely *question*, and in so doing add little to the depth and breadth of cognitive processing. The absence of exploratory talk results in little development of groups' ideas that could extend to open up the scientific reasoning behind their thinking.

Open tasks

Although Azmitia et al (1993) has indicated, and I predicted, that open tasks would support the most cognitively productive interactions, it appeared that this potential was not realised. Dialogue was often 'cumulative'. For example, 3 girls (1F: half a minute into the problem) at the beginning of an open task:

B "If you light a candle under each of them, right, in order of size, erm, find out which one goes out quicker"
A "Yeah, see how much air in it"
C " turn that upside down" (pointing to largest gas jar)
A "Yeah" (picks up jar)
B "So what you do is light a candle and then you put it on like that" (indicating by moving hand and arm over candle)
A (picks up gas jar and moves it over candle)
C "Yeah, so shall we light the candles with the splint?"
C reaches for splint, A picks up another gas jar, B fiddling with gas jar.

The girls do not extend the conversation to verbalise exactly what they mean. B has suggested that the candles should be lit, under the gas jars. She says do in order of size, and find out which goes out quickest. B has outlined roughly what they should do, A augments her ideas, and tries to link B's statement to the task, by saying 'see how much air in it', C is confirming a practical point that they will need to turn the jars over from their current position. B is reiterating again that the candle needs lighting first, and then the jar should be lowered over the candle. A demonstrates. C agrees and asks a rhetorical question about using the spills to light the candles. No-one replies, but they all respond by 'doing' something.

In this episode it appears that not only can speech be 'cumulative', each girl adding to what the others have said, but that 'action' can also 'add' to the dialogue. Through this un-confrontational talk, the girls are less likely, it seems to be 'sparked' or stimulated into considering carefully step by step what they should do; as a result they are not co-ordinated when they lower the jars over the candles.

Their mode of cumulative talk is not only commonplace at the onset of the practical, but also when the task is in progress.

The three girls above are watching the candles burn in the three gas jars:

B	(Points to large gas jar) "That's gone out...but we lit that...that went out quicker than that" (Pointing to the two jars)
C	"And the middle went out last"
B	"But that wasn't a fair test because we didn't put them on all together did we"
A	"No"
B	"So we can't call it a fair test"
	(A + B lift off gas jars)
C	"So shall we do it again" (Reaching for splint)
B	"Yeah"
C	"Just to make sure"

B suggests that the test hasn't been fair because the jars were not lowered together. They do not explicitly share that this may explain why the medium sized jar still supports a burning candle longer than the larger jar, and they do not each enter into discussion about what they did that wasn't 'fair' and how they should ensure it is 'fair' next time. Typical of these working friendship groups, when a plausible reason is provided by one of the group, it is apparently accepted by the others without question. In open tasks, it seems, that the frequent episodes of cumulative talk that fall 'flat' or peter out and do not develop into more cognitively challenging discourse, without more expert intervention to stimulate ideas or provoke further deliberations.

7.5 Type of task, interactions and quality of science outcomes

The quality of science outcomes developed as a result of social interactions were explored in each task situation (and are summarised below in table 7.1). The pupils generally took the longest to complete the semi-structured tasks and the highly structured tasks were finished much more quickly. Open tasks were generally completed somewhere between the two (not quickly, but not as extensively as semi-structured tasks).

Is there recognition of relevant independent and dependant variables? Are appropriate variables recognised? Size of jar/amount of air/volume of oxygen? Length of burning time?
What methods are used? How are burning times compared? Are the candles and jars used sequentially, randomly or simultaneously?
Are the appropriate influential variables controlled or considered? E.g.: size of candle, position of candles, which candles, standardised initial flames; replenishing of air in jars; speed of lowering; end point of burning? Is there understanding of fair testing?
What data is collected? The nature of data collected. Is it qualitative or quantitative data? Is the data valid, reliable, and accurate? Is anomalous data recognised and considered?
How is the data collated? Is it written? Recorded as generated? Into pre-structured table? Randomly jotted somewhere?
Is the data pattern described? Is the relationship between air space and burning time recognised? Are the links between longevity of combustion, decreasing amount of oxygen, increasing amount of carbon dioxide, size of flame, brightness of flame considered?
Is the data pattern explained? Has the relationship between independent and dependent variable been explained clearly, accurately, scientifically?
Has the solution to the problem been clarified? Is it appropriate, reliable and valid? Is it based on good/some/no scientific evidence? Is the scientific explanation that relates to the problem clear and accurate?

Table 7.1 Criteria used to compare the quality of scientific outcomes between groups.

Evidence of scientific conceptual or procedural development evidenced through predictions, conclusions and explanations provided either verbally or in written form.

The highly structured tasks

The highly structured tasks have a high degree of scaffolded support which enabled the pupils to complete quickly. There was very little discussion or negotiation about methodology, because there were step by step instructions on the task sheet, pupils did not have to enter into decision making about what to 'do'. However, they could have deliberated and discussed who would do what, and then enter into debate, toward the end of the task, regarding their explanations, conclusions and justifications. Two groups adapted the method identified on the sheet, but interestingly did not verbalise why they chose a differing approach. One group had difficulty lighting one of their candles, so then adapted the given method. This recipe-like approach to a practical (typical of many secondary science texts, e.g.: Spotlight Science, Eureka etc.......) prompted the pupils to consider why it was best to repeat the task a number of times, identify which candle burnt the longest and which extinguished most quickly (being given some information about oxygen in air). They were then asked to explain their results. The resultant discussions did provoke some cognitive engagement (group 2D:after nine minutes), but when trying to explain unexpected results because they had not immersed themselves so fervently with the decision making process to identify methods they could use, their explanations did not recognise a lack of fair-testing (i.e.: controlling the possible influential variables). They are discussing why they should repeat the task several times.

C	"So we could know what the difference is between, you know"
B	"..what...average is"
C	"Yeah"
C	"And then what has happened" (Talking over each other)
B	".. the smaller one because there is less erm..."
A	"Oxygen"
B	"Oxygen in it so it goes out quicker than that one, cos that's got less air in it than that one" Pointing to smallest gas jar first, then middle one and then largest one.
C	"Yeah"
A	"The time difference of one second is just because...?"
B	"The candle wouldn't light"
A	"Yes, the candle wouldn't light"
C	"yea..we...can explain this one well.."
A	"The candle didn't light in the first jar"
B	"Yeah"
C	"Yeah"

They don't realise that suggesting the candle didn't light is not an explanation for the anomalous results. This is an example of cumulative talk. The girls do not extend into exploratory conversation...to elucidate reasoning for the observations, even though they are being asked to explain what they have seen (and they have been given a useful hint; i.e.: amount of oxygen in air). Encouragement to enter into exploratory talk (by more able peer or teacher) may have helped here to suggest to the girls that they should think about reasons as to why they achieved the results they did.... this would have developed the cognitive engagement with the task to consider a much wider range of influences on the outcomes of the result.

Another example of the confidence a highly supported task can develop is when pupils are discussing the 'patterns', trends or relationships between variables elucidated through their data. The following extract provides an insight into how a group (9D) clarify their observations:

B Reading task sheet "What pattern can you see between the masses in the shoe and the force ...... It's every two hundred really.."
A "No"
B "It is.., most..., the average is every two hundred"
A "Yes, but, the ave..., yes, it goes up in two hundreds, it's between...., it either goes up one hundred, two hundred or three hundred, so the average ...... "
C Tidies up weights
B "So, the average will be ....."
A "......Goes higher or lower than that"
B "Yes, so it goes two hundred, three hundred...." Points to sheet.
C "Yes two..., because it goes up between one hundred and two hundred..."
B "So the average is two hundred. Right, now is that it?"

There is some initial disagreement between A and B, but as the data pattern shows quite clearly as mass increases so does the force, they are sufficiently confident to try and identify more exactly the relationship between the independent and the dependant variable.

Other cumulative talk at the culmination of the practical work resulted in misconceptions becoming more obvious. This added an interesting dimension to Mercer's 'common knowledge' concept, in this case what became clear was 'common misunderstandings' as well as 'understandings' (group 4D: after five minutes):

A Writes. "...was it best to repeat a number of times?" Reading from script.
C "uh?"
B "So you'll have more reliable answers"

A "Yeah, you can have more of a reliable answer ……and it depends how big the flame was didn't it because..... on the last two this flame was smaller" (Indicating largest gas jars candle)

C "Mmm"

A "What has happened?" Reading from script.
"Well the smaller ones went out faster because there wasn't enough oxygen to feed the flame in them"

B "Mmm"

A "So the oxygen would have worn out faster and it would have just suffocated the flame"

C "They all went out because of suffocation"

A "And they all did go out.."

A "..... Eventually because of lack of oxygen and they got suffocated"

B "Medium one had a bigger flame than the large jar"

A "Bigger wick"

B "Yeah"

B and A accumulate understanding of reliability of results through repeating the collection of data.

A thinks the smaller jar extinguished first because there wasn't sufficient oxygen to feed the flame, neither B nor C refine this. A proposes that oxygen wears out! And that the flames then suffocate, C thinks suffocation is then what happened to all of the candles.

B then mentions flame size, presumably because it can explain their anomalous result, if there was not a standardised initial flame issue, but the others do not pick up on it as an issue of fair-testing, A however, does elaborate on the wick determining flame size.

Semi-structured tasks

The groups given the semi-structured tasks to carry out, tended to develop a wider range of tactical strategies (see Figure 7.2 a,b,c : Tables to show comparative science outcomes from groups given either open, semi-structured or highly structured tasks) ; they usually 'trialled' and checked their ideas and methods practically more times than others; there was much more obvious cognisance (through discussion and adaptation of methods) of possible variables that could affect the outcomes; they were more likely to 'predict' what was likely to happen and thus engage more deeply with the expected data pattern, and its meaning (it appeared that these pupils inherently held a clearer idea of the 'whole' experiment). As a result of more 'involvement' in the activity it appears that the whole scientific process and the science were more generally discussed.

Group 2C discuss a number of variables at the beginning they should consider controlling:

Pupil C first suggests how they could place the jars over the candles...

C	places small jar over a candle.
B	says "yes"
C	" ,,,then that end....." indicating that could place jar over other candles. Lines up neatly small, medium and large jar. Picks up spill to light the candle.
A	finishes reading task sheet "...it true"
B	"What we going to do now?"
A	"We're going to put this...in the flame and burn it.....how long it burns". He picks up a jar and places it over a candle to try to emphasize what he thinks.

B then asks 'How can we accurately measure?' promoted by the task sheet. He answers how own question:

B " So how can we accurately measure? ..light all candles ..and then in the jar"
A leans over and lights spill then lights candle in front of him. Blows out spill and candle

A obviously agrees although does not say so, and proceeds with lighting the candles. In being prompted to think about measuring their results they are likely to get, they begin to talk about making a table for the data. In the process of writing their results tables they predict in turn to each other how they think they should do it, and what they think will happen:

	All 3 still writing
C	mutters
B	"we just have to make a table ...what have you written ?"
C	"The smaller jar....,the quicker it burns, bigger jar longer it takes to burn out"
B	"put the jar over the flame and time the small, medium and large ...time before the flame goes, what have you put A?"
A	"I put...exactly what I've put ....(reading from his sheet) put a jar over a lit candle and see how long it takes to burn out....the smaller jar quicker it...burns out."

Each boy in turn has made explicit to the other what they predicted would happen and how they thought the experiment should be done.

B then reads the next step in the scaffolded support..."how can you make sure that it is a fair test?'

B answers the question first again, but C and A do add their views as well:

B reads from sheet " ....How can you make sure that it is a fair test? start the stop watch at the same time **and**..."
A "use the same size candles"
B "yea, same sized candles"
A "you agree C?"
C "I do"

They jot down notes and continue talking...

A "..use the same size candles and start the stop clock at the same time"
C " same sized candles and....."
B " same sized candles and start time...."
A "To start and stop at ....."

They have considered here controlling the variable candle, and considered that timing needs to be synchronised.

B Re-reads the task sheet. "How will you present your results?...this is where we have to draw a table"
The boys delve into pencil cases.
A "right"

The boys are stimulated to think further about their scientific method through the next question:

B Reading from sheet. "How many times do you need to repeat the experiment so you know...your results are reliable? "
C "three times"
B "repeat it?"
C "twice?"
A "Twice.....repeat twice"
All write it down.
A "I'll have the big one"
C "I think we should put all the jars on this (indicating nearest candle; then on that one (indicating next candle), then on that one (indicating third candle) it'll be fairer then..."
A "yea...more..fairer then"
B " All candles the same size" put on smallest first.....are you timing C?"

They consider whether trialling their method twice or three times renders the data reliable. C clarifies exactly how they could place a jar at a time over sequential candles, A agrees that would be a fair test. B re-iterates that candles of the same size important and that they should proceed with smallest jar first. Trial 2 and 3 (group 2C) produce results whereby the candle in the medium jar burns the longest, not in the largest jar. B is also perplexed by the results not being exactly the same each time for each of the jars. As a result of this they re-visit (but not explicitly) an earlier suggestion from C, which is a more comprehensive method to check whether their predictions can be verified:

B "….not one is the same"

B is reflecting on the data gathered so far in three trials.

A	"Shall we try it again. This on that (indicating large jar over candle in front of B, i.e.: rotating the jars over different candles)
C	"That's what I said all jars over each candle"
A	"That one on that one (indicating large jar on next candle). That one on that one (indicating medium jar over candle in front of C), that one on that one (indicating small jar over candle nearest him)."
A & B	move the jars around.
A & C	reach to light the spills and re-light the candles
B	'Shall we put fourth time?" writing on results table All candles are light in front of each boy.
A	sings "for another day"
B	"three of each on each one"
C	"yea, that's what I said"
A	"but you've gotta be sure haven't you?……..another six.." indicates each jar in turn over each candle "three of them on that one…three of them on that one….three of them on that one…"
B	mutters "three on each…that's another nine!"

So this group have controlled the variable, candle, as they try each jar over each candle in turn. What they do not realise is that if they then calculated the averages their results would be validated and verified, and provide the evidence they are looking for. They obtain some anomalous results, and are swayed by the non-conformity of the data, convinced they have done something wrong, (it does take them a significant length of time, however) so they begin to look at what they are doing more carefully and how they could measure more accurately, A first notes synchronising start times (group 2C: after twenty four minutes on task):

All three boys re-set their timers
A lowers large jar "as soon as glass hits the floor that's when it counts"
C "yea"
All three time

And B recognises they need to focus on the 'end-point' of burning:

A "five point thirty three"
C "five point fifty five"
B "six point seventeen, and this time shall we wait until the smoke goes up?"
C "yea"

Another group on a semi-structured task (1D:after six minutes) also use the occurrence of smoke as the 'end-point' of burning:

A	*lowers large jar*
B	starts timing
B	"When the smoke comes out then we do it..then we stop"

Other groups do not use the smoke as their end-point but do realise they have to be sure about when the flame has extinguished otherwise their readings are inaccurate. Group (3F: after four minutes) also have some unexpected data (the medium jar last time supported a candle burning for 15 seconds, this time it is much shorter than that) and one of the boys suggests C has lowered the jar too quickly, which may have caused a draught and blown the candle out:

A	"Nought point 2.84...it's a bit weird that is "
C	"Yeah, I know, before ??? time" moves candle to re-light it
B	"The big one"
C	"..maybe , I put it in a bit too hard"
B	"Quick"
A	"Yeah"
C	"Like blew the candle out at the same time"
A	"Time" Writing "It's going to be nought point something isn't it?"
B	"It might not, because the other one took 15 before...... seconds"
C	Lights candle "yes, put it in slower this time, should we try the middle one again?" brings back candle.

The groups engaged on semi-structured tasks tend to repeat their methods several times to attempt to verify their predictions.

Open tasks

Given open ended tasks to do groups sometimes produced more ingenious ideas or practical strategies that differed to expectations; often they considered (verbally) a wider range of influencing variables than the highly structured groups, but not as extensively as the semi-structured groups and they were less likely to modify their methods and repeat for validation and reliability. They did not always collect quantitative data, evidence was sometimes gathered in a more comparative, qualitative way, thus the data collected from these groups was sometimes more questionable in terms of its validity, accuracy and verifiability.

One group 1C, for example, only lowered all three jars over the candles for one trial the results they derived were roughly what they expected, so they didn't repeat it. They discussed the results, during which time their misconceptions became apparent (group 1C:after five and a half minutes):

C	"Yes, look" (Examines small jar) (A takes off large and medium jars)
B	"Smaller, the large jar had a lot of space and a lot of oxygen, so it took longer to go out, it took..." (Writing) "It took longer to go out, yes?"
A	"Yes, so the....so put, the conclusion is, our conclusion is it, Joe was right"
B	"Conclusion is..."
A	"Or was it that John, yes, Joe was right"
C	"So just put our conclusion is..."
A	"You just need..."
C	"Our conclusion is that the one, more space, I mean air..."
A	"Yes"
B	"It depends on the space of, the light is..."
A	"If it's got more oxygen it goes out........ it takes a longer time, it burns for longer, that's it"
B	"Yes, so our conclusion is that if the lantern has more room"
A	"More oxygen..."
C	"No, our conclusion is that the.."
A	"The candle will stay alight...."
C	"The jar with the more oxygen would make the candle, the candle, the jar..."
B	"With the less oxygen"
C	"Will make the candle blow out first, this is because it hasn't got enough oxygen in it...."

Initially A is a little confused about the relationship between the amount of oxygen and how long the flame burns, she does correct herself, after some reflection. Through the verbal exchanges they piece together in a cumulative way how the size of the jar determines the amount of oxygen and how that in turn influences how long the flame burns. From C's contribution however, she is still not absolutely clear, she appears to associate less oxygen with blowing out in the smaller jar first. Later discussions further elucidate that B and C have not yet developed the correct scientific understandings:

B	"Yes, our conclusion is that the, (writing again) small jar..."
A	"Why don't you just put went out first..."
B	"No, shouldn't the oxygen go out first, will a lot of oxygen make it go out first?"
A	"No, because oxygen helps it burn doesn't it?"
B	"Oxygen makes it breathe, yes"
C	"Well it's water isn't it?"
B	"Our conclusion is that the small jar..."
C	"With the least amount of oxygen in"
A	"Burnt out first because it didn't have..."
B	"With the least amount" (Still writing)
C	"It will burn out first because it means that the..."
B	"Our conclusion is that the small jar with the least amount of oxygen in..." (Reading aloud from notes)
C	"Would..."

A "Burn out"
B "Would burn out"
C "Out first because there isn't enough light to make, because there isn't enough light to make because..."
B "There isn't enough oxygen to keep it alight, yes?"
A "Oxygen to keep it alive, yes, alight"
B "Because it, there isn't enough oxygen...."

During the process of making their thinking more explicit, they expose their incorrect ideas (they do not whole-heartedly develop exploratory talk, because they don't explain and rationalise the little 'chunks' of information and opinion they each contribute), but through the accumulation of their contributions eventually they decide (1C : after nine minutes):

B ".... to keep it burning?"
A "Yes, that's right"
B "The light burns..." (Writing)
A "So with more oxygen"
C "Yes, so with more oxygen.."
A "The candle, the candle stays alight more"
B "The candle has more chance of staying alive, staying alight"
C "The candle stands more chance of staying alight for longer"
B "Chance.."
A "It's light here" (Points to sheet)
B "Chance of staying..."
C "Alight for longer"
B "Alight, for most, for longer"
C "Right, let's just read it out"
B "Right, the smaller jar didn't have a lot of oxygen so it went out in 2 seconds, the medium jar also didn't have a lot of oxygen so that went out in 7 seconds, but it had more oxygen than the smaller jar. The larger jar had a lot space and a lot of oxygen so it took longer to go out. It went out in 11 seconds..."
B "Our conclusion is that the smaller jar with the least amount of oxygen in would burn out first because there isn't enough oxygen to keep it burning. With more oxygen the candle has more chance of staying alight longer".

7.6 Conclusions

The findings indicate that levels of in-task structure (differentiated scaffolding) can impact on the nature and extent of discourse and thus by inference the cognitive gains. Prescriptive or highly structured activities or tasks appear to constrain engagement in the procedural aspects of practical work. Providing step-by-step instructions, however, appears to support more consistent experimental data collection that is likely to be more reliable and verifiable, enabling pupils to engage in describing and explaining evidence more readily. This could be because their 'confidence' in the evidence they have collected is higher. The extent to which they are able to evaluate the evidence is sometimes constrained though, because the opportunity for *experiential* reflection of different practical approaches (to the same problem) is limited. Some task scaffolding appears to offer more opportunity for the development of more widely ranging dialogic patterns to emerge (Tolmie et al, 1993) which focuses much more on procedural and methodological matters. It appears that the diverse strategic direction of group activity and discourse can be strongly influenced by task structure. More comprehensive discussion includes foci on procedural and methodological matters. The scaffolded support appears to generally engage the pupils more deeply with scientific ways of thinking about a task. It also appears to support development of both creative and critical thinking. Creative in that more diverse problem solving strategies are developed. Critical in that the pupils appear to evaluate more effectively how and why procedure has influenced the findings. The more evaluative thinking often results in modification and refinement of the methods initially developed to verify and/or validate findings.

As Cohen (1994) suggests the optimal task for effective learning together must invite negotiation and if problems are too constrained then this is unlikely to happen. If on the other hand, if the limits of the problem space are too ambiguous, then the students require more support from the teacher. Anderson, Palinscar and Kurth (1996) suggest open problem-solving situations require support that attends to; a) techniques, through which students engage in inquiry in which they are trying to make reliable and accurate observations; b) observations through which they are recording, comparing and communicating about phenomena in the inquiry; c) patterns through which students are seeking to make rules or generalisations that characterise what they have observed; and d) explanations, through which students are developing arguments using models or theories to make sense of the patterns they have observed. These problem-solving issues are resolvable through appropriate scaffolding that guides students to consider pluralistically (Reiss, 1998) pertinent concerns, without directing routes to solutions.

However, even with in-task support, there are *missed* opportunities for cognitive development through social interaction. In contradiction to Azmitia and Montgomery (1993), but supported by Kutnick and Kington (2005), evidence of spontaneous Socratic evaluation of processes and outcomes was not widely prevalent. These peers were more likely to agree and 'conform' to plausible reasoning provided by a high status pupil (Bianchini, 1999 who considered personality and status as well as scientific capability). Historical behavourial patterns (Bauersfeld, 1988) or even cultural ways of working can develop between *friends* that regularly, co-operatively work together. Faced with difficult intellectual challenges, pupils are less confident and more likely to *agree* with another's view, rather than suggest alternate viewpoints that may result in an uncomfortable situation that could interfere with social relationships. The lack of confrontation between pupils and little exploratory talk has shown interactions to be supportive and socially intuitive rather than cognitively conscious. Azmitia claims that if groups of pupils are given demanding tasks then 'friends' exhibit more of a cognitive developmental dialogue (justifying; explaining; etc).

I would argue, from the evidence here, that this could be likely as long as the pupils have been *encouraged* or *enculturated* into ways of developing this kind of *working-with-each-other* and are *comfortable* with and accept that it is *normal* and *acceptable* to *disagree* and discuss contrasting ideas and associated reasoning. It appears that in the schools observed, there is little or no *culture* of pupils readily questioning each others ideas. Anecdotally, I overheard one boy say to another in a school corridor, 'It shows you're thick if you ask questions'. This kind of peer-peer comment reflects a school culture that does not value the cognitive activity underpinning pupil development of constructive questioning and curiosity.

It appears that in these schools where the groups have been observed that there is no 'culture' of pupils readily questioning each other, asking for clarification of suggestions and daring to propose alternative approaches (or interpretations) for consideration.

To achieve effective intra-group discussion that supports cognitive development much more explicit verbalisation of thought is required, not only whilst the task is in progress, but also for preparatory planning and post-task-reflections. The findings suggest that the level of in-task scaffolding could affect the subsequent discourse and resultant learning outcomes. The kinds of questions that are posed can be used to sharpen the focus of pupils' minds on issues they often find difficult or are not likely to consider without intervention of some kind. Scaffolding could purposely suggest alternative and challenging ideas regarding tactics or methods of data collection, interpretations of evidence and a range of possible scientific explanations.

There are many incidences when intervention by a more expert other (peer or teacher) could enhance the within-group zpd through interjecting to deliberately provoke explicit pupil inter-thinking. Cognitive conflict or socio-conflicts could be purposely introduced or highlighted to be resolved through discussion. Groups could be supported to ensure explicit articulation of all (hitherto silent/unspoken) ideas, opinions, proposals and justifications of participating members in a group, each taking a turn to share their views. Pupil participation should be encouraged to ensure more open, unhindered contributions. The pupils could be encouraged to consider how *others* may interpret data or evidence and offer explanations from another's perspective. They should not feel it inappropriate to ask questions to clarify understandings. This approach is now widely promoted at primary schools through the use of concept cartoons (Naylor, Keogh and Mitchell 2000) which presents learners with several alternate and contrasting interpretations of scientific ideas. Argumentation is also promoted with younger children through various strategies (Simon and Maloney 2007). These approaches however, do not highlight how differentiating in-task support can vary the cognitive nature of discussion that pupils engage in. Teachers realising that the nature of talk and discussion can be influenced in particular ways by scaffolded-in-task-support that can subsequently result in pupils achieving more autonomous learning appears to be possible from the findings so far.

Chapter eight

8.1 Reflecting on the interactions

The nature of the interactions observed when pupils were offered varying levels of scaffolded support was not quite as I anticipated. I assumed that open ended tasks (as Roth, 1998; Watson and Wood-Robinson, 1998; Watson et al 1999 define), would provide the opportunity for more autonomy in decision making, and consequently support more exploratory talk. I expected to observe more explicit reasoning and sharing of ideas in these open tasks. I anticipated that through social interactions and problem solving together the pupils would communicate to share their perspectives and understandings to reach agreements regarding procedures and meanings of evidence. As Bruner (1996:174-183) so eloquently describes, without *intentions* of pupils (working together), being made explicit to each other, how can they interpret the understandings each other have of the task in hand. However, it appeared from the analysis in chapter 7 that subjective understandings were regularly more explicit in tasks, illustrated through exploratory talk, where some scaffolding (rather than none at all) was provided. Reflecting on Bruner's (ibid) discussion of 'theories of mind', where he (and I agree) questions the Piagetian view of knowledge of the world, growing out of direct hands-on contact with it, rather than learning about it through interaction with others (pupils or teachers). I came to realise that through my analysis of *inter-talk* and *inter-action*, I was attempting to measure the extent to which the pupils were *enacting* and engaging in the processes that achieve 'intersubjectivity'. Intersubjectivity is a term developed by theorists to describe

> 'the process of interchange, a dynamic during which meanings are chosen from a repertoire of language tools' (Solomon, 1994:15).

I had theorised that open tasks offering more opportunities to consider subjective ideas would result in intersubjectivity being achieved.

8.2 From interaction to intersubjectivity

As a consequence of reviewing literature regarding 'intersubjectivity' I re-visited my observations of the pupils interactions. The following discussion of intersubjectivity informed how I subsequently re-reviewed pupils' interactive talk and action to then guide teachers to support its development in science classrooms. Intersubjectivity described by Rogoff (1990:71) could be verbal or non-verbal, but is essentially 'a bridge between one and another's understanding'. Explicit communication is therefore presumed. My analysis illustrates that there appears to be almost constant 'action' when pupils work together, usually related to 'carrying out the practical work' and 'preparing the equipment'. These 'actions' are often the 'silent' response to others' comments or suggestions. Unspoken actions and a lack of explicit rationale for ideas (especially in open tasks), indicate bereft communication. Vygotsky (1987) points out that intersubjectivity cannot subsequently extend children's understanding to new activities without overt communication. The exchange between pupils, visibly considering each others' views was hardly evident in the prescriptive task and lacking in the open tasks. The lack of meaningful and purposeful exchange regarding scientific ideas in un-structured tasks highlights a relevant issue requiring further consideration, especially as teachers often 'expect' pupils to engage in holistic complex investigations (chapter 5, section 5.4) with little previous practice (chapter 5, section 5.2) planning and reflecting on results in-task. As pupils also indicate (chapter 6, section 6.6) teachers do not regularly 'intervene' to support learning together and, they [the pupils] recognise they need help in understanding others' views. In re-considering the evidence, intersubjectivity and supporting teachers to develop more effective learning, I am attempting to suggest what may be done regarding pedagogical support for pupils in the context of science investigations. This is pertinent, because as Murphy (2000:158) identifies,

> 'currently models of practice available to teachers and learners are narrowly conceived. Hence practices have not been developed to support negotiation in social interaction in subject cultures. The issue is whether there is potential to reconceptualise approaches to science education in ways that recognise the cultural process of meaning making.'

She continues to explain how 'simplistic models of mind' and 'nationally prescribed pedagogic approaches' constrain *possibilities* for science learning. Her view is that a cultural approach allowing children to develop more useful, robust understanding is needed. My task here is to begin to suggest how that might manifest itself through pupils-working-together and the understanding teachers [themselves] require to understand their role in supporting effective peer-peer learning.

Active negotiation illustrated through dialogic exchanges appeared to be best supported in the semi-structured tasks that offered scaffolded support, suggesting that pedagogic intervention to help pupils focus on particular aspects of a problem is important. Rogoff (1990: 71) highlights how 'shared understanding' is based on a 'common focus of attention' and some 'shared presuppositions' that form the 'ground for communication'. In other words if the pupils, in open learning situations are not sure what is significant to focus on, they will be hesitant in their decision making. This lack of focus at the onset of a task is borne out by the evidence in this study, showing groups, spending little time discussing the best method or planning strategically before engaging in evidence collection. The support in the semi-structured tasks guides the pupils to consider specific issues, thus highlighting the pertinent foci for attention. The guidance was designed (e.g.: figure 7.4) to prompt consideration of; i, measurement of the dependent variables; ii, controlling appropriate variables; changing relevant variables (fair testing); iii, presentation and subsequent consideration of the evidence and iv, reliability of the evidence. This scaffolding (in work sheets illustrated in Appendix 7) appeared to impact, significantly, in some cases, (Appendix 7 and 10) on the range and number of tactical approaches developed, utilised and compared; controlling a range of appropriate variables (often simultaneously); accuracy of judgements (e.g.: 'start' and 'end-points' for measurements); reliability and validity of evidence; and the improved likelihood of 'describing' a data pattern and 'explaining' what the evidence means to reach a good task solution, by collecting quality scientific evidence that can be appropriately explained. It appeared that whilst focussing on particular concerns, each pupil contributed their understanding, through a more explicit 'back and forth' discussion, which enabled the group to collaborate in a shared construction zone (Roth 1995:183).

I began to reflect on how teachers could come to realise that if there is no development of shared understandings then participants couldn't engage in joint decision-making and begin to appropriate meaning. My evidence from chapter 5 indicated that the teachers in this study perceived learning from an individualistic (Piagetian) perspective.

Which as Rogoff (1990: 150) describes:

> "is thus a limited version of social impact on the individual's cognitive development; in taking the individual as the base unit, it does not reach a collective perspective on the social context of cognitive development."

She points out that this view does not embrace any cognisance of social meaning making. A point, she extends (ibid) :

> "....it is necessary to grant that meaning is more than a construction by individuals."

Chapter 5 findings suggest that teachers perceive working-together predominantly as an opportunity to efficiently utilise resources, share ideas and develop social skills. They have not reflected carefully on the nature of the social and cognitive interactions they wish to nurture within groups.

Collaboration and intersubjectivity

The beginning of intersubjectivity is the exchange between co-learners of ideas, and subsequent thoughts to clarify how each is juxtaposed to the other. To enhance understanding of others' ideas or different perspectives, however, Rogoff (1990) argues greater shared communication is essential. To see a problem from a qualitatively different vantage point, requires a person to become aware that there is another perspective. For development of understanding (and skills) individuals may more easily realise that there is information they do not know or tactics they could become aware of through explicit exchange of differing perspectives. Social interaction, then, is fundamental to directing the individual to recognise another's view (and maybe even internalise it), through presentation of the alternatives and consideration of the merits of each. Intersubjectivity, facilitated through engagement in the exploration of possibilities, is only likely to occur if participants allow others to describe and justify their alternate views and in so doing enter into cognitive development through social interaction.

Intersubjectivity is fundamental to developing shared understandings about the nature of the task itself, as well as agreement about how to perform the task, and any interpretations that may be accrued through engagement in the task or findings or outcomes developed through reflection of the task. In other words to enter into intersubjectivity participants (pupils) need to exchange thoughts through language (and actions) that portrays their logic and reasoning. As Ding and Flynn (2000:11) suggest from their work assessing the links between theory-of-mind and collaborative learning. The acquistion of collaborative skills could be underpinned by intersubjectivity skills. Thus in order to collaborate effectively pupils (and the teacher) must have a shared understanding of the task and goals. Intersubjectivity thus underpins collaboration.

Roth (1995: 183) describes how learning together is developed in a Piagetian sense.

> 'learning……is facilitated by the continual conflict between antagonistic forms of thinking….. resolution of these conflicts is achieved ….. through reciprocal consideration of alternative views'.

Piagetian constructivists would argue the comparison of minds involves two separate individuals, each operating on the other's ideas, using the back-and-forth of discussion to advance his or her own thinking. This portrays the co-operative nature of individuals reflecting on another's suggestions. The discussion is the product of two individuals considering alternatives provided socially, rather than the construction of a joint understanding between partners achieved through intersubjectivity. From a Vygotskian point of view, knowledge is collaboratively constructed between individuals. From this shared construction zone,[24] knowledge can be appropriated by individuals into their personal repertoires. This process of appropriation is equivalent to the intra-individual construction of knowledge. Forman (1987) defines the differences by describing Piaget's view that problem solving is explained by deriving both cognitive and social processes from the same central intrapsychological process, whereas in Vygotsky's theory, the correspondence

[24] Construction zone, occurs in ZPD (Newman, Griffin and Cole 1989).

between cognitive and social processes is due to the derivation of individual cognitive processes from joint cognitive processes in social contexts.

For Piaget, advancement of one another's cognitive development through attempts to resolve personal cognitive conflict or discrepancy is derived from differences in their perspectives. Thus individual appropriation of socially constructed meaning advances intra-cognitive development.

In the Vygotskian perspective, in contrast, the individual makes use of the joint decision-making process itself to expand understanding and skill. The Piagetian constructivist's view is thus a narrow perspective of the social impact on the individual's cognitive development (much like the teachers perceptions, it seems); in taking the individual as the base unit, it does not reach a collective perspective on the social context of cognitive development (Rogoff 1990). It does not make the necessary shift in perspective to encompass the social construction of meaning through intersubjectivity.

Shared problem solving and intersubjectivity

Even though the tasks were presented to the pupils in a standardised fashion (specific context and structure), the ways in which the pupils interpreted the goals or task was often difficult to discern. This is significant because, as Newman, Griffin and Cole (1989), point out, laboratory subjects and school pupils are often judged to be stupid or not to have learned anything when they might equally well be seen as having been doing something different than anticipated by the researcher or teacher.

> 'In everyday situations, people are not always presented with clearly stated goals. They often have to figure out what the problem is, what the constraints are, as well as how to solve the problem once they have formulated it'
>
> (Newman, Griffin and Cole (1989:33).

Quite appropriately, they highlight that, maintaining control in a laboratory can veil the crucial process of *formulating the task and identifying the goal(s).* An investigation includes figuring out what the task actually is. Pupils clarifying their interpretation of the task (and associated intentions) is then a crucial focus for the development of intersubjectivity. As Lave and Wenger (1991) describe, it is the process of intersubjectivity that is pivotal for learning.

> 'Learning is a process that takes place in a participation framework, not in an individual mind. This means, among other things, that it is mediated by the

> differences in perspective among co-participants. It is the community, or at least those participating in the learning context, who 'learn' under this definition' (Lave and Wenger, 1991:15).

Rogoff (1990) identifies that the most productive interaction appears to result from arrangements in which peers' decision making occurs jointly, with a balanced exploration of differences of perspective (Bos 1937; Glachan and Light 1982; Light, Foot, Colbourn and McClelland 1987). Learning occurs as each group member's perspective is analysed, inferior ideas rejected and superior propositions accepted (Kruger 1993). As Murphy and Spence (1997) propose collaborative learning relies on students engaging with each others' ideas and sharing what they consider to be salient[25]. The intersubjective discussion centred around issues of significance in a task, is the crux of learning in a social setting. Through collaboration, partners may develop ways to communicate about difficult problems that advance the definition or solution of the problems.

With this purpose of social interaction in mind I reviewed the transcripts to re-examine the social nature of the interactions and incidence of shared understanding of the task, shared projections, shared decision making, shared appreciation of the findings and shared reflective perspectives, all of which, I perceived, would demonstrate the development of intersubjectivity between peers.

[25] Salient is taken to mean the pupils subjective interpretation of the relevant and important aspect(s) of the task.

Re-viewing the potential opportunities for intersubjectivity

I re-viewed the interactions between pupils that attempted to solve problems with no scaffolding in the light of missed potential (Murphy and Hennessey 1999). I identified these as potentially pivotal moments for collaborative interaction to develop 'intersubjectivity'. These opportunities were potential moments for intersubjectivity to develop before enacting decisions.

Open task analyses indicate that there is a lack of intersubjectivity focussed around i, clarifying the tasks; ii, identifying what the independent and dependent variables are; iii, considering what methods or procedures are appropriate and possible to collect (independent and dependent variable evidence) to address the task; iv, what are the likely outcomes (predictions/propositions) of the nature of the relationship between variables; then v, reflection on the meaning of the data.

Thus it appears that pupils tackling open tasks, offered a range of opportunities to develop intersubjectivity, do not consistently fulfil expectations at these key moments in the problem solving process.

Dynamic exchanges between pupils involved in solving problems with *some support* more frequently illustrated engagement in the process of intersubjectivity, evidenced by more extensive and intensive exploratory talk (Appendix 7 and 19). Evidence of intersubjectivity leading up to decision-making moments in their problem-solving situations was more evident. This indicated pupils were capable of intersubjective discussions, but not without support.

Reflecting on the tasks and the nature of science I considered that the process of scientific enquiries should, as Hodson (1998:117) explains (re-iterated by many other science educators) connect 'doing science' with 'learning from science' as well as 'learning about science'. I considered also, Blagg's (1991:153) view of scaffolding problem solving, informed by Sternberg (1997) and Feurstein (1980). He identified strategic steps or critical stages that could inform the design of problem solving tasks: 1. Recognising (a problem exists); 2. Defining (the problem); 3. Generating (alternative approaches); 4. Planning (selecting the most viable approach); 5. Evaluating (solutions and approaches); 6. Communicating (the outcomes to self and others); 7. Transferring and Generalising (actively reflecting on the application of skills and procedures learnt in one context to many others, and where possible deducing general principles or rules that can help with future learning or problem solving). Holding these perspectives in mind I reviewed the potential opportunities to develop intersubjectivity in science investigations. In Sc 1 (Scientific enquiry; DFEE and QCA, 1999:28-29) consideration regarding evidence and interpretation of data; planning investigations (including identification of key factors, controlling variables, considering the extent and range of data to be collected); obtaining and presenting evidence (from investigations); considering (the meaning of) evidence and evaluating (evidence obtained and procedures used to gather data) are the key skills (pupils should develop), described in the National Curriculum. Revisiting Roth's (1995) criteria (from chapter 4:24) in which he highlights potential problem solving opportunites, there appear to be, critical points at which, or particular issues about which, proffered propositions should be carefully considered before collaborative decisions are made. My synthesis of Sternberg, Feurestein, Roth, Watson et al, DFEE, QCA and others suggest 5 key decision making opportunities (outlined below), that appear to be significant issues in open task situations, such as science investigations. These appear to be potential opportunities for pupils to participate in active negotiation to culminate in justified and thoughtfully reasoned decision-making, fundamental to intersubjectivity.

1. Clarification of the task.

Evidence that illustrates pupils are clear about the intent of the task, explicitly sharing their perceptions concerning the goals they are aiming for. I looked for shared understanding of the questions they needed to address.

2. Shared thinking about tactics or methods they could use.

Describing the different ways the problem could be solved. Do they consider the possible tactics they could employ to solve the problem. Do they consider any one way is better than another? Do they exchange views about the differing approaches? Do they develop a shared view of the best approach? Do they justify their opinions?

3. Shared predictions and projections

Does each pupil state or clearly infer what he or she expects should happen. As a group do they agree what findings they are anticipating?

4. Sharing perspectives on the evidence

Do they share with each other what the evidence means to them? Do they compare it to their expectations? Lack of clarity in their explicitly reasoned initial predictions that findings are often 'fuzzy' (Bassey, 2000:52) and participants are then unclear about what to expect and thus less able to describe and explain patterns of behaviour. Without explicit sharing of conceptual expectations it is difficult to consider whether they conceive plausible explanations.

5. Evaluation and review

Do they re-consider whether their tactics were appropriate for the task set? Do they review their success? Without unambiguous discourse exposing their views of prospective procedural and conceptual outcomes, judgements about relative success are based on unclear expectations. Thus task endpoints are often reached without clear outcomes in sight. Vague notions, it seems, are held by the pupils, without clarity about what evidence *exactly* constitutes their solutions to the problem posed. The inclusion of intersubjectivity as a cultural expectation in the process of collaborative problem solving would mean that dialogically explicit clarification, consideration and evaluation of all participants' differing views inform the joint decision making about whether their data illustrate their expectations or not.

8.3 Reflecting on task performance

Reconsideration of intersubjectivity at significant stages in the problem solving process led me to review the pupils' interactions at these junctures. I reconsidered only the open tasks, at this point, because there were numerous potential opportunities for subjective discussions, and this type of task typifies Sc1 investigations, specified by the Science National Curriculum. Scaffolded intervention from the teachers appears to be uncommon (Chapter 5:19), so pupils' capacity to work autonomously in groups, without further support is of relevant concern. I wished to clarify, as a teacher-researcher, how under-utilised potential opportunities were to support collaborative interactions between pupils. The following extracts are selected to be illuminatory, focussing on potentially 'critical happenings' (Hitchcock and Hughes 1995) or not. I am applying Tripp's (1993) qualitative approach to focus on issues and ideas upon which to base future practice. The following reflective discussion is intended to inform the rationale for the structure of professional development activities to enable teachers to empathise with pupils' learning-together. My intention is to engage teachers in appreciating learners' *missed opportunities* when working collaboratively on practical activities.

8.3.1 Clarification of the problem

Differing perceptions of the problem are illustrated through the following extract, from Group 1C, at the beginning of their task:

A	"You're going to use them aren't you, them jars" (Points to jars)
C	"Yes, you need it to light one don't you?" (Points to candle and picks up small jar)
A	"Yes, I think you have to..."
B	"Don't you want to use that one (A takes jar from B) because that..." (Points to candle then picks up small jar from C - places over candle). "You have to..."
A	"No, so you have less oxygen in each of them don't you?"
B	"Yes"
C	" Because that will be less oxygen, so if you have more oxygen it will light out longer"
B	"We'll just use these then" (Picks up spill)
A	"C you go first" (A and C take spills)
C	"I'm doing it. We'll do one each." (All light candles)
B	"Mind, mind......I'll get this one, careful with the paper"
A	"I don't think it's going to go and light"
C	"It wunna light, now you leave it on this don't you, you do, you do it on this" (Places spill on mat next to candle to extinguish"
A	"Do you?" (B tries to blow out spill)
B	"To blow it out, (A and B place spills on mat to extinguish) that's it, it's out"
A	"Can we put it back?"

Several sentences are left un-finished, as if there is an expectation on behalf of the speaker that the others will know what she is intending. The listeners rarely ask for clarification of a half-completed or even complete statement. It appears that they assume each will know what the others mean without explicitly saying so. Questioning of each others' postulations' or suggestions appears to be very infrequent. Consider this extract, where the girls are thinking about how the jars should be placed over the candles (initially one at a time). Pupil A suggests there is less oxygen in each of them (meaning jars), and pupil C offers the idea that if there is more oxygen it will 'light out longer'.

Neither A nor B refines or comments on C's postulation that is not correctly articulated. They don't ask C what does she mean?, or does she mean it won't burn for so long?, in other words there is very little or no deliberation over an individual's contribution of an explanation. They have not defined or clearly identified the dependant and independent variables, or agreed the task strategy. They launch unpreparedly into lighting the candles before they have carefully considered their practical tactics. Pupil C determines they will do one each, again neither of the others pause and ask why or supportively agree. They don't at this point consider whether to time the candles, or any other aspects of fair-testing methodology (lowering jars in synchrony etc). They do not explicitly think through and plan their experimental strategy. They do not 'expose' their individual thoughts about procedure, so there is little opportunity to consider, modify or refine ideas and suggestions, because no initial plan is clearly constructed. Thus the quality of subsequent discourse and connected cognitive processing appears rather impoverished.

Another group (1F) have some discussion about what to do, but they don't clearly share with each other what the independent and dependent variables are, i.e.: *what* are they investigating. One pupil suggests they need to consider lighting a candle in each jar, and find out which goes out quickest. A thinks its to do with how much air is in it. They don't develop the discussion into how the length of burning (dependent variable) is indicative of the volume of oxygen (independent variable) available for combustion, and that if there is more oxygen or air available the candle will burn longer; with less the candle is not likely to burn as long. For them it appears that there is a limited view of the outcome (because they haven't re-formulated the investigation), their objective is just to see which candle extinguishes first.

B	"If you light a candle under each of them, right, in order of size, erm, find out which one goes out quicker"
A	"Yeah, see how much air in it"
C	"turn that upside down" (pointing to largest gas jar)
A	"Yeah" (picks up jar)
B	"So what you do is light a candle and then you put it on like that" (indicating by moving arm over candle)
A	(picks up gas jar and moves it over candle)
C	"Yeah, so shall we light the candles with the splint"

At this point the girls then carryout the procedure with virtually no discussion about whom does what. There are huge assumptions, implicit thinking, here about who will do what, and when.

C	Reaches for spill.
A	Picks up another gas jar.
B	Fiddling with gas jar.
B	Reaches for watch glass. "Put that on the bottom .....stick your candles on there"
C	"OK." Puts candle on watch glass.
A	Puts candles on other watch glasses.
B	Puts on safety goggles.
C	Lights candles.
B	Picks up gas jar.
A	Holding another gas jar ready.

It appears that they are so used to working together they do not need to make explicit to one another what should be done next! This lack of discourse indicates discussion to exchange thoughts is not at all spontaneous.

Another group (1A) that exhibits much implicit communication:

	All read the task sheet
A to **B**	'You work the timer'
A	"Let's do the smallest tube, then the middle then the biggest"
A, **B** and **C** spend a minute or so writing.	
A	Looks at **C**'s writing
A	"Let's do this one first". Reaches for smallest jar and spill.
C	"I'll light one of the candles"
B to **A**	Referring to timer. "How do I start this?"
A *to* **B**	"Just press start then I'll tell you to go"
A	Lights first candle with spill.
B to **A**	"Tell me when go"
A	"Not yet"

There is no shared view that is made explicit about what each pupil thinks they are investigating. Pupil A, a rather dominant child, instructs the other two, who do not ask for clarification, they just appear to follow instructions. It appears that the apparatus is acting as a prompt for what to do. They do not explicitly 'plan' at all, they launch into lighting the candles with no shared task objectives.

The group (1C) lit all the candles and then discussed, after one minute, practical considerations. Pupil A, rather unusually asks a question:

A	"Are we going to go at the same time?"
B	"1, right"
C	"No, OK, 1.."
A	"2"

C & A	"3" (All place jars over lit candles)
B	"Right just wait a minute, like that went out"
A	"Yes"
B	"There's not a lot of air in that one, no there's not a lot of air in that one, that will go out"
A	"See, so..."
C	"Yes, it's the bigger one"
B	"Yes, it's the bigger one, like say, you need to write down..."

A asks a very valid question, but this appears to be prompted by the action of lighting the candles, when thinking about what they should do next, so the need for discussion was encouraged or mediated by artefacts, as Vygotsky would identify, not (it seems) autonomously brought about by a culture of social interaction. Because they haven't discussed the various ways they could do the experiment, they haven't reached an agreed way forward. Thus they are not consciously clear about why it's a good idea (or not?) for each to lower a jar simultaneously. B initially wasn't sure they should do it any way and says no. They do not pause and openly consider the difference of opinion at all.

Only after lighting the candles and all lowering jars together, through seeing the candles extinguish in turn, and then spotting the timer, they consider that timing 'how many seconds' the candles burn is useful. They appear to use the 'evidence' to reflect on what they are doing, ie: consider what might matter. As a result of launching rather un-thinkingly into practical work, they do not consider timing how long each candle burns for. The following comes later in their discussion about using the timer, when they realised that after the first attempt at comparing the burning in the different jars, they could have measured how long each remained alight.

B	"Just leave it there" (Returns spills to jar)
A	"Are we supposed to use them things to time them, are you?" (Looks at teacher)
B	"You're supposed to, yes, well it is a clock" *(Teacher: "You decide what you think that you'd like to do")*
A	"Right, how stupid can you get, man"
C	Picks up timer.
B	"Yes, but we watched it go out last so what shall we..."
C	"Yes, now we don't know which one's how many seconds"
A	"Yes, but then we can use our scientific knowledge"
B	"Yes, OK"
C	"What's scientific knowledge?"
B	"Alright then, we'll try again and we'll count it this time"
A	"Be more specific"
C	"Alright, I'll time it"

Another group (2F) did discuss some aspects of the procedure, but again much consequent 'action' taken by the pupils appears to be prompted by the apparatus and 'evidence' gathered from initial observations. Again clarification of the variables to be investigated, before practical action, is lacking:

	All read through script
B	points to particular point on the task sheet
A	".... a few"
C	"Try it." Pointing to equipment.
	All move towards equipment.
A	Picking up small gas jar. "Put them over that". Lowers jar over candle.
B	"Light the candle"
	All three put on safety goggles
A	Picks up spill and lights it, then lights a candle.
B	"Small...first"
C	Lowers small gas jar over candle and looks at watch.

The lack of shared focus, i.e.: developing their understanding of the nature of the task itself, limits the process of intersubjectivity at the onset. The bereft discussion regarding each other's perspective of the task means that only as they experience and incrementally consider what has happened do they develop their method.

8.3.2 Shared thinking about tactics

Another group (1A) that does not readily engage in the process of intersubjectivity is illustrated below. One child notices that the candle flames are not all prepared equally (in fact she focuses on how long it takes to light the candle) but correctly realises that each candle hasn't been prepared in exactly the same way. She points this out, but A has a different view of what is 'unfair', B doesn't say anything about whether it is fair or not, but suggests a pragmatic approach of using the same candle:

C** to **A	"Hang on 'cause it isn't a fair test 'cause you've taken longer to get that ready than you did on the other one" (pointing to 2nd lit candle)
A	Puts lit spill on the lit candle "I'll just put a little bit more on ... make it a bit bigger..... come on .... light .... that's it now... no it's not"
B to **A**	"Why don't you use that same candle?"
A *to* **B**	"Hang on" - blows out spill, candle not lit
B	repeats to **A** "Use the same candle ... if you use the same candle, then it'll be fair"
A	"Yeah"
B	Swaps 2nd candle for first one and A lights it with spill
A	Picks up medium sized jar
B to **A**	"..... ... say go"

From the dialogic exchange, it appeared that C's perception of 'fair' was to hold the spill lighting the candle wick for a standardised time; A's view was that the flame sizes should be the same (bigger in this instance) and B's idea was that the candle itself should be standardised by being re-used for each trial. At no stage either here in the verbal interactions or later in this activity do they explicitly describe and thus verbally 'expose' their differing interpretations. This lack of explicitly shared juxtaposed views between friends is not spontaneous in the culture of these peers working together. Exploratory talk or critically reviewing peers' views is obviously not entered into easily.

Another group (1F) also reflected on 'fairness' after running one trial:

A + B	Place gas jars on two of the candles,
C	Reaches across and puts a gas jar on the third candle
A	Points to smallest gas jar. "That ones gone out"
B	"There's' less..."
A	"Carbon air in it"
B	"Yes there's less oxygen in it"
A	Points to large gas jar. "And that ones gone out"
B	Points to large gas jar. "That's gone out...but we lit that...that went out quicker than that". Pointing to the two jars.
C	"And the middle went out last"
B	"But that wasn't a fair test because we didn't put them on all together did we"
A	"No"
B	"So we can't call it a fair test"

Because they didn't consider the synchronicity of placing jars over the candles simultaneously, their results don't quite reflect their expectations. Although, as with other groups, these pupils don't clearly describe what they expect before it happens. Lack of discussion in their planning about how to construct a fair test meant the girls overlooked this in their procedure.

Another tactical issue is that of agreeing 'starting strategies' and 'end-points'. This group here have trialled the small and medium jar. They are now observing to see how long the candle burns in the large jar. They have not so far discussed when the flame is 'out'.

B	Puts large gas jar over candle.
C	Starts timing with his watch.
A	"It's not lit properly is it?"
B	"Not really"
C	"Not really"
B	"But I think like keep going for a bit won't it"
	All 3 watch the flame intently.
B	"It's flickering a bit isn't it"

C "Mmm….."
B "It's still flickering a bit.. it's gone"
C Stops his watch.
A "No! it's not gone yet, it's still there"
B "Is it?"
A "No it's gone now"
C "26.50" Records results.

Listening to their discussion, they have not decided when the 'end-point' of burning is. Some pupils watch the flames, which dwindle to a very small amber glow, but are still alight, the pupils however, have judged the flame to be out often before this, as exemplified above. In their discussion, they don't describe exactly how the flame is changing and in so doing enter into a more meaningful and informed judgement about when it is out, and thus measure 'time of burning' more accurately.

Another tactical issue is that of validity; recognising whether one set of data is enough. Group 1A and 1C do not consider repeating data gathering at all. They ascertain just one trial is sufficient for them to draw their conclusions. Another group 1F repeat their trials 4 times, spurred on to a second trial because one pupil recognises they didn't synchronise the lowering of the jar. One of the girls suggests that they should repeat the trial to 'make sure', the others agree, but do not explicitly reason why. The second trial produces a differing order of extinguishing candles. Pupil C suggests they should try it one more time, again B and A agree, but they do not qualify their agreement. There is no discussion regarding the number of times they should repeat the experiment before they accept the results are verifiable or valid. There is no consideration by any group about the quantity of reliable data that should be gathered before an average or general trend can be identified with confidence and relative certainty. This group do not enter into timing the burning, they just remember the sequence of extinguishing flames.

8.3.3 Sharing predictions and projections

These were uncommon. Very few pupils described what they thought would happen before it did, most waited to see the results and then some attempted to explain the findings. One pupil in group 1F typically offers a prediction after one trial:

A (points to smallest gas jar) "That ones gone out"
B "There's' less..."
A "Carbon air in it"
B "Yes there's less oxygen in it"
A (Points to large gas jar) "And that ones gone out"
B (Points to large gas jar) "That's gone out...but we lit that...that went out quicker than that" (Pointing to the two jars)
C "And the middle went out last"
B "But that wasn't a fair test because we didn't put them on all together did we"
C "So shall we do it again" (Reaching for splint)
B "Yeah"
C "Just to make sure"
A "That ones not out yet... " Points to candle still smoking. "I reckon this ones going to go out first because it's got less air in it" Holding smallest gas jar.
B "Yeah less oxygen"
A "And that one will go out last" Pointing to largest.
C Lights candles.
B "Smell the candle"

Typically there is very limited and constrained spontaneous discussion regarding the prediction and the underpinning rationale. C does not even engage in verbally agreeing with A or B, she focuses on the pragmatics of candle lighting. However, her actions in progressing with the practical activity, could arguably be interpreted by regularly working partners as silent acquiescence.

After lowering the candles over the jars, the third trial of observed results differ again to the first and second trial. The peers enter into limited conceptual discussion regarding this:

B "We can say there's...the bigger one goes out first"
A "Yeah but...the first time we did it that one went out first, didn't it" *(Pointing to smallest gas jar)*
B "Yeah"
A "And then that one" *(Pointing to biggest)* "then that one" *(Pointing to middle)*
B "It's something to do with carbon dioxide and oxygen"
C "Yeah inside the, inside the, inside the"
A "..jar..."
B "Yeah"
B "Is that" *(Pointing to smallest)* "Because it's got less oxygen"
A *(picks up smallest jar to examine...she turns it around to examine from different angles)*
C "They are all the same candles aren't they? So"
B "That's got less oxygen" *(Pointing to smallest)* "So that means the candles going to burn more carbon dioxide....or something"
A *(puts smallest jar down and picks up medium jar)*
C "Yes" *(Picking up smallest gas jar)* "It's all steamed up inside hasn't it"
B "Yeah"
A & B *(pick up large jar together & examine)*
A "Yeah, that one in the middle hasn't got much on it" *(Puts down the large jar, picks up medium jar to examine)*

B "No"
A "That ones got loads" (Pointing to large) "That ones quite...hasn't it"
C (Puts down small jar) "Do you want to try one more time then"
B "Yeah if you like"
A "Yeah..."
(C+B light candles, A resets stop clock)

There is very little symmetrical contribution from each group member, and only B really 'connects' the observations with scientific concepts. A and B converse at a relatively descriptive level, not exposing what their ideas might be regarding the link between the composition of the air in the jars and its affect on the burning candle, and also in trying to explain why there might be differing levels of condensation on the inside of the jars. There appears to be no spontaneous entering into sharing their individual understandings to contribute to the group's thinking and negotiated explanation for the phenomena observed.

8.3.4 Sharing perspectives on the meaning of the 'evidence'

In a typical secondary science classroom of possibly 10 triads working-together, meaningful teacher-led verbal-intervention to ensure the development of intersubjectivity for each group at strategic points in a practical situation will be difficult. Pupils may *appear* to be working-together, but without *careful listening* and consideration of the *nature of the discussional exchanges*, to ensure *egalitarian exploratory talk* is occurring at particular stages in a problem-solving situation, teachers will be unsure whether intersubjectivity has been achieved. In group 1C, for example, pupil A thinks that the amount of air is important in influencing burning time, but pupil B thinks it is the amount of carbon dioxide produced through burning, but pupil C thinks it is about the amount of space in the jar, providing opportunity for gases to easily move around. When the data collected then shows that the large jar always supports a candle burning for the longest, and the smallest the shortest, because they haven't agreed their independent variables and it's values (size of jar: small, medium or large or amount of oxygen: some, more lots respectively) they each develop a unique explanation. These explanations are developed independently in the pupils' minds (Figure A4.5: 24). Without explicitly describing and sharing their ideas, they are not likely to realise that all three ideas could plausibly explain their results and thus be interrelated and be used in a much more sophisticated, and scientific way, to better explain the phenomena observed.

If pupils do not carry out a fair test (perhaps inadvertently) and one lowers a jar earlier than another, or doesn't flush the large jar, anomalous data can be collected (like group 1F and several others). 1F did not explicitly discuss their experimental strategy, pupil B suggested what they should do, A & C acquiesced through their actions (there was little verbal debate about possible tactics). As a result of the lack of explicit clarity regarding their method and the rationalisation regarding in what way and why, there was no shared thinking about what the evidence meant, which for them, then rendered the results more difficult to explain.

Pupils engaging in reviewing and evaluating their task resolution was very limited and uncommon. Once plausible answers had been offered, there was usually quiet acquiescence and often almost unspoken agreement that the task was completed. There was little debate about whether the best solution had been arrived at, whether the approach and tactics used could have been improved. There was little discourse that re-focussed on the initial task, to reflect both procedurally and conceptually on what had been achieved.

Group 1A, just silently wrote their own individual conclusions when they had completed the task, there was no sharing of conceptual outcomes at all, but their conclusions were each unique and would have contributed to intersubjectivity had they offered verbally their views for review and reflection. Another group 2F, just agree...'its true' they re-visit the original task, but implicitly assume their evidence supports and explains it. A third group are a little more collective in their thinking, they don't offer differing views, but as is often the case with regular working partners, they are swayed, and appear to agree with, the more dominant pupils view.

These vignettes are intended to highlight how teachers need to be attentive to the nature and extent of discussion between pupils that arises (or not!) through experimental work, to try and intervene and ensure the development of intersubjectivity at key moments when learning through peer-peer interactions could be maximised.

8.4 Discussion

Culturally there appears to be little or no spontaneous asking questions of each other, trying to establish what another means by their comment or statement. Because of this lack of open, explicit cognitive processing or convention to pluralistically discuss and consider each others' ideas when working together, there is little or no debate regarding possible and plausible solutions to propositions. Pupils generally appear to be reluctant to offer or are not aware that there may be several ways to approach a task and that consideration of alternatives is an appropriate activity to engage in. As Bricheno, Johnston and Sears (2000:146) point out, the 'factual' nature of scientific knowledge and the implication therefore, that there are 'correct' or wrong answers influences pupils' learning. Working alongside teachers in classrooms, it has become evident that pupils often perceive problems in this way, with only one possible solution. Pupil perceptions of only one possible solution to open-ended tasks should be challenged, so that they feel comfortable when co-workers make alternate propositions. Teachers' views should encompass this and recognise that the evaluative process engaged in, which develops intersubjectivity, is a crucial step to supporting cognitive development. Both pupils and teachers need to recognise where and when it is appropriate and useful to engage in this kind of inter-actional learning. The reflections of 'missed opportunities' suggests that the 5 steps revolving around the significant issues in problem solving described earlier are a form of scaffolding appropriate to exemplify (in professional development activities) to teachers the potential for productive discussion and scientific learning. Reflexively applying Clark's (1996:193) ideas, underpinned by Vygostsky's notion of language as an intellectual tool. He highlights how mind and social setting may be interrelated in transactions. He considers the role of language as a tool which he argues acts as an adjunct of the brain in task resolution 'a tool that alters the nature of the computational tasks involved in various kinds of problem solving'. To develop the reflectivity, in teachers, to understand the importance of intersubjectivity when pupils-work-together-on-tasks they need to engage in similiar (but not direct replicate) activities themselves. As it is they, the teachers who can then construct (double hermeutical) meaning about the social influences of others on their learning and recognise how pupils themselves will bring their unique experiences to their learning situations too.

Pedagogy and intersubjectivity

There appear to be many missed opportunities regarding significant issues in problem solving tasks, such that the common focus of attention may need emphasizing for pupils to develop a shared construction zone. Teachers' recognising and realising these potential opportunities to subsequently ensure pupils develop the process of intersubjectivity at these pivotal junctures is fundamental to cognitive development through social interaction. The development of a pedagogical approach that can successfully support open, unthreatening exchange between pupils requires teachers to become reflective practitioners able to discern whether intersubjectivity is occurring. The teachers also need to recognise how to encourage reluctant or hesitant pupils to share their cognitive resources.

To teach effectively, to support sharing juxtaposed perspectives, contingently (to support perspective taking) Ding and Flynn (2000:10) suggest the teacher has to be knowledgable regarding the lack of knowledge possessed by collaborators. As Wood (1998) describes to teach contingently, the tutor must reflect between his or her own knowledge and that of the tutee, and be able to plan from this reflection.

It appears then, that classroom culture needs developing to enable groups to become more collaborative through engagement in intersubjectivity to inform collective understandings, thus increasing opportunities for more autonomous learning (Murphy and Spence 1996).

To create a less threatening culture where pupils feel comfortable sharing their reasoning and logic teachers need to appreciate how important social interactions are in developing intersubjectivity. As Lave and Wenger (1996 : 145) would emphasise participation in learning, involves peers in developing understanding and meaning that should be "socially negotiated through the engagement of the thought and actions of persons-in-activity". It appears that there is little of this kind of spontaneous behaviour, possibly as a result of a lack of culture existing between pupils in the groups and schools studied here.

Hogan (1999) indicates from her work in analysing discourse and reasoning levels reached within groups, on consideration of the nature of matter, she raises issues about how (unfocussed) social interactions can impede cognitive advancement. She does not however, elaborate on the kinds of 'intervention' a teacher could constructively offer the working groups. Mercer (1999) claims that

> "given clear guidance from teachers, it seems that children are able to use group work activities to practice and develop independent strategies for learning and formulating knowledge"
>
> (Galton 1989; Bennett and Dunne 1992; Gipps 1994).

Thus implying that empowering teachers with particular pedagogic tools that support interactive group work influences cognitive development. Mercer et al (1999) report on case studies where learning and understanding is promoted through modelling effective use of social interaction and language in group work.

As a practitioner I reflected on my practice whilst in the classroom, often providing tasks, then leaving the pupils 'autonomously' to *hopefully* work collaboratively, circulating around the classroom, attending only when groups requested or obviously required practical support. My previous practice and the observations analysed in chapter 7, led me to consider, as Bruner (1986), how could the learning experience for the pupils be improved? Reflecting on development of one's impact on the learner's learning experience, Bruner (1986:129) talks about how distancing one's self from one's thoughts to reflect and gain better perspectives. He says this is about forming and knowing one's self. In this study, I reflected as Bruner suggests and contemplated the constraints of the interactive cognitist perspective. It appeared to me that it was limited, in that it considered only what had happened (in the form of talk and action) in the context of the tasks, and didn't consider the wider potential of social influences, and more importantly as a teacher-researcher how to support, engender and engage pupils into intersubjectivity regarding significant issues at pivotal junctures in the problem solving process.

It appeared that I needed to re-visit a more social emphasis on learning theory.

As Bruner says (1986:130) 'I am by long persuasion a constructivist', a philosophy which, to some extent I am still committed, i.e.: the child has to engage in some kind of activity (actional or dialogic) to construct or construe their meaning of the world. Bruner adds that 'transaction' of self and knowing requires reflection, (implying a reflecting agent) and metacognition requires a master routine that knows how and when to break away from straight processing to corrective processing procedures. I reflected on pedagogic practice modelled and analysed (in my thesis), indicative of teacher practice (in the Keele ITT consortium) i.e.: providing a potentially collaborative task for pupils to complete together that allows them to share ideas.

To enable teachers to recognise how to engage in supporting *effective learning interactions*, that address and clarify subjectivities to impact on cognitive development, requires reflexivity that recognises the constraints of current practice, but can envisage what kind of social and mental 'interactions' they wish to nurture in scientific enquiries.

Claxton (1999:191) describes this becoming reflective as 'the consciousness of good learning'. He goes on to say that :

> 'Being reflective means looking inward as well as out, making explicit to ourselves the meanings and implications that may be latent within our store of originally unreflective know-how.

In this sense he says....

> "In periods of reflection......ruminating on experiences .....to see what larger significance they may have. At the same time ...theories ....can be re-examined in the light of personal history."

So I reflected on others' and my previous personal practice to review how to support teachers becoming more informed practitioners. It appeared to me I was then engaging in applying a perspective echoing that of Habermas, action research as critical praxis. Grundy (1987:154) defines 'technical' action research as designed to render an existing situation more efficient and effective. In the sense that current pedagogical practices when supporting small groups of pupils in practical science, here are demonstrated to influence dialogic exchange and subsequent cognitive development. The view taken is that of informing and improving classroom practice. To further 'inform' classroom practice, the findings presented so far indicate that teacher intervention or some form of mediation is needed to support the 'focus of attention' for collaborating pupils on appropriate significant issues in problems solving. At various junctures in the problem solving process the (re) focus of attention should involve examination of strengths and weaknesses of multiple ideas considered from multiple perspectives (Murphy 1999:259) so that learning occurs as each group member's perspective is analysed, inferior ideas rejected and superior views proposed and accepted (Kruger 1993). Clarifying the task, recognising what matters in terms of the independent variable(s) and dependent variable(s), identifying how the solution might be reached, predicting anticipated outcomes, considering what the evidence means and finally reviewing and evaluating the task solution (including the interrelatedness of scientific method and data). Hitchcock and Hughes (1995) when they talk about reflective practitioners suggest that reflection is about looking again at a situation from a different perspective (ibid: 11). They suggest that this reflectivity is about, as Dewey (1933) would say, moving from 'routine action' to 'reflective action'. Schon (1983) would say it is about moving beyond 'habitual action' to consider other factors such as social, political and cultural influences. In this instance, I am attempting to highlight what are important issues for teachers to re-consider when supporting effective pupil collaborations, ie: a 'social' and scientific view of the pupils' learning interactions that embraces the notion of 'intersubjectivity' that is appropriate to strategically develop at pivotal junctures in problem solving activities.

Recognising the social nature and influence on learning interactions and realising how to enculturate them into normal classroom practice is my next challenge. As Mercer (1999) states, in reviewing his use of a teaching program to improve pupils' reasoning ability,

> "teachers very rarely offer their pupils explicit guidance on.....ways of using language for seeking, sharing and constructing knowledge".

Mercer also notes that where pupils are not clear about their tasks and lack shared understandings, talk is often confused, unfocussed and unproductive (Edwards and Mercer, 1987; Sheeran and Barnes, 1991; Barnes and Todd,

1995) he adds it may result in the interactional use of language being reduced and even 'squandered' (Galton and Williamson, 1992; Christie and Martin, 1997). Murphy (1997) points out that the 'situated nature of students' understandings and interpretations of tasks means that teachers need to consider students prior experiences as well as social, cultural and cognitive influences. Murphy (2000:140) suggests that when collaborating in learning situations, pupils 'situate themselves in relational activities with others' and that is recognised as significant in the 'interpretation of children's behaviours in social interactions.' 'Childrens actions are understood to be shaped and realised as they resolve the tensions between the influences of various and divergent social representations' (Ivinson and Murphy, 1999). Murphy (2000) goes on to explain that through the process of socialisation children develop different ways of responding to the world and making sense of it, these different patterns of socialisation then influence how they learn and what they learn. The behaviours associated with learning are potentially influenced by the notion of conformity amongst friends, a questioning culture of each other's ideas may damage social relationships and thus curtail challenging learning. It appears that less threatening cumulative talk (rather disputational or exploratory) is the most comfortable amongst friends, because it does not entail discord, criticism or critique of another's close social peers. To encourage peers to engage in a more Socratic, debative discourse, entailing justifications and reasoning, a more open, discursive culture needs to be developed without fear of retribution (that could damage self-esteem of the participants), so that plausible 'alternative' viewpoints are solicited from pupils. The less closed ethos embraces the notion that any propositions are acceptable and debatable if they can be clearly articulated and logically argued. Another social or historically-cultured factor that appears to influence eqalitarian discourse are asymmetrical groupings where one personality is (traditionally) more dominant than others and retains within the group more egocentric thinking, constraining participation and task engagement by others. The nature and expectations about learning in a school can influence these behavioural patterns of learning together. In school 4, for example, where examination success is good, there is, in science, a tradition of a knowledgeable didactic, instructional style teaching. Often practical opportunities are offered, the activities are tackled in similar sex friendship groups and pupils are *guided* to the teacher's perceived *correct* scientific outcomes. There is little or no thought as to how pupils process information and *arrive* at appropriate conclusions, but 'expert teachers provide quality information' (OFSTED, 2000) and 'thus achievement is high'.

In contrasting groups from each of the schools involved in the third stage of the study, it is clear that empathetic and relational perspectives of pupils engaged in collective meaning making has not been appropriated by the teachers. In fact many teachers typify the social expectations exemplified by staff in the schools studied. As Murphy (1999) indicates children's understandings of the values, rules and common representations of school, the routines and rituals of science classrooms will influence interactions with each other and their ability to negotiate and develop shared reference.

Typical interactions represented by the groups studied here indicate how common practice in classrooms informed by teachers' expectations in these kinds of learning situations have influenced interactional behaviour. If pupils are not actively encouraged to engage in learning together with the purpose of cognitive development in mind inter-actional behaviours will be constrained with a paucity of verbal exchange to question, clarify, debate, and decide on problem solutions. As Mercer (1995:98) summarises collaborative or exploratory talk focussed around sharing information, planning together, presenting ideas explicitly, engaging in joint reasoning, offering alternatives, requesting clarification is the kind of discourse practice pupils should be encouraged to engage in. Some pupils (chapter 6) recognised that teacher support was needed to successfully engage in interactions of this kind, one recognised they [the pupils] needed help to 'agree on ideas'...so that they 'can get on with each other and try feel the same way about the project', and thus to develop shared goals and outcomes, highlighting the lack of cultural collaboration. Another recognised that an integral aspect of pupils working more collaboratively in this way required them to behave toward each other in particular ways 'they have to be co-operative, listen and respect others view, help each other out, laugh with not at the person' obviously currently lacking in school. Another pupil recognising that mutual support and cognitive development can arise through social interaction said 'I think its better working in groups because I get more help'. It appeared that pupils themselves recognised they needed more mediational support from their teachers to achieve more effective learning together.

My findings (chapter 6) indicate that both pupils and teachers recognise they spend little time on 'planning' and 'reflection', but concentrate mostly on co-operatively 'doing' practical work. This practice belies the view that working in groups is purposely to 'share' ideas. The lack of conscious initial group investment in 'tackling' the tasks set by jointly clarifying and agreeing what the group hope to achieve, inherently leaves 'individual' pupils within the group working, possibly co-operatively together, but most definitely not developing intersubjectivity and collaboration. Without the establishment of joint responsibility for the ultimate learning outcomes, there is no overt recognition that each pupil has to actively participate and contribute both cognitively and socially to reach a solution to the problem set. Typically the teachers assume 'on task' behaviour and talk, with no mis-behaviour or argument indicating a group working well together. The teacher view of collaboration is apparently constrained to successful 'co-operative' working.

Insight into the limited cognitive benefits that develop as a result of co-operative peer-peer interactions should be extended to enlighten them of the value of a more 'social' view of learning collaboratively. If classrooms are seen as mini-cultures (Murphy, 2000:141) then peer-peer and pupil-teacher interactions should be considered more carefully because their '*perceptions of tasks and solutions and the consequences of these for negotiation with a collaborative learning situation*' are not obvious to the individuals concerned. Both pupils and teacher need to be more aware of the processes involved in successful collaboration and the principles that underpin effective learning in this way.

Charles Crook (2000:162) draws parallels between 'Ecology' the 'study of the interactions between organisms and their environment'; arguably the series of small communities of learners, working together, considered in this research project here, through their interactions with each other and that of the more expert teacher are 'mini-communities' of learners. If we think of interactions resulting in 'forms of productive joint engagement' (Crook; ibid) then in our mini-communities of learning we would wish to support 'collaboration', arguably resulting in more effective learning outcomes. Accepting this view requires a review of the way the 'learning environment' is orchestrated and enculturated, crucial to support effective mini 'learning cultures'.

Developing teachers' awareness of cognitive and social influences on learning

Teachers need to understand how social interactions; both through discourse and 'action', in different practical contexts, can influence cognitive development. They also need to appreciate that factors such as gender, conformity, and dominance can influence the character and extent of the discourse and action, and how these may be underpinned by the learning 'culture' of the school. They need to understand how important shared 'articulation' of thoughts are, to the development of collective knowledge and understanding. They need to appreciate and understand how non-threatening the classroom culture needs to be to enable informed shared decision-making in the problem-solving process in practical aspects of secondary science. Teachers need help in supporting this culture of 'explicitness' as (Mercer 1999:95) defines it, because it is something not normally required in 'everyday' discourse. Cognitive dialogic exchange requires proposals, ideas, opinions and explanations to be clearly described and justified, i.e.: utterances must be supported with reasoning. In this way alternate interpretations and understandings are made available for consideration within the group. Teachers need to understand these cognitive processes to be able, not only to 'scaffold' practical work, but also more effectively 'mediate' cognitive development. They need to extend and enhance pupils' expectations such that they recognise the value in reasoning and justifying ideas and in so doing begin to support cultural classroom change to one of much more open discussion, inter-thinking and shared meaning making.

Chapter nine

9.1 Changing current practice to support more effective learning interactions.

This chapter discusses suggestions about how to support teachers to encourage more effective collaborative learning in secondary science. This is stage five of my research project. In this chapter I will begin by reviewing the nature of the support teachers (in my study) appear to need. I will then describe the in-service provision at Keele, developed to offer appropriate support. I will then discuss the teachers' reflections of their changed practice through participation in in-service training. Finally I intend to examine (as a case study) the impact of changed teacher practice on pupils-working-together (through videoed observations) in school C which participated in an in-service programme July 1998 – July 2000. This school is also involved in Initial Teacher Training within the Keele partnership and was the setting for some of the initial pupils-working-together observations discussed in chapter 7 and 8 (groups with suffix 'C' indicates the groups from that school). This aspect of the study took a case study approach, typical of a more socio-cultural perspective of both learning and research, and involving observing 12 triads from two Y7 classes of the same teacher from school C (who had been trained and noted her changed pedagogy) carrying out the same tasks, three years later. The post-teacher-intervention observations of pupils-in-action were analysed in a qualitative way to illuminate how the nature of interactions were influenced to improve cognitive development and scientific learning. School C was involved as a result of their departmental interest and curiosity in science, regarding the effects of training on their practice in the classroom. Observing pupils-in-action attempting similar tasks, post-teacher-training, was a measure of the impact of in-service on happenings in the classroom. As Joyce and Showers (1995) have illustrated effective in-service for teachers is that which improves pupils' performance in the classroom. My intention was to examine whether there was any evidence of the impact of developing teachers' appreciation of the importance of intersubjectivity and whether or not it had manifest itself in pedagogic practice. I explored teachers' perceptions of their changed pedagogy and examined after intervention pupils-in-action to discern the effectiveness of the training.

Chapter 8 examined the constrained nature of intersubjectivity when pupils-working-together on open scientific investigations were observed. The cognitive gains (reviewed in Appendix 7 and 10) when other collaborating peers were offered scaffolded support appears to be significant, because there was guidance about what was important to consider or focus upon. Rogoff, Newman, Griffin and Cole and Murphy recognise that it is a lack of 'focus' on appropriate issues that limits pupils' social engagement on open tasks and thus impairs cognitive development. Thus, besides enabling teachers to recognise how to guide peers' 'foci' on relevant issues in problem solving situations, they also need to develop a supportive environment in which pupils are encouraged to offer their cognitive resources for collective consideration. Culturally teachers need to understand how to cultivate a more open, dialectic, classroom community to nurture intersubjectivity and collaborative working-together in small groups.

My intention was to model for teachers, by enacting a cognitively-sensitive pedagogic approach, using a variety of tactics to mediate learning through social interactions, so that they could 'experience' [like pupils] learning-together. In reflective discourse and collective reflections I hoped to objectify and make explicit the cognitive purpose of social exchanges underpinning intersubjectivity. As Cobb, Boufi, McClain and Whitenack (1997) explain I was attempting to engage the teachers in actions or processes which were then transformed into conceptual (scientific and cognitive) objectives. Through collective reflection of their active participation, my intention was to involve them in the 'communal activity of making what was previously done in action an object of reflection' (Cobb, Boufi, McClain and Whitenack 1997:258). The explicit reflections of the modelled experience were intended to provide the opportunity for the teachers to empathise, as learners, with their pupils' learning situations. As a teacher-researcher myself, when first considering how to teach 'Thinking Science' lessons, I recognised that to make legitimate knowledge claims, having 'lived' and 'experienced' my 'material in some fashion' (Collins 1990:232) I found myself in a position that was 'empowering and illuminating' because I could 'reflect on' and 'speak about my experience' in ways not available to some-one 'outside' the experience. Thus through modelling pedagogic practices, within particular contexts, I hope to enlighten and empower teachers in *understanding* the learning processes engaged in by their pupils (issues about which pupils, rather than their teachers, appeared to more readily relate to as 'participators-on-action' in their reflections of working-together; Chapter 6).

I reflected that didactically instructing them [teachers] about how to mediate effectively only provides 'abstract', de-contextualised guidance regarding classroom practice.

INSET programme philosophy

At Kings College London, Adey, Shayer and Yates (1989) developed a two year training programme for science teachers. This programme was based around teachers constructing for themselves, through reflections on their personal thinking, how pupils might reason and logically solve problems. The essential methods to develop pupils cognitively, Adey (1998) describes as challenge, reflection, construction and bridging. He emphasises how the programme is centred around placing the 'pupil in the position where she has to construct herself – slowly and often painfully – the type of thinking needed to tackle all sorts of scientific problems and investigations' (Adey, 1998:71). He also describes how *the child* is reflectively encouraged to 'unpack her own thinking', and consider additional contexts where ratio; proportionality; correlation (Piaget's schemata, chapter 3, section 3.3) would be useful. Adey et al (2001) suggest that pupils should work together in groups of five or six and that teachers should become adept at classroom management skills to maximise opportunities for pupils to work and talk as 'peer coaches'. In teaching 'Thinking Science' activities to local children, in local schools, my 'experience' enabled me to conceive how to more effectively interact with the pupils to support their working-together collaboratively (and thus more inclusively). I provided clear 'enactments' of my experiences during in-service training sessions. In a professional capacity I have now developed this philosophy and applied it to teaching technology, physical education and other general thinking programmes. Thus within the two year in-service tutoring the

'Thinking Science' programme becomes the 'arena' within which pedagogic practice supporting pupils' cognitive development is 'enacted' (Lave, 1988; 179). The professional development activities have been developed through experience and are designed to be appropriate 'settings' in which to 'enact' the development of intersubjectivity in a scientific context (e.g.: Appendix 9.2), they provide the opportunities for the teachers to become 'persons acting'. Their 'active participation' and direct involvement in authentic activities such as those referenced in Appendix 9 are key to teachers understanding how to develop intersubjectivity in their classrooms.

The in-service programme structure

To become an effective teacher, who effectively supports cognitive development through collaboration, requires significant professional development in the form of a two year INSET programme, which runs parallel to the implementation of the 'Thinking Science' programme. The pattern of the Keele in-service Training (INSET) programme is detailed in McGregor and Gunter 2001.

In two years there are 6 INSET days (one per term), and 6 school visits which could consist of additional in-service sessions for the whole science department or school, lesson observations, coaching sessions and pedagogic feedback.

Review of INSET requirements

A report published by the Department of Trade and Industry (2000) analysing the professional development views and needs of science teachers identified high priorities to be subject knowledge, pedagogy, pupil learning and classroom management. Teachers also wanted more opportunities to share good practice, in their own and different schools. They wished for high quality INSET that emphasised more practical activity rather than pure theory and provided classroom focussed support and advice from top class tutors/mentors. They indicated they would appreciate the opportunity to try out new teaching strategies, approaches, styles, methods and materials in their classes. They valued extended courses where there was time for reflective learning with colleagues from other schools. All these elements are embraced within the Keele INSET programme.

In-service tasks and the development of intersubjectivity

The following discussion concerns an exemplar activity (Appendix 9.2 and 9.3) that has been developed to make explicit through social interaction and engagement (how to attend to intersubjectivity and recognise the) various socio-cultural influences that shape cognitive development; and highlight how the process of intersubjectivity underpins development of shared understandings. In reflection the activities would also be contrasted with Vygotskian and Piagetian accounts of learning, including the issue of intersubjectivity.

As Roth (1995, 1999), Cobb (1994, 1997) and others describe, learning activities need to be authentic, that is to make sense and have meaning for the learners (in this case the Science teachers). With authenticity, context, uniqueness and unpredictability very much in mind, I attempted to create original learning experiences (mimicking pupils' learning opportunities) for science teachers. However, in working with a colleague, Barry Gunter, true collaboration developed that modified and refined the various INSET approaches and activities I had already worked on. The exemplar activity (Appendix 9.2 and 9.3) and various other carefully constructed activities (McGregor and Gunter 2006) have been developed to present information (and evidence) that could be interpreted in a variety of ways. The intention was to offer opportunities for widely differing propositions and explanations to be developed by teachers in non-threatening situations. Engaged on task teachers are encouraged to analyse their juxtaposed perspectives and reach a group 'consensus'. As Mercer (1995:104) illustrates this approach appears to absorb participants in exploratory talk, rejecting inferior ideas, proposing and negotiating superior views. Through conflict (of a social and evidential nature) and the open sharing of ideas; Mercer's ground rules were applied, that required views of all participants to be considered, proposals to be explicitly stated and evaluated. These rules appear to develop explicit agreement which precedes decision-making and action. Teachers' collective reflections on how they discussed, negotiated meaning and developed understanding through their active engagement in-task, provided 'real' experience to empathise with pupils. It is through after-participation-reflection of the appropriation of personal understandings that they come to realise the importance of social interactions in the learning process. My intention to remove teachers from their usual 'expert' role and re-situate them as 'novices' in collaborative learning situations, allows them through 'learning in practice' (Wenger 1998: 95) to recognise how to sustain 'mutual engagement' of participants in pursuing an enterprise. My hope was that from this active participation they begin to appreciate the value and socio-historical nature of contributions that pupils themselves can bring to a learning situation. Thus, given *opportunities* they [the pupils] can develop intersubjectivity, applying their everyday and regular life experiences, to illuminate their scientific understandings. Developing teachers' appreciation that *their* role of enculturating this kind of autonomous, mutually beneficial way of learning together is applicable and appropriate in science teaching (particularly Sc 1 investigations) is significant.

Pedagogic strategies and development of socio-cultural perspectives

To develop teachers' awareness of social and cultural influences on intersubjectivity and consequent cognitive development asymmetrical peer-peer grouping is overtly modelled. Triads of teachers (recognised as 'usual' practice; chapter 5), but arguably influential for groups working towards a common consensus, from differing schools are organised to work-together. This ensures that the contrasting asymmetrical 'experience' of participating staff serves as 'experience' for reflection on social and cultural influences. This experience provides conceptual 'evidence' for collective reflections on rationale for 'grouping' and organising pupils-working-together in particular ways for cognitive purposes. A pedagogic issue not clearly addressed in the National Curriculum (see chapter 2; section 2.6).

Pedagogic strategies, overtly modelled to support teachers' developing understandings regarding intersubjectivity are those that support: clarification of the tasks; collective consideration of solutions to tasks and proposition of likely outcomes (prediction); consideration of learner [pupil] responses encouraged through different types (and frequency) of interventional questioning; consideration of conflict through evidence that provides dissonance with likely pre-conceptions; exaggeration of socio-conflict (through description of others' alternate views); deliberate teacher mis-interpretation of descriptions, explanations or propositions; the need to reach a 'consensus' agreement through the process of dialogic reasoned argumentation and negotiation participated in by all members of the group; intra-group post task evaluative reflection of conceptual and procedural processes; influential contributions by participants in the group to the final collective solution.

9.2 Modelling pedagogic approaches to develop intersubjectivity

In the process of (long-term) engagement (over two years) I anticipated that teachers' understandings and knowledgable skills regarding pedagogy and learners' cognitive capabilities develop from, as newcomers, legitimate peripheral participation to that of fully engaged practitioners (Lave and Wenger 1991:94).

The in-service 'experience' begins with an interactive activity designed to raise awareness of learners' cognitive diversity (described in Appendix 9; McGregor and Gunter 2006). The F's activity (as described by McGregor 2007: 282) developed from Carter's 1998 book 'Mapping the Mind', is enacted by me to engage the teachers personally, at an individual level and then to collectively reflect on its meaning and purpose. This attention grasping activity, stimulating teachers to cognitively reflect upon their experience (as well as those of other participants) and the implications for learning in their classroom creates an engaging, open, discursive ethos. This nature of this ethos is maintained throughout the in-service programme, reflected by the numerous opportunities for teachers to pause, share their experience and then relate it to the learners' situation.

Another interactive in-service activity

The apparatus is presented on a table (for all to see) and participants' attention is drawn to the three different sized beakers and three similar sized candles (like the candle race activity, used with the pupils in chapter 7).

The teachers are already introduced to effective ways of working as a group, including the concept of intersubjectivity (Appendix 9). Presented with the three different sized jars and three candles teachers are asked to consider 'What could be investigated?', thus providing the opportunity to define the independent and dependent variable(s) and clarify their focus of attention. In their groups they are then asked to predict what they think will happen (in the above setting). Qualified teachers offer a range of predictions including 'all will extinguish at the same time'; 'the candle in the largest jar will extinguish first, the candle in the smallest jar last' and 'smallest jar flame first, largest jar flame last'. The groups then have to justify and explain their predictions. Their ensuing discussion attempts to reach a consensus. All propositions are collectively noted.

The practical activity is then carried out, all candles are lit (simultaneously) and the differing sized jars lowered simultaneously. A timer can be used to measure burning times until all the flames extinguish or the order of flame extinction noted. Usually the candle in the smallest jar extinguishes first, and that in the largest jar last. Each group reviews their propositions in the light of the evidence and is asked to proffer an explanation of the happenings. The second part of the activity is illustrated, below, in Figure 9.1 :

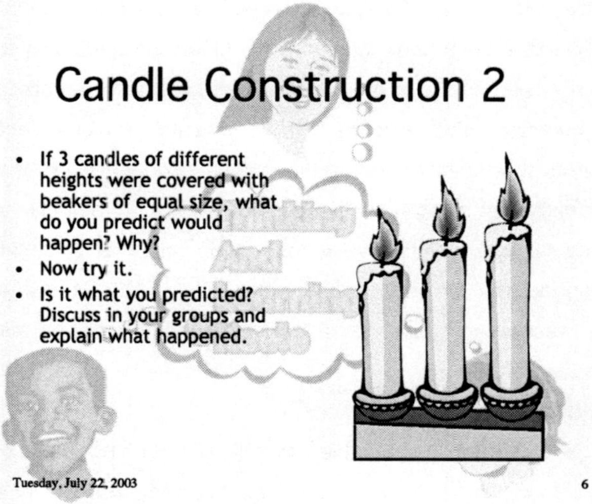

Figure 9.1 : An extract from a subsequent slide in the power point presentation used to develop teachers' appreciation of intersubjectivity.

This time the groups are asked to reach a consensus regarding the three different sized candles in the similar sized jars. Qualified teachers suggest a similar range of predictions as before, 'all extinguish at the same time', 'the smallest candle flame will extinguish first'; 'the largest candle flame will become extinct first'. Because very few science teachers have carried out this practical, they are not likely to 'know' the correct answer. They have to apply their experience (as a teacher and scientist) to develop a prediction. In this unique learning situation juxtaposed perspectives become more explicit and rationalisation of propositions more debatable. It is possible for teachers to develop quite complex justifications of proposals: movements of more or less dense gases, influenced by developing convection currents within the jars that will result in tallest candle, closer to top of jar burning longest or, more simply, the smaller the volume of the jar the less oxygen available for combustion, which is influenced by the size of the candle, so the bigger the candle the less oxygen proportionally in the jar, so the quicker the flame extinquishes. There have been various other suggestions proffered too, the point is, however, that in situations where teachers don't 'know' the correct answer (in common with our pupils much of the time) they are more likely to engage in developing intersubjectivity to collaboratively construct plausible solutions. Discussion regarding controlling all appropriate variables, leads teachers to realise that some, like temperature, can not be controlled, and thus the results are less reliable. Given a constant cool temperature, and a consistently burning candle that is half the height of the beaker it is possible to regularly ensure that the middle sized candle burns for the longest time. This evidential 'conflict' engages the teachers even longer in developing intersubjectivity, for many more, increasingly complex explanations begin to evolve between co-partners.

This is one of several models of enactment developed to demonstrate to the teachers what to do to engage pupils, and why socially exchanging predictions and explanations to develop an agreed group consensus or shared task outcome supports cognitive development.

The enactment of pedagogy that explicitly supports the development of exploratory talk or inter-thinking is not just confined to the professional development activities, the lessons in 'Thinking Science' are also deliberately modified to 'open-up' scientifically justified plausibilities. In the very first

Thinking Science lesson, I enacted how to create opportunities for intersubjectivity to develop. I purposely explain how the pupils should be clear about the differing expectations for learning when they are collaborating in small groups to develop their cognitive capability. Below is an extract from a powerpoint presentation I have used with pupils when demonstrating to teachers how pupils need support in understanding how to work more effectively together to support cognitive development.

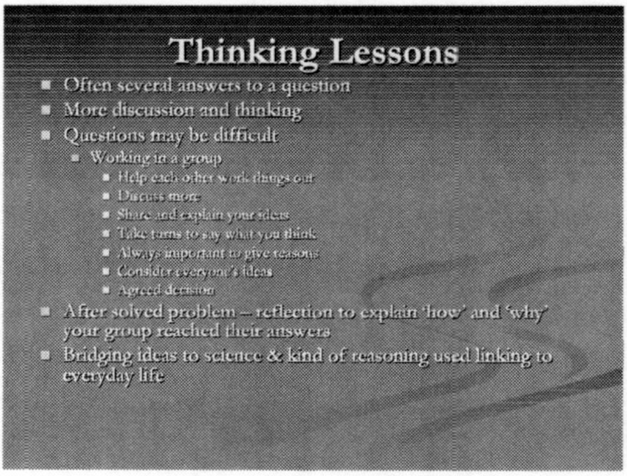

Figure 9.2 : Extract from powerpoint presentation used to raise pupils' awareness of different expectations in thinking lessons.

Where there were any possible alternative views of data, observations or other phenomena I encouraged the teachers to participate in thinking like pupils. All plausible suggestions are described (on flipchart for public scrutiny) and associated reasoning annotated. Progression through activities is thus supported by overt written and verbal articulation of cognitive processing. Collective reflections of the outcome and processes of a mental nature manifest as 'conceptual objects' (Cobb, Boufi, McClain and Whitenack, 1997). The development of this collaboratively mediated approach to teaching Thinking Science developed as a result of my supporting a 'novice' teacher educator (Barry Gunter) to also engage in 'thinking' professional development activities. We collaboratively refined activities through sharing our subjectivities (regarding scientific interpretations of tasks and scientific phenomena), as Lave and Wenger (1991: 29) describe, he was a legitimate peripheral participant when he first arrived at Keele, as a classroom teacher embarking upon involvement in professional development. He participated in many in-service sessions with me, engaging in discussions that drew attention to the social and cognitive processes resulting in others' appropriating (scientific) meaning. He has now mastered full participation in learning situations associated with supporting cognitive development and recognises the socio-cultural relationships between activities, identities, artefacts and communities of knowledge and practice (ibid). He recognises that the nature of learning tasks, that their openness and authenticity are significant; that participating (pupils or teachers) in learning situations bring to collaborations their own personal life experiences (scholastic or not), influencing the subjective interpretations they make; that 'objects' can also influence the success or not of the educative process, and that the perception of collaborators sharing cognitive resources through explicit talk (and action) can result in effective learning (ibid). Through engagement in enactments with me as a collaborator we have advanced the (previously successful) in-service training (initiated at King's College, London) to influence teachers' understandings about learners (illustrated to be lacking in chapter 5).

The sample of teachers involved

The teachers involved in this (third part of the study) were an elective, voluntary sample, they were engaged in the 2 year Thinking Science professional development programme, run at Keele University. The first cohort of teachers engaged in the in-service were reported on in 2001 (McGregor and Gunter 2001a). Each school enrolled on the course, usually sent two representatives from their science department, often the Key Stage 3 co-ordinator or Head of science and another Year 7 or 8 Science teacher. Although a similar in-service approach has been developed for other phases and other subjects, i.e.; secondary Technology teachers, primary Science teachers, secondary Physical Education teachers, and secondary Science technicians (McGregor and Gunter 2001b); the sample reported on here are 6 cohorts of science teachers. Each of the teachers attending the final INSET day (of the two year programme) were asked to complete the reflective questionnaire (Appendix 9.1). Of the 162 questionnaires distributed, 97 were returned (Appendix 4.7a-f). The sample of teachers responding included five from Stoke-on-Trent schools, that are also involved in the Keele ITT programme and a mix of staff predominantly from Cheshire, Staffordshire, Shropshire and Nottinghamshire, with a few from further afield (Derbyshire, Yorkshire, Lancashire, Leicestershire, and Manchester). Teachers were asked to complete their questionnaires 'in-situ' at lunchtime to minimise (postal and temporal) costs for the teachers and Keele and to attempt to maximise the response rate. Non-responses were usually those teachers not able to attend the final training day, those that took the questionnaire with them (explaining they would return it at a later time) and those that had to leave promptly at the end of the day (due to pressure of parents evenings, staff meetings etc). I extended the range of teachers involved in this stage of the project (compared to the initial ITT sample described in Chapter 5), to explore whether particular pedagogic changes were affected to a wider range of teachers, in a generalisable way and not subject to localised influences. To try and assess the extent of some of the anticipated reflective changes, I developed closed questions with optional responses (e.g.; Appendix 9.1) so that I could measure pedagogical developments in a semi-quantitative way (Cohen, Manion and Morrison 2000:248). I recognised that these kinds of questions may not explore all changes and be exhaustive, Oppenheim (1992:115), so I also included open questions intended to provide the opportunity for teachers to describe other pedagogic changes not anticipated.

The reflections I sought from the teachers were centred around how they had recognised, through their changed pedagogic 'actions', they had affected pupils' cognitive development.

The nature of the pedagogic reflections

The teachers were asked about *their* perceptions of *their* changes in practice. I was concerned with how they 'enacted' CASE in their classrooms, to develop *their* pupils' cognitive abilities. I was particularly interested in whether they thought more carefully about grouping the pupils to develop intersubjectivity; how their questioning (frequency and type) may have changed to encourage pupils to share and explain their thinking; whether or not they encouraged the pupils to engage more intra-psychologically with the scientific evidence by asking them to predict what they thought could happen; by guiding them [the pupils] to reflect more often on the meaning and derivation of evidence; and by generally encouraging discussion to contrast subjectivities within groups.

9.3 Reported impact on practice

This section of chapter 9 builds on the reported pedagogic changes of an initial cohort of teachers, already described by McGregor and Gunter (2001b). The reported responses of the 97 teachers, in this project, indicate that in-service provision has impacted on their practice in a variety of ways. After INSET a much larger proportion more regularly organised their pupils into purposeful working groups in science.

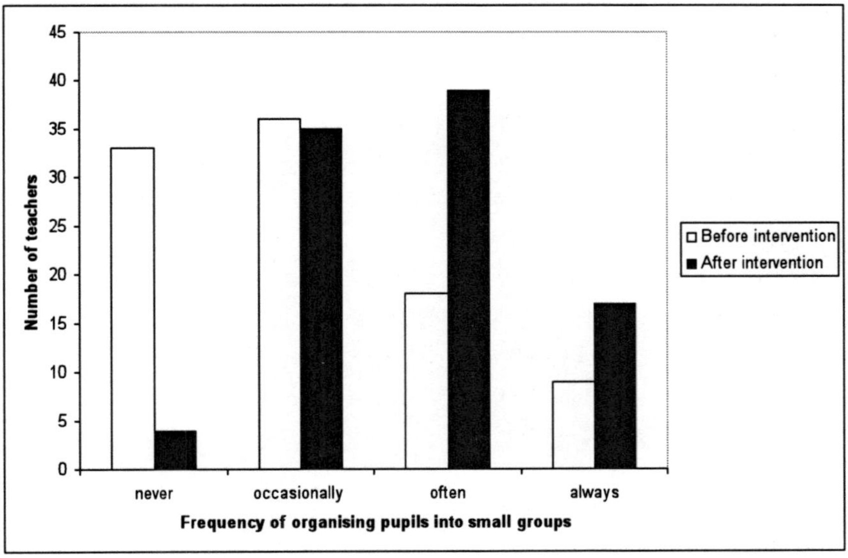

Figure 9.3 : Extent of change in teachers organising pupils to work in small groups (n = 96).

Before training nearly 75% of the teachers never or occasionally 'grouped' their pupils to work together. It appeared that modelling the influence of persons-working-together with varied socio-historical experience enriching the intersubjective discourse impacted on teachers 'actions'.

In professional discussion with them, they frequently mentioned they now considered a raft of issues when placing pupils in particular groups to work together. They realised dialogue was likely to be richer if pupils changed working partners regularly; they anticipated boys made quite different contributions to girls in discussions as a result of varied life histories; they recognised that mixing abilities could augment zpd development as a result of the complementary increase in discursive exchange of ideas and reasoning. Teachers also appeared to cultivate their questioning approaches (see Figure 9.4; 9.5; 9.6 below).

They generally asked more questions, regardless of type, indicating that they perceived this was an applicable and useful strategy to engage pupils cognitively. The proportion of open[26] questions asked more regularly was markedly increased, complemented, it appeared by a significant decrease in the ratio of closed[27] questions.

[26] Open questions defined as those that could have a variety of responses. Usually more than one right or appropriate answer to the question. Potentially there could be a range of responses that comprise the right answer.

[27] Closed questions are those that have only one 'correct' answer. Pupils often answering these have a 50% chance of opting for the right response.

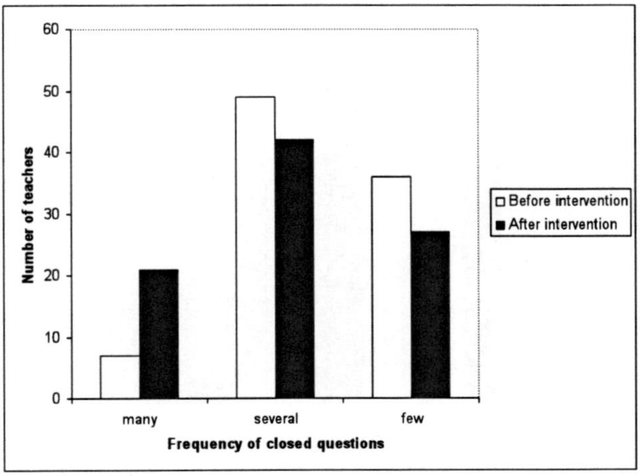

Figure 9.4 : Change in frequency of closed questions (n = 94).

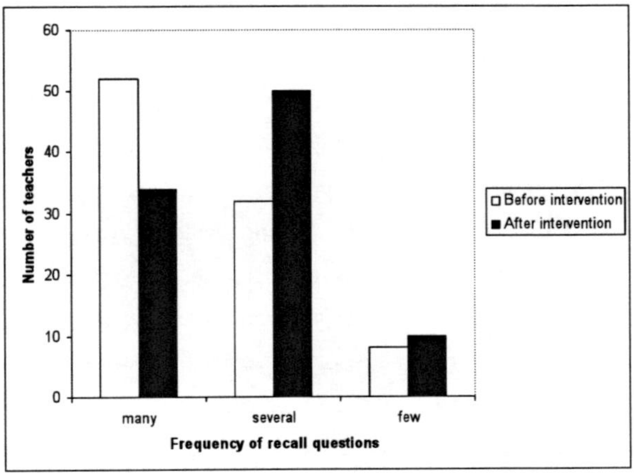

Figure 9.5 : Change in frequency of recall questions (n = 94).

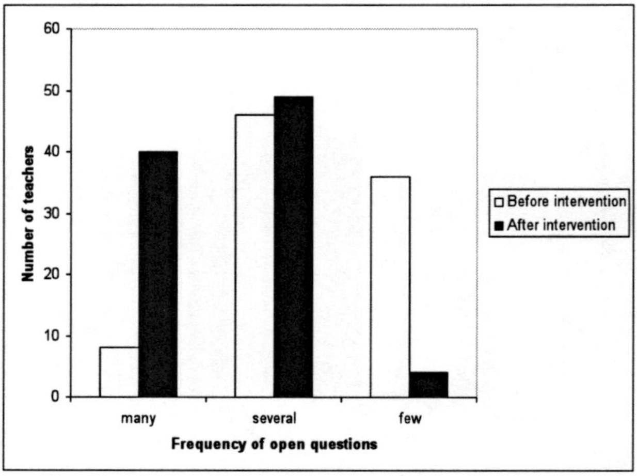

Figure 9.6 : Change in frequency of open questions (n = 94).

The teachers appeared to shift from asking closed questions to asking more open questions. During in-service sessions they often commented that they had begun ask 'what do you think?' and 'why' (an open form of questioning) more often to elicit from pupils their reasoning behind their answers to questions. The strategy of asking more open questions (and collecting a range of possible replies or answers before giving any negative or positive responses) is a technique that encourages the pupils to develop intersubjectivity. Although there was no opportunity on the questionnaire to explain why they decreased the proportion of closed questions asked, previous interviewees (McGregor and Gunter 2001b) suggested 'closed' questions constrained the thinking, because the response may only require a selection from limited possibilities, often only one 'right' answer. More than half the teachers (57%) reported some *other change(s)* in their questioning too.

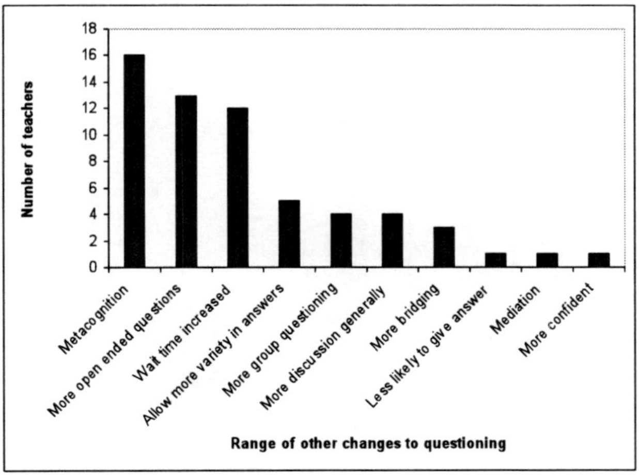

Figure 9.7 : Additional changes to questioning techniques and strategies (n = 60).

These notable shifts in changing questioning type and techniques were accompanied by 29% stating that they asked pupils to reflect or metacognate more on their answers and that they allowed more 'wait-time' (Tobin, 1984) to allow pupils the opportunity to elaborate (and discuss) their responses (Dillon, 1988) before expecting a reply. A technique it seems to support the development of reflective habits of mind (Zessoules and Gardner 1991). Another strategy for developing intersubjectivity is to support more opportunities for pupils to openly share their current understandings, by predicting what should or could happen next. Teachers appeared to change the frequency with which they did this significantly.

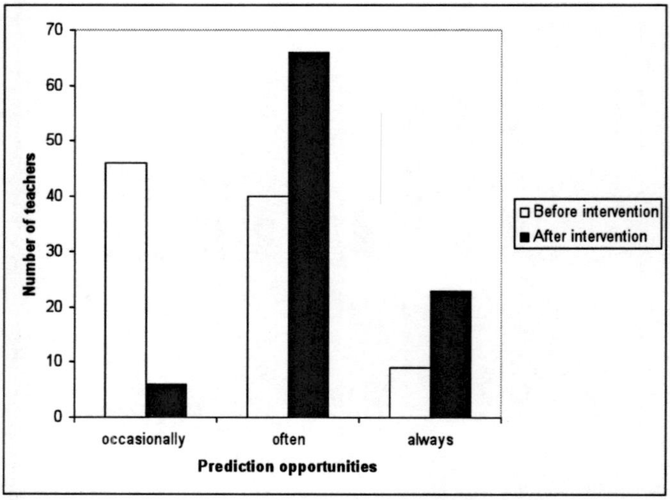

Figure 9.8 : Illustration of the increase in frequency of opportunities created for pupils to predict (n = 95).

The most overt change in practice, of over 60% of the teachers, was to encourage the pupils to regularly predict (and reason what might happen next) in experimental situations. After in-service intervention a fifth enculturated this way of working (asking pupils for propositions) all the time. Teachers appeared to utilise less straightforward opportunities to encourage pupils to predict too. In professional discussions they would say that where they knew particular practicals were unlikely to produce reliable results they would utilise the opportunity to collect a range of predictions from pupils knowing that 'unexpected' evidence may materialise which would engage pupils further into intersubjective discussion. Anomalous results or contradictory evidence also became a more prominent focus for discussion (Figure 9.11), offering lots of opportunities for subjective prepsectives to be described, considered, compared, justified and reasoned.

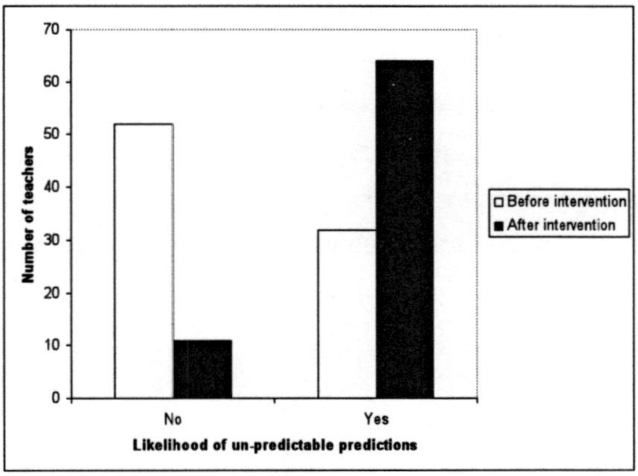

Figure 9.9 : The change in teachers developing straightforward prediction opportunities (n = 85).

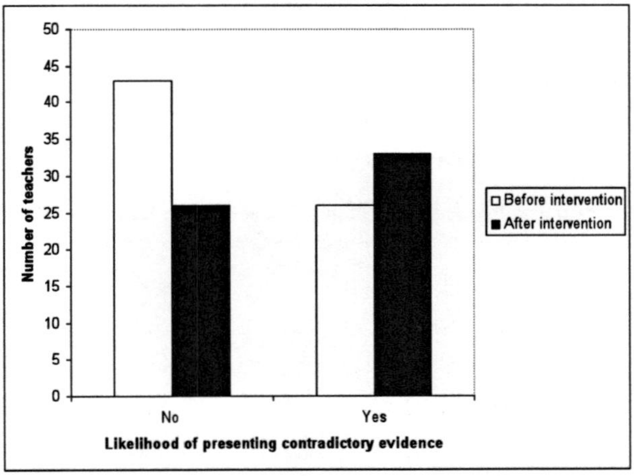

Figure 9.10 : Change in teachers likely to present contradictory evidence to pupils for consideration (n = 69).

There appears to be significant evidence of teachers using a range of pedagogic strategies to develop intersubjectivity.

A further finding was that teachers provided more opportunities and potential for pupils to contemplate and exchange their ideas than before (see Figure 9.11 and 9.12 below).

In their reflections the teachers reported that they were more pro-actively encouraging pupils to discuss their ideas and were also requiring them to justify their solutions too. It appeared that more than half the teachers notably increased the frequency with which they asked pupils for explanations. The increase in propositions being justified was not only related to the teacher but also increasingly discussed between peers by more than 60% of the teachers.

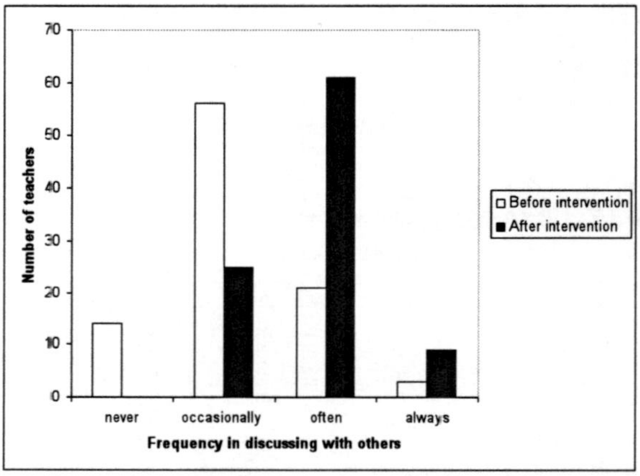

Figure 9.11 : Change in occurrence of pupils discussing ideas with others (n = 93).

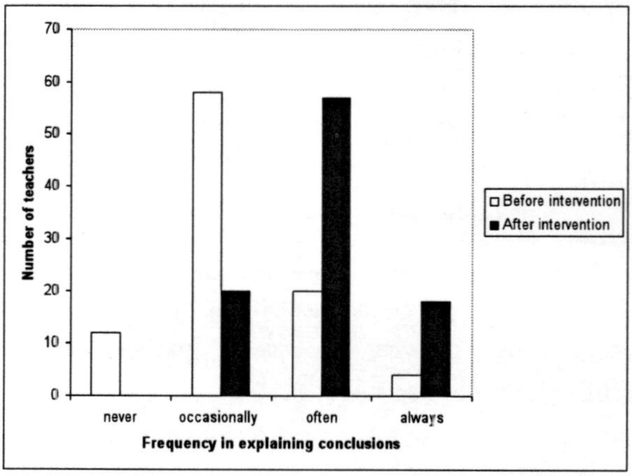

Figure 9.12 : Change in teachers asking pupils to explain their conclusions (n = 94).

Teachers much more readily ask their pupils to justify or explain their findings. With more than two thirds of the staff questioned always or often expecting pupils to clarify or elucidate on evidence. The interventional in-service appears to address the lack of discussion evidenced in chapter 5, focussed around planning, consideration of the meaning of evidence and attempting to explain findings scientifically. These were points of focus previously ignored by teachers that are now recognised and collaboratively considered in the schools included in this study.

Another notable change was that of increased opportunities for pupils to relate their conclusions to new situations.

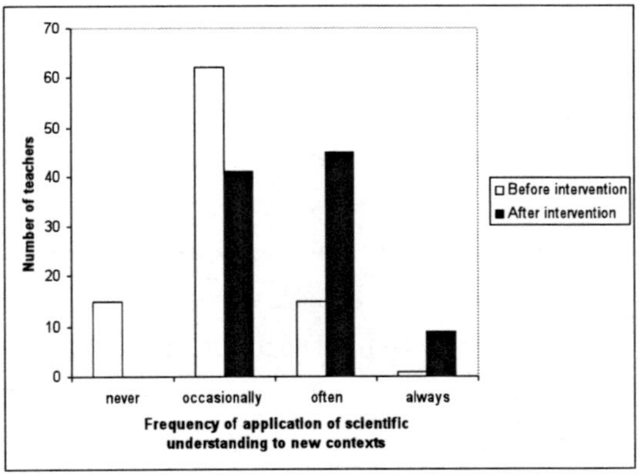

Figure 9.13 : Regularity with which teachers ask pupils to apply their scientific understandings to new contexts (n = 93).

It appears that they recognised these were effective strategies to engage and stimulate pupils cognitively and conceptually to develop and apply scientific understanding.

The range and frequency of the application of the pedagogic strategies described above, indicates teachers are supporting more effective social interactions to develop intersubjectivity in a more collaborative way than pre-in-service training. There appears to be a dramatic shift in teachers' practice in classrooms, presumably underpinned by their change of views and understandings about how to develop pupils' cognitive development and subsequent learning.

I reflected on the subjectivity of the teachers' views of their personal change in praxis over time, likely to underestimate actual change because of the long-term, continual and subtle nature of the changes involved, and their only being able to make relative judgements.

I decided therefore to triangulate, to view the changes from a more objective perspective (Denscombe 1998:84) to assess the pedagogic influence in a more comprehensive way. I reflected that observations of pupils-in-action from a school trained and involved in professional development at Keele could illustrate how the pedagogic developments impacted on pupils' learning. The second series of observations of pupils-in-action involved school C (Chapter 4: Section 4.6.1) because they had volunteered interest, were engaged in Keele ITT partnership work and had attended the two year CASE in-service programme at Keele. School C is a reasonable school academically and does not notably utilise groupwork strategies in an experimental context (Chapter 6).

Assessing the impact of in-service on pupils' learning in science

Evidence of the development of a cultural change in the classroom was investigated using Y7 triads from School C. The groups were randomly chosen (typical ability within the class, but usual working partners). I collected data from 12 groups (36 pupils from a possible 60). Four groups were to attempt the highly scaffolded candle task, another four the semi-scaffolded candle task and a final four the open candle task (as described in chapter 7). I hoped to compare the nature of the interactions and cognitive outcomes, to assess whether intersubjectivity was being developed more readily at significant junctures, than the group interactions suggested in chapter 7 (that were reflected upon in chapter 8) to improve cognitive gains. I am reporting on nine of the groups studied, due to technical issues that curtailed quality recordings of transcribable conversations. The triads were videoed in a naturalistic way, in a science laboratory, adjacent to their usual classroom, without teacher intervention. In common with my analysis in chapter 7, I analysed the scientific outcomes alongside the nature of the interactions to examine whether the development of intersubjectivity and levels of collaboration had improved post in-service training.

Scientific outcomes and task structure

To compare the quality of cognitive outcomes between groups I used the same criteria for analysis as in chapter 7 (Table 7.1; Appendix 7.5, 7.6, 7.7; Appendix 9) to enable direct comparison of pre and post intervention effects. The findings suggest improvements in the performance on open tasks. The groups concerned illustrated a wider range of tactical approaches to the ways in which they attempted to solve the problems compared with those observed before teachers were trained to develop cognitive capability. They also gathered more reliable data by collecting more extensive evidence. Group 3C carried out numerous trials and measured the affects of reducing jar size (air/oxygen volume) on two dependent variables not just one, their results table indicates they have recognised a more complex relationship between connected variables than other pupils (Appendix 9). 3C also develop a unique 'paired' or comparative method, where they burnt two candles simultaneously to see which remained alight the longest. Another group 5C repeated their trials on several occasions. Each of the groups attempting open tasks appear to gather more reliable, verifiable data than previously. These are outcomes I had anticipated would be evident in classrooms pre-in-service. However, final task solutions appear to be lacking, without intervention or mediation in some way to focus their attention on developing meaning of and explanation for their results they do not explicitly link their evidence to well argued, plausible scientific, explanations.

The semi-structured tasks appear to maintain supporting the development of a range of methods to solve the problem (including consideration of 'start' and 'end' points for measuring the dependant variable, burning time). The aspect of problem solving the semi-scaffolded groups appear to develop (beyond the extent of the previous groups) is the use of data analysis to describe the patterns or trends existing between the dependent and independent variables, they develop presentations of their results in graphical formats, as well as considering calculating outcome averages. An example of this came from group 6C who represented the relationship between "seconds the candles is lit" and "size of the jar" in the form of a bar chart (even though line of best would be more appropriate), demonstrating their understanding of the connection between the related variables. All three girls were operating at level 5 (in National Curriculum terms). Their resultant task outcome (ie: their strategy) included not only which factors to control (candle lighting, jar lowering), how to measure the changing dependent variable and record it in tabulated form, but also recognised that they should repeat their data collection (totally spontaneously without teacher intervention) and use a graph to enable interpretation of the evidence, which indicated they can clearly demonstrate, present and describe the nature of the relationship between burning time and size of jar. Group 7C showed clearly how they averaged the data from three trials to show how burning time changed with jar size. These boys were operating at level 4/5 (National Curriculum) too, but collectively they appeared to be functioning at a more secure level 5, because they were making judgements about the number of times to measure length of burning, they recorded observations systematically, they offered a simple explanation that could explain the data pattern. Group 9C's strategy showed they thought a number of steps further, controlling more variables and calculating averages of their trials before plotting graphs. Group 8C consider how many times to repeat the experiment, they discussed the pattern and variation of the data, the relative accuracy of their results and then they considered how to illustrate their conclusions graphically. They attempt a line of best fit to show variation in their data. Their discussions about the procedure indicate they are operating at level 7, but their discussion touches on aspects of level 8 attainment (when they discuss whether line, bar chart or tally is the best method to display their results). They also indicate how they have internalised the more discursive cultural approach, when towards the end of the task they are discussing their conclusions:

B "No, no, no, ...that's just our results from the actual test, the actual conclusion is that the more air there is in the ......"
A (interprupts) "Yes, but what results are we going to from 10? "
C "No"
A "we have come to ....",
B "No .. we've shown our three experiments, we haven't got to write ...let them form a decision about them..."
A "Yes,"
B "That's all we actually had to do for the experiment to find out the conclusion. Not the actual results."

C "No, **we have to give our own decision** about them"

The highly scaffolded tasks appeared to continue to constrain intersubjectivity centred around method, description, presentation and meaning of the results or evidence (Appendix 9).

The cultural shift appears to impact significantly on the quality of task outcome (Appendix 9) in open and semi-scaffolded situations. The open task groups improved their methods, extended the range of approaches and developed rigour within their strategies. The semi-scaffolded groups extended their resolutions to include the use of graphical interpretations to explore the meaning of the data. They also gave more consideration to methods and the development of more comprehensive ways to collect data than hitherto, and there was more in-depth discussion of the meaning of the evidence. It appeared to me that through their collective pooling of analytical skills they were improving the quality of both their investigational strategy and their learning about the phenomena investigated.

9.4 The impact of in-service training on the relationship between the nature of the talk and task outcome.

I have assumed here that the outcomes of pupils' learning is a measure of the impact of the teacher intervention. The transcripts of the groups (analysed post-in-service impact) indicated there was an increase in dialogic exchange (which appeared to be 'richer' in its cognitive nature) between pupils. Peer-peer questioning appeared to be more evident, as well as more explicit reasoning (predicting, justifying, explaining) and more in-depth consideration of the science involved. It appeared that the pupils had begun to collaborate more effectively because the teaching staff had re-focussed their pedagogic approach to encourage pupils to 'debate' and make decisions as a 'group', thereby providing opportunities for pupil to compare individual contributions and justify what was important to solve problems. This resulted in higher quality science investigations and solutions.

For example, the following extract (from group 10C) illustrates how discussion between pupils develops to clarify understanding of the task. This appeared to be spontaneous even though the task was highly scaffolded:

A "What to do?"
C "Go on"
A *Pulls task sheet closer.*
A "Right (reads from sheet) with a bunsen burner, remember you have wear goggles. It means you have to use these? ' *Points to spills in jar.*
C "Erm, hang on a min, bunsen burner, you have to wear...., number 2, set out in each of the candles with a jar close by and light with a spill. What's a spill?" *Examines gas jars and jar of spills.* "Is this a spill?" *Picks up spill from container and replaces it.* "So we have to put one by each jar, do they have to go in order?"
C "So, put this on there, they look about..." *Rearranges candles.*
A "Right, yes, start the clock"
C "Oh I think we're supposed to do this" *Places jars over candles to demonstrate.*
A "We're supposed to light them first"
A, B and **C** *all reach for a spill.*
B "Do you want me to...? "

In this extract (group 10C) the beginnings of a cultural change is evident. They seek clarification through questioning dialogical exchange, each seeking for agreement with the others before embarking on the practical. C also makes explicit her ideas through action, by placing the jars over the candles. In the following extract A then confirms exactly what they need to do next:

A "That's it, that's it, right, start the clock and at the same time place jars over each candle as in the diagram above, right"
C Places medium jar over centre candle, large jar over right candle, small jar over left candle
A "Start??" Starts timer

More subsequent situations are evident where they seek confirmation from each other:

B "Take that back, shall I do this one?" (Picks up smaller jar)
A Resets timer. "Right, ... right are you ready, put it down"

And then later A says:

A "Then are you going to do the last jar now?"
C "Yes"
A "It's what, the size of the jar isn't it, because of the air?"
C "Yes, because more air's in the bigger jar"

The dialogic exchange is much more open, and there appears to be more thinking out-loud. Their conversation continues to include another illustration of this kind of exposed cognitive processing when C continues to discuss their presumptions:

A "Yes"

C "..longer, well that's what we're presuming"
A "Yes, that's what we're going ...., yes, because this will probably be longer won't it?"
C "Yes" Tries to blow out spill.
A "That's it, it's blowing"

C and A have clarified how they think the size of jar and amount (volume) of air will affect burning time.

They continue to make obvious the way they connect the observations they have made previously and the consequence on burning time of the candle:

C "Ready, steady, go"
A *Starts timer.*
C *Places large jar over candle.*
A "It gradually gets higher doesn't it and then it suddenly drops because the air goes"
C "Yes, ready, it's going down now and...it's gone"
A *Stops timer.* "That's 11 seconds"
C "So that's only 1 second difference"
A *Begins to write.*
C *Blows out candle.*
A "Right, we've got to do it again now"

Another example of pupils' increased willingness to share ideas (through speech and action) and to begin to clarify what should be done at the beginning of a task is taken from group 3C:

They read the task sheet aloud together.
A reads some parts solo...."is this true?"
B "Yes...'
C Mutters inaudibly
B *Lifts large jar and puts it down.*
A "You can use ...." *Reaches for goggles to put them on.*
B & C *also put goggles on.*
C *Pulls task sheet to her. Moves candles and then lines them up.*
B "I think you have to put the jar over it" *Attempts to put the candle in the jar, but places it back down on the table.*
They all pause as teacher checks they have equipment.
C *puts a candle up-side down into a jar.*
B "I think ...." *Points to each candle.*
C "Yes, but could put that there...." *Places candle up-side down again into a jar. She then lights the candle, with B's help, and places it into the top of the jar.*
A *Takes goggles off.*
B *Picks another candle up and lights it.*
A "Let me have a look at that" *She copies C, picks up a third candle and lights it and places it in the top of another jar.*
B & C *study the candles.*
The candles extinquish.
B *"go out.."*
C "Should ... do it again shouldn't we?"
B "Shall we do it together?"

A "You need to time it" *Picks up timer.* "You light yours and put it on when I say go."

When the girls (group 10C) are discussing the results after three trials, they make their reasoning very explicit:

C "Put that one on there" Puts large jar at left, small jar in middle and medium jar on right.
B "So are they, is this the first one, is that the third one"
A "No, it's going to be the same though isn't it, because the bigger the jar, the smaller the jar, but all the candles are the same size. It's the amount of air in the jar"
C "Yes, but if you swap them round...?"
B "Yes, but it's like the bigger the jar the longer the light..."
C "The longer the light lasts"
A "Yes because there's more air in it"
B "And then the smaller the jar..."
C "The less air in it, so the less the, so the less of the thing isn't it, the flame?"
C "Yes, so shall we just, we've got to try again anyway"
A "We've got to try it again"
C "Because it might last longer now because we've left these jars standing longer, more air in it"

Later on there is evidence of more collaborative behaviour when through asking questions of each other they are seeking agreement, their decision making process is becoming more explicit:

A "Are we ready"
C "Go" (A Starts timer) "Now that's lasting longer see and now it's dying down, ready and stop" (A stops timer, C takes off jar)
A "9 seconds"
C "Oh no it's lit again"
B "Put it back on"
A "No, because you took the lid off"
C "Do I have to blow it out?"
A "Do you want to do it again?"
B "Shall we do it again? ....leave it there, are you ready?"

During the activity there are many offers of support, again illustrating a more collaborative nature to their interactions:

C to B "Do you want me to do it?"
C lights spill, then A, then B
C "One at a time, mine won't light"
C lights candle

Several seconds later.... (because A and B are still struggling to light their candles):

C to A "Come here, do you want me to help you?"
A and C take out spills
C to A "That's it, ... A"
B blows out spill
C "Do you want me to help you B?"
C lights B's candle
B "I'll put that there on the table" Puts down spill "Look at mine".

Several minutes later C struggles to light her candle:

C Lights spill and tries to light closest candle (right) then puts spill out. "It's burning my fingers" Lights another spill.
B "Come here..."
C "It's not working"
B "Let me show you how to do it"
C "Should be lighting ???"
B "Come here...."
C "No, I can do it, it's just that"
B "Hold it to the side like that, ...yes, ...it's done, ...no it's not"
C "It won't light"
B "Careful of your tie"

It appears then that the 'cultural shift' for pupils to more openly discuss and verbalise thinking, and to support each other to clarify practical procedures is more evident (than examples discussed in chapter 7). Even in highly scaffolded tasks (where there are arguably less potential opportunities for effective social interactions to develop intersubjectivity) pupils appear to more readily share their ideas.

The groups involved in the semi-scaffolded tasks illustrated even more examples of spontaneously engaging in appropriate constructive collaborative discussions.

Group 8C are beginning to be explicit in describing what they are intending to do. Unlike, many groups before intervention (chapter 7) who launched into handling and manipulating apparatus without careful planning and fore-thought. This is the initial part of their discussion:

B "light these three candles and place one on each one and a jar on each one and see which one lasts the longest which is probably the .."
C (interrupts) "yes, so we're going to draw..."
B (interrupts) "...so we need like um..."
A "I'll light these" Indicating the spills.
B "Do you want to?"
C "This is what you do, A, put that down. I'll light one, you light one."

The pupils are more inclusive in the way that they invite each other to participate, B provides an initial overview of a possible procedure, checks with A that she does want to light the spills. C then offers guidance about how to do the lighting and considers how they should then share the task.

Throughout the investigation (as with other groups after intervention) there is generally more open discussion, whereby peers are invited to offer suggestions.

In-task discussion and participation is also more evident from a variety of groups including the all male 5C, who were tackling an open task:

B	*places the small jar over the lit candle.*
C	*reaches across the table to pick up some paper)*
B	"Stop. Now."
A	"Three seconds."
B	"Three seconds, right."
A	"The small jar ???? in three seconds. The small jar has gone ......"
B	*lifts the small jar up but replaces it back down on the table)* "........We haven't got time, we've got ...."
A	".....C, just write down small jar three seconds."
C	*writes down on paper.*
B	*Lifts the medium jar up* "........jar."
A	*Mutters and presses the timer as **B** places the medium jar over the lit candle)*
B	"This is going to last because there's more oxygen in there." *Observes the medium jar and waits until the lit candle goes out.* "Now."
A	*stops the timer.* "Eleven seconds."
B	"Eleven seconds."
C	*takes instructions from **B** and writes on the paper in front of him.*
A	"Medium jar."
C	"Medium jar." ***A** picks up the large jar and places it over the lit candle then lifts it up again.*
B	*Mutters.*
A	*Stops the timer and takes the medium jar away from the candle whilst **B** replaces the large jar over the lit candle.*
A	*Presses the timer.* "Looks as though its' going to take ages." *Watches intently the large jar.*
B	"No, it won't, no.."
A	*Mutters.*
B	"Now, now."
A	*presses the timer.*
C	*touches the large jar.* "No, don't it's still going." *Speaking to **A*** "Oh, ...now."
A	*Stops the timer again.*
A	"It's gone." *Points to the paper which **C** is writing on.* "So that's seventeen"
B	".... large jar ..seventeen." *Dictates to **C** who in turn writes on the piece of paper in front of him.*
A	"No, but that's .... different candles." *(takes the large jar away from the candle)*

Within the discussion, both B and A postulated how long they thought candles in different jars would burn, indicating they had developed some level of pattern recognition at least of the relationship between the volume of the jar and time for burning. B also offers an explanation as to why this might be so. A also recognises the issue of using different candles which B & C had hitherto not mentioned. Although the dialogue does not consider fair testing here – there is an implication that it is a concern. The boys continue to engage in a similar, more explicit kind of discussion for the second and third trial.

A further group 8C have carried out the practical work, and discussed the task related questions they should have considered.

A	"Anyway lets have a look at what we've got to do."
C	"Design…"
A	(interrupts) "How can you make sure your tests are fair?"
B	"Well we did it three times …..make sure"
C	"How will you present your results?"
B	" Put them in a …"
C	(interrupts) "In a big table.."
A	"its says how many times do you need repeat it?"
B	"We did it three times"
C	"Yes, and we got two the same so.."
B	"And one was only one mark off, so.."
A	"Shall we do one more…'cos it says just think about how many times you need do it. That's all you need to do…."

C and B agree here that the data they collected was sufficiently similiar to obviate the need to repeat and collect more. B supports C by adding that one reading (for each of the three trials) only was different to the others. B and C have therefore justified their ideas. A suggests they perhaps should do another trial, but doesn't explain why.

They do however, later re-consider the reasoning behind the number of trials (and not just the similarity or validity of the data) they begin to consider the reliability of the data, and one member of the group even suggests that they should consider the probability of the outcomes (and therefore their relative reliability):

C	"Put it back in the tub, otherwise it'll look a mess."
A	"Right shall we do it one more time, or shall we just leave it as the conclusion."
B	"Umm"
C	"I think we should do it one more time"
A	"..'cos it says how many times if you need to be reliable"
B	"three or more "
A	"so you need it like four or five"
B	"well we've got fairly similar results on all …of ….all ….and, but if you think about that, it can't be a coincidence that we got it wrong three times when we

each had a go at recording... erm ....actually doing the experiment and writing" (meaning that because each had taken a turn in each role therefore results consistent)

A "But if you think about it miss said out of a hundred times you need to do it at least 25 times..... it's a quarter....remember when we were talking about that other man (in a previous lesson) so if you..."

B "But that was like probability, this is how often you expect to get the same thing each time"

C "Right! ....so"

B "So, so far we've got a 100%. " Writing.

C "Yes, so write it on the piece of paper now"

They discuss at length also how to present their data before making decisions (although discussions are not highly symmetrical):

B "And do you want to underline and that.."

A "No, ta I'm fine, how are we going to .... though..getting a graph we're going to have do three different colours aren't we?"

B "Yes, why can't we find an average of the results, they are all the same, 10, 3, 7 pretty much. You see like that's only two off. "

C moves to other side of B to see results she has written.

A "Thirteen though, that's three off, and that's one off. That's one down"

C "Here you are use a pencil and a ruler"

A "I think umm Harriet wasn't it yours? That thingy..."

B "Wasn't as accurate, cos all the others are OK."

A "Both of the others are exactly the same."

B "So we'll say 10, 7, 3 'cos that's pretty much what we got...because I mean 7 & 8 and 2 & 3"

A "just write it just experimenting 2,3 and then write conclusion."

B "And then for the thingy, the graph we'll do it just with the 10, 7 & 3 yea?"

A "I'll draw the graph, now while we're waiting 'cos I've got a good idea, can I borrow a ruler?"

C "Why don't you do a line graph?"

A "That's what I'm doing with all three a different colour" Pulls piece of paper closer to her.

B still writing.

Although the single sex male groups don't discursively exchange so often and quite so explicitly as the girls there is still evidence that indicates that the boys in a group are more actively involved in the decision making processes, they appear to offer more explicit reasoning and explain their ideas more often as a result of the teachers changed pedagogy.

9.5 Discussion of effects of teacher mediation

There appears to be some emerging evidence that teachers are able to change their practice in an informed way to influence the culture and thus nature of peer-peer interactions. It seems that with appropriate INSET they can recognise and put into practice pedagogic strategies that can engender more spontaneous discourse, that addresses the issue of intersubjectivity, and although variable in nature, it can impact significantly on the level of cognitive engagement in-activity and the resultant collective task outcomes. This cultural shift appears to support development of scientific understanding, of both investigational strategies and the science of the phenomena being investigated.

It appears that although teachers 'action' supporting peers engaging on task and sharing perspectives, it is not clear why they do this. Tudge and Rogoff (1989) identify this central characteristic of effective interaction to establish intersubjectivity, being supported either because the teachers create learning situations which incorporate cognitive conflict (Piagetian) and/or joint problem solving (following Vygotsky). The reasoning or beliefs that the teachers hold, that inform and determine their practices are not clear. It is possible that the teachers appreciate and enact elements of both these theories.

The extended and enhanced nature of the peer-peer social interactions, influenced by changed teacher practice, appear to suggest that through developing intersubjectivity more often, (at appropriate junctures offering multiple perspectives) joint task understanding, inherent decision making and group construction of meaning are all improved through augmented communication (via both action and speech) and become more collaborative. Thus as Murphy (2000:140) would describe, what the teachers are succeeding in supporting here are the pupils beginning to be engaged in generating and evaluating and modifying solutions or outcomes through a multi-dimensional[28] 'seesaw' of interconnected dialogue and action. Thus through the teachers 'seeing children as thinkers' and promoting the 'development of intersubjective exchange' that Bruner (1996:56) describes,

[28] Multi-dimensional meaning not on one plane, the toing and froing of discussion maybe asymmetrical interweaved by threads of explicit thinking on the procedural, conceptual and social interactions required to co-operatively solve a problem.

the teachers are successfully supporting effective interactive learning in groups, that enhances cognitive development.

> "concerned with understanding what the child thinks and how she arrives at what she believes. Children ....are seen as constructing a model of the world to aid them in construing their experience. Pedagogy is to help the child understand better, more powerfully, less one-sidely. Understanding is fostered through discussion and collaboration, with the child encouraged to express her own views better to achieve some meeting with others who may have other views."

He goes on to explain how

> "Such a pedagogy of mutuality presumes that all human minds are capable of holding beliefs and ideas which, through discussion and interaction, can be moved toward some shared frame of reference. Both child and adult have points of view, and each is encouraged to recognise the other's, though they may not agree. They must come to recognise that differing views may be based on recognizable reasons and that these reasons provide the basis for adjudicating rival beliefs. Sometimes you are 'wrong', sometimes others are – that depends on how well reasoned the views are. Sometimes opposing are both right – or both wrong. The child is not merely ignorant or an empty vessel, but somebody able to reason, to make sense, both on her own and through discourse with others. The child.....is capable of thinking about her own thinking, and of correcting her ideas and notions through reflection – by 'going meta', as it is sometimes called."

Chapter ten

10.1 Initial reflections

I began this thesis in a very straightforward manner eliciting teachers' perspectives on their pedagogy to inform how they actively supported effective group work in practical secondary school science. The results of surveying sixty nine teachers (from 38 schools) led me to recognise they paid scant attention to the types of learning interactions that arose, between pupils in their classrooms, as a result of either their organisational practices, structured activities or verbal interventions. The findings highlighted (in chapter 5) how little they valued either peer interactions in the development of understanding or the vital role of language in cognitive development.

To explore corroboration between learners' and teachers' perspectives I surveyed 652 high school pupils (from 5 schools). The most successful school, academically, appeared to support significant working together (91% of the time). The other less academic schools supported group work much less frequently. The pupils indicated that they usually worked with friends, in triads, when carrying out practical work. It became apparent that they did not normally *plan* or *reflect* with-others when engaged in practical activities. It appeared that teachers, undervaluing the impact of peer-peer discussion, did not organise classes for pupils to regularly share and develop ideas together. Most opportunities for discussion appeared to centre around examination papers or test questions. Pupils described many more benefits of working-together than the teachers, including valuing each other's contrasting views and learning with different people. Almost half of them recognised they learnt from others and perceived that collectively they worked more enthusiastically and efficiently. Asked about difficulties encountered when working-together 70% of the pupils highlighted decision-making. My intention was then to observe small groups of pupils working together to solve problems and consider how they could be better supported to become more autonomous, effective decision-makers, mutually engaged in deeper deliberations over the processes and outcomes of task resolution. In questioning six hundred and ninety six pupils (from 5 schools) and observing, in-detail the interactions, of thirty six pupils (from 5 differing schools) it became clear to me that there was no culture of explicit verbal exchange, discussing their subjective ideas. As Mercer (1999) suggests teachers rarely offer pupils explicit guidance on such matters of the nature and purpose of discourse in the classroom. Rather as Galton and Williamson (1992) and Christie and Martin (1997) would claim opportunities for quality discourse are squandered. Reflectively, I then considered how teachers could be helped to understand the importance of talk and its probable influence to improve peer-peer learning. Applying Mercer's view of talk (1995) was informative (in an interactional-cognitist sense), but it did not address **why** pupils tended to speak mostly at a 'cumulative' level rather than in an 'exploratory' way. I re-focussed taking a more Vygotskian stance to social interaction (which included the notion of socio-conflict) provoking cognitive development, and thus defined in my mind (rather vaguely at that moment) that talking, discussing, sharing ideas and developing 'inter-thinking' was a good use of group work. Further reflection and concluding reading of Roth's work influenced the social nature of my study. Consequently I developed my approach to, and design of professional development activities for teachers so that they could come to understand (in an experiential way) what was happening in a child's mind as they were being directed to solve problems in small groups with peers.

My aim was to develop an empathetic awareness of the learner's situation by guiding teachers through reflection on their personal experiences. Through our discursive reflections of their engagement in interactive activities I attempted to elucidate how the characteristics of particular pedagogic practices can influence cognitive development. I was able to illustrate theory-in-practice or as Bleakley (1999) describes it practice-as-theory, not only generally, (i.e.: social construction, to co-construct understanding that would not have been possible with partners working as individuals) but also to recognise how to generalise regarding the impact of effective teaching strategies (e.g.: questioning approaches; timing of intervention; task structure; expert/novice working partnerships; context and content of activity). This realisation empowered the teachers to share with pupils why discussion is central to intersubjectivity, that then underpins collaboration to co-construct group resolutions. My thesis finally triangulates teachers' perceptions (after in-service, through 97 reflective questionnaires) with observational evidence of the development of reflexivity in pupils (from re-focussed analysis of [36] pupils [in school C]) and the teacher-researcher, me (through the process of this study).

10.2 Critical reflection on some methodological aspects of the work undertaken

10.1.1 Choice of schools and groups involved in the case studies

Lack of funding to support this project, often resulted in data being collected from conveniently located schools. Situated nearer the University occasionally meant teachers and their pupils were conveniently sampled (Blaxter, Hughes and Tight, 2001:163), being involved in ITT and CASE training resulted in purposive sampling (ibid). Recognising that claims from studies of this nature are thus limited and localised. Systematic sampling of schools nationally and the groups within would ensure no bias. This would provide data of a more quantitative nature to enable reporting on *typical* group work practices nationally.

10.2.2 Sampling teacher and pupil perspectives

The initial teacher questionnaire (Annex 4: Figure A4.1) constrained the extent to which I could *interpre*t teachers' actions. Within the interpretative paradigm, seeking to understand why 'persons act' in the ways they do, my questions in the survey elicited *what* teachers *do* in a variety of learning situations. They were also asked about their views of pupils working together and what they perceived benefits and constraints to be. I omitted to seek *why* they engaged in particular practices, e.g.: not placing pupils in particular working groups; supporting very little discussion when planning investigations; minimal collective discourse and reflecting on meaning of evidence from multiple perspectives; not ensuring *all* pupils explained their propositions.

10.2.3 Naturalistic observations

Ideally I would have preferred to video the pupils-in-action 'in-situ' amongst class mates with the teacher. However, in a naturalistic situation (adjacent classroom, no teacher intervention, just myself as non-participant observer) it could be argued that the groups working apart from the rest of the class are to some extent 'artificial' observations of reality. However, each group offered an indication of the maximal learning that could take place in a mini-learning-community of this kind. The aspiration of autonomous, focussed, creative, thoughtful collaborators immersing themselves in scientific discourse, analysing problems, developing a range of potential solutions, even identifying sub tasks, to make decisions about which is best and why, perhaps even prioritise a series of ideas; were illustrated by the groups of pupils taught by the teachers involved in my in-service courses (chapter 9). These more advanced, complex, spontaneous (compared to earlier findings in chapter 7) cognitive processes engaged in, through social exchanges, are the kind educators and teachers should realise are the kinds of outcomes we desire of independent productive learning interactions.

10.3 My contribution to knowledge

10.3.1 The different perspectives of teachers' and pupils' views

The study of teacher's perspectives of pupils learning together provides corroboration with other studies that indicate teachers organise pupils working together as a result of concerns regarding practical constraints rather than primarily focussing and orchestrating for maximal educational benefits. The juxtaposed perspectives of pupils as learners reflecting on their personal experiences, in classrooms, can make more informative suggestions about the help they need, than teachers who focus on resourcing and behavioural issues. As Fullan (2001: 153) reports a minority of high school students (25%) think teachers understand their point of view. My evidence also suggests that teachers under estimate the benefits of peer-peer interactional learning and therefore do not appreciate why many pupils are motivated when working with others. This constrained view of learning appears to limit teachers' pedagogic repertoire. My thesis addresses this issue and suggests how teachers can be supported to overcome this. My final analysis also suggests that the in-service support I offer at Keele (in collaboration with others) affects teachers practice to improve the ways pupils work together.

10.3.2 Lessons learnt from the effects of scaffolded tasks on the quality of learning interactions

Some scaffolded support appears to extend and enhance task discussion. The discussion centring around tactical strategies and methods to gather evidence is better developed than highly scaffolded or open tasks. The approaches the pupils develop are more imaginative, more carefully considered, valid and reliable than those attempting tasks of a very prescriptive nature or with no help at all. Before teachers were trained to support pupils working more effectively together, the *open* tasks were not completed as well as anticipated, the discussion of possible and plausible solutions was limited. After teachers had *experienced* effective collaboration and problem-solving themselves (through my in-service training approach) they supported group learning much more effectively. Their pupils improved the ways in which they solved the open, Sc 1 type investigations, with higher quality learning outcomes. They devised a wider range of tactical approaches, developed more rigorous methods, than previously, to gather their evidence and thought more carefully about the meaning of their data. Collective pooling of their cognitive resources became more commonplace, and consequently improved both the quality of their investigational strategy and their learning about the phenomena investigated.

Highly prescriptive practical work (frequently used in science education) does little to develop pupils cognitive capability.

10.1.3 Importance of different kinds of talk in a science investigational context

My analysis of pupils' talk (in chapter 7) provided evidence that few groups were engaging in exploratory discourse, that is, critically but constructively, reviewing each others' ideas and clarifying what each intended before the teachers were trained. After teachers' involvement in my training approach the pupils engaged in 'exploratory' talk more regularly. This resulted in more challenges to others' ideas which had to be explained and justified. Alternative propositions were more frequently offered for the others to critically evaluate it. The pupils began to talk about investigations at a much deeper level than hitherto. Other kinds of talk, e.g.: 'cumulative' or 'disputational' which do not involve critical justifications and rationalisation (only tacit agreements or disagreements or undisputed directives), so subjective ideas are not exposed in the same way for collective consideration. Thus scientific investigations requiring consideration of appropriate methods to explore the problem posed are better resolved through mental (and verbal) exchanges of the kind entered into by 'exploring' each other's scientific reasoning. Applying the 'ground rules' Mercer (1995:104) suggests, that is to reach a group 'consensus', appears to support the development of exploratory talk.

Ogborne, Kress, Martins and McGillicuddy (1996) describe the nature of 'explanatory' talk in a limited way that offers pupils opportunities to share their views, through a variety of narratives, but does not engage the children in comparing and contrasting others' suggestions to subsequently clarify and justify the 'best' ideas or explanations. The absence of this limits the extent to which pupils develop their understanding of scientific concepts.

Teachers supporting exploratory talk can augment their pupils cognitive development and also enhance their performance in Sc 1 investigations. This is because there appears to be a link between the nature of talk and the cognitive processes required to solve a problem, if pupils are guided to focus on appropriate issues.

10.3.4 Impact of changed talk and understanding of intersubjectivity informing effective in-service

Modelling for teachers how important *talk* is in developing thinking; demonstrating how they have differing interpretations of the same scientific phenomena (see in-service activities described in chapter 9), dependant upon their expertise and life experience, and then engaging them in 'exploratory' talk which enables them to recognise how the nature of discussion can affect cognitive engagement, appears to affect their practice. They experience that 'revealing' juxtaposed subjectivities in scientific contexts is piquing. Exploration of the derivation of differing views through see-sawing discussion in small groups stimulates consideration of a wider range of factors influencing a situation. Providing practical activities that offer vexing evidence (e.g.:

second stage of candle activity described in chapter 9) further engages the teachers in discourse to propose several alternative explanations. Collective reflection enables the teachers to recognise that it is the development of 'intersubjectivity' that is *key* (not reaching a consensus, which is a *technique* to reveal subjectivities and begin the process of intersubjectivity) in engaging learners to critically and discerningly consider scientific explanations, and in so doing 'extend' their cognitive commitment to the problem, thereby expanding their zpd. Modelling how to extend teachers thinking and reflection through questioning and discussion elucidates how the type of intra-verbal exchange influences inter-mental activity. It appears that teachers supporting more, open talk of an exploratory nature can affect pupils' subsequent performance in open-ended tasks.

10.3.5 Summary of components of effective INSET provision that can impact on practice

i. The problem solving approach in science to engage and motivate.

A common argument for problem solving is that good problems are motivational and that intriguing or relevant problems will pique the interests of students and engage them (Hiebert et al, 1999). The problems presented to teachers are designed to be unique in a reliable but vexing (through unexpected data patterns; unpredictable happenings) way.

The problematising of science provides an opportunity for teachers to 'recognise the inventiveness of their own practice' (Lave and Wenger, 1988:69) and for them to enable pupils to see science as an intellectual activity in which they participate.

ii. Organising collaborators

Teachers usually allow pupils to chose their working partners. My evidence here, supported by Bauersfeld (1988), suggests that regular partners develop particular patterns of working together, their social interactions have developed with 'friendship' in mind, not learning. As Bauersfeld suggests, and I found from my evidence of friends working together (chapter 7), these historically informed interactional patterns often result in 'dominant' characters asymmetrically influencing the collective ideas, actions and solutions. The lack of equitable contributions from all group members often limits the outcomes of solutions (evidenced by individual written work articulating different (sometimes more informed ideas) to those discussed in groups *before* teachers were trained. Thus creating groupings that take account of the social and cultural bases of students' experiences situation them in different ways in relation to activities. After training teachers are more sensitised to social and cultural influences that learners may bring to problem solving situations. Co-learners with more varied life histories (eg: boys or girls; Londoners or Scots; housewives or businessmen) will offer juxtaposed views. Encouraging open, non-threatening sharing of cognitive resources between dissimilar learners is likely to develop more extensive and intensive intersubjectivity. In open enquiry situations where intersubjectivity underpins collaboration; the composition of the working group is influential.

iii. Active participation

All members of a group are expected to actively participate. Symmetrical contributions should be encouraged to retain equity in actively learning. Participation may develop from an initially, legitimate peripheral position (as a novice teacher developing learners' thinking) to more full engagement (Lave and Wenger, 1988) as an experienced teacher of cognitive development.

iv. Developing a culture of open and non-threatening exchanges underpinned by the belief (of the teachers as learners) that working together is mutually beneficial. Interactions developing intersubjectivity (explicit pluralistic sharing of suggestions; consideration of each others' propositions; justifying plausible and prioritised ideas; reflecting and evaluating task resolution) that underpin affective collaboration are constantly supported.

v. Opportunities for problem solving

The heterogeneic nature of learning suggests that in different situations, different strategies can work for different teachers and pupils to solve problems. Elucidating 'subjectivities' and engaging in evaluative reflection of propositions develops the cognitive quality of discourse. There are some, generalisable junctures at which interventional pedagogy could support effective collaboration. Intervening in teachers' and pupils' discussions at strategic points in investigations or open tasks can ensure purposeful deliberation, clarification and justification of tactics or approaches. This discursive reflection should arise at the onset of the task, throughout its' progress, during the concluding stage and evaluatively after the task is resolved. This framework could provide a useful 'beginners' psychological 'scaffold' for science teachers coming to understand better how to continually engage pupils in sharing 'subjectivities' and raise the quality of interactional scientific and cognitive discourse. As Reiss (1998) explains to teach for all pupils to actively engage in learning science, 'requires a continual degree of reflection'.

I have identified five *key* or *pivotal* decision making opportunities at which it would be useful for teachers to purposely develop intersubjectivity to absorb pupils in reflection on pertinent issues as described in Figure 10.1. The under-pinning psychology would be to ensure that as task engagement proceeds, problem solving tactics, rationalisation and explanation are clarified by reflecting upon suggestions, negotiating decisions and refining solutions.

Stage in task	**How to develop 'intersubjectivity'**
Preparing for the task	All participants contribute their clarification of the purpose of the activity (What are they trying to find out?). Encourage each collaborator to re-formulate the task to verify correct 'focus' or 'foci'. Participants should agree and clarify what matters and identify the relevant variables, (independent and dependent) and possible values.
Planning the task	All participants contribute suggestions of *possible* tactics to achieve the task outcome. Consider all propositions, their strengths and weaknesses. All should agree a justifiable decision about what should be done. Participants contribute their ideas about the methods to achieve the tactics. What should be measured? (Independent Variable(s) and Dependent Variable(s)), when? (how often? For how long? (interval and extent of data collection). How should evidence be collected (which equipment?).
Sharing projections and prediction	All participants should share their expected outcomes (predict/project possibilities with justifications). Describing rate at which 'evidence' accrued, as well as type of data develops *anticipation* of the 'outcome', application and understanding of the science involved.
During-in-task-engagement	Assess in task whether tactics, methods and evidence proposed are developing as expected. Is the adopted scientific approach (process)

	being enacted? Is it still appropriate? Do any methods require refinement? Do predictions, justifications and explanations 'fit' the emerging data? Negotiated reflection is needed to decide whether or not to continue as originally planned (or follow an adapted tactic or method).
Reflecting on the completed task	Evaluation of the quality of task resolution (was the tactic and methods employed successful? How could they be improved? Is any more evidence needed?) Can the data pattern be described and explained? What does the evidence mean? Does it support or confuse existing understanding?

Figure 10.1 : Important junctures at which to address pupils' (and/or teachers') subjectivities when problem solving.

For each of these potentially, pivotal, junctures in a science investigation (or open task), symmetrical contributions, of subjective opinions and justifications, from each participant should be encouraged and supported. Regular development of this approach can result in exploratory talk becoming more culturally spontaneous. The considered discussion and deliberation of each participant's views, resulting in sharing cognitive resources to resolve problems, points of dissonance and establish joint referents and subsequent understanding should be encouraged at each stage to culminate in mutual decision making. How (and to some extent when) intersubjectivity is developed, is a key endeavour (for teachers to support) so that learning collaboratively is successful. Engaging pupils (and teachers) in this way reflects the experience of 'science-in-the-making' (Latour 1987) rather than constraining active participation and interaction in learning and teaching 'ready-made-science' (Roth 1995:202). Hodson (1998) describes this enculturation model of learning as:

> 'understanding something to the extent that we use it appropriately for the purpose for which it was designed' (Hodson 1998:117);

and that

> 'we come to understand it as we use it appropriately, or as our attempts to use it [……] are monitored and supported by others more expert than ourselves. In other words, we do not understand and then use, we understand *as we use, and we use* (properly) as we come to understand' (ibid).

10.3.6 Extending understanding of opportunities and applications for formative assessment

In developing teachers' understandings about how to influence ways of talking and discussing science, they are reflecting on the nature of the discussion. In becoming reflexive in-action to guide and steer the focus and nature of talk to ensure that intersubjectivity is developed, teachers are supporting pupils to become reflective about the subject being learned. As Black and William (1998: 11) describe 'opportunities for pupils to express their understanding should be designed into any piece of teaching, for this will initiate the interaction whereby formative assessment aids learning'. In parallel with my study, exploring the impact of intersubjectivity being developed (given the appropriate cultural context) within other subject domains (as well as into later and/or earlier key stages) lends itself to both teacher and learner development. Exploring with teachers (who have developed understanding of intersubjectivity) how to create effective problem solving situations, particularly around subject matter of conceptual difficulty or concepts about which there are known frequent mis-understandings or misconceptions. The subsequent impact of this approach to learning could be assessed through both qualitative (transcription, interpretation of meaning and outcomes or similar) and quantitative (akin to summative) assessments of pupil performances.

10.4 Personal reflections

Reflexivity and myself

This study has impacted personally on my methodological perspective to recognise how views of learning influence the methods one would utilise to support investigations and experimental design. My view has developed from an initial scientific, truth-searching like stance, to a more relativist, reflective way of viewing outcomes and processes in solving scientific problems. In coming to appropriate for myself the meaning of intersubjectivity, I recognise that for the teachers, it will be understood in various ways, as Bruner (1996:13) describes when considering perspective and meaning making.

> 'The meaning of any fact, proposition or encounter is relative to the perspective or frame of reference in terms of which it is construed. ....to understand well what something 'means' requires some awareness of the alternative meanings that can be

> attached to the matter of scrutiny, whether one agrees with them or not. Understanding something in one way does not preclude understanding it in other ways. Understanding in any one way is only 'right' or 'wrong' from the particular perspective in terms of which it is pursued. But the 'rightness' of particular interpretations, while dependent on perspective, also reflects rules of evidence, consistency and coherence. ...there are inherent criteria of rightness, and the possibility of alternative interpretations does not license all of them equally.'

Therefore teachers and other academics working in the field of learning theories will read this thesis and interpret, using *their* frames of reference, whether, in their view I have taken a *right, wrong or appropriate* stance at particular junctures in this study. They themselves will develop intersubjectivity when critically engaging with the progress of my arguments described in the text. Reflecting on how my teaching has changed and been informed by my research I realise that my beliefs (and associated frames of reference) have shifted, subtly and incrementally from a Piagetian constructivist stance to consider various social influences of a Vygotskian perspective and finally to develop a deeper understanding and appreciation of socio-cultural views of learning. I have come to recognise that praxis is dialectically developed through the interplay of 'action' and 'reflection' (Schon 1991); in that many pedagogic strategies can be utilised for mediation, to ascertain intersubjectivity, and that various ways in which differing teachers may apply similar tactics could result in greater or lesser impacts on pupil's cognitive development. What I have appropriated from this study is that given the opportunity to experience 'in-action' learning and reflect on the power of sharing collective views, teachers come to recognise their role in supporting peers to problem solve more effectively. They recognise how as 'expert' teacher they should encourage co-learners to debate, negotiate and explain outcomes to become autonomous and mutualistic. Teachers and I have become reflexive through recognising that these cognitive and social outcomes are not realised through a single strategy alone. As Bourdieu and Wacquant (1992), Lawson, (1985) and Steier, (1991) identify through deriving the meaning of reflexivity from its latin definition, "to turn back on oneself", which can be interpreted to indicate that people have to think about their own concepts and what they bring to any situation. In hindsight from their own experience they can reflexively re-construct a parallel learning experience for their pupils. In contrast to the view that people can be objective, reflexivity argues that we have a social and intellectual unconsciousness-and-consciousness-that we bring to any situation. Hence, we need to be self-aware in order to extend and further our understanding of situations (Matthew and Jessel 1998).

In my study I have critically self-reflected on the application of my theoretical suppositions or frames of reference. Which Schwandt (1997) describes as reflexive, I recognise that my early questionnaires were positivist in nature and as such did not probe deeply teachers educational beliefs and rationale for encouraging pupils to work together. The findings provided information of a descriptive rather than illuminatory nature. Methodologically, within the interpretative paradigm, I would wish to have sought much richer reflections-in-action of both teachers and pupils whilst engaged in solving investigational tasks in science.

So, my reflexivity has extended beyond the teaching and learning process, to permeate research methodology. I agree with Kleinasser (2000;1), who identifies that 'as a researcher reflexivity represents a methodological process of learning about self as researcher, which in turn, illuminates deeper, richer meanings about personal, theoretical, ethical and epistemological aspects of the research question.' As I have come to realise 'Qualitative researchers engage in reflexivity because they have reason to believe that good data result' (Kleinasser (2000; ibid).

Reflexivity and learning theory

As Siraj-Blatchford (1997) describes reflexivity, she refers to the process by which observations we make are dependant upon our prior understandings of the subject. In our observations we 'refer back'. It is a concept of central importance to philosophical, social scientific and psychological constructivism. As a sociological concept it should be clearly distinguished from the notion of independent self-reflection (however critically conceived), which is sometimes presented as a strategy for overcoming the problems that reflexivity poses to research designs. She goes on to consider the Piagetian theory of learning, and describes how Piaget's 'reflexive abstraction' is a mechanism of cognitive equilibrium and it is always the perception of novelty, disequilibrium or disturbance that provides the motor process for learning. Reflexivity, the teachers in this study might also perceive dissonance as that arising socio-cognitively or as data offering conflicting or surprising evidence or as the teacher deliberately 'getting it wrong', they conceived of it as a 'motivatory mechanism', that enthralled and engaged the pupils on task; quite unlike Piaget's perception as the 'motor that drives a learning process'. One of the important implications Blatchford (1997;ibid) emphasises is the 'double hermeneutic' (Giddens, 1993) process it involves. The notion of the 'double hermeneutic' relates to the way in which everyday concepts of social science come to be appropriated uniquely by individuals within their everyday action. Thus how teacher's behaviours were moderated according to their interpretations of observations of 'events', reflexively informs, how 'acting' as 'novice' instead of 'expert' in learning situations can influence beliefs and consequently pedagogic actions.

Reflexivity, learning and teaching science

In attempting, like Dawkins (1998) who 'unweaves the rainbow', I have endeavoured to 'un-ravel' the nature of the entwined teacher–pupil and peer-peer learning interactions to enable key, influential aspects of pedagogy to become more explicit.

I have also come to appreciate, as Bruner (1996:57) who discusses when considering 'Children as thinkers: the development of intersubjective interchange', ' The child, in a word, is seen as an epistemologist as well as learner.' He elaborates further by adding "Knowledge (in the child's world) is what is shared within discourse............truths are the product of evidence, argument and construction rather than authority, textual or pedagogic." The model of education he explores is that which reflexively I have been attempting to (re)create for teachers, so they in turn support their pupils in mini-learning communities, which 'are mutualistic and dialectical, more concerned with interpretation and understanding than with the achievement of factual knowledge or skilled performance.'

Three strands of entwined reflexivity

The three strands of intertwined reflexivity in this study have been, first and foremost, my reflexivity as a teacher-researcher coming to recognise the importance of intersubjectivity and how to address it, study it through a qualitative, interpretative paradigm to subsequently inform and empower learning in secondary science. Secondly, the science teachers to see why and how to support dialogic exchange to reveal pupil subjectivities, and to be aware of appropriate situations in which to intervene. Thirdly the pupils who, having engaged in more spontaneous discourse, come to recognise that to contribute personal cognitive resources augments better collaborative task resolution.

10.5 Areas for future research

10.5.1 How far have teachers' beliefs developed?

From the analysis in chapter 9 there are the beginnings of evidence that illustrate how through influencing teachers learning experiences, their beliefs and volitions it appears are altered, reflexively resulting in their changed pedagogic techniques to influence more effective peer-peer interactions and subsequently augment pupil cognitive development. As Schon (1991) would explicate these teachers are 'reflecting-on-action'. Further research extending more deeply into how their beliefs affected their practice, could then ascertain whether they were developing 'reflection-in-action' and thus becoming truly reflexive in their praxis. As Bleakley (1999) emphasises 'reflection-on-action' is retrospective, pondering an event and its consequences after it has happened, whereas 'reflection-in-action' is an intuitive reflectivity informed by the retrospective, but involving the prospective, where thinking and doing coincide in a moment-to-moment adaptation. Reflectively the reasons for their change in pedagogy could be explored to investigate what is it about the teachers' changed beliefs or understandings that have underpinned their change in praxis? Do they take Brown and Campione's (1990;94) view that through socially interacting each pupil engages in a peer-generated zone of proximal development and within the classroom, in the small working groups there are subsequently "multiple overlapping zones of proximal development " (and therefore retain a more cognitist, absolutist, individualistic perspective of learning) or do they internalise a more socio-cultural stance (that permits reasoned relativist perspectives to co-construct scientific meanings and appropriate understandings), which Bruner (1996:56) would argue is 'to achieve some meeting of minds".

I wonder too, if they 'internalise' the development of intersubjectivity to 'reveal' pupils subjectivity as a *mechanism* to elicit mis-conceptions (Driver, 1983, 1985, 1994), rather than alternate perceptions, thus retaining an individualistic (Piagetian) perception of developing cognition or do they believe that openly, contributing ideas for the benefit of the group as a whole, is a step to improving collective performance (thus retaining a more social perspective of learning)? Exploration of the happenings (and developing beliefs) in teachers' minds when collaborating with others, and demonstrating changed praxis in their classrooms would be an appropriate development of this study.

What is often apparent is that through their own self-reflexivity they come to know what consciously they were un-aware of. Empathy as a learner, developed through reflection of (new) direct experience, can re-invigorate experienced staff. This empowering perspective can fundamentally change perspectives of learning, so much so, at the end of an INSET day (March 2003), the Head of science (a teacher of 22 years experience) from Lacon Childe High school in Shropshire said to me "this is like Viagra for science teaching". This is true vindication of my aim, set out earlier in the study, to empower teachers (Roth, 1995), through developing their understanding of the nature of cognitive development arising through social interactions, when actively engaged in innovative problem solving activities. Her piqued enthusiasm motivated and stimulated her to reflect on adapting current lessons to replicate learning experiences, modelled at in-service sessions, for her pupils.

10.5.2 Further exploration of the influence of the composition of triads.

The single sex case studies examined here, suggest the girls tend to facilitate intersubjectivity and thus collaborate more readily. Boys are often more adventurous and less tentative in their 'actions' and the way they carry out 'trials by error'. Girls are often more focussed on the social context of a problem (Murphy 2000). The different ways that boys and girls behave in problem solving situations suggestions (because of different social influences) suggests that they could contribute complementary cognitive resources. Supported in appropriate classroom cultures it would be interesting to explore the impact of BBG and GGB triads and their relative success in solving scientific investigations.

10.5.3 Exploring further links between questioning and thinking

Further exploration of the frequency, distribution, sequence, nature and timing of questions impacting on cognitive development would be fruitful in the area of scientific practical work, to assess the subtle differences between supporting investigations and illustrative practicals. Questioning is a key skill in teaching (Kyriacou 1995), that needs further exploration in the context of practical learning in science. Morgan and Saxton (1991) have argued that teachers should make more use of open-ended (which my study has shown is possible to support) and higher- order questioning to stimulate pupils' thinking and understanding. Detailed observations of 'changed' teachers-in-action would provide illuminatory examples of the distribution, sequence and nature of questions supporting cognitive activity. Information of this kind could inform whether there are generalisable scaffold(ing) questions that can be suggested to pupils (and teachers) to further encourage collaborative discussion, support autonomous learning through subjective, but justified exchanges and discerning decision-making. Developing from this, can a framework for cognitive development be conceptualised in the form of particular types of questions at strategic junctures of problem solving activities?

10.5.4 Further development of scientific enquiries and investigations.

There is evidence that students who engage in reflective inquiry, who are allowed to treat mathematics as problematic, develop a positive disposition towards mathematics (Carpenter et al 1989; Cobb et al 1991). Investigating whether this is also the case in science could inform curriculum reform to address current concerns regarding the declining motivation in science lessons (Bricheno, Johnston and Sears 2000), particularly at KS 3 and 4. Research on the effective aspects of such a course currently being developed by McGregor, Gunter and Twist (see Appendix 10) would support teachers developing practise that embraces many aspects of learning together in small groups, outlined and justified in this study.

10.6 Concluding remarks

I have illustrated through the work in my study, how I have developed as a teacher and a researcher, to support both educators and pupils in their ways of working together in science. I have provided insights into the social and cognitive processes arising when learners endeavour to work on practical tasks together. I have explained how to develop effective collaboration, through the development of intersubjectivity. I have shown how teachers can influence the quality of learning that arises through peer-peer interactions. Pedagogic strategies and psychological tactics developed and described in this study can improve pupils' understanding of *doing science* as well appreciation *about science*. The findings discussed from a pedagogical and learning perspective in this study are applicable in both investigational and illustrative practical science situations.

References

Adelman, C., Kemmis, S. and Jenkins, D. (1980) Rethinking case study : notes from the Second Cambridge Conference. In Simons, H. (Ed) *Toward a science of the singular.* Centre for Applied Research in Education, University of East Anglia. 45 - 61

Adey, P. (1991) Pulling yourself up by your own thinking. *European Journal for high ability.* 2 28-34

Adey, P. (1997) It all depends on the context doesn't it? The search for general, educable dragons. *Studies in science education.* 29 45 - 92

Adey, P. (1997) Factors influencing uptake of a large scale curriculum innovation. *American Educational Research Association (AERA) conference paper.* March 1997

Adey, P., Shayer, M. and Yates, C. (1989) *Thinking Science INSET pack.* British Petroleum

Adey, P.S., Shayer, M. and Yates, C. (2001) (3rd edition) *Thinking Science: The Curriculum Materials of the CASE project.* London : Nelson Thornes

Adey, P. and Shayer, M. (1990) Accelerating the development of formal thinking in middle and high school students. *Journal of research in science teaching.* 27 (3) 267 - 285

Adey, P. and Shayer, M. (1994) *Really Raising Standards.* London : Routledge

Aguirre, J. M., Haggerty, S. M. and Linder, C. J. (1990) Student-teachers' conceptions of science teaching and learning : A case study in pre-service science education. *International Journal of Science Education* 12 (4) 381-390

Alexander, R. (1998) The problem of good primary practice. In Murphy, P. Selinger, M. Bourne, J. and Briggs, M. (Eds) *Subject Learning in the Primary Curriculum. Issues in English, science and mathematics* Buckingham : Open University Press 50 - 69

Alexopoulou, E. and Driver, R. (1996) Small-group discussion in Physics: Peer Interaction modes in pairs and fours. *Journal of research in Science Teaching* 33 (10) 1099 – 1114

Anderson, J.R. (1982) Acquisition of cognitive skill. *Psychological Review* 98 (4) 369 - 406

Anderson, A., Foot, C.H., Howe, C., Low, J. and Tolmie, A. (2000) Computer support for peer-based methodology tutorials. *Journal of Computer Assisted Learning* 16 41 - 53

Atkinson, T. and Claxton, G. (2000) *The intuitive practitioner. On the value of not always knowing what one is doing.* Buckingham : Open University Press

Ausubel, D. (1968) Educational Psychology. Holt, Reinhart and Winston, New York.

Azmitia, M. and Montgomery, R. (1993) Friendship, transactive dialogues and the development of scientific reasoning. *Social Development* 2 (3) 202-221

Baines, E., Blatchford, P., Kutnick, P., Chowne, A., Ota, C., & Berdondini, L. (2008). *Promoting effective group work in primary schools: developing relationships to enhance learning and inclusion. A guide for teachers.* London: Routledge.

Bakhtin, M. M. (1986) Speech genres and other late essays. Austin, TX: University of Texas Press.

Barnes, D. (1976) *From communication to curriculum.* Harmondsworth : Penguin.

Barnes, D and Todd, F (1977) *Communicating and Learning in Small Groups* London: Routledge and Kegan Paul.

Barnes, D., Britton, J., and Rosen, H. (1969) *Language, the learner and the school.* Harmondsworth : Penquin.

Bassey, M. (1999) *Case study research in Educational Settings.* Buckingham : Open University Press

Bauersfeld, H. (1988) Interaction, Construction and Knowledge : Alternative perspectives for mathematics education. In Cooney, R. and Grouns, D. (Eds) *Effective Mathematics teaching.* 27 - 46

Bauersfeld, H. (1995) The structuring of the structures : Development and function of mathematizing as a social practice. In Steffe, L. P.(Ed) *Constructivism in Education.* Hillsdale. NJ : Lawrence Erlbaum

Bearison, D. J. (1991) Interactional contexts of cognitive development : Piagetian approaches to sociogenesis. In L. Tolchinsky (Ed.) *Culture, cognition and schooling.* Norwood, NJ. Ablex.

Bearison, D. J., Magzamen, S. and Filardo, E. K. (1986) Socio-cognitive conflict and cognitive growth in young children. *Merrill-Palmer Quarterly* 32 51 - 72

Bell, J. (1999) *Doing your research project.* 3rd Edition. Buckingham : Open University Press

Bennett, N. (1985) Interaction and achievement in classroom groups. In Bennett, N and Desforges, C. (Eds) Recent Advances in Classroom Research, *British Journal of Educational Psychology*, Monograph Series No. 2 105 – 119

Bennett, N. (1991) Co-operative learning in classrooms : processes and outcomes. *Journal of child psychology and psychiatry* 32 581-94

Bennett, N. and Blundell, D. (1983) Quality and Quality of work in rows and classroom groups. *Educational Psychology* 3 (2) 93 - 105

Bennett, N. and Cass, A. (1989) The effects of group composition on group interactive processes and pupil understanding. *British Educational Research Journal* 15 (1) 19-32

Bennett, N. Desforges, C., Cockburn, A. Wilkinson, B. (1984) *The quality of pupil learning experiences.* London : Lawrence Erlbaum Associates.

Bennett, N. and Dunne, E. (1989) *Implementing Cooperative Groupwork in Classrooms.* Exeter: University of Exeter School of Education (Monograph).

Berge, Z. (1990) Effects of group size, gender and ability grouping on learning science process skills using microcomputers. *Journal of research in Science Teaching* 27 747-759

Bianchini, J. A. (1999) From here to equity: The influence of status on student access to and understanding of science. *Science Education* 83 (5) 577 - 602

Bianchini, J. A. (1997) Where knowledge construction, Equity and context intersect: Student learning of science in small groups. *Journal of research in science teaching* 1039 – 1065

Bidell, T. R. (1992) Beyond interactionism in contextualist models of development. *Human development* 35 306-15

Biott, C. (1987) Co-operative Groupwork : Pupils and teachers membership and participation. *Curriculum* 8 5-14

Bishop, P. (1994) Task difficulty and effectiveness of group work. In Foot, H. C., Howe, C.J., Anderson, A., Tolmie, A. K., Warden, D. A. (Eds:) *Group and Interactive Learning.* Computational Mechanics Publications. 399-404

Black, P. J. and Lucas A. M. (1993) *Children's informal ideas in science.* London : Routledge.

Black, P. (1993) Formative and summative assessment by teachers. *Studies in Science Education.* 21 49 - 97

Black, P. and Wiliam, D. (1998) *Inside the black box: Raising standards through classroom assessment.* London : School of Education. Kings College

Blagg, N. (1991) *Can we teach intelligence?* Lawrence Erlbaum Associates Hillsdale New Jersey

Blaxter, L., Hughes, C. and Tight, M. (2001) *How to research.* 2nd edition. Buckingham : Open University Press

Bleakley, A. (1999) From reflective practice to holistic reflexivity. *Studies in Higher Education* 24 (3) 315 - 331

Bloom, B. S., Krathwohl, D. R. and Masia, B. B. (1956) *Taxonomony of Educational Objectives: Cognitive Domain.* New York : McKay

Blumer, H. (1969) *Symbolic Interactionism. Perspective and Method.* Englewood Cliffs, New Jersey : Prentice-Hall

Boaler, J. (1998) Sets maniacs. *Education Guardian.* November 24th

Boaler, J., Wiliam, D. and Brown, M. (2000) Students' experiences of ability grouping – disaffection, polarisation and the construction of failure. *British Educational Research Journal* 26 5 631 - 648

Boaler, J. (1997) *Experiencing school mathematics : teaching styles, Sex and setting.* Buckingham: Open University Press.

Bonanno, H., Jones, J. and English, L. (1998) Improving group satisfaction: making groups work in a first-year undergraduate course. *Teaching in Higher Education* 3 (3)

Bossert, S. (1988) Co-operative activities in the classroom. *Review of Research in Education.* 15 225-250

Boydell, D. (1975) Pupil behaviour in Junior Classrooms. *British Journal of Educational Psychology*. 45 122 – 129

Bredo, E. (1999) Reconstructing educational psychology. In Murphy, P. (Ed) *Learners, Learning and Assessment*. 23 – 45 Buckingham : Open University Press

Bricheno, P., Johnston, J. and Sears, J. (2000) Children's attitudes to science. Beyond men in white coats. In Sears, J. and Sorenson, P. (Eds) *Issues in science teaching*. RoutledgeFalmer

Brotherton, P. and Preece, P. (1996) Teaching science process skills. *International Journal of Science Education* 18 (1) 65 - 74

Brown, A. (1997) Transforming schools into communities of thinking and learning about serious matters. *American Psychologist* 52 (4) 399 - 413

Brown, A. and Campione, J. C. (1990) Communities of learning and thinking, or a context by any other name. In Kuhn, D. (ed.) *Developmental perspectives on teaching and learning thinking skills 21. Contributions in Human development*. Basel : Karger.

Brown, A. and Campione, J.C. (1994) Guided discovery in a community of learners. In McKilly, K. *Classroom lessons : Integrating cognitive theory and classroom practice*. Cambridge, Mass : MIT Press

Brown, A. L. (1974) The role of strategic behaviour in retardate memory. In N. R. Ellis (Ed) *International Review of Research in Mental Retardation*. 7 55 – 111

Brown, A. L. (1975) The development of memory: Knowing, knowing about knowing, and knowing how to know. In H.W. Reese (Ed) *Advances in child development and behaviour*. New York : Academic Press. 103 - 152

Brown, A. L. (1978) Knowing when, where and how to remember: A problem of metacognition. In R. Glaser (Ed) *Advances in instructional psychology* 10 77-165

Brown, A. L., Bransford, J. D., Ferrara, R. A. and Campione, J. C. (1983) Learning, remembering and understanding. In Flavell, J. H. and Markman, E. M. (Eds) *Handbook of child psychology*. 4th Edition. New York : Wiley

Brown, A. L. and Reeve, R. A. (1987) Bandwidths of competence : the role of supportive contexts in learning and development. In Liben, L. S. (Ed)

Development and learning : Conflict or congruence? Hillsdale, NJ : Erlbaum 173 - 223

Brown, C.R. (1995) *The effective teaching of Biology.* New York : Longman.

Brown, J., Collins, A. and Duguid, P. (1989) Situated cognition and the culture of learning. *Educational Researcher.* 18 32 - 42

Brown, R. (1988) *Group Processes : Dynamics within and between groups.* Oxford : Basil Blackwell

Bruner, J. S. (1985) Vygotsky: A Historical and Conceptual Perspective' in J. V. Wertsch (Ed.), *Culture, Communication and Cognition: Vygotskyian Perspectives.* Cambridge : Cambridge University Press

Bruner, J. S. (1966) *The process of Education.* Cambridge, MA : Harvard University Press

Bruner, J. S. (1971) *The relevance of Education.* New York : W.W. Norton

Bruner, J. S. (1983) *Child's talk : Learning to use language.* Oxford, England : Oxford University Press.

Bruner, J. S. (1986) *Actual minds, possible worlds.* Cambridge, MA : Harvard University Press

Bruner, J. S. (1990) *Acts of meaning.* Cambridge, MA : Harvard University Press

Bruner, J. S. (1996) *The culture of education.* Cambridge, MA : Harvard University Press

Carey, S. (1992) The origin and evolution of everyday concepts in Respiration. In Giere (ed) *Cognitive models of Science. Minnesota Studies in the philosophy of science.* Minnesota: University of Minnesota Press.

Carey, S. (1985) *Conceptual change in childhood.* Cambridge MA : MIT Press

Carey, S., Evans, R., Honda, M., Jay, E. and Unger, C. (1989) An experiment is when you try it and see if it works : a study of grade 7 students' understanding of the construction of scientific knowledge. *International Journal of Science Education* 11 (5) 514-29

Carraher, T. N. (1986) From drawings to buildings : working with mathematical scales. *International Journal of Behavioural development.* 9 527 - 544

Carter, R. (1998) *Mapping the Mind.* London : Weidenfeld and Nicholson.

Cavendish, S., Galton, M., Hargreaves, L., and Harlen, W. (1990) *Observing activities.* London : Paul Chapman

Christie, F. and Martin, J. (1997) *Genre and Institutions : social processes in the workplace and school.* London, Cassell

Clancey, W. J. (1992) *Situated means coordinating without deliberation.* Santa Fe, NM : McDonnel Foundation Conference.

Claxton, G. (1990) *Teaching to Learn: A direction for Education.* London : Cassell Educational Ltd

Claxton, G. (1999) *Wise-up. The challenge of lifelong learning.* London : Bloomsbury.

Cobb, P. (1994) Where is the mind? Constructivist and sociocultural perspectives on Mathematical development. *Educational Researcher* 23. (7) 13 - 20

Cobb, P. (1989) Experiental, cognitive, and anthropological perspectives in mathematics education. *For the learning of Mathematics* 9 32 - 42

Cobb, P., Boufi, A., McClain, K. and Whitenack, J. (1997) Reflective discourse and collective reflection. *Journal for Research in Mathematics Education.* 28 (3) 258 - 277

Cobb, P., Wood, T., Yackel, E. (1991) Analogies from the philosophy and sociology of science for understanding classroom life. *Science Education* 75 23 - 44

Cobb, P., Yackel, E., Wood, T. (1992) A constructivist alternative to the representational view of mind in mathematics education. *Journal for Research in Mathematics Education.* 23 (1) 2 - 33

Cohen, E. G. (1994) Restructuring the classroom. *Review of Educational Research* 64 (1) 1 – 35

Cohen, L., Lawrence, M. and Morrison, K. (2000) (2nd edition) *Research methods in education.* London : RoutledgeFalmer

Collins, P.H. (1990) *Black Feminist Thought.* Boston, MA : Unwin Hyman.

Collins, A., Brown, J.S. and Newman, S. (1989) Cognitive apprenticeship : Teaching the craft of reading, writing and mathematics. In Resnick, L. et al (Eds) *Cognition and instruction : Issues and agendas.* Hillsdale, NJ : Lawrence Erlbaum Associates 453 - 494

Confrey, J. (1995) How compatible are radical constructivism, sociocultural approaches, and social constructivism? In L.P. Steffe and J. Gale Eds. *Constructivism in education.* Hillsdale. NJ : Lawrence Erlbaum 185 - 226

Conwell, C. R. (1989) *Assessing shared leadership with the Co-op learning Interaction Instrument.* Raleigh, NC : Center for research in Math and Science Education

Conwell, C. R. Griffin, S. and Algozzine, B. (1994) Gender and racial differences in unstructured learning groups in science. *International Journal of Science Education* 15 (1) 107 – 115

Cotton, J. and Cook, M. (1982) Meta Analyses and the effect of various systems : Some different conclusions from Johnson et al. *Psychological Bulletin* 92 176 - 183

Council for Science and Technology (March 2000) A report on supporting and developing the profession of science teaching in primary and secondary schools. Department of Trade and Industry.

Cosgrove, M. and Schaverien, L. (1996) Children's conversations and learning science and technology. *International Journal for Science Education* 18 (1) 105-116

Cowie, H. and Ruddock, J. (1988) *Co-operative Groupwork : An overview.* London : BP Education Service.

Craft, A. (2000) (2nd edition) *Continuing professional development. A practical guide for teachers and schools.* London: RoutledgeFalmer.

Crook, C. (1994) *Computers and the collaborative experience of learning.* London : Routledge.

Crook, C. (2000) Motivation and the ecology of collaborative learning. In Joiner, R., Littleton, K., Faulkner, D. and Miell, D. *Rethinking collaborative learning.* London : Free Association Books

Crotty, M. (1998) *The Foundations of Social Research.* Sydney : Allen and Unwin

Damon, W. and Killen, M. (1982) Peer interaction and the process of change in children's moral reasoning. *Merrill-Palmer Quarterly* 28 347 - 378

Damon, W. and Phelps, E. (1989) Critical distinctions among three approaches to peer education. *International Journal of Educational Research* 5 331 - 343

Damon, W. (1984) Peer education: The untapped potential. *Journal of applied Developmental Psychology* 5 331 - 343

Daniels, H. (Ed) (1996) *An introduction to Vygotsky*. London : Routledge

Daniels, H. (Ed) (1993) *Charting the agenda*. London : Routledge

Daniels, H. (2001) *Vygotsky and Pedagogy*. London : RoutledgeFalmer

Dart, B. and Clarke, J. (1988) Sexism in schools : a new look. *Educational Review* 40 41 - 49

Davis, E. and Linn, M. (2000) Scaffolding students' knowledge integration : prompts for reflection in KIE. *International Journal for Science Education* 22 (8) 819 - 837

David, M. (2002) From Keighley to Keele : personal reflections on a circuitious journey through education, family, feminisim and policy sociology. *British Journal of Sociology of Education*. 23 (2) 249 - 269

Davidson, J. (1970) Outdoor Recreation surveys : The design and use of questionnaires for site surveys. Countryside commission, London.

Davydov, J. L. and Markova, A. K. (Eds) (1982) Ausbilding der Lerntatigkeit bei Schulern [Development of learning]. Berlin : Volk and Wissen 14 - 27

Dawkins, R. (1998) *Unweaving the Rainbow*. London : Penquin

DfEE (1999) *The National Curriculum Science*. London : HMSO

DfEE (1997) *Excellence in Schools*. London : HMSO

Denny, M. and Chennell, F. (1986) Science Practicals: what do pupils think? *European Journal of Science Education* 8 (3) 325 – 336

Denscombe, M. (1998) *The good research guide for small scale research projects*. Buckingham : Open University Press

Des-Fountain, J. and Howe, A. (1992) Pupils working together on understanding. In Norman, K. (Ed.) *Thinking Voices : The work of the National Oracy Project*. London : Hodder and Stoughton.

Department for Education and Employment and Qualifications, Curriculum and Assessment. (1999) Science. The National Curriculum for England. Key Stages 1 – 4. London : HMSO

Dewey, J. (1916) *Democracy and Education*. New York : The Free Press
Dewey, J. (1938) *Experience and Education*. New York : Touchstone
Dewey, J. (1991) *How we think*. Amherst, NY : Prometheus Books
Diederich, H. and Lingelbach, K. (Eds) (1977) *Erfahrungen mit schulischen Reformen*. Kronberg/Taunus.
Dillon, J.T. (1988) *Questioning and teaching : a manual of practice*. London : Croom Helm.
Ding, S. and Flynn, E. Collaborative Learning: An underlying skills approach. In Joiner, R., Littleton, K., Faulkner, D. and Miell, D. (2000) *Rethinking collaborative learning*. Free Association Books.
Doise, W. et al (1976) Social interactions and cognitive development. *European Journal of Social Psychology*. 6 245 - 47
Doise, W. and Mugny, G. (1984) *The social development of the Intellect*. Oxford : Pergamon Press.
Doise, W. (1985) Social regulations in cognitive development. In R. Hinde, A. N. Perret-Clermont and J. Stebenson-Hinde, (Eds) *Social relationships and cognitive development*. Oxford : Oxford University Press.
Doise, W. and Mugny, G. (1979) Individual and collective conflicts of centrations in cognitive development. *European Journal of Psychology*. 9 105-108
Doise, W., Mugny, G. and Perret-Clermont, A. N. (1975) Social interaction and the development of cognitive operations. *European Journal of Social Psychology* 5 367 - 383
Donaldson, M. (1978) *Children's Minds*. Glasgow : Fontana/Collins
Drever, E. (1995) *Using semi-structured interviews in small-scale research*. Edinburgh : Scottish Council for Research in Education
Driver, R. (1983) *The pupil as scientist*. Buckingham : Open University Press
Driver, R. (1997) The application of science education theories : A reply to Norris, Stephen and Kvernbekk, Tone. *Journal of Research in Science Teaching* 34 (10) 1007-1018
Driver, R., Guesne, E. and Tiberghien, A. (Eds) (1985) *Children's ideas in Science*. Buckingham : Open University Press.

Driver, R., Asoko, H., Leach, J., Mortimer, E., and Scott P. (1994) Constructing scientific knowledge in the classroom. *Educational Researcher* 23 (7) 5-12

Driver, R., Squires, A., Rushworth, P. and Wood-Robinson, V. (1994) *Making sense of Secondary Science*. London. Routledge

Driver, R., Leach, J., Millar, R. and Scott, P. (1996) *Young peoples images of science*. Buckingham : Open University

Driver, R. (1995) Constructivist Approaches to Science Teaching. In Steffe, L. S and Gale J. (Eds) *Constructivism in Education*. Hillsdale. N J : Lawrence Erlbaum. 385 - 400

Driver, R., Leach, J., Scott, P. and Wood-Robinson, C. (1998) Young peoples understanding of science concepts. In P. Murphy, M. Selinger, J. Bourne and M. Briggs. Eds. *Subject Learning in the Primary Curriculum. Issues in English, science and mathematics* 158 - 183

Dunne, E. and Bennett, N. (1990) *Talking and learning in Groups*. London : Macmillian

Duggan, S. and Gott, R. (1995) The place of investigations in practical work in the UK National Curriculum for Science. *International Journal for Science Education* 17 (2) 137 - 147

Durkin (1995) *Developmental Social Psychology* Oxford : Blackwell

Duveen, G. (1999) Representations, identities, resistence. In K. Deaux and G. Philogene (Eds) *Social representations : introductions and explorations.* Oxford : Blackwell.

Gruber, H.E. and Voneche, J.J. (Eds) (1977) *The Essential Piaget*. Northvale, NJ : Jason Aronson

Edwards, A. (2000) Researching pedagogy : a sociocultural agenda. Inaugural lecture. University of Birmingham. November 7th 2000

Edwards, D. 1997 Towards a discursive psychology of classroom education. In D. Edwards (Ed) *Teaching, learning and classroom discourse.* Madrid : Fundacion infancia y Aprendizaje

Edwards, D. and Mercer, N. (1987) *Common knowledge*. London : Methuen

Edwards, R. and Miller, N. (2000) Go your own way : lifelong learning and reflexive autobiographies in post modernity. *International Journal of Lifelong Learning* 19 (2) 126 - 140

Eichinger, D. C. Anderson, C. W., Palinscar, A. S., and David, Y. M. (1991) An illustration of the roles of content knowledge, scientific argument and social norms in collaborative problem solving. Paper presented at the annual meeting of the American Educational Research Association, Chicago, IL.

Engestrom, Y. (1999) Activity theory and individual and social transformation. In Y. Engestrom, R. Miettinen and R. L. Punamaki. *Perspectives on activity theory.* Cambridge : Cambridge University Press

Emler, N. and Valiant, G.L. (1982) Social interaction and cognitive conflict in the development of spatial coordination skills. *British Journal of Psychology* 73 295 - 303

Ernest, P. (1994) What is social constructivism in the psychology of mathematics education? In P. Ernest (Ed.) *Constructing Mathematical Knowledge: Epistemology and Mathematics Education.* London : Falmer Press 62 - 72

Fensham, P, Gunstone, R. and White, R. (eds) (1994) *The content of science: A Constructivist approach to its Teaching and Learning.* Lewes : Falmer Press

Feurstein, R., Rand, Y., Hoffman, M. and Miller, R. (1980) *Instrumental enrichment.* Baltimore, MD : University Park Press

Flanders, N. (1970) *Analysing Teaching Behaviour.* Reading, MA : Addison-Wesley

Foot, H. C., Howe, C. J., Anderson, A., Tolmie, A. K. and Warden, D. A. (1994) *Group and interactive learning.* Southampton : Computational Mechanics Publications.

Forman, E, and Larreamendey-Joerns, J. (1995) Learning in the context of peer collboration. *Cognition and Instruction* 13 (4) 549 - 564

Forman, E. and Cazden, C. (1985) Exploring Vygotskian perspectives in Education : the cognitive value of peer interaction. In J. Wertsch (Ed) *Culture, communication and cognition : Vygotskian perspectives.* Cambridge : Cambridge University Press 323 - 347

Forman, E. A. and McPhail, J. (1993) Vygotskian perspective on children's collaborative problem-solving activities In Forman, E. A. Minick, N., Stone, C.A. (Eds) *Contexts for learning : sociocultural dynamics in children's development.* Oxford : Oxford University Press. 213 – 229

Forman, E. and Kraker, M. J. (1985) The social origins of logic : the contributions of Piaget and Vygotsky. In Berkowitz, M. W. (Ed) *Peer conflict and psychological growth.* San Francisco : Jossey Bass.

Fosnot, C.T (1989) *Enquiring teachers, enquiring learners : A constructivist approach for teaching.* New York : Teachers College Press.

Fuchs, L., Fuchs, D., Hamlett, C. L. and Karns, K. (1998) High-achieving Students' interactions and performance on complex mathematical tasks as a function of homogeneous and heterogenous pairings. *American Educational Research Journal* 35 227 - 267

Fullan, M. (2001) *The new meaning of educational change.* London : RoutledgeFalmer.

Gabbert, B. Johnson, D.W., Johnson, R. T. (1986) Coooperative Learning, Group-to individual transfer, Process Gain and the acquisition of cognitive reasoning strategies. *The Journal of Psychology* 120 (3) 265-278

Gallagher, J. J. and Tobin, K. (1987) Teacher management and student engagement in high school science. *Science Education* 71 (4) 535-555

Galton, M. and Hargreaves, L. (2009) Group work : still a neglected art? *Cambridge Journal of Education* 39 (1) 1 - 6

Galton, M., Hargreaves, L. & Pell, T. (2009) Group work and whole-class teaching with 11 – 14 year olds compared. *Cambridge Journal of Education.* 39 (1) 119 - 140

Galton, M. and Patrick, H. (Eds) (1990) *Curriculum Provision in Small Primary Schools.* London : Routledge

Galton, M. and Williamson, J. (1992) *Group work in the primary classroom.* London : Routledge

Galton, M., Simon, B. and Croll, P. (1980) *Inside the Primary school.* London: Routledge and Kegan Paul

Galton, M., Hargreaves, L. and Pell, T. (2009) Group work and whole-class teaching with 11 – 14 year olds compared. *Cambridge Journal of Education* 39 (1) 119 - 140

Gardner, M., Greeno, F., Reif, A.H., Schoenfeld, A. H., diSessa, A., Stage, E. (1990) Toward a scientific practice of science education. Hiilsdale, NJ, Lawrence Erlbaum, 203-217

Garton, A. F. (1984) Social interaction and cognitive growth : Possible causal mechanisms. *British Journal of Developmental Psychology* 2 269-274

Gauvain, M. and Rogoff, B. (1989) Collaborative problem solving and children's planning skills. *Developmental psychology*. 25 131-151

Gilbert, J. K. (1995) Studies and fields: Directions of research in science Education. *Studies in science education*. 25 173 – 197

Glachan, N. M. and Light, P. H. (1982) Peer interaction and learning. In Butterworth, G. E. and Light, P. H. (Eds) *Social cognition : Studies of the development of understanding*. Brighton : Harvester Press.

Gott, R., Duggan, S., Millar and Lubben, F. (1998) Progression in investigative work in science. In Murphy, P. Selinger, M. Bourne, J. and Briggs, M. (Eds) *Subject Learning in the Primary Curriculum. Issues in English, Science and Mathematics* 184 - 196

Good, T., Cooper, H. and Blakely, S. (1980) Classroom interaction as a function of teacher expectations, student sex and time of year. *Journal of Educational Psychology*. 72 378 - 385

Good, R. (1993) The many forms of constructivism. *Journal of Research in Science Teaching*. 30 (9) 1015

Gott, R. and Duggan, S. (1994) *Investigative Work in Science*. Buckingham, Open University Press.

Grima, G. (2002) *Group assessment : exploring the influences of group gender composition*. EARU. University of Otago

Gruber, H. E. and Voneche, J.J. (Eds) 1995 *The essential Piaget. An interpretative reference and guide*. New Jersey : Aronson.

Gunter, H., McGregor, D., Gunter, B. (2001) Teachers as leaders : a CASE study. *Management in Education* 15 (1) 26-28

Habermas, J. (1974) *Theory and practice*. London : Heinemann

Harlen, W. and Malcolm, H. (1999) *Setting and streaming.* Edinburgh : Scottish Council for Research in Education

Hardman, F. and Beverton, S. (1993) Co-operative groupwork and the development of metadiscoursal skills. *Support for Learning* 8 (4) 146 – 150

Harnqvist, K. and Burgen, A. (Eds) (1997) *Growing up with science.* Cambridge : Jennifer Kingsley

Hatano, G. and Inagaki, K. (1992) Sharing Cognition Through Collective Comprehension Activity in Resnick, L. et al (eds) *Perspectives on Socially Shared Cognition.* American Psychological Association.

Hatano, G. (1993) Time to merge Vygotskian and constructivist conceptions of knowledge acquisition. In Forman, E. et al (Eds) *Contexts for learning.* New York : Oxford University Press.

Hedegaard, M. (1996) The zone of proximal development as basis for instruction. In Daniels, H. (Ed) *An introduction to Vygotsky.* London : Routledge

Hiebert, J., Carpenter, T. P., Fennema, E., Fuson, K., Human, P., Murray, H., Olivier, A. and Wearne, D. (1999) Problem solving as a basis for reform in Curriculum and Instruction: the Case of Mathematics. In Murphy, P. (Ed.) *Learners, Learning and Assessment.* Buckingham : Open University Press.

Hadow Report (1931) *Report of the consultative committee on primary schools.* London : HMSO

Hammersley, M. and Atkinson, P. (1995) 2nd edition. *Ethnography. Principles in practice.* London : Routledge

Heathfield, M. (1999) How to assess student groupwork. THES Issue 1377 p.40

Helsby, G. (1999) *Changing teachers' work.* Buckingham : Open University Press

Henderson, J. and Wellington, J. (1998) Lowering the language barrier in learning and teaching science. *School Science Review* 79 (288) 35 - 46

Hendley, D. and Lyle, S. (1995) The potential of collaborative group work to increase pupils' learning in the implementation of design and technology in the National Curriculum. *The Curriculum Journal* 6 (3) 363 – 373

Hennessey, S. (1993) Situated cognition and cognitive apprenticeship : Implications for classroom learning. *Studies in Science Education.* 22 1 - 41

Hennessy, S. and Murphy, P. (1999) The potential for collaborative problem solving in Design and Technology. *International Journal of Technology and Design Education.* 9 1 - 36

Hill, G. W. (1982) Group versus individual performance: Are N + 1 heads better than one? *Psychological Bulletin* 91 (3) 517-539

Hitchcock, G. and Hughes, D. (1995) *Research and the teacher. A qualitative introduction to school-based research.* 2nd edition. London : Routledge

Hodson, D. (1990) A critical look at practical work in school science. *School Science Review.* 71 (256) 33-40

Hodson, D. (1992) Redefining and reorienting practical work in school science. *School Science Review.* 73 (264) 65 - 78

Hodson, D. and Hodson, J. (1998) From constructivism to social constructivism: a Vygotskian perspective on teaching and learning science. *School Science Review* 79 (289) 33 - 41

Hofstein, A. A. and Lunetta, V. N. (1982) The role of the laboratory in Science Teaching: Neglected Aspects of Research. *Review of Educational Research* 52 (2) 201-217

Hogan, K. (1999) Sociocognitive roles in science group discourse. *International Journal of Science Education* 21 8 855 – 882

Hopkins, D. (1993) *A teacher's guide to classroom research.* 2nd edition. Buckingham : Open University Press

Howe, A. C. (1996) Development of science concepts within a Vygotskian framework. *Science Education* 80 (1) 35-51

Howe, C. (1993) Peer interaction and knowledge Acquisition. *Social development* 2-3

Howe, C. (1997) *Gender and Classroom interaction. A research review.* Edinburgh : Scottish Council for Research in Education

Howe, C. (1998) Learning about physics through peer interaction. Interaction in Primary school. In Murphy, P. Selinger, M. Bourne, J. and Briggs, M. (Eds) *Subject Learning in the Primary Curriculum. Issues in English, Science and Mathematics.* 197 - 204

Howe, C., Rodgers, C. and Tolmie, A. (1990) Physics in the primary school: peer interaction and the understanding of floating and sinking. *European Journal of Psychology of Education* 4 459-475

Howe, C., Tolmie, A. and Rodgers, C. (1992) The acquisition of conceptual knowledge in science by primary school children: group interaction and the understanding of motion down an incline. *British Journal of Developmental Psychology* 10 113-130

Howe, C., Tolmie, A., Thurston, A., Topping, K., Christie, D., Livingston, K., Jessimen, E. & Donaldson, C. (2007) Group work in elementary science : Towards organisational principles for supporting pupil learning. *Learning and Instruction.* 17 549 - 563

Howe, C., Tolmie, A., Anderson, A. and Mackenzie, M. (1992) Conceptual knowledge in physics: The role of group interactions in computer – supported teaching. *Learning and instruction* 2 (3) 161-183

Howe, C. J. Tolmie, A., Greeer, K. and Mackenzie, M (1995) Peer collaboration and conceptual growth in physics : task influences on children's understanding of heating and cooling. *Cognition and Instruction* 13 483 - 503

Ireson, J. (1999) *Innovative grouping practices in Secondary schools.* DFES research report No. 166

Ireson, J. and Hallam, S. (2001) *Ability grouping in Education.* London : Paul Chapman Publishing

Inhelder, B. and Piaget, J. (1958) *The growth of logical thinking from childhood to adolescence.* New York : Basic Books

Issroff, K., Jones, A., and Scanlon, E. (1994) Case studies of children cooperating with computers: A time based analysis. In Foot, H.C.; Howe, C. J., Anderson, A., Tolmie, A. K. and Warden D. A. (Eds) *Group and Interactive Learning.* 73 - 79

Seers, J. (Ed.) *Issues in science teaching.* (2000) London : Routledge

Johnson and Johnson, R. (1987) *Learning together and alone.* Englewood cliffs, NJ : Prentice Hall.

Johnson, D. W. (1981) Student-student interaction : the neglected variable in education. *Educational Researcher* 10 (5) 10

Johnson, D. W. and Johnson, R. T. (1994) Constructive conflict in the schools. *Journal of Social Issue.* 50 (1) 117 - 137

Johnson, D. W. and Johnson F.P. (1975) *Joining together : Group theory and group skills.* Boston, MA : Allyn and Bacon

Johnson, D. W. and Johnson, R.T. (1995) Positive interdependence : key to effective co-operation. In Hertz-Lazarowitz, R. and Miller, N. (eds) *Interaction in Co-operative Groups: The theoretical Anatomy of Group Learning.* Cambridge : Cambridge University Press.

Johnson, D. W., Johnson, R.T., Roy and P., Zaidman, B. (1985) Oral interaction in Co-operative learning groups : Speaking, Listening, and the nature of statements made by High, Medium and Low achieving students. *Journal of Psychology* 119 (4) 303-321

Johnstone, A. H. and Wham, A.J.B. (1982) The demands of practical work. *Education in Chemistry.* May 71 – 73

Joiner, R., Littleton, K., Faulkner, D. and Miell, D. (2000) *Rethinking collaborative learning.* London : Free Association Books

Jones, M. and Gerig, T. (1994) Silent sixth-grade students: characteristics, achievement and teacher expectations. *The Elementary School Journal* 95 169 - 182

Joyce, B. and Showers, B. (1995) *Student achievement through staff development.* New York : Longman

Kagan, S., Hertz-Lararowitz,, Webb, C. and Schmuck, R. *Learning to Co-operate. Co-operating to learn.* New York : Plenum Press 177 – 209

Keats, D. W. (1994) Task based small group learning in large classes. *Higher Education* 27 (1) 59 – 73

Kelly, A. V. (1978) *Mixed-ability grouping. Theory and practice.* London : Harper and Row

Kelly, G. J. and Crawford, T. (1996) Students interactions with computer representations: analysis of discourse in Laboratory groups. *Journal of Research in Science Teaching* 33 (7) 693 – 707

Kelly, G. J. (1997) Research Traditions in comparative Context : A philosophical Challenge to Radical Constructivism. *Science Education* 81 355-375

Kempa, R.F.K. (1979) Studying curriculum implementation in the classroom. In P. Tamir, A. Blum, A. Hofstein, N. Sabar, (Eds) *Curriculum implementation and its relationship to curriculum development in Science*. Jerusalem, Israel : Rehovot

Kempa, R.F. (1994) Learning from group work in science. *International Journal of Science Education.* 1069 - 1080

Kempa, R.F.K. and Ayob, A. (1994) Learning from group work in science. *International Journal of Science Education*.

Kempa, R.F.K. and Ayob, A. (1991) Learning interactions in group work in science. *International Journal of Science Education* 13 (3) 341-354

Kempa, R.F. and Orion, N. (1996) Students' perception of co-operative Learning in Earth Science Fieldwork. *Research in science and technological Education.* 14 (1)

Kerry, T. and Sands, M. K. (1982a) *Mixed ability teaching.* Basingstoke : Macmillan

Kerry, T. and Sands, M. K. (1982b) *Handling classroom Groups.* Basingstoke : Macmillan

Kerry, T. (1981) Thinking in Science Lessons. *School Science Review* 63 223 355-360

Kieren, T. E. (2000) Dichotomies or binoculars : Reflections on the papers by Steffe and Thompson and by Lerman. *Journal for research in Mathematics Education.* 31 (2) 228 - 233

Kimbell, R., Stables, K., Wheller, T., Wosniak, A. and Kelly, V. (1991) *The Assessment of performance in Design and Technology.* London : School Examinations and assessment Authority

King, L. H. (1994) High and Low achievers perceptions and co-operative learning in 2 small groups. *Elementary School Journal.* 93 (4) 399-416

Kleinasser, A. M. (2000) Researchers, reflexivity, and good data : writing to unlearn. *Theory into practice.* 39 (3) 155 - 163

Kobayashi, Y. (1994) Conceptual Acquistion and change through social interaction. *Human development.* 37 233-241

Kourilsky, M. (1994) Generative teaching - an enhancement strategy for the learning of economics in co-operative groups. *American Educational research Journal.* 29 (4) 861-876

Kourilsky, M. and Wittrock, M. (1992) Generative teaching: An enhancement Strategy for the learning of economics in cooperative groups. *American Educational Research Journal* 29 4 861-876

Krathwohl, D., Bloom, B. and Masia. B. (1956) *Taxonomy of educational objectives. The Classification of Educational Goals.* New York : Longman

Kruger, A. (1993) Peer collaboration: conflict, collaboration or both? *Social development* 2 (3) 165-182

Kuhn, D. and Brannock, J. (1977) Development of the isolation of variables scheme in experimental and 'natural experiment' contexts. *Developmental Psychology* 13 (9) 13

Kuhn, D. (1989) Children and Adults as Intuitive Scientists. *Psychological Review* 96 (4) 679-89

Kuhn, T. S. (1962) *The structure of scientific Revolutions.* Chicago : University of Chicago Press.

Kutnick, P. and Rodgers, C. (Eds) 1994 *Groups in schools.* London : Cassell.

Kutnick, P., Blatchford, P., Clark, H., MacIntyre, H. & Baines, E. (2005) Teachers' understandings of the relationship between within-class (pupil) grouping and learning in secondary schools. *Educational Research* 47 (1) 1 – 24

Kyriacou, C. (1997) *Effective teaching in Schools. Theory and Practice.* 2nd Edition. Stanley Thornes

Latham, P. (1992) Oracy in the National Curriculum. In Norman, K. (Ed) *Thinking voices – the work of the National Oracy Project.* London : Hodder and Stoughton

Latour, B. and Woolgar, S. (1986) *Laboratory Life : The construction of scientific facts.* Princeton, NJ: Princeton University Press

Laurence, R. (1998) Co-operative learning: Prevalence, conceptualisations, and the relation between research and practice. *American Educational Research Journal* 35 419-454

Lave, J. and Wenger, E. (1991) *Situated learning: Legitimate peripheral participation* Cambridge : Cambridge University Press

Lave, J. and Wenger, E. (1996) Practice, person, social world. In Daniels, H. (Ed.) *An introduction to Vygotsky* 143-150

Lave, J. (1988) *Cognition in practice, Mind mathematics culture in everyday life.* Cambridge : Cambridge University Press.

Layder, D. (1994) *Understanding Social Theory.* London : Sage Publications

Leach, J., Driver, R., Scott, P. and Wood-Robinson, C. (1996) Children's ideas about ecology 2 : ideas found in children aged 5 –16 about the cycling of matter. *International Journal Science Education* 18 (1) 19 – 34

Leach, J. and Moon, B. (1999) *Learners and pedagogy.* Buckingham : The Open University and Paul Chapman Publishing

Lerman, S. (2000) A case of interpretations of *Social:* A response to Steffe and Thompson. *Journal for Research in Mathematics Education.* 31 (2) 210 - 227

Leont'ev, A. N. (1981) The problem of activity in psychology. In Wersch, J. (Ed.) *The concept of activity in soviet psychology.* 37 - 71

Light, P., Littleton, K., Messer, D. and Joiner, R. (1994) Social and communicative processes in computer-based problem solving. *European Journal of Psychology of Education* 9 (1) 93 – 109

Light, P. and Glachan, M. (1985) Facilitation of individual problem solving through peer interaction. *Educational Psychology* 5 217 - 225

Lincoln, Y.S. and Guba, E. G. (1985) *Naturalistic Inquiry.* London : Sage Publications

Lockhead, M. E. and Hall K. P. (1976) Conceptualising sex as a status characteristic. *Journal of Social Issues* 32 111-124

Lockheed, M. E., Harris, A. M. and Nemceff, W. P. (1983) Sex and social influence. *Journal of Educational Psychology.* 75 877-888

Lunzer, E. and Gardner, K. (Eds) (1979) *The effective use of Reading.* Schools Council Project. London : Heinemann.

Luria, A. R. (1976) *Cognitive development : Its cultural and social foundations.* Cambridge, MA : Harvard University Press.

Malinowski, B. (1922) *Argonauts of the Western Pacific. An account of the Native Enterprise and Adventure in the archipelagoes of Melanesian New Guinea.* London : Routledge and Kegan Paul

Marginson, S. and Mollis, M. (2002) "The door opens and the tiger leaps": theories and reflexivities of comparative education for a global millennium. *Comparative Education Review.* 45 (4) 581 - 615

Marin, N, Benarroch, A., Fimez-Gomez, E. (2000) What is the relationship between social constructivism and Piagetian constructivism? An analysis of the characteristics of the ideas within both theories. *International Journal of Science Education* 22 (3) 225-238

Matthew, B. and Jessel, J. (1998) Reflective and reflexive practice in initial teacher education : A critical case study. *Teaching in Higher Education.* 3 (2) 231 - 244

McAllister, W. (1995) Are pupils equipped for group work without training or instruction? *British Educational Research Journal* 21 (3) 395 - 495

Mcauliffe, T. J., Dembo, M. (1994) Status rules in scenarios of peer learning. *Journal of Educational Psychology.* 86 (2) 163 -172

McCaslin, M. (1994) Gender composition and small group learning in 4th grade mathematics. *Elementary School Journal.* 94 (5) 467 – 482

McCormick, R. and Paechter, C. (1999) *Learning and Knowledge.* Buckingham : The Open University and Paul Chapman Publishing

McGilly, K. (1994) *Classroom Lessons : Integrating cognitive theory and classroom practice.* Cambridge, MA : The MIT Press

McGlynn, R. (1982) A comment on the Meta-Analysis of goal structures. *Psychological Bulletin* 92 184-185

McGregor, D. (1999) Group work in secondary science. Some elements of the teachers' perspective. *ASET Conference Proceedings 1998.* Hatfield : Association of Science Education.

McGregor, D. (2008) The influence of task structure on students' learning processes : observations from case studies in secondary school science. *Journal of Curriculum Studies. 40 (4)* 509 – 540.

McGregor, D. and Gunter, B. (2006) Invigorating pedagogic change : Initiating development of secondary science teachers' practice and cognisance of the learning process. *European Journal of Teacher Education*. Vol 29 (1) 23-48

McGregor, D. and Gunter, B. (2001a) Changing pedagogy of secondary science teachers. *Journal of Teacher Development*. 5 (1) 59 - 74

McGregor, D. and Gunter, B. (2001b) The CASE for technicians. *School Science Review* 82 (300) 103 – 108

McGuinness, C. (1999) *From thinking skills to thinking classrooms : a review and evaluation of approaches for developing pupils' thinking.* Research report No 115 Department for Education and Employment.

McKinney (1994) The use of collaborative learning groups in the large class - is it possible? *Teaching Sociology* 21 (4) 403 – 408

McMahon, A. (2000) The development of professional intuition. In Atkinson, T. and Claxton, G. (eds) *The intuitive practitioner. On the value of not always knowing what one is doing*. Buckingham : Open University Press

Mead, G.H. (1934) *Mind, self and society from the standpoint of a social behaviourist*. Chicago : University of Chicago Press.

Meece, J., Blumenfeld, P. and Hoyle, R. (1988) Students' goal orientations and cognitive engagement in classroom activities. *Journal of Educational Psychology* 80 (4) 514-523

Mercer, N. (2000) *Words and Minds: How We Use Language to Think Together.* London : Routledge

Mercer, N. (1995) *The guided construction of knowledge: talk amongst teachers and learners.* Clevedon : multilingual matters.

Mercer, N. and Littleton, K. (2008) *Dialogue and the development of children's thinking*. London : Routledge

Mercer, N., Wegerif, R. and Dawes, L. (1999) Children's talk and the development of reasoning in the classroom. *British Educational Research Journal* 25 (1) 95-111

Messer, D., Joiner, R., Loveridge, N., Light, P. and Littlejohn, K. (1993) Influences on the effectiveness of peer interaction : children's level of cognitive development and the relative ability of partners. *Social Development* 2 (3) 279 - 294

Millar, R. (1989) Constructive criticisms. *International Journal of Science Education.* 11 587 – 596

Millar, R. and Driver, R. (1987) Beyond processes. *Studies in Science Education.* 14 33 - 62

Minick, N., Stone, C.A., Forman, E.A. (1993) Integration of individual, social and institutional processes in accounts of children's learning and development. In Minick, N., Stone, C.A., Forman, E.A. (Eds) *Contexts for Learning : Sociocultural dynamics in children's development.* Oxford : Oxford University Press 3 - 16

Moll, L. and Greenberg, J. B. (1990) Creating zones of possibilities: Combining social contexts for instruction. In Moll, L. (Ed) *Vygotsky and education.* Cambridge University Press 319 - 347

Moll, L.C. and Whitmore, K.F. (1993) Vygotsky in classroom practice : moving from individual transmission to social transaction. In Minick, N., Stone, C.A., Forman, E.A. (Eds) *Contexts for Learning : Sociocultural dynamics in children's development.* Oxford : Oxford University Press

Moll, L.C. (Ed) (1990) *Vygotsky and education : instructional implications and applications of sociohistorical psychology.* New York : Cambridge University Press.

Monk, M. and Osbourne, J. (2000) (Eds) *Good practice in science teaching. What research has to say.* Open University Press

Moon, B. and Murphy, P. (1999) *Curriculum in context.* The Open University and Paul Chapman Publishing

Morgan, N. and Saxton, J. (1991) *Teaching, Questioning and Learning.* London : Routledge

Munn, P. and Drever, E. (1990) *Using questionnaires in small-scale research.* Edinburgh : Scottish Council for Research in Education

Murphy, N. and Messer, D. (2000) Differential benefits from scaffolding and children working alone. *Educational Psychology* 20 (1) 17 - 31

Murphy, P. (1999) *Learners, Learning and assessment.* Buckingham : Open University Press

Murphy, P. (1999) Supporting Collaborative Learning. In Murphy, P (ed) *Learners, Learning and assessment.* Buckingham : Paul Chapman in Association with Open University

Murphy, P. and Hennessey, S. (1999) Realising the potential and lost opportunities for peer collaboration. *International Journal of Technology Education.*

Murphy, P., Selinger, M., Bourne, J., and Briggs, M. (1989) *Subject Learning in the Primary Curriculum.* Buckingham : The Open University.

Murphy, P. and Spence, M. (1997) *The influence of task on social interaction.* Paper 7th Earli conference 26-30 August in Athens.

Murphy, P. (2000) Equity, Assessment and Gender. In Salisbury, J. and Riddell, S. (Eds) *Gender, Policy and Educational Change.* Routledge. 134 - 152

Murphy, P. and Davidson, M. (2002) *Exploring the characteristics of effective teaching and learning: a study of primary science classrooms.* Paper presented at Annual meeting of NARST 7 – 10th April p. 1-26

Murphy, P. and Hennessy, S. (2001) Realising the potential – and lost opportunities – for peer collaboration in a Design and Technology setting. International *Journal of technology and design education* 11 203 - 237

Needham, R. (1987) *Teaching strategies for developing understanding in science.* Leeds University : Children's Learning in Science Centre for Studies and Mathematics Education .

Newman, D., Griffin, P., and Cole, M., (1989) *The construction Zone: Working for cognitive change in school.* Cambridge : Cambridge University Press.

Newson, J., and Newson, E., (1975) Intersubjectivity and the transmission of culture : On the social origins of symbolic functioning. *Bulletin of the British Psychological Society* 28 437-446

Norman, O. (1997) Investigating the nature of formal reasoning in chemistry: testing Lawsons' Multiple Hypothesis theory. *Journal of Research in Science Teaching* 34 (10) 1067 - 1081

Norris, S. and Kvernbekk, T. (1997) The application of science education theories. *Journal of Research in Science Teaching* 34 (10) 977 - 1005

Novick, S. and Nussbaum, J. (1981) Pupils understanding of the particulate nature of matter : A cross-age study. *Science Education* 65 (2) 187-96

Nussbaum, J. and Novick, S. (1982) Alternative frameworks, conceptual conflict and accommodation : towards a principled teaching strategy. *Instructional Science.* 11 183-200

Nussbaum, E. M. (2002) Scaffolding argumentation in the Social Studies Classroom. *The Journal of Social Studies* 79 - 83

Nunes, T. (1991) *Cognitive invariants and cultural variation in mathematical concepts.* Paper given at ISSBD conference.

O'Loughlin, M. (1992) Rethinking science education : Beyond piagetian constructivism toward a sociocultural model of teaching and learning. *Journal of Research in Science Teaching* 29 (8) 791-820

Ogborne, J. Kress, G. Martins, I., McGillicuddy, K. (1996) *Explaining Science in the classroom.* Buckingham : Open University Press

Ogden, L. (2000) Collaborative tasks, Collaborative children: an analysis of reciprocity during peer interaction at key stage 1. *British Educational Research Journal* 26 (2)

Okebukola, P.A. (1985) *Science Education.* Buckingham : Open University Press.

Oppenheim, A. N. (1972) *Questionnaire design and attitude measurement.* Buckingham : Open University Press

Panofsky, C., John-Steiner, V. and Blackwell, P. (1990) The development of scientific concepts and discourse. In Moll, L.C. (Ed) *Vygotsky and education. Instructional Implications and applications of socio-historical psychology.* Cambridge : Cambridge University Press 251-267

Parkinson, J. (1994) *The effective teaching of secondary science.* London : Longman

Parkinson, J. (2002) *Reflective teaching of science 11 – 18.* London : Continuum

Pheasey, K. and Underwood, G. (1994) Collaboration and discourse during computer-based problem solving. In Foot, H.C.; Howe, C. J., Anderson, A., Tolmie, A. K., Warden D. A. (Eds) *Group and Interactive Learning.*

Piaget, J. (1923) *Language and thought of the child.* Neuchatel : Delachaux et Niestle.

Piaget, J. (1926) *The language and thought of the child.* New York : Harcourt, Brace

Piaget, J. (1929) *The child's conception of the world.* New York : Harcourt, Brace

Piaget, J. (1950) *The psychology of intelligence.* London : Routledge and Kegan Paul.

Piaget, J. (1973) *To understand is to invent : The future of education.* New York : Grossman

Piaget, J. (1977) *Les operations logiques et la vie sociale. In Etudes sociologiques.* Geneva : Libairies Droz.

Pizzini, E.L., Shepardson D.P. and Abell, S.K. (1991) The enquiry level of junior high activities : Implications to science teaching. *Journal of Research in Science Teaching* 28 111-121

Plowden Report (1967) Children and their primary schools. London : HMSO

Pollard, A. (1999) Towards a new perspective on children's Learning? *Education* 27 (3) 56 – 60

Pollard, A. (2002a) *Reflective Teaching. Effective and evidence informed professional practice.* London : Continuum

Pollard, A. (Ed) (2002b) *Readings for Reflective Teaching.* London : Continuum

Pozzi, S., Healy, L. and Hoyles, C. (1993) Learning and interaction in groups with computers : when do ability and gender matter? *Social development* 2 (3) 222 - 241

Provak, D., Gottschalk, T., Pollastro, M., (1994) Teaching method and psychological type in Bibliographic instruction - effect on student learning. *Research Quarterly* 33 (4) 484-495

Pryor, J. (1995) Gender issues in group work – a case study involving computers. *British Education Research Journal* 21 (3) 277 - 284

Radziszewska and Rogoff, B. (1988) Influence of adult and peer collaboration on childrens planning skills. *Developmental Psychology* 24 840-48

Ratcliffe, M. (Ed) (1998) *ASE Guide to secondary Science Education*. Cheltenham : Stanley Thornes.

Ratcliffe, M. (1998) Discussing socio-scientifc issues in science lessons – pupils' actions and the teacher's role. *School Science Review* 79 (288) 55 - 59

Reiss, M. (1998) Science for all. In Ratcliffe, M. (1998) *ASE Guide to secondary science education*. Cheltenham : Stanley Thornes. 42-51

Reiss, M. (2000) *Understanding science lessons*. Buckingham : Open University Press

Repman, J. (1994) Collaborative, computer-based learning-cognitive and affective outcomes. *Journal of educational computing* 9 (2) 149-163

Resnick, L.B. (1989) *Knowing, learning and instruction. Essays in honor of Robert Glaser.* Hillsdale, NJ : Lawrence Erlbaum Associates

Resnick, L.B., Levine, R., and Teasley, S. (1991) *Perspectives on socially shared cognition*. Washington DC : American Psychological Association

Resnick, L. (1992) Perspectives on Socially Shared Cognition 'Sharing Cognition Through Collective Comprehension Activity. Washington DC : American Psychological Association.

Richmond, G. and Striley, J. (1996) Making meaning in classrooms : Social processes in small-group discourse and scientifc knowledge building. *Journal of Research in Science Teaching* 33 839 - 858

Rieber, R.W. and Carton A. S. (eds) (1987) *Thinking and speech in 'The collected works of LS Vygotsky.'* New York : Plenum Press.

Rogoff, B. (1990) *Apprenticeship in Thinking : Cognitive Development in Social Context.* New York : Oxford University Press

Rogoff, B. and Lave, J. (Eds) (1984) *Everyday Cognition : Its Development in Social Context* Cambridge, MA : Harvard University Press

Rommetveit, R. (1985) Language acquisition as increasing linguistic structuring of experience and symbolic behaviour control. In J.V. Wertsch (Ed) *Culture, communication, and cognition : Vygotskian perspectives*. Cambridge : Cambridge University Press.

Roseberry, A.S., Warren, B. and Conant, F. R. (1992) Appropriating science discourse : Findings from language minority classrooms. *The Journal of Learning Sciences* 2 61-94

Ross, D. and Kyle, D. (1987) Helping pre-service teachers learn to use teacher effectiveness research. *Journal of Teacher Education. 38 40 - 4*

Roth, W. M. and Roychoudhury, A. (1993) The nature of scientific knowledge, knowing and learning : The perspectives of four students. *International Journal of Science Education.* 15 (1) 27-44

Roth, W. M. (1993) Metaphors and conversational analysis as tools in reflection on teaching practice : Two perspectives on teacher-student interactions in open-inquiry science. *Science Education* 77 351-373

Roth, W. M. (1995) *Authentic School Science. Knowing and learning in open-enquiry science laboratories.* Netherlands : Kluwer Press

Roth, W.M. and Bowen, G. M. (1995) Knowing and interacting : A study of culture, practices and resources in a grade 8 open-inquiry science classroom guided by a cognitive apprenticeship metaphor. *Cognition and Instruction* 13 73-128

Roth, W. M. and Robbie, C. (1999) Lifeworlds and the 'w/ri(gh)ting' of classroom research. *Journal of Curriculum Studies* 31 (5) 501 - 522

Roy, A.W. and Howe, C. (1990) Effects of cognitve conflict, socio-cognitive conflict and imitation on children's socio-legal thinking. *European Journal of Social Psychology* 20 241-252

Sands, M.K. (1981) Group-work in Science : Myth and Reality. *School Science Review* 62 (221) 765-769

Scanlon, E., Issroff, K. and Murphy, P. (1999) Collaborations in a primary classroom. In Liitlejohn, K. and Light, P. *Learning with computers : Analysing productive interaction* London : Routledge.

Schliemann, A.D. and Nunes, T. (1990) A situated schema of proportionality. *British Journal of Developmental Psychology* 8 259-268

Schon, D. A. (1983) *The reflective practitioner : How professionals think in action.* New York : Basic books.

Scott, P. (1998) Teacher talk and meaning making in science classrooms: a Vygotskian analysis. *Studies in Science Education.* 32 45 - 80

Scribner, S. (1984) Studying working intelligence. In Rogoff, B. and Lave, J. (Eds) *Everyday cognition : its development in social context* Cambridge MA, Harvard University Press 9 - 40

Scribner, S. (1986) 'Thinking in Action': some characteristics of practical thought. In R.J Sternberg and R. K. Wagner (Eds.) *Practical intelligence : Nature and Origins of competence in the everyday world.* Cambridge : Cambridge University Press 13 - 30

Sears, J. and Sorenson, P. (Eds) (2000) *Issues in Science Teaching*. London : RoutledgeFalmer

Selley, N. J. (2001) Alternative models for dissolution. *School Science Review* 80 (290)

Sharan, S. and Sharan, Y. (1976) *Small-group teaching*. Englewood Cliffs, NJ : Educational Technology Publications.

Sharan, S. (1980) Co-operative learning in small groups: recent methods and effects on achievement, attitudes and ethnic relations. *Review of Educational Research* 50 241-249

Sharan, S. (1985) Cooperative learning and the multiethnic classroom. In Slavin, R., Sharan, S., Kagan, S., Hertz-Lararowitz,, Webb, C. and Schmuck, R. *Learning to Co-operate. Co-operating to learn*. New York : Plenum Press 255 - 262

Shayer, M. (1976) The distribution of Piagetian stages of thinking in british middle and secondary school children. *British Journal of Educational Psychology* 46 164 - 173

Shayer, M. (1993) Piaget : Only Galileo of cognitive development? Comment on Niaz and Lawson on genetic epistemology. *Journal of Research in Science Teaching.* 30 (7) 815 – 818

Shayer, M. (1997) Piaget and Vygotsky : A necessary marriage for effective educational intervention. In Smith, L.; Dockrell, J. and Tomlinson, P. (Eds) *Piaget, Vygotsky and beyond. Future issues for developmental psychology and education.* 36 – 59

Shayer, M. (1999) Cognitive acceleration through science education II: Its effects and scope. *International Journal of Science Education* 21 (8) 883 - 902

Shayer, M. and Adey, P. (1992) Accelerating the development of formal thinking in middle and high school students II : post project effects on science achievement. *Journal of Research in Science Teaching.* 29 (1) 81-92

Shayer, M. and Beasley, F. (1987) Does Instrumental Enrichment work? *British Educational Research Journal.* 13 (2) 101 - 119

Shepardson, D. P. (1999) Learning Science in a first grade science activity : A Vygotskian perspective. *Science Education* 83 621 - 638

Shotter, J. (1992) *In dialogue ; Social construction and radical constructivism.* Paper presented at conference on Alternative Epistemologies in Education. Athens GA

Showers, B. and Joyce, B. (1996) The evolution of peer coaching. *Educational Leadership* 53 12 – 16

Shulman, L. S. (1987) Those who understand : knowledge and growth in teaching. *Educational Researcher.* 15 4 - 14

Silverman, D. (2000) *Doing qualitative research. A practical handbook.* London : Sage Publications

Silverman, D. (2001) *Interpreting qualitative data. Methods for analyzing talk, text and interaction.* 2nd edition. London : Sage Publications

Simpson, M. and Tuson, J. (1995) *Using observations in small-scale research.* Edinburgh : Scottish Council for Research in Education

Sinacore, A. L.; Blaisure, K., R., Justin, M., Healy, P. and Brawer, S. Promoting reflexivity in the classroom. (1999) *Teaching of Psychology* 26 (4) 267 – 271

Siraj-Blatchford, I. (1997) Reflexivity, social justice and educational research. *Cambridge Journal of Education.* 27 (2) 235 - 249

Slavin, R.E. (1980) Cooperative learning. *Review of Educational Research* 50 315 - 342

Slavin, R.E. (1983) *Cooperative learning.* New York : Longman

Slavin, R.E. (1983) When does cooperative learning increase student achievement. *Psychological Bulletin* 94 429 - 445

Slavin, R. (1985) Team assisted individualization : combining cooperative learning and individualized instruction in mathematics. In Slavin, R., Sharan, Slavin, R., Sharan, S., Kagan, S., Hertz-Lararowitz,, Webb, C. and Schmuck, R. (1985) *Learning to Co-operate. Co-operating to learn.* New York : Plenum Press

Smith, A. and Glynn, T. (1990) Contexts for boys and girls learning mathematics : teacher interactions and student behaviour in two classrooms. *New Zealand Journal of Psychology* 19 9 – 16

Smith, C., Carey, S. and Wiser M. (1985) On differentiation: a case study of the development of the concepts of size, weight and density. *Cognition* 21 177-237

Smyth, J. (1989) Developing and sustaining critical reflection in teacher education. *Journal of Teacher Education* 40 (2) 2 - 9

Solomon, J. (1987) Social influences on the construction of pupil's understanding of science. *Studies in Science Education* 14 63-82

Solomon, J. (1991) Partners in cognition: extending human intelligence with intelligent technologies. *Educational Researcher* 20 (3) 2-9

Solomon, J. (1994) The rise and fall of constructivism. *Studies in Science Education* 23 (1) 19

Solomon, J. (1994) What's happened to biology investigations? *Journal of Biological Education.* 28 (4) 261 - 265

Solomon, J. (1998) Constructivism and quality of science education. In Murphy, P., Selinger, M., Bourne, J. and Briggs, M. (Eds) *Primary Curriculum. Issues in English, Science and Mathematics.* 144 – 157

Steffe, L.P. and Gale, J. (Eds.) (1995) *Constructivism in education.* Hillsdale, NJ : Lawrence Erlbaum

Steffe, L. P. and Thompson, P. W. (2000) Interaction or intersubjectivity? A reply to Lerman. *Journal for Research in Mathematics education* 31 (2) 191-209

Sternberg, R. (1996) *Successful intelligence.* New York : Simon and Schuster

Sternberg, R. (1997) *Thinking Styles* Cambridge MA : Cambridge University Press

Sternberg, R.J. and Wagner. R. K (Eds.) (1986) *Toward a broader conception of human intelligence. Practical intelligence : Nature and Origins of competence in the everyday world.* Cambridge MA : Cambridge University Press

Stevens, R. J. and Slavin, R.E. (1995) The co-operative elementary school : effects on students achievement, attitudes and social relations. *American Educational Research Journal* 32 321 - 351

Stewart, J. and McCormack (1997) Experiencing and supporting change: from lecture to interactive groupwork. *Teaching in Higher Education* 2 (2) 167 - 181

Stone (1998) The metaphor of scaffolding : its utility for the field of learning disabilities. *Journal of learning Disabilities* 31 (4) 34 - 64

Strang, J. and Shayer, M. (1993) Enhancing high school students' achievement in chemistry through a thinking skills approach. *International Journal for Science Education* 15 (3) 319 – 337

Strough, J. (2000) Dyad gender and friendship differences in shared goals for mutual participation. *Child Study Journal* 30 (2) 103 - 127

Swatton, P. (1990) Process and content in the Science National curriculum. *School Science Review.* 72 (259) 19 - 28

Tamir, P. (1981) Classroom interaction analysis of high school biology classes in Israel. *Science Education* 65 (1) 87-103

Tann, S. (1981) Grouping and Group Work. In Simon, B. and Willcocks, J. (Eds) *Research and practice in the Primary Classroom.* London : Routledge and Kiegan Paul. 43-54

Taylor, A. (1997) Learning science through creative activities. *School science Review* 79 (286) 39 - 46

Tharp, R. and Gallimore, R. (1988) *Rousing Minds to life : teaching and learning and schooling in social context.* Cambridge : Cambridge University Press

Tizard, B., Blatchford, D., Burke, J. Farquhar, C. and Plewis, I (1988) *Young children at school in the Inner City.* Hove: Lawrence Erlbaum.

Tobin, K. (1984) Effects of extended wait time on discourse characteristics and achievement in middle school grades. *Journal of Research in Science Teaching.* 21 (8) 779-791

Tolmie, A and Howe, C. (1993) Gender and dialogue in secondary school physics. *Gender and education* 5 (2) 191-209

Tolmie, A., Howe, C., Mackenzie, M. and Greer, K. (1993) Task design as an influence on dialogue and learning : primary school group work with object flotation. *Social development* 2 (3) 183 - 201

Tough, (1977) The development of meaning : A study of use of Language. London : Allen and Unwin

Toulmin, S. (1972) *Human Understanding*. Princeton : Princeton University Press

Tripp, D. (1993) Case study generalization : an agenda for action. *British Educational Research Journal* 11 (1) 33 - 43

Trumper, R. (1993) Children's energy concepts : a cross age study. *International Journal of Science Education*. 15 (2) 139-48

Tuckman, B. (1965) Developmental sequence in small groups. Psychological Bulletin 63 384 – 399

Tuckman, B. and Jensen, M. (1977) Stages of small group development revisited. *Group and organizational studies*. 2 419 - 427

Tudge, J.R.H. and Rogoff, B. (1989) Peer influences on cognitive development : Piagetian and Vygotskian perspectives, in M.H. Bornstein and J.S. Bruner. *Interaction in Human Development*. Hillsdale, N. J.: Lawrence Erlbaum.

Tudge, J. and Winterthoff, P. (1993) Can young children benefit from collaborative problem solving? Tracing effects of partner competence and feedback. In C. Howe (ed) *Social development. Special issue: peer interaction and knowledge acquisition*. 2 (1) 242 - 259

Underwood, G. McCaffrey, M., Underwood, J. (1990) Gender differences in a cooperative computer-based language task. *Educational Research* 32 (1) 44-49

Underwood, G. Underwood J., Turner, M. (1993) Children's thinking during collaborative computer-based problem solving. *Educational Psychology* 13 (3) 345-357

Veenman, S., Kenter, B. and Post, K. (2000) Cooperative learning in primary Dutch classrooms. *Educational Studies* Sept 26 (3) 281

Venn, C. and Walkerdine, V. (1977) The acquisition and production of knowledge. *Ideology and consciousness* 3 67-94

Von Glaserfeld, E. (1984) An introduction to radical constructivism. In Watzlawick, P. (Ed) *The invented reality*. New York : Norton. 17 - 40

Vygotsky, L. S. (1979) Consciousness as a problem in the psychology of behaviour. *Soviet Psychology* 17 (4) 3 - 35

Vygotsky, L.S. (1981) The genesis of higher mental functions. In Wertch, J. V. (Ed) *The concept of activity in Soviet psychology*. Armonk. NY : Sharpe 147 – 188

Vygotsky, L. S. (1986) *Thought and Language*. Kozulin, A (Ed.) Revised Edition. Cambridge, MA : The MIT Press

Vygotsky, L.S. (1978) *Mind in Society: The development of higher Psychological Processes.* Cambridge, MA: Harvard University Press

Vygotsky, L. S. (1962) *Thought and Language*. Cambridge, MA : MITPress

Watson, J. R. (1994) Students engagement in practical problem-solving: a case study. *International Journal of Science education.* 16 (1) 27 – 43

Watson, J. R., Swain, J R. L. and McRobbie, C. (1999) The interaction between teaching styles and pupil autonomy in practical science investigations: a case study. In Leach, J. and Paulsen, A. (Eds) *Practical work in Science Education : Recent research studies.* Roskilde: Roskilde University Press

Watson, R. and Wood-Robinson, V. (1998) Learning to investigate. In M. Ratcliffe (Ed) *The ASE Guide to Secondary Science Education.* Stanley Thornes

Watson, R. (2000) The role of practical work. In M. Monk and J. Osbourne, (Eds) *Good practice in science teaching. What research has to say.* Buckingham : Open University Press

Watts, M., Gould, G. and Alsop, S. (1997) Questions of understanding : categorising pupils' questions in science. *School Science Review* 79 (286) 57 – 63

Watts, M. and McGrath, C. (1998) SATISfactions : approaches to relevance in science education. *School Science Review* 79 (288) 61 - 65

Webb, N. (1989) Peer Interaction and Learning in small groups. *International Journal of Educational Research* (13) p.21-39

Webb, N. (1980) An analysis of group interaction and mathematical errors in heterogeneous ability groups. *British Journal of Educational Psychology* (50) 266-276

Webb, N. (1983) Predicting Learning from student interaction : Defining the Interaction variables. *Educational Psychologist* 18 (1) 33 - 41

Webb, N. (1984) Sex differences in interaction and achievement in cooperative small groups. *Journal of Educational Psychology* 76 (1) 33 - 44

Webb, N. (1985) Verbal Interaction and Learning in Peer Directed Groups. *Theory into practice 24 (1) 32 - 39*

Wegerif, R., Mercer, N. and Dawes, L. (1999) From social interaction to individual reasoning : an empirical investigation of a possible socio-cultural model of cognitive development. *Learning and instruction.* 9 493 - 516

Wellington, J. (1994) *Secondary science. Contempary issues and practical approaches.* London : Routledge

Wellington, J. (1989) *Skills and processes in Science Education. A critical analysis.* London : Routledge.

Wells, G. (1981) *Learning through interaction* Cambridge : Cambridge University Press

Wenger, E. (1998) *Communities of practice : Learning, meaning and identity.* Cambridge : Cambridge University Press

Wertsch, J.V. (ed.) (1981) The concept of activity in Soviet psychology. Armonk, NY: M.E.

Wertsch, J.V. (1985) Vygotsky and the social formation of the mind. Harvard University Press

Wertsch, J. V. (1985) Culture, Communication and cognition: Vygotskian perspectives. Cambridge University Press

West, L. and Pines, A. (1985) Cognitive structure and conceptual change. Orlando, FL. Academic Press

Wittgenstein, L. (1958) Philosophical Investigations. New York : Macmillan.

Wood, David (1998) *How children think and learn.* 2nd edition. Blackwell Publishers Ltd

Wood, D. and O'Malley, C. (1996) Collaborative learning between peers : An overview Pairs/small groups. *Educational psychology in practice.* 11 (4) 4 - 9

Wood, D., Bruner, J. S. and Ross, G. (1976) The role of tutoring in problem solving. *Journal of child psychology* 17 89 - 100

Wolcott, H. F. (1990) *Writing up qualitative research.* London : Sage Publications

Woolnough, B. E. (1994) *Effective science teaching.* Buckingham : Open University Press

Zander, A and Van Egmond, E. (1958) Relationships of intelligence and social power to interpersonal behaviour of children. *Journal of Educational Psychology* 49 257 – 268

Zeichner, K. M. and Liston, D. (1990) *Traditions of reform and reflective teaching in US Teacher Education.* East Lansing, MI : National Center for Research on Teacher Education

Zessoules, R. and Gardner, H. (1991) Authentic assessment: beyond the buzzword and into the classroom, in Perrone, V. (ed.) *Expanding Student assessment.* Alexandria, VA : Association for supervision and curriculum development 47 - 71

Appendices (Numbered with pre-fix relating to chapter where referenced)

Appendix 4.1 : Investigating group work at Key Stage 3 and 4 : The teachers questionnaire

Investigation into group work in Science at Key Stage 3 and 4
(Questionnaire for teachers)

The purpose of this questionnaire is to collect information about the extent to which you conduct your group work activities in Science teaching, with your Key Stage 3 and 4 pupils. We should also like to know about the nature of such activities and your opinion concerning group work practice in your school.

'Group work' here is defined as **'activity in which groups of two or more pupils work together in collaboration, either on identical activities or different aspects of the same activity, usually without direct supervision or control by the teacher'.**

Please complete the questionnaire by providing the information asked for in the various questions. Any additional information that you may provide will be most welcome.

We do assure you that any information you give will be treated as **confidential** and **used for research purposes only.**

May we thank you for your co-operation in completing this questionnaire.

SECTION A: GENERAL INFORMATION

In this section we would like you to provide some information about yourself and the school in which you work.

1 Your name:____

2 Sex: *(Please tick as appropriate)*

Male	
Female	

3 Number of years teaching experience:____________________________

4 Your teaching qualifications: *(Please tick as appropriate)*

B.Sc. + P.G.C.E.	
B.A. + P.G.C.E.	
B. Ed.	
Certificate of Education	
Other(s) (please specify)	

5 Please indicate by placing a tick in the appropriate boxes, the science courses you are currently teaching Key Stage 3 and 4:
(If you offer a combination of resources could you indicate the approximate component of the course in % terms.)

Key Stage 3		Key Stage 4	
Active Science		Action Science	
Bath Science 5 - 16		Active Science	
Blackwell Modular		Bath Science	
New Horizons		Blackwell Modular Science	
Nuffield Science (Yrs 7,8,9)		Cambridge Co-ordinated Science	
Oxford Science programme		Co-ordinated Science (Oxford)	
Q Science		Co-ordinated Science - Suffolk development	
Science Focus - The Salter's Approach		Modular Science for GCSE	
Science Scene		New Horizons	
Science World		Nuffield Co-ordinated	
Spotlight Science		Oxford Science programme	
Staring Science		Pathways through Science	
Understanding Science		Salter's Science	
Others (please specify)		Science at Work	
		The Sciences for GCSE	
		Understanding and Applying Science	
		Others (please specify)	

6. Name and address of the school where you are employed:

SECTION B: THE EXTENT AND NATURE OF GROUP WORK

In this section, we would like to know the extent to which you use **group work** in your teaching and your reasons for choosing to organise your science class(es) in this way.

1. The following list presents a number of learning activities that may be organised in the form of **group work** done by pupils.

   Indicate, by means of a tick (/), the extent to which you make use of them in your own science teaching with KS 3 and 4.

Learning activities	Extent of use at KS 3					Extent of use at KS 4				
	never	rarely	ocass-ionly	fairly frequ-ently	always	never	rarely	ocass-ionly	fairly frequ-ently	always
a. Conduct of practical work, including the collection of data and information										
b. Discussion of data/information collected from practical work										
c. Planning of practical investigation										
d. Discussion of theoretical problems, e.g. examination type questions										
e. Debates on reading assignments										
f. Science games/simulation exercises										
g. Science quizzes										
h. Other(s) please specify ______ ______										

2. Please indicate, by ticking the appropriate box, approximately what proportion of pupil-based actvities are organised by you as group work.

	At Key Stage 3	At Key Stage 4
Less than 10%		
10 - 25%		
25 - 50%		
more than 50%		

3. What group size(s) do you use when organising pupil-based practical activities as group work? Please tick as appropriate.

Group size (students per group)	Extent of use at Key Stage 3			Extent of use at Key Stage 4		
	frequently	occasionall y	never	frequently	occasionall y	never
two						
three						
four						

4. There may be a variety of reasons why teachers arrange science activities in the form of group work. Please indicate your main reasons, in relation to:

a. practical activities (give up to three reasons)

i. ______________________________

ii. ______________________________

iii. ______________________________

b. non-practical activities (give up to three reasons)

1. ______________________________

ii. ______________________________

iii. ______________________________

SECTION C: ORGANISATION OF GROUP WORK

In this section, we are interested in finding out about the way you organise your working groups with particular interest to group formation, composition and flexibility (in this question, please **select the response that most closely applies to you**).

1. When organising group activities in science do you usually:

a. allow your pupils to select their own working partners, without 'intervention' from you?	
b. instruct your pupils to work with their neighbour(s) , i.e., those seated next to them?	
c. form the working groups by placing the pupils together for particular (educational or other) reasons?	

If you have ticked option c, please give the main criteria that you use in forming working groups.

____

____

2. What is your preferred practice in relation to 'mixed' working groups?

	Yes	No
a. I like to see boys and girls interacting in science working groups, and encourage 'mixing' of the sexes.		
b. I have no particular preferences in relation to this matter		
c. As far as possible I prefer boys and girls to work in 'single-sex' groups.		
d. I prefer to have 'mixed ability groups wherever possible		
e. I prefer to have mixed 'personality' groups where possible.		

3. In your science classes, do the working groups usually remain the same?

Yes	No

If the answer is NO, what changes occur or can occur?

____

____

Are these changes initiated mainly:

by yourself?	
by the pupils?	

What in your judgement, are the main reasons for the changes?

____

____

4. We should like to know of any major difficulties or problems that you have encountered when organising group work in science. Please describe briefly up to three such difficulties or problems.

   i. ____

   ii. ____

   iii. ____

Section D: Management of Group Learning

In this part of the questionnaire, we are seeking information about the strategies you use in organising learning tasks and in supervising your working groups.

1. The following statements explore different approaches to the way in which practical tasks can be introduced in science lessons. Please indicate, by means of appropriately placed ticks, the extent to which you employ these approaches in your teaching.

Strategy for introducing practical tasks	frequency of use			
	normal	occasional	exceptional	never
a. Practical task is pre-determined. Pupils are expected to follow instructions provided.				
b. Practical tasks are generally pre-determined, but modifications are required in the light of outcomes of prior class discussion.				
c. Practical tasks are only loosely pre-structured. Actual practical strategies emerge from discussion with pupils.				
d. Practical work is not pre-structured, but arises from the context of the lesson topic and in the light of suggestions received from pupils.				
e. Other(s) (Please specify) ______ ______				

2. To what extent do you usually involve yourself in the organisation of learning tasks for working groups? Please indicate, by placing a tick in the appropriate box, the response that most clearly describes your practice.

a. I try not to involve myself, instead, I make the groups responsible for task organisation and distribution among themselves.	
b. I ask one group member to be responsible for task allocation	
c. I suggest how tasks can be divided, but leave the task distribution to each group to decide.	
d. I assign specific tasks to different members of the group	
e. Any other procedure (please specify): ______ ______	

3. The following are strategies frequently used by teachers when supervising group work. Choose the **one** that best describes your own practice.

a. I move around the classroom/laboratory to monitor the general progress of pupils, without intervention unless I think it is necessary.	
b. I systematically move around to all working groups and discuss their work with them.	
c. I keep a general overview of the class, but I focus attention especially on those groups which contain pupils of low ability or 'slow workers'.	
d. i monitor the work of the class in general, but I stay close to working groups that tend to 'deviate' from the task set.	
e. Any other procedure (please specify): ______________________ ______________________	

If none of the above applies to you, please describe in your own words how you supervise your pupil's work.

____

____

4. Groups generally differ with regard to the pace at which they complete learning tasks assigned to them. briefly indicate your main strategies for dealing with:

a. 'fast working groups'

____
____
____

b. 'slow working groups'

____
____
____

5. Some of the practical work undertaken by pupils is likely to be the result of their own planning. Please indicate which **one** of the following **best** describes your normal practice in allowing your pupils progression from the planning to the 'doing' (implementation) stage.

a. I tend to allow pupils to proceed strictly to practical work once they have completed their planning.	
b. I generally allow pupils to proceed to their practical work after completion of their planning, but tend to check that their practical method is safe.	
c. I tend to discuss plans with individual working groups, in order to establish the safety of proposed procedure as well as it's appropriate feasibility in relation to the work set.	
d. There is a class discussion of proposed plans in order to focus on 'best' or 'most suitable' strategies.	
e. Any other procedure (please specify): ______________________ ______________________	

Section E: Views and opinions about group work

In this section, we would like to explore your personal opinion about aspects of group work.

1.a. From your point of view as a science class teacher, what do you consider to be the main **educational advantages and benefits** of group learning activities. Please give up to three points.

i. ______________________________

ii. ______________________________

iii. ______________________________

b. Are there any definite **disadvantages** that you associate with group work in science? Please specify.

i. ______________________________

ii. ______________________________

iii. ______________________________

2. In the light of your experience, which kind of working group tends to be educationally most effective? Please tick **one** of the following boxes.

a. Groups composed of pupils of similar academic aptitude ('homogeneous' groups)	
b. Groups composed of pupils of widely differing ability ('mixed ability' groups)	
c. Groups composed of pupils with strong social links ('friendship groups')	
d. Groups composed of pupils who 'get on' with one another in terms of personality ('compatibility groups')	
e. Groups in which at least one pupil can exhibit leadership qualities ('leadership groups')	
f. Groups with some other characteristics(please specify) ______________________________ ______________________________	

3.a. In your view, are there any types of experimental work or other learning task for which group work is particularly suitable? Please specify.

i. ______________________________

ii. ______________________________

iii. ______________________________

b. Are there any types of experimental work or other learning tasks that you consider **unsuitable** for group work? Please specify.

i. ____________________

ii. ____________________

iii. ____________________

4. It is common for pupils working in groups to engage in 'task-unrelated talk' or activities.

a. What in your view, is the approximate percentage of pupil time spent 'off-task' during their practical work? (Do not include in your estimate time used for class discussion, review of methods, results etc.) Please tick the appropriate box.

< 10%	
10 - 24%	
25 - 50%	
> 50%	

b. What proportion of time spent 'off-task' do your regard as reasonable or acceptable? Please tick the appropriate box.

< 10%	
10 - 24%	
25 - 50%	
> 50%	

ADDITIONAL COMMENTS/OBSERVATIONS

If there is any additional information you feel is likely to help in our enquiry, please note it in the space below (continue on a separate sheet if necessary).

Should we require any further information or help with this study, would you be willing to assist us further? Please indicate.

Yes	No

May we thank you for your co-operation in completing this questionnaire. Would you please return it ASAP to:

D.McGregor
Education Department
Keele University
Keele
Staffordshire
ST5 5BG

Appendix 4.2 : Analysis of open responses from Teacher's questionnaire.

Open ended questions, allowing free responses from the teachers were listed and then typed in a word processed file, e.g.; in response to question B4a 'There may be a variety of reasons why teachers arrange science activities in the form of group work. Please indicate your main reasons, in relation to practical activities.'

Typical teacher responses were:

- to share roles, observing, timing, recording - to make task easier
- to develop idea of team work and sharing ideas and practices
- practicalities of amount equipment required
- availability of equipment
- complexity of task needs 'pairs' of hands
- sharing ideas

After reading through a large sample of responses, they were categorised and classified, e.g.:

Categories of response (for question B4a):

10 Class management (relating to class size/no of pupils etc.)

20 Resources sharing/shortage of resources/limited space

21 resources

22 space

23 resources and space

24 safety

30 Time management idea (constraints of time)

31 progress

32 complex tasks (subdivision of labour/sharing the work load)

33 more results

34 speed

40 Sharing - of ideas/results/findings/learning efficiency/task related

41 ideas

42 results/findings/observations

43 more efficient/effective learning (can learn from one another/less able assisted)

44 task related (communication/more opportunity for individual input/active involvement)

50 Social interaction/social skills, collaborative team working etc.

51 social skills

52 personal skills (happier/confident)

60 Alternative approach (vary teaching strategy)

Each rejoinder was then allocated the corresponding category reference, e.g.

'to share roles, observing, timing, recording - to make task easier' categorised as 32

'to develop idea of team work and sharing ideas and practices' 51

'Practicalities of amount equipment required' 21

'Availability of equipment' 21

'Complexity of task needs 'pairs' of hands' 44

'Sharing ideas' 41

The numerical equivalent of the data was then entered into an SPSS so that quasi, semi-quantitative statistical and graphical analysis could be carried out.

Appendix 4.3 : Pupil's 'Working together in Science' questionnaire. Distributed as A5 booklet.

University of Keele
Education Department

Pupils working together in Science

(Questionnaire for pupils)

- This is not a test, there are no right or wrong answers. Your responses will remain private.

- This is a survey to try and find out **what you do** and **what you think about working with others in science.**

- The questions ask you about working in a group. In each case, a **group means two or more of you working together**, i.e.; not working by yourself, but with at least one other person.

Please fill in the boxes below.

Your name	
Are you boy or girl?	
Your class	
Your school	

INTRODUCTION AND INSTRUCTIONS

IN EACH SECTION THERE MAY BE DIFFERENT KINDS OF QUESTION TO ANSWER, E.G.:

I TICK THE BOX THAT INDICATES WHAT USUALLY HAPPENS IN SCIENCE CLASS
E.G.: How many teachers do you have for science in a normal week?

1	
2	
3 or more	

2 TICK ONE OF THE THREE BOXES THAT IS CLOSEST TO WHAT USUALLY HAPPENS IN SCIENCE CLASS

	Lots of times	Occasionally	Rarely or never
Carry out a practical or experiment, including collecting results			

3 WRITE DOWN WHATEVER YOU CAN
ii If these groups change, either occasionally or regularly, what do you think are the reasons for the change? (Feel free to give more than one reason):

____

____

____

PLEASE read all the questions carefully.

THANK YOU FOR YOUR HELP.......

SECTION A: GENERAL INFORMATION

1 Tick the box which best describes you?

I can cope easily with my science work	
Usually I can cope, but sometimes I struggle	
I usually struggle, but sometimes I cope	
I always struggle in science	

2 How many teachers do you have for science in a normal week?

1	
2	
3 or more	

3 Is your main science teacher a man or a woman?

man	
woman	

SECTION B: WHEN DO YOU WORK IN A GROUP?

1. Here are some activities that can be carried out as a group. Tick all those you have done as a group. Put the tick in the column which fits best:

	Lots of times	Occasionally/ some-times	Rarely or never
Carry out a practical or experiment, including collecting results			
Discuss the results or how the experiment has gone			
Plan a practical or investigation			
Discussing questions, problems set or information provided by the teacher			
Creating a piece of written work (e.g.; poster or letter) together			
Role-play, using drama/acting in some way			
Finding out something together, using CD-ROM or encyclopaedia, library			
Other			

2. In a typical science lesson, how much time do you think you spend working in a group?

over half the lesson	
between a quarter and a half	

less than a quarter	

3. In your science course, how often do you work in groups?

in every science lesson	
in most science lessons	
in some science lessons	
never	

4 How often do you work in groups when not doing practical work or doing things other than practical work?

often	
occasionally	
rarely or never	

SECTION C: HOW IS YOUR WORK IN GROUPS ORGANISED?

1. Tick which statement best describes what usually happens when you work with others in groups:

the teacher tells us exactly which other pupils to work with	
the teacher tells us to work with our neighbour	
the teacher allows us to choose whom to work with	

2. When working with others what is the usual size of your group in a science lesson?

2	
3	
4	
more than 4	

3i. Do the people in your working group:

usually remain the same	
change sometimes	
change often	

ii. Please answer this question if you ticked the 2nd or 3rd answer. What do you think are the reasons for the change? (Feel free to give more than one reason):

____

____

____

4. If you could chose who to work with in your group, which **one** of the following would you choose?

pupils of about the same ability as yours	
pupils who are better at science than you are	
my friends	
pupils who will listen to you	
you don't mind at all who is in your group	

SECTION D: HOW DO YOU WORK AND LEARN IN GROUPS?

1. When you do practical work in groups which one of the following statements best describes how your teacher usually introduces the work you have to do:

our teacher gives us clear instructions about what each individual in a group should do	
our teacher describes what has to be done, but leaves us to decide what each of us does	
our teacher provides general information about an experiment, but we have to work out how to do it	

2. When working with others in groups, which usually applies to you:

I learn a lot from my partners	
I learn a little from my partners, but they learn just as much from me	
I don't think I learn much from my partners, but they learn a lot from me	
We don't really learn a lot from each other because we just follow our teacher's instructions.	

3. When working with others in groups doing practical work, chose which statement best describes what happens:

we are usually left to ourselves	
our teacher walks around the class and occasionally talks to us	
our teacher regularly checks on our progress	
our teacher helps us when we are in difficulties	

4. When you are working in a group, what best describes how you feel?:

I always know what we have to do	
I mostly know what we have to do, but sometimes I am are not clear	
I am often unclear and tend to be lost	

5. Here are a number of statements about working in groups. For each statement, tick the box the best describes what happens to you when working with others:

	Always applies to me	Sometimes applies to me	Rarely or never applies to me
We work more quickly in a group than on our own			
We produce more ideas than working on our own			
We share our ideas about the work to be done			
When discussing the work to be done I usually say alot			
We work out our results together			
I think more about the science because we discuss it more			
I am more enthusiastic than working on my own			
I feel more confident than working on my own			
We argue about who does what			
I don't work as hard as I could			
We more often talk about things not related to task set			

6. When working in groups which statement best describes how much of your time you usually spend **talking about things not connected with the science work set**.

I talk only a little	
I talk between a quarter and a half of lesson	
I talk about a half of the lesson	
I talk more than half of the lesson	

SECTION E: WHAT DO YOU THINK ABOUT WORKING IN GROUPS?

1. When working in groups, pupils sometimes experience difficulties. In the following list some of the difficulties are given. Tick the box which best describes how often you have had these problems.

	Lots of times	Sometimes	Rarely or never
Deciding who does what			
One of the group members always wants to be the leader			
My partner(s) don't listen to my thoughts			
I find it difficult to see what I have to do			
I don't always get on with my working partners			
We don't make enough effort to discuss our work together			
Please add any other difficulties you have had not listed here: ________ ________ ________ ________			

2. Have you been given any guidance or help on how to work with others in a group?

Yes	
No	

3. Please answer this question if you ticked yes to question 2. Who has given you guidance or help? Please tick the boxes that best describe how much guidance or help they have given you.

	A lot	some	none
Present science teacher			
Previous science teacher			
Form tutor			
Someone else			

4. Do you feel that you should have more advice on how to work with others in groups?

Yes	
No	

5. Are there any aspects of working with others in groups you would like advice or help on? Please feel free to write what you can.

____

Appendix 4.4 : Script for teachers to introduce question booklets to pupils.

Dear Science Teacher,

Thank you very much for allowing your pupils the time to answer the questions on how they work and learn in groups in science.

Could you please remind them of the following:

- This is not a test - but conditions under which they will **not copy** each other's responses is appropriate.
- It is intended that the responses are **entirely** the **pupils own** - so there should be no advice about answers to be given.
- Their responses will remain confidential.
- There are 3 types of responses required (explained on inside cover of questionnaire):

I TICK THE BOX THAT INDICATES WHAT USUALLY HAPPENS IN SCIENCE CLASS
E.G.: How many teachers do you have for science in a normal week?

1	
2	
3 or more	

2 TICK ONE OF THE THREE BOXES THAT IS CLOSEST TO WHAT USUALLY HAPPENS IN SCIENCE CLASS

	Lots of times	Occasionally	Rarely or never
Carry out a practical or experiment, including collecting results			

3 WRITE DOWN WHATEVER YOU CAN
ii If these groups change, either occasionally or regularly, what do you think are the reasons for the change? (Feel free to give more than one reason):

____

- Please remind pupils that **groups** are **2 or more pupils**. When answering questions they need to remember this.

Could you please return questionnaires in envelope provided.

Thank you for your time.

Yours faithfully,

Debbie McGregor
Science (Biology) Education Tutor

Appendix 4.5 : Initial analysis (including transcript of actions and discussion and subsequent interactive-cognitist analysis) of the interactions between a triad of girls (group 1A) from School A.

Overview of group (1A) activity (Open candle race)

They read problem sheet in silence.
Immediately after reading problem, A allocates timing task to B and decides that 'do tubes' in order, 'smallest first, then the middle, then the biggest'. *(There is no discussion about either of these directives from A.)*
They all write for about a minute.
A lights first candle.
B asks A how to operate stop clock.
A places smallest jar over candle. B starts stop clock.
Candle extinguishes. B stops timer.
All write down results.
A lights second candle.
C recognises flame not same size as previous candle and states not fair test.
B suggests using the first candle again, she swops them.
A relights first candle.
A lifts medium jar ready.
B says 'say go' when ready.
A and B sychronise beginning to time and lowering jar.
They watch flame.
B stops timer as flame extinguishes.
They all write down answer.
A re-lights candle again.
C says 'go' as she lowers large jar. B starts timing.
All write down result.

Individual recording of results.

A's written record:
'Smallest: Time 5 seconds
Middle: Time 7 seconds
Large: Time 9 seconds
Conclusion
The candle stays lit longer if there is more air because fire needs air to flame. Jo gest right.'

B's written record:
'Three candle race
Little tube: Time 5 seconds
Middle tube Time 7 seconds
Large tube time 9 seconds
Conclusion the candle that had the large tube around it with the most air stayed lit the longest. So Jo's prediction was correct. A candle needs air to stay lit.'
Most accurate response in written format – but weaker in contribution to discussion on methodology – even though better idea of fair test when asked post-filming.

C's written record:
'Little tube: 5 secs time to go out
Medium tube: 7 secs time to go out
Large tube: 9 secs time to go out
Conclusion: The candle in the large tube stayed lit a lot longer than the other two. Jo's predicment was correct. The candle did get a bit brighter at about half way through the timing.'
Altho's this is the weakest re: analysis, in discussion she was probably the strongest on evaluation (of a fair test)

Relative engagement of pupils for duration of task

Continous judgements made not at regular half minute intervals as on 'Action recorded every half minute'.

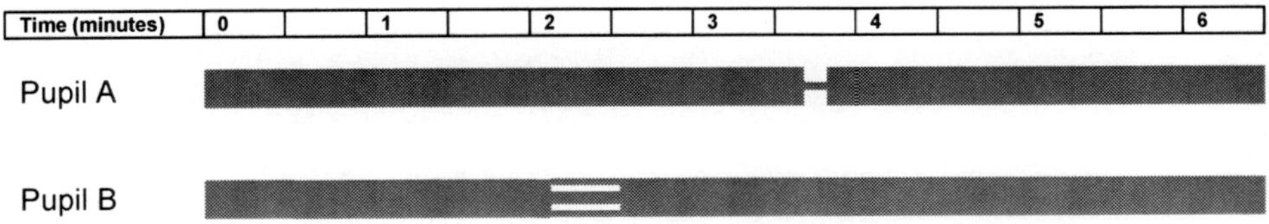

Pupil C

Indicates 'active engagement' whereby the pupils are engaged in some kind of obvious action directly linked to the task.

Indicates intermittent 'active and passive engagement'. The pupils are not engaged in either active or passive continously for more than 30 seconds.

Indicates 'passive engagement' whereby the pupils are engaged with the task as illustrated by observing or listening.

——— Indicates 'no engagement' whereby the pupils are not engaged in any kind of obvious action directly linked to the task.

These general categories of active/passive and no engagement are evident in a number of ways and review of the various aspects of these can elicit some patterns in interactions.

Active engagement:
Includes 'actions' whereby pupils are 'doing' something directly related to the task, such as:
reading the worksheet,
explicitly discussing issues (what to do; how to do it; what it means) related to the task,
setting up, testing, using or handling the equipment,

Passive engagement:
This is when pupils are still focussed and on task but not actively carrying out an 'action' related to the task.
Indicative behaviour would include observing and listening, perhaps others or events occurring in the course of the task.

Non-engagement:
This would involve behaviours not linked to the task. Either actions or words that are 'off task' such as telling a joke, clowning behaviour etc would be included.

The following three diagrams illustrate how the behaviours of three pupils in a triad were monitored and assessed along a time-line.

Action of pupil A recorded each half minute

Behaviour of Pupil A:		Time (minutes during activity)											
Levels of engagement – indicated through 'action'		**0.5**	**1**	**1.5**	**2**	**2.5**	**3**	**3.5**	**4**	**4.5**	**5**	**5.5**	**6**
Active engagement:													
1.Talking (Thinker:mind on) On task talk:	makes initial suggestions* (what to do/write/record)		■										
	evaluator/reflector* (reviews where at/success etc)												
	idea generator*												
	asks provoking questions*												
	Improves technique*												
	suggests improvement/modification to practical*												
	agreement/ acquiescence*												
	idea developer*												
	gives instruction to another												
2. Doing (Hands on)	preparation/dev familiarity with/ assembling/handling apparatus												
	carrying out expt			■	■	■							
	hands apparatus to another												
	cleaning/tidying												
On task writing:	i. preparatory	■											
	ii. recording results							■					
	iii. other – explanation								■	■	■	■	
Passive engagement:	reading (instructions)												
	observing others in group												
	observing events												
	listening to others												
	(appears to be) contemplating						■						
Non-engagment:	not doing anything –'vacant'												
	off task talk												
	off task behaviour (not contributing to task outcome,ie:joke,daft behaviour,non-constructive fiddling with equipment)												

Co-operative behaviour coded in black type
Collaborative behaviour coded in purple type

Action of pupil B recorded each half minute

Behaviour of Pupil B:		Time (minutes during activity)											
Levels of engagement – indication through 'action'		**0.5**	**1**	**1.5**	**2**	**2.5**	**3**	**3.5**	**4**	**4.5**	**5**	**5.5**	**6**
1. Talking (Thinker:mind on) On task talk													
	makes initial suggestions* (what to do/write/record)												
	evaluator/reflector* (reviews where at/success etc)												
	idea generator*												
	asks provoking questions*												
	Improves technique*												
	suggests improvement/modification to practical*												
	agreement/ acquiescence*												
	idea developer*												
	gives instruction to another						■						
2. Doing (hands on)	Preparation/dev familiarity with/ assembling/handling apparatus												
	carrying out expt			■	■	■							
	hands apparatus to another												
	cleaning/tidying												
On task writing:	i. preparatory	■											
	ii. recording results							■					
	iii. other - explanation								■	■	■	■	
Passive engagement:	reading (instructions)												
	observing others in group		■										
	observing events												
	listening to others												
	(appears to be) contemplating												
None engagement:	not doing anything –'vacant'												
	off task talk												
	off task behaviour (not contributing to task outcome,ie:joke,daft behaviour,non-constructive fiddling with equipment)												

Co-operative behaviour coded in black type
Collaborative behaviour coded in purple type

Action of pupil C recorded each half minute

Behaviour of Pupil C:		Time (minutes during activity)											
Levels of engagement – indicated through 'action'		**0.5**	**1**	**1.5**	**2**	**2.5**	**3**	**3.5**	**4**	**4.5**	**5**	**5.5**	**6**
Active engagement:													
1.Talking (thinker;mind on) On task talk:	makes initial suggestions* (what to do/wnte/record)												
	evaluator/reflector* (reviews where at/success etc)					■							
	idea generator*												
	asks provoking questions*												
	Improves technique*												
	suggests improvement/modification to practical*												
	agreement/ acquiescence*												
	idea developer*												
	gives instruction to another												
2. Doing (hands on)	preparation/dev familiarity with/ assembling/handling apparatus												
	carrying out expt												
	hands apparatus to another												
	cleaning/tidying												
On task writing:	i. preparatory	■											
	ii. recording results							■					
	iii. other - explanation									■	■	■	
Passive engagement:	reading (instructions)												
	observing others in group		■		■				■				
	observing events						■						
	listening to others			■									
	(appears to be) contemplating												
None engagement:	not doing anything –'vacant'												
	off task talk												
	off task behaviour (not contributing to task outcome,ie:joke,daft behaviour,non-constructive fiddling with equipment)												

Co-operative behaviour coded in black type
Collaborative behaviour coded in purple type

Transcript of pupils' (verbal and actional) interactions with commentary using the interactional-cognitist perspective

Time (minutes :second s)	**Transcript**	**Commentary on interactions and science processing**	**Interactional-cognitist perspective** (different colours indicat different episodes c discussion)
0 0.05 0.30	All read papers **A** to **B** "you work the timer" **A** "let's do the smallest tube, then the middle then the biggest" **A**, **B** and **C** spend a minute or so writing. **A** looks at **C**'s writing	A deciding what needs doing, who should do it and how they should do it – illustrating **organiser**/leader qualities Is A as confident as she initially portrays?…referencing what C has written, A could just be checking she's ready for the practical work. No collaboration – solo writing – preparing to write results in a table. All take on board A's suggestion of order of trial – smallest – medium – largest size. No challenge to A's ideas.	*}* *} Disputational* *} As A directs she makes the* *} decisions. B and C do not tak* *} opportunity to 'dispute'*
1.00	**A** "let's do this one first" reaches for smallest jar and spill ***C*** "I'll light one of the candles" ***B*** to **A** referring to timer "how do I start this?" **A** *to* **B** "just press start then I'll tell you to go" **A** lights first candle with spill ***B*** to **A** "tell me when go" **A** "not yet" ***C*** "you've got wait, you've got wait until it goes" **A** *to* **B** "you've got to wait until I go light this" **A** blows out spill **C** 'that's it' **A** "oops" as she blows too hard ***C*** *to* **A** "put it on the other one as well" **A** *to* **B** "time to go" ***C*** *to* **A** "why don't you do them all at once?"	A initiates the practical work by reaching for and stating 'lets do this one first'. C says I'll light one of the candles …but A doesn't pass a spill – C anticipates having a turn but doesn't happen – she doesn't assert herself. B has picked up timer ->intuitive task allocation?for A and B -no discussion and therefore consideration of tasks/process/best way to solve problem. B requesting help from A-reinforcing C and B acceptance of A as leader and more capable? A leading/organising again. A determines what should be measured;ie: when timing should start and finish. C means wait until candle lit. A means until candle alight too C means light other candle too. C persisting – light all candles together. A answers with pragmatic response – using level of resourcing/equipment as indicator of whether to light candles or not. B choosing not to challenge-although later recognises why better to light all 3 candles simultaneously.	*}* *Disputational* *} Again A directs, no discussio* *} of her decision regarding* *} order of jars to investigate* *}Disputational* *} A deciding when to time. B* *} does not ask for clarification* *} or question what to do when.* *}* *} Disputional* *} C questioning whether tin right* *} to start timer* *} A then asserts when to time.* *} No inclusive discussion an }agreement about when is be and } why* *}* *} Disputational* *} C attempting to direct that a* *} candles should be lit togethe* *}*

1.30	**A** *to* **C** "because there's only one timer" **A** "ready? One, two three" places jar over candle **B** starts timer ***B*** to **A** "I'll stop it..." **A** to **B** "stop" **B** stops timer **A** *to* **B** *"*5 seconds" ***B*** to **A** "hang on..." **A** *to* **B** *"*5 seconds" ***A*** **B** and **C** write down results **B** whispers "5 seconds" **A** removes jar from candle "right then" **A** lights spill	Because A and B have possession of equipment they are involved in gathering data, C observes acquiescingly. Absence of any commentary regarding results, no…comment re: expectations of next jar, will it burn for longer or not?	*} Disputational* *} A directs again, does not enter into discussion and reasoning with C why to do it a particular way*
2.00	***B*** to **A** "wait a sec" adjusting timer **A** tries to light second candle with spill "I don't think this one wants to light" ***C*** to **A** when candle is lit "ok" **A** tries to shake out flame "it won't go out" ***C*** *to* **A** "blow on it" **A** blows it out 'That's it" ***B*** to **A** "right let's have another go" **A** picks up medium sized jar	A has not asked others about using the second candle, she has assumed that they should. First time C has contributed for a while – just confirmatory comment C offers suggestion that A then carries out.	*} Cumulative* *}* *} Pupils affirm each* *} others actions or* *} comments, but they do* *} not enter into discussion* *} regarding the procedure* *} or results so far*
2.30	***C*** *to* **A** - "hang on 'cause it isn't a fair test 'cause you've taken longer to get that ready than you did on the other one" (pointing to 2nd lit candle) **A** puts lit spill on the lit candle "I'll just put a little bit more on ... make it a bit bigger..... come on .... light .... that's it now... no it's not" ***B*** to **A** - "why don't you use that	C spots that preparation, burning time etc could affect candle, mentions fair test. Challenge to size of flame before place jar. A accepts C's suggestion here….but perceives making it fair is to leave the spill on the candle wick longer. B has notion that fair test if use same candle – challenges A.	*} Disputational* *} C points out not doing a fair test* *} Neither A nor B ask for elaborat-* *} tion, or verbally agree* *}* *} Cumulative* *} B uncritically suggests*

	same candle?" **A** *to* **B** "hang on" - blows out spill, candle not lit	A acquiescence of B's suggestion – no discussion, just acceptance that what suggested is OK.	*} an alternative - carrying* *} on with same candle. The girl* *do } not discuss this*
3.00	**B** repeats to **A** "use the same candle ... if you use the same candle, then it'll be fair" ***A*** "yeah" **B** swaps 2nd candle for 1st one and **A** lights it with spill **A** picks up medium sized jar ***B*** to **A** - "..... ... say go" **A** to ***B*** "ready one, two, three go" places jar over candle **B** starts timer They watch flame **B** stops timer **A** and **B** "7 seconds"	B explains rationale, A agrees. Interesting - no discussion or dis-agreement as to the 'end point' of timing. There is quiet pacificity and acquiescence from B and C.	*} Cumulative* *} B suggests again that* *} same candle OK to use.* *} Again that girls do not discuss* *} and consider the pros and* *} cons of same candle, o* *another* *} with same initial flame. The* *do* *} not explore what each think* *they* *} could do to ensure it is a fai* *test.* *}*
3.30	***A*** **B** and **C** write it down **B** prepares timer **A** puts large jar in the middle of the table and picks up lit spill ***C*** *to* **A** "can I light this one?" **A** *to* **C** "you can put the thing on" - lights same candle ***B*** "you'll have to say go" **C** places large jar over lit candle and says "go" **B** starts timer Wait ***B*** "that's it" stops timer ***A*** **B** and **C** "nine" they all write it down and **C** says "it goes up by two every time"	No challenge or discussion regarding large jar next. No predictions about likely outcomes. Second time C asked to light candle. A gives permission this time. Appears that A makes decisions and usually directs proceedings. No reflective discussion between all 3, regarding procedure and validity and reliability of results. There is unspoken acceptance that the 3 readings sufficient data. C quickly describes pattern in data.	*} Disputational* *}* *}A directing again, with n* *prior* *} contributions or discussion* *}from other two* *}* *}* *}Cumulative* *} All having repeated the result* *} C affirms this by adding how* *} much she perceives th* *dependant variable ha* *changed each time*
4.00	All still writing **A** removes large jar from candle **C** mutters "it's like (???) **A** "right ... conclusion... and I know how you do this" **C** "I do" all are writing	A articulates that she knows what to do, C says she does too. B says nothing (but written evidence indicates that she has best understood the task)	*}Disputational* *} They do not 'share'* *} their reasoning. A* *} and C both state* *} they know without* *} explaining what (their writte* *explanations indicate they d* *not understand all that the* *have been doing).*
4.30 5.00 - 5.30	someone says "the candle stays......" all writing for about 2 mins **A** looks over to **B** and **C**'s writing **C** finishes first – asks about	Their end point as judged individually	

6.00	writing method		

Early measures taken to compare performance and outcome between groups

Group Comp-osition (gender age ability)	**Intra-group inter-actions** see following table	**General organisation of task what? whom? how? when? for how long? rotation?**	***Timed aspects*** * on task * off task * to complete task	**Quality of outcome** • *correct* scientific concepts • experimental methodology • fair test • safe procedure • written record • results? verbal/written/organised • results valid/reliable/accurate • solution to task found? • end point/ conclusion?
3 girls Y7 High		**How long before start talking/discussion?** 0.40 familiarisation with equipt?- yep - timer - few seconds approx 20 **Discussion/clarification of task?** A little:14 seconds (2 x 7 seconds) **Starting task proper(as defined on sheet)?** as above 1 min 48 seconds **Are tasks identified?** No discussion - unspoken understanding about what needs to be done. **What tasks/roles are identified?** A – Organiser/ideas and does (lighting candle jar lowering initially) B - does (timing) and some ideas C - facilitator, refiner. Articulates explanations, does lowering jar for last candle. **Whom identifies the tasks/jobs/roles?** No-one **How decide whom does what?** ? presume used to taking on particular roles	No off task talk or action. Completed task (in their eyes) in 6 mins 42 seconds.	• *correct* scientific concepts - No discussion of concept more air therefore candle will burn longer. *(Incorrectly thought would be quicker if lit a candle sequentially rather than all 3 simultaneously)* • experimental methodology - Lit one candle 3 times, timed length of burning once in each jar. • fair test - thought OK as same candle lit. *(didn't consider other factors, eg:how well candle burning before jar lowered)* • safe procedure - *goggles worn throughout.* • written record - varied; used different descriptors for jars, presented results and conclusion in similar way • results? verbal - by C - spotted pattern, all wrote results, units mixed with numerical values/ didn't organise them in a tabular format • results not repeated • solution to task found. A - rather inarticulate, but right nuance,, B best specific and addressed science correctly, C - correct answer, wrong explanation (confused by brightness and timing). • end point/ conclusion - was reached - but prompting to consider validity of results needed. Cognitive capability (Bloom/IEA): Pupil A=2.1.1; 2.2.1; 2.2.2; 2.2.3; 2.3.1; 2.3.2; 2.4.3; 2.4.5 Interpretation – of data to see trend, the more air there, the longer the candle burns. Application – recognised that more air means the flame burns for longer. That flames need air to burn. (No

		Once role(s) defined do they remain in that guise? No C changed, took over lowering jar – sought permission twice. Refused first time. **Is there rotation of roles/organised sharing of tasks?** Not explicitly. Limited change of 'doer'.		mention of oxygen in air, or that increase in co2 might affect rate of extinquishing.) Analysis – some of this – not all steps clearly identified (ie:larger jar=more air) Synthesis – yes but not explicitly...linked length candle burns and amount of air. Evaluation – none.(post discussion – some) Pupil B=2.1.1; 2.2.1; 2.2.2; 2.2.3; 2.2.4;2.3.1; 2.4.3; 2.4.4; 2.4.5 Interpretation – of data to see trend, the larger the jar, the more air is in it, the longer the candle burns. Application – recognised that more air means the flame burns for longer. That flames need air to burn. (No mention of O_2 in air, or that increase in CO_2 might affect rate of extinguishing.) Analysis – link between jar, air and candle flame clearly stated. Synthesis – yes explicitly...linked length candle burns and amount of air in jars. Evaluation – none.(post discussion – some) Pupil C=2.1.1; 2.3.1; 2.5.2; 2.4.5 Observed the pattern in the data (increasing 2 seconds in each successive jar) Interpretation – not consistent. Initially size of 'tube' and length candle burnt recognised, but then reference to brightness and span of timing. Application – no Analysis – not consistent Synthesis – hasn't linked quantity of air and length of burning flame. Evaluation – none written. Some methodological points raised in videoed discussion.

Early analysis of the ways pupils interacted with each other verbally.

	Measurements from transcript: Time to complete task. Total verbal contributions by pupils: A B C Challenges from: A B C Acceptance (affirmation) of another's comment/action/statement (without challenge) i.e.: agreements: A B C Questions from: A B C	 5 mins 50 secs 22 11 13 0 1 3 4 8 9 0 2 2

Cognitist perspective:
A takes on role as leader, both B and C accept many of her ideas and suggestions with out question, although C and B challenge with regard to fair testing, C asks about standardising the flame before placing jar over it and B challenges the use of different candles.

Assessment of the quality of scientific processing and outcomes achieved by groups whilst working on-task.

Evidence of scientific conceptual development can also be evidenced through predictions, conclusions and explanations provided either verbally or in written form. Groups (labelled according to tape numbers)	Group 16A1
Prodcedure (Methodology) **C**andles: 1 candle sequentially 2 each candle sequentially 3 all candles simaultaneaously **J**ars: 1 sml – med – lge 2 lge – med – sml 3 random	C1 J1
Control of variables (eg:fair testing) 1. Same sized candles 2. Same candle 3. Same start time 4. Standardised intial flame 5. Flushed jars 6. Lowering of jar 7. Extinguished (end piont) flame	2 ,3
Measurements 1: Data collection 1. organised:sml/med/lge 6. Qualitative -> Quantitative valid (repeat if problem/?) 7. Qualitative (relative time) reliable (repeated) 5. accurate measurements	1,4
Measurements 2: Data organisation 1. recorded as generated 3. Not recorded 2. recorded in table (pre-strucured?)	1
Data analysis 1: Describe data pattern a) incr space so flame burns longer b) incr in volme -> incr in air so flame burns longer c) incr in volume -> incr in O2 so flame burns longer	b
Data analysis 2: Explain data pattern a) Candle flame needs air to burn b) Candle flame needs air to burn, so the more air the longer it burns c) Combustion requires oxygen in the air, so the more oxygen	b
Solution – reliable and valid 1. Complete with good scientific evidence and explanation 2. Complete with some scientific evidence and explanation 3. Complete with some scientific evidence, but no explanation 4. Complete, but no scientific evidence 5. Not complete, but some evidence and explanation	2

Appendix 4.6 : Example of a collated pattern of interactions between the participants in a group.

		Pupils activities					
		(mins during activity below)					
		1	2	3	4	5	6
'Thinking' role - includes reflector and idea generator	makes initial suggestions - what to do/write/record						
	evaluator - reviews where at/sucess etc						
	idea generator						
	asks provoking questions						
	improves technique						
'Doing'	reading (instructions)						
	dev familiarity with/ handling apparatus						
	carrying out expt						
observing:	i. measurments						
	ii. others in group						
	listening to others						
writing:	I. recording results						
	ii. other						
contemplating	results/writing						
Not doing anything - 'vacant'							
'Facilitator' - includes implementor, complimentor, finisher							
	suggests improvement/modification to prac						
	gives instruction to another						
	hands apparatus to another						
	cleaning/tidying						
	preparation						
	agreement/ acquiescence						
	developer of ideas						
On task talk							
Off task talk							
Off task behaviour (not contributing to task outcome,ie:joke,daft behaviour,non-constructive fiddling with equipment)							
Key:		A=		B=		C=	

Appendix 4.7a : Responses from cohort of 28 teachers from Stoke-on-Trent LEA (engaged in INSET between July 1998 and July 2000) to teacher 'End of INSET programme QUESTIONNAIRE'.

Each school issued with 2 questionnaires.

Name of school	Reflective end of course questionnaires completed and returned	
	Male	Female
Berryhill High School		1
Birches Head High School	1	1
Blurton High School	2	
Brownhills High School	1	
Haywood High School		1
Holden lane High School		
James Brindley High School		
Longton High School	2	
Mitchell High School	1	
St Margeret Ward High School	1	1
St Peter's High School	1	1
Sandon High School		1
Trentham High School		
Thistley Hough High School		
Total	15	

**Blank indicates no return from the school.*

Appendix 4.7b : Responses from cohort of 26 teachers from assorted LEAs : (engaged in INSET between July 1998 – July 2000) to teacher 'End of INSET programme QUESTIONNAIRE'.

Each school issued with 2 questionnaires.

Name of school	Reflective end of course questionnaires completed and returned	
	Male	Female
Belpher School, Derbyshire	2	
Charlton School, Shropshire	1	1
Cheadle Hulme College, Cheshire		2
Bishops Castle School, Shropshire		
Harrytown RC School, Cheshire		1
The Heath School, Cheshire	1	1
Kingsway High School, Cheshire	1	
The Pingle School, Derbyshire	2	
Ryles Park School, Cheshire	1	1
Robert Sutton Catholic, Staffordshire	1	
Shavington School, Cheshire		
Shirebrook Community School, Nottinghamshire	2	
St Benedicts School, Derbyshire		
Total returned	17	

**Blank indicates no return from the school.*

Appendix 4.7c : Responses from cohort of 24 teachers from three LEA's (engaged in INSET between July 1999 and July 2001) to teacher 'End of INSET programme QUESTIONNAIRE'. Each school issued with 2 questionnaires.

Name of school	Reflective end of course questionnaires returned	
	Male	Female
Avondale High School, Cheshire	1	
The Bishop's C of E High School, Cheshire		1++
Coppenhall High School, Cheshire	1	
Edensor High School, Stoke	2	
Firth Park School, South Yorkshire		
Lymm High School, Lancashire	1++	
Norton Priory High School, Cheshire	1	1
Poynton High School, Cheshire	1	1
Trentham High School, Stoke		1++
Westlands High, Cheshire		
Wilmslow High, Cheshire		
Whitby County High, Cheshire		1
Total returned	12	

** Blank denotes no response from the school*
++ Denotes two teachers completed questionnaire

Appendix 4.7d : Responses from cohort of 14 teachers from the Wirral LEA (engaged in INSET between July 2000 and July 2002) to teacher 'End of INSET programme QUESTIONNAIRE'.

Each school issued with 2 questionnaires.

Name of school	Reflective end of course questionnaires completed and returned	
	Male	Female
Hilbre High School		
Plessington Catholic High School	1	
St Mary's College		
St Benedict's Catholic High School	1	1
Upton Hall School	1	1
Weatherhead High School		1
Woodchurch High School	2	
Total returned	8	

**Blank indicates no return from the school.*

Appendix 4.7e : Responses from cohort of 32 teachers from Nottingham LEA (engaged in INSET between July 2000 and July 2002) to teacher 'End of INSET programme QUESTIONNAIRE'.

Each school issued with 2 questionnaires.

Name of school	Reflective end of course questionnaires completed and returned	
	Male	Female
Alderman White School		
All Saints RC School	1	1
Bigwood School	1	
Bircotes and Harworth Community School		
Chilwell School	1	1
Holgate School		1
Joseph Whittaker School	2	1
Matthew Holland School	1	
Meden School		
Minster School		
Redhill School	2	
South Wolds School		
The Weldon School	1	
Trinity RC School	1	1
Valley School		
William Sharp School	1	
Total returned	16	

*Blank indicates no return from the school.

Appendix 4.7f : Responses from cohort of 38 teachers from various LEAs (engaged in INSET between July 2000 and July 2002) to teacher 'End of INSET programme QUESTIONNAIRE'. Each school issued with 2 questionnaires.

Name of school	Reflective end of course questionnaires completed and returned	
	Male	Female
Bankfield School, Cheshire	1	
Clough Hall Technology College, Staffordshire	1	
Derby Moor Community School, Derbyshire		
Ellesmere Port Catholic High School, Wirral		1++
Granville School, Derbyshire	1	
Great Sankey High School, Cheshire	1	1
Henbury High School, Cheshire		
Ilkeston School, Derbyshire		
Levenshulme High School, Manchester	1	
Madeley High School, Staffordshire	1	
Mary Hill School, Staffordshire		
Neston County High School, Cheshire	1	1
Palatine School, Lancashire		1
Riverside Community College, Leicestershire		1
Rivington and Blackrod High School, Manchester		
Tytherington High School, Cheshire	1	
Weaverham County High School, Cheshire		
William Brookes School, Shropshire		
Wilnecote County High School, Staffordshire		2
Total returned	15	

**Blank indicates no return from the school.*
++ indicates 2 staff completed the form

Appendix 7

SPORTING SHOES

Sam and Mary both have new training shoes of the same type and size.

They were both running, but Mary slipped.

Mary asked 'Why should I slip and not you?'

Sam replied 'Perhaps it's because I'm heavier than you.'

Can you design and carry out an investigation to see if there is any truth in Sam's suggestion?

Equipment you might use:

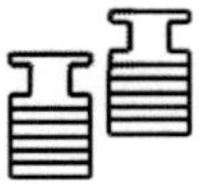

Think carefully about the following before you start to carry out the experiment.

- How will you measure the slippiness of the shoe?
- How will you make that shoe heavier and lighter?
- How many measurements will it be useful to make?
- How will you record your results?

Appendix 7.1 : Semi-structured Sporting Shoe task sheet

SPORTING SHOES

Sam and Mary both have new training shoes of the same type and size.

They were both running, but Mary slipped.

Mary asked 'Why should I slip and not you?'

Sam replied 'Perhaps it's because I'm heavier than you.'
This is an investigation to find out how the heaviness of a shoe can affect its slippiness.

You will need:

a training shoe | a force meter | a set of masses

What to do:

1. Set up the apparatus as shown above in diagram, with a 100g mass in the shoe.
2. Record your findings in the following table:

Mass in shoe (g)	Force needed to start shoe moving (N)

3. Now pull gently on the forcemeter until the shoe moves.
4. At this time take a reading from the forcemeter and record this in the table, together with the mass in the shoe.
5. Now add another mass. Repeat steps 3 and 4.
6. Continue until you have added all the masses. Record all your results in the table.
7. What relationship can you see between the masses on the shoe and the force needed to move the shoe

Appendix 7.2 Highly structured sporting shoe task sheet

DENSITY RATINGS

A group of teenagers were discussing floating and sinking.

Sarah said "rubber will sink in water, but cork will float".

Peter said " I agree, but would it be the same in oil? or syrup?"

Sarah replied "Umm, and would other objects like a nail, paper clip, pasta, piece of candle and a grape all sink in any liquid?"

Can you design an experiment to find out which of the liquids and solids mentioned are more or less dense than each other?

Equipment you might use:

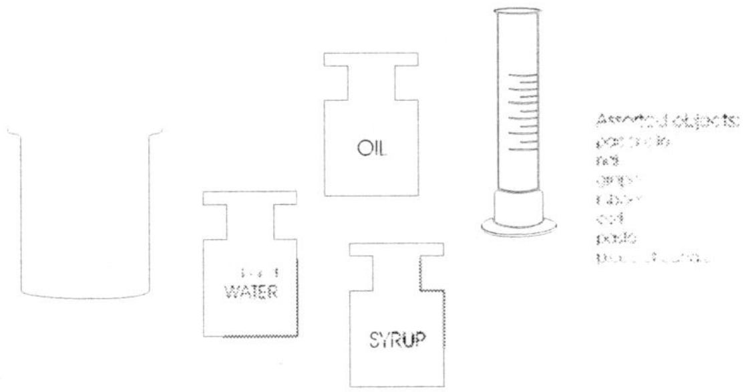

Think carefully about the following before you start to carry out the experiment.

- How can you fairly compare the density of the liquids?
- How will you compare density of the seven objects?
- How will you present your results?

Appendix 7.3 Semi-structured (some in-task scaffolding) Density Ratings work sheet

DENSITY RATINGS

This is an experiment to compare the density of a range of liquids and solids.

You will need:

syrup
desert size spoon
coloured water
oil
measuring cylinder
glass beaker

small screw/nail
grape
rubber
cork
piece of pasta
paper clip
piece of candle

What to do:

1. Measure out 70cm3 syrup and pour into the beaker.
2. Repeat for the coloured water and then the oil.
3. Gently float onto the liquids in turn the screw, grape, rubber, cork, pasta, paper clip and candle.
4. Wait until each object has settled before adding the next. Try and guess where you think each thing will rest.
5. On the diagram below label the liquid layers. Which is the least dense and which the most?

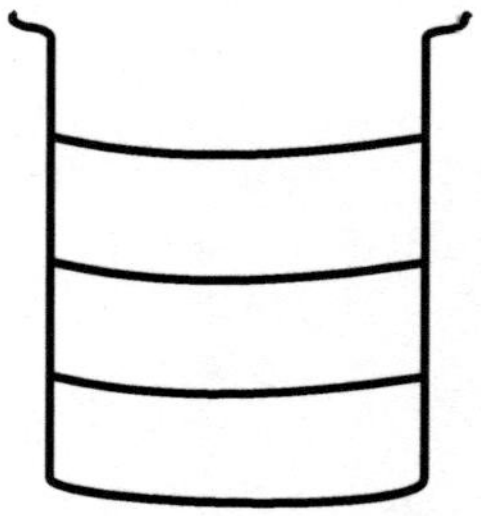

6. Add on the diagram the position of each of the objects...then list them in order, the least dense first:

____
____
____
____
____
____
____

Appendix 7.4 : Highly structured Density ratings task sheet

Triads (number denotes the group within W, X, Y or Z school)	Conceptual and procedural science evidenced through observations of interactions (actional or verbal) between students or from their written notes						
	Procedure (Methodology) Candles: 1 candle sequentially 1. each candle sequentially 2. all candles simultaneously Jars: 1 sml – med – lge 2 lge – med – sml 3 random	Control of variables (e.g.: extent of fair testing) 1. Same sized candles 8. Sequential candles used 2. Same candle 3. Same start time 4. Standardised initial flame 5. Flushed jars 6. Lowering of jar 7. Extinguished (end point) flame	Measurements 1: Data collection 1. valid (repeat if problem?) 2. reliable (repeated) 3. accurate measurement 4. Qualitative -> Quantitative 5. Qualitative (relative time)	Measurements 2: Data organisation 1. recorded as generated 2. recorded in table (pre-structured?) 3. not recorded	Data analysis 1: Description of data a. increased space so flame burns longer b. increase in volume -> incr in air so flame burns longer c. increase in volume -> incr in O2 so flame burns longer	Data analysis 2: Explanation of data a. Candle flame needs air to burn b. Candle flame needs air to burn, so the more air the longer it burns c. Combustion requires oxygen in the air, so the more	Solution – reliable and valid 1. Complete with good scientific evidence and explanation 2. Complete with some scientific evidence and explanation 3. Complete with some scientific evidence, but no explanation
2Z (10 mins)	C3	6	Completed table provided. Repeated 3x as instructed.	1	a	No explanation that linked to combustion	3
4Z (6 mins)	C2 J1	4 + wick	Completed table provided. Repeated 3x as instructed.	1			2 but explanation was somewhat confused.
3Z (13 mins)	C2 then C1 J1	2,7	? accurate ? reliable A stopped timer before flame went out (not reliable). Some inaccuracy.	1	a,b,c	a,b	3
5Z (5.5 mins)	C3	6	Completed table provided. Repeated 3x as instructed.	1	b	c	2 but anomalous data not explained at all

The numbers and letters in the cells, indicate which aspects of task tactics, methods, results or solutions (described in column headings) were evident during task engagement. No entry indicates those elements of task tactics, methods, results or solutions were not evident.
Time to complete tasks in parentheses after group identification.

Appendix 7.5 : Quality of science outcomes – comparison of a series of case studies : students participating in resolving prescribed (or highly structured) tasks.

		Procedure (Methodology) Candles: 1 candle sequentially 1. each candle sequentially 2. all candles simultaneously Jars: 1 sml – med – lge 2 lge – med – sml 3 random	Control of variables (e.g.: extent of fair testing) 1. Same sized candles 8. Sequential candles used 2. Same candle 3. Same start time 4. Standardised initial flame 5. Flushed jars 6. Lowering of jar 7. Extinguished (end point) flame	Measurements 1: Data collection 1. valid (repeat if problem?) 2. reliable (repeated) 3. accurate measurement 4. Qualitative -> Quantitative 5. Qualitative (relative time)	Measurements 2: Data organisation 1. recorded as generated 2. recorded in table (pre-structured?) 3. not recorded	Data analysis 1: Description of data a. increased space so flame burns longer b. increase in volume -> incr in air so flame burns longer c. increase in volume -> incr in O2 so flame burns longer	Data analysis 2 : Explanation of data a) Candle flame needs air to burn b) Candle flame needs air to burn, so the more air the longer it burns c) Combustion requires oxygen in the air, so the more oxygen	Solution – reliable and valid 1) Complete with good scientific evidence and explanation 2) Complete with some scientific evidence and explanation 3) Complete with some scientific evidence, but no explanation 4) Complete, but no scientific evidence 5) Not complete, but some evidence and explanation
		Conceptual and procedural science evidenced through observations of interactions (actional or verbal) between students or from their written notes						
Triads (number denotes the group within W, X, Y or Z school)	2W (14 mins)	C1 J1 then C2	2,3,4,5,7	1,2,3,4	1	a,b	b	3
	3W (13.5 mins)	C3 then C1 J1 [J3]	1,2,3,4,5,6,[7]	1,3,4	1 (and altered)	a,b	a,b,c	2
	1Z (7.5 mins)	C2 + J1	1,2,3,4,7 Smoke off wick denotes candle out	1,3,4	1	a,b	a,b	2
	2Y (31 mins)	C2 + J1 - 6 trials	1,2,3,6,7 Smoke off wick denotes candle out	1,2,3,4,5	1 + 2 (own table)	a.b	a,b	2 Lots of evidence (6 trials)

The numbers and letters in the cells, indicate which aspects of task tactics, methods, results or solutions (described in column headings) were evident during task engagement. No entry indicates those elements of task tactics, methods, results or solutions were not evident.
Time to complete tasks in parentheses after group identification.

Appendix 7.6 : Quality of science outcomes – comparison of a series of case studies : students participating in resolving scaffolded (or partially structured) tasks.

Triads (number denotes the .group within W, X, Y or Z school)	Conceptual and procedural science evidenced through observations of interactions (actional or verbal) between students or from their written notes.						
	Procedure (Methodology) 1. Candles: 1 candle sequentially 2. each candle sequentially 3. all candles simultaneously Jars: 1 sml – med – lge 2 lge – med – sml 3 random	Control of variables (e.g.: extent of fair testing) 1. Same sized candles 8. Sequential candles used 2. Same candle 3. Same start time 4. Standardised initial flame 5. Flushed jars 6. Lowering of jar 7. Extinguished (end point) flame	Measurements 1: Data collection 1. valid (repeat if problem?) 2. reliable (repeated) 3. accurate measurement 4. Qualitative -> Quantitative 5. Qualitative (relative time)	Measurements 2: Data organisation 1. recorded as generated 2. recorded in table (pre-structured?) 3. not recorded	Data analysis 1: Description of data a. increased space so flame burns longer b. increase in volume -> incr in air so flame burns longer c. increase in volume -> incr in O2 so flame burns longer	Data analysis 2 : Explanation of data a. Candle flame needs air to burn b. Candle flame needs air to burn, so the more air the longer it burns c. Combustion requires oxygen in the air, so the more	Solution – reliable and valid 1. Complete with good scientific evidence and explanation 2. Complete with some scientific evidence and explanation 3. Complete with some scientific evidence, but no explanation 4. Complete, but no scientific evidence 5. Not complete, but some evidence and explanation
1X (6 mins)	C1 J1	2, 3	1, 3	1	b	b	2
2X (8 mins)	C3	6, 7	4	1	a		2 very weak evidence. No re-trials.
3X (10 mins)	C1, 3	1, 4 mention wick affects	5	3	a	b/c	4 very weak evidence
4X (6.5 mins)	C2 J1	Not explicitly considered	1 No repeating	1	Not overtly described	Not explicitly discussed. Only 1 pupil mentions air	Set of three data values – useful but not validated or verified

The numbers and letters in the cells, indicate which aspects of task tactics, methods, results or solutions (described in column headings) were evident during task engagement. No entry indicates those elements of task tactics, methods, results or solutions were not evident.

Time to complete tasks in parentheses after group identification.

Appendix 7.7 : Quality of science outcomes – comparison of a series of case studies : students participating in resolving open (no structure) tasks.

End of INSET programme QUESTIONNAIRE : Sample questions focussed on reflections about teaching

Teacher Details:

Name: ______________________________

School: ______________________________

Could you please reflect on the following to comparing your teaching now with 2000:

Q1a. Did you used to record any thoughts on your lessons for use in the following year? If so, could you describe an example?

____

____

____

____

____

____

Q1b. Do you record any thoughts on your lessons for use in the following year? If so could you describe an example?

____

____

____

____

____

____

Q2a. What was the average time you spent on planning and preparing Y7 lessons? (Please tick (✓) as appropriate)

5 – 10 mins	10 – 30 mins.	30 – 60 mins.	60 – 90 mins.	Other

Q2b. What is the average time you now spend on planning and preparing Y7 lessons? (Please tick (✓) as appropriate)

5 – 10 mins.	10 – 30 mins.	30 – 60 mins.	60 – 90 mins.	Other

Q3a. Did you ask pupils to make predictions in practical science lessons? (Please tick (✓) as appropriate)

Always	Occasionally	Often	Never

Q3b. Do you ask pupils to make predictions in practical science lessons?
(Please tick (✓) as appropriate)

Always	Occasionally	Often	Never

Q4a. Did you develop situations in which pupil predictions were likely to be wrong? If so could you describe an example?

Q4b. Do you develop situations in which pupil predictions are likely to be wrong? If so could you describe an example?

Q5a. Did you develop situations where pupils gathered evidence that contradicted what they already knew? If so could you describe an example?

Q5b. Do you develop situations where pupils gather evidence that contradicts what they already know? If so could you describe an example?

Q6a. Did you ask pupils to discuss their conclusions with others?
(Please tick (✓) as appropriate)

Always	Occasionally	Often	Never

Q6b. Do you ask pupils to discuss their conclusions with others?
(Please tick (✓) as appropriate)

Always	Occasionally	Often	Never

Q7a. When pupils came to conclusions, did you ask them to explain their thinking?
(Please tick (✓) as appropriate)

Always	Occasionally	Often	Never

Q7b. When pupils have come to conclusions, do you ask them to explain their thinking?
(Please tick (✓) as appropriate)

Always	Occasionally	Often	Never

Q8a. When pupils came to conclusions, did you ask them to apply their ideas to new situations?
(Please tick (✓) as appropriate)

Always	Occasionally	Often	Never

Q8b. When pupils have come to conclusions, do you ask them to apply their ideas to new situations?
(Please tick (✓) as appropriate)

Always	Occasionally	Often	Never

Q9a. Did you plan how to organise pupils into small groups for science?
(Please tick (✓) as appropriate)

Always	Occasionally	Often	Never

Q9b. Do you plan how to organise pupils into small groups for science?
(Please tick (✓) as appropriate)

Always	Occasionally	Often	Never

Q10a. How long did you spend at the beginning of the lesson explaining what was to be done?
(Please tick (✓) as appropriate)

5 – 10 mins.	10 – 20 mins.	20 – 30 mins.	Other*

Q10b. How long did you spend at the beginning of the lesson explaining what is to be done?
(Please tick (✓) as appropriate)

5 – 10 mins.	10 – 20 mins.	20 – 30 mins.	Other*

Q11a. What proportion of recall, open and closed questions did you ask?
(Please tick (✓) as appropriate)

RECALL:		
Many	Several	Few

OPEN:		
Many	Several	Few

CLOSED:		
Many	Several	Few

Q11b. What proportion of recall, open and closed questions do you ask?
(Please tick (✓) as appropriate)

RECALL:		
Many	Several	Few

OPEN:		
Many	Several	Few

CLOSED:		
Many	Several	Few

Q12. Are there any other ways you think your questioning technique or general teaching or view of learning or impact on the department has changed since 2000?

____
____
____
____
____
____

Appendix 9.1 : Example of questions on reflective questionnaires given to the teachers after their INSET

The **Titanic** Activity

- ***What will happen when I add the two liquids to the syrup?***
- ***What will happen when I drop in Leonardo di Grapio?***
- ***Why do you predict this?***

Discuss why this happened

What will happen with these objects?

- ***Nut Winslet?***
- ***Billy Grain?***
- ***Jenny Pasta?***
- ***Tom Harto?***

What would happen if I dropped a raisin into the jar? Explain your prediction.

Discuss, debate and decide as a group what you think.

- ***What about a glass of water?***
- ***What about sparkling water?***

Now try it.

- ***Can you explain how this happened?***

Discuss, debate and decide as a group what you think.

Explain the following:

  - ***How does a Lava Lamp work?***
  - ***Why is it easier to swim in the sea than in the swimming pool?***
  - ***Which of these two questions was a better 'bridge' to everyday life and why?***

Discuss, debate and decide as a group what you think.

Appendix 9.2 Example of the activity used to develop teachers' understanding of social and cultural impacts on pupils' thinking.

Specific area of Titanic activity	Pedagogic and mediational illustrations for teachers	Socio-cultural features explicitly discussed
Pre-activity group organisation	Each teacher is given a symbol token, so that groups of three are co-ordinated to work together	Non-school colleagues working together. Overcome issues of 'conformity' held within the local school community.
Distribution of questions	Each group has the various tasks and questions posed to them. They are encouraged to 1. Tell the others what they think in turn. 2. Consider, compare and contrast each contributors ideas. 3. Agree as a group what is the best strategy, procedure, solution to the tasks set.	What will happen when I add the two liquids to the syrup? This question has even had Heads of science predicting that the resultant mixing of syrup, coloured water and cooking oil would result in three layers being formed: Syrup, oil, coloured water (it appears to be holding in mind a notion of viscosity of fluid, rather than density). Because each of the group members can 'consider' the question and debate it before responding to the tutor, there is opportunity for each to contribute their experience and expertise. For example chemists may more readily (because of their experience with calculating oil droplet surface area on water) tend to contribute that element of the hypothesis. Others may note they have used syrup and/or jam not dissolved in water in a jar to tempt wasps etc in the summer. In other words through their life experience professionally or socially they can bring to bear some previous relevant observations.
Nature of the questions	More open-ended questions are deliberately asked to pose, much less 'leading' challenges and thus provide opportunities to develop	*What will happen when I drop in Leonardo di Grapio? Why do you predict this?* Questions with this pre-fix, 'what

	more diverse cognitive processing.	will happen?' create very open-ended possibilities, with no fettering or constraints on the anticipated response. Frequent use of this type of question engenders a more reasoned 'open' culture of offering proposals with justifications, rather than the less obvious implication of will the oil float on the water and/or the syrup? A more closed question provides less opportunity for cognitive processing. Frequent examples are given of open questions.
Explicit metacognition/reflection of discourse patterns and contributions	Reflective discussion once the task has been completed provides the opportunity for all group participants to share how their constructions and understandings developed as a result of both engaging in the activity and entering into discursive consideration about meaning and explanation.	Teachers reflect on how their experience of relative densities of 'food stuffs' has never been formally taught, therefore they don't 'know' the answers. They recognise that engaging in an activity where they are 'novice' means they can enter into learning and constructing new knowledge together (social construction). They reflect on how each participant has contributed differing facets of their solution, and how the collaborative nature of their interactions contributes to shared referents and the development of mutual understandings.
Emphasis of integral nature of language and thought, through explicit demonstration of 'inner speech' becoming purposeful external communication	Each participant offers a proposal that contributes to the group prediction.	Through articulating a prediction involving 'unknown' influences (ie: don't know exact composition of grape, nut, tomato etc, therefore do not know absolute densities) requires more thought and thus

		more explicit linguistic description and explanation
Importance of cognitive conflict	Creating this in an activity is a factor that can contribute to 'engagement' on task, and stimulate discussion of intersubjectivity.	Possible through a variety of routes: Purposely provide "conflicting" or anamolous data or evidence. Differences in perspectives between co-learners. teacher mediation – twisting/changing deliberately what the pupil has said to check for 'firm' volition of understanding (not just positive reinforcement clues from teacher).
Importance of co-construction of meaning by peers	Through overcoming intersubjectivity the 'peers' move into a construction zone, negotiating and debating what their agreed group solution should be.	Each peer is likely to predict the buoyancy of the grape, tomato and nuts to be different. Through argumentation and justification they should eventually agree a consensus
Importance of intra-group conscious reflection	Reflection on how the group solution was reached, and why that particular resolution was judged appropriate.	For each of the objects dropped into the liquids how did the group construct the pattern of different densities (of different objects) illustrating a particular trend.
Authentic task or authentic experience?	By dropping various objects that have every-day-life relevance, all participants should be able to offer some suggestions based on life experience. For example, cooking risotto may contribute to predictions about Billy grain (single and clumped rice grains); peanut tossing in the local hostelry may contribute to notions about nut winslet's behaviour; having boiled dried pasta, and washed tomatoes other	What will happen when I drop in Leonardo di Grapio? Why do you predict this? Discuss why this happened What will happen with these objects? Nut Winslet? Billy Grain?

	experience of food preparation or cooking could contribute to ideas regarding Jenny and Tom.	Jenny Pasta? Tom Harto?

Appendix 9.3 : How the Titanic activity provides explicit opportunities for the noted mediating strategies

Measures of the nature of interactive talk between pupils whilst engaged on task									
Groups of pupils	Extent of discussion required to reach solution (Minutes)	Total number of verbal exchanges between members of the group	Purposeful questions[29] asked by members of the group	Number of episodes of disputational talk	Average extent of disputaton episodes	Number of episodes of cumulative talk	Average extent of cumulative episodes	Number of episodes of exploratory talk	General commentary
1B	6.0	50	4	12	x = 2.1; range 1 - 6	3	x = 3.3; range 1 - 4	None	Talk more disputational at the beginning, becoming of increasingly cumulative towards the end of the task.
2B	8.0	142	4	8	x = 1.25; range 1 - 3	13	x = 8.8; range 3 - 20	None	Longer episodes of cumulative talk towards end of task.
3B	10.0	180	9	8	x = 2.5; range 1 - 5	10	x = 11.7; range = 2 - 14	None	Much more cumulative toward end of task.
4B	6.5	78	3	8	x = 1.9; range 1 - 4	8	x = 4.1; range = 2 - 7	None	Some increase in cumulative talk towards later part of task.

Appendix 10.1 : The measures of the nature of social and cognitive interactions between pupils in groups carrying out the same practical before teacher participation in interventional in-service.

29 A purposeful or challenging question is a statement that is proposed to others in the group, in the expectation that they will be answered. The response requires some thought, for example, 'How do you do this now?' or 'Do we need to do it again?' or 'Will a lot of oxygen make it go out first?' Rhetorical questions such as 'Yes, so we could write that down couldn't we?' or a managerial or organisational question such as 'Are you ready?' or 'Where are my goggles?'; 'Have you got my pencil?' or 'Do you want me to help you?' are not counted as cognitively purposeful questions.

Measures of the nature of interactive talk between pupils whilst engaged on task										
Groups of pupils	Extent of discussion required to reach solution (Minutes)	Total number of verbal exchanges between members of the group	Purposeful questions asked by members of the group	Number of episodes of disputational talk	Average extent of disputaton episodes	Number of episodes of cumulative talk	Average extent of cumulative episodes	Number of episodes of exploratory talk	Average extent of exploratory episodes	General commentary
5A	27.0	446	13	14	x = 2.9; range 1 - 9	18	x = 7.1; range 3 – 16	11	x = 5.3; range 2 - 11	Generally more discursive exchanges. Balanced nature of discussion. Exploratory talk evident.
6A	13.0	214	13	9	x = 3.6; range 1-7	6	x = 4.2; range 2 – 7	11	x = 7.6; range 2 – 21	Very explicit verbalization of ideas and thoughts generally.
7A	11.0	82	1	4	x = 2.25; range 1 – 4	5	x = 4; range 3 – 5	2	x = 4.5; range = 4 - 5	Development of explicating thoughts.
8A	23.5	314	25	7	x = 1.9; range 1 - 4	7	x = 4.7; range 2 - 8	19	x = 8.7; range 4 - 32	Very open conversation generally. Frequent invitations to each other to share/confirm/ discuss ideas.

Appendix 10.2 : Measures of the nature of social and cognitive interactions between pupils in groups carrying out the same practical after teacher participation in interventional in-service.

	Effects on pupils learning and understanding in the science classroom				
	Clarity of task	**Development of potential solutions**	**Application of scientific procedures**	**Discussion of the findings and explanation of the evidence collected.**	**Evaluation of task solution**
Before teacher participation in interventional in-service	Rarely re-iterated so all clearly understand. Often 'actional' participation.	Once plausible (often initial) suggestion made, likely all in agreement.	Some consideration of standardizing candle flame, timing techniques, flushing jars in between trials etc.	Data pattern usually recorded clearly but evidence not explained.	Once solution reached there is little or no reflection.
Post teacher participation in interventional in-service	More social interaction and verbal exchange by pupils about meaning of the task. More 'exploratory' talk.	More suggestions, offered by more pupils in total. More varied (creative) tactics developed.	More comprehensive consideration regarding the control of influencing variables	More careful recording of evidence and scientific discussion of the meaning of the data.	Validity and verifiability of solution considered by some groups.

Appendix 10.3 : A summary of the impact of teacher participation in interactive in-service: a comparison of scientific learning developed between pupils before and after the interactive teacher intervention.

1. Deriving a formal model:
    a. A simple formal model (compound variable; e.g.: as temperature increases, in fixed shape vessel, gas pressure increases)
    b. A more complex formal model (multi-variant; e.g.: photosynthesis requiring carbon dioxide, water and light)
2. Classifying or categorising using a variety of properties (not directly visible) (e.g.: reactivity series, pre-historic organisms and evolutionary trends) to predict properties or generalise about 'unknown' objects.
3. Comparing two concrete differing models to 'reality' i.e.: comparative formal modelling (e.g.: the vinegar and bicarbonate model of larva compared to the wax and sand model of volcanic action).
4. Refining/adapting a formal model:
    a. In light of a little more evidence (e.g.: 'nothing'/particles in air explaining what happens when balloon warmed or tyre pressure changes in cold weather).
    b. Lots more evidence, several changes required (e.g.: various models of electrical circuits).
5. Connecting models. Recognising how one model is connected or influenced by another (e.g.: photosynthesis and respiration).
6. Recognising a model within a model (e.g.: diffusion is a part of osmosis; particulate theory is part of atomic theory).
7. Comparing two abstract models, exploring how they are different (eg: using land-line phone and walky talky workings to explain mobile phone workings).
8. Restructuring a formal model:
    a. Changing evidence/information over a long **temporal** period (e.g.; wrinkled apple hypothesis -> tectonic plates; Lamarckian ideas about change -> Darwinian evolution)
9. Evaluating a formal model. Given a model to explain a phenomena, determining its reliability, verifiability and bias (E.g.: Lincoln index, how reliably does it determine the population number).

Appendix 10.4 Possible classification of types of formal modelling that could inform cognitive outcomes for Thinking Science at KS 4. Proposal of underpinning thinking of Reflective Science, a Key Stage 4 programme, designed to develop cognitive ability within science (informing a research project funded by Esmée Fairbairn).

Lightning Source UK Ltd.
Milton Keynes UK
23 September 2010

160256UK00001B/100/P

9 783639 187625